"Research in the controversial area of homosexuality is fraught with ideology and plagued by a dearth of science. This study has broken new ground in its adherence to objectivity and a scientific precision that can be replicated and expanded, and it opens new horizons for investigation. It is the kind of scientific research I had in mind when in the mid-1970s I introduced my successful resolution in the APA Council of Representatives that homosexuality is not a disease, but a complex constellation of factors that requires scientific investigation to further our understanding of its etiology, its many parameters and its subjectivity to change. I have waited over thirty years for this refreshing, penetrating study of an imperative, though controversial human condition. This book is must reading for psychotherapists and counselors, as well as academic psychologists studying human behavior and sexuality."

Nicholas A. Cummings, Ph.D., Sc.D., Former President, American Psychological Association; Distinguished Professor, University of Nevada, Reno; President, Cummings Foundation for Behavioral Health

"This is clearly the best scientific study yet conducted on change of homosexual orientation and on the question as to whether attempts at such change are inherently harmful. My academic peer review found this investigation to be the most rigorous, well-designed empirical study to date on these questions. This study meets the high research standards set by the American Psychological Association that individuals be validly assessed, followed and reported over time with a prospective, longitudinal outcome research design.

"Using well-accepted, standard psychological measures, Jones and Yarhouse found solid evidence that homosexual orientation can be significantly changed. And their careful scientific research found no evidence that spiritual or psychological harm directly results from attempting such change. Because so many secular psychologists and psychiatrists mistakenly assume the opposite of these clear scientific findings, this groundbreaking scientific study sets a new landmark in the field of therapeutic change for unwanted homosexual orientation.

"Given the practical constraints facing any scientist for these research questions, Jones and Yarhouse employed a prospective and longitudinal research design that measures up to widely accepted professional standards. This study's authors are cautious, basing their conclusions only on systematically gathered and appropriately analyzed scientific data. Jones and Yarhouse assessed individuals who met fairly rigorous standards of 'homosexualness,' using every established measure of sexual orientation that has empirical support in past scientific research as well as standard psychological measures of distress and spirituality that are among the best currently available.

"This study demonstrates with convincing scientific evidence that the Christian ministry interventions of Exodus International produced strong and clinically meaningful changes in homosexual orientation in a large percentage of individuals. Furthermore this careful clinical research investigation of a significant number of individuals yielded no evidence to support the common assumption that attempts to change sexual orientation cause harm or psychological distress."

George A. Rekers, Ph.D., Th.D.; Fellow of the American Academy of Clinical Psychology; Professor of Neuropsychiatry and Behavioral Science Emeritus, University of South Carolina School of Medicine; Diplomate in Clinical Psychology, American Board of Professional Psychology

"With this landmark study, Drs. Jones and Yarhouse have made a major contribution to a controversial area. The findings from their study support the importance of client autonomy and client self-determination as therapists provide a range of options to those who seek help for unwanted same-sex attraction. The book is required reading for those interested in the best practices and evidence-based care."

Dr. A. Dean Byrd, University of Utah School of Medicine

"Professors Jones and Yarhouse provide a well-designed, conceptually and philosophically sophisticated longitudinal study of intervention efforts aimed at changing homosexual orientation. Their data address the question, Is such change possible? They also cogently address related controversial questions such as the ethical issues involved. They embody all the characteristics of first-rate scholarship (for example, they modestly note the methodological limitations of their study). However, this is a groundbreaking study that will hopefully be judged by the normal standards of scholarship rather than be prejudged by its religious element or its tentative positive results."

William O'Donohue, Ph.D., Nicholas Cummings Professor of Organized Behavioral Healthcare Delivery, University of Nevada, Reno

"Can some motivated people alter aspects of their sexuality through religious ministry? With the publication of *Ex-Gays?* Stanton Jones and Mark Yarhouse have produced the most rigorous study to date to address this question. Knowing their results would generate controversy, the authors have thoroughly described the rationale for their procedures. While the authors fully acknowledge that change in sexual attractions did not occur for some individuals, they offer cogent and compelling reasons to believe that participation in religious ministry resulted in durable changes for others. The Jones and Yarhouse study will set the standard for all future work in this field and demands a serious reading from social scientists. For anyone interested in the study of sexuality, values and human change, this book is a must-read."

WARREN THROCKMORTON, PH.D., Associate Professor of Psychology and Fellow for Psychology and Public Policy, Grove City College, coauthor of "Sexual Identity Therapy Framework," and producer of *I Do Exist*

"This study is a groundbreaking classic—scientifically erudite and clearly presented. It shares irrefutible data gained over time that serve to explode arguments based on ideology and anecdotes. Its irenic and thoughtful discussion invite an open forum where scientific evidence and rational thinking are allowed to dominate discussion of the subject."

MERTON P. STROMMEN, PH.D., Founder of Search Institute and Fellow in the American Psychological Association

"Psychologists have long championed and cared for the 'other' of our society—the weird, the abnormal, the minority and the less powerful. Although this book may at first appear to attack the other—in this case, those who consider themselves gay—this book *is* the other of psychological research. This book addresses ideas that are other than the ideas of psychology's power centers and power brokers. It addresses questions about homosexuality that are not asked by the mainstream and the majority of our discipline. Yet, like most any 'other,' it deserves a hearing, whether or not we agree with it. It especially deserves a hearing because it follows the principles of those who deserve hearings in psychology—careful scholarship and empirical rigor."

BRENT D. SLIFE, PH.D., Clinical Psychologist and Professor of Psychology, Brigham Young University

"Congratulations on your book. It is well and thoughtfully done, and the meticulous adherence to your experimental design gives added weight to your findings. Your carefully executed research demands a substantial and credible reexamination of current, politically driven, politically correct dogma that homosexual orientation is immutable and that therapeutic address thereof threatens patient well-being. In a best-case scenario, your research might even persuade the organized mental health movement to return to almost forgotten principles that it is *the patient's right to choose,* and that *the patient has the capacity to do so.*"

ROGERS H. WRIGHT, PH.D., Fellow and Past President of Divisions 12 and 31 of the American Psychological Association, Founding President, Council for the Advancement of the Psychological Professions and Sciences, Diplomate in Clinical Psychology, American Board of Professional Psychology

EX-gays?

A Longitudinal Study of
Religiously Mediated Change
in Sexual Orientation

Stanton L. Jones
Mark A. Yarhouse

InterVarsity Press
P.O. Box 1400, Downers Grove, IL 60515-1426
World Wide Web: www.ivpress.com
E-mail: email@ivpress.com

InterVarsity Press® is the book-publishing division of InterVarsity Christian Fellowship/USA®, a student movement active on campus at hundreds of universities, colleges and schools of nursing in the United States of America, and a member movement of the International Fellowship of Evangelical Students. For information about local and regional activities, write Public Relations Dept., InterVarsity Christian Fellowship/USA, 6400 Schroeder Rd., P.O. Box 7895, Madison, WI 53707-7895, or visit the IVCF website at <*www.intervarsity.org*>.

Design: Cindy Kiple

ISBN 978-0-8308-2846-3

Printed in the United States of America ∞

Library of Congress Cataloging-in-Publication Data

Jones, Stanton L.
Ex-gays?: a longitudinal study of religiously mediated change in sexual orientation/Stanton L. Jones and Mark A. Yarhouse.
p. cm.
Includes bibliographical references and index.
ISBN-13: 978-0-8308-2846-3 (pbk.: alk. paper)
1. Homosexuality—Religious aspects—Christianity. 2. Homosexuality—Treatment—Moral and ethical aspects. 3. Ex-gay movement. 4. Sexual reorientation programs. 5. Ex-gays. 6. Sexual orientation. I. Yarhouse, Mark A., 1968- II. Title.
BR115.H6J655 2007
306.76'6—dc22

2007026747

P *21 20 19 18 17 16 15 14 13 12 11 10 9 8 7 6 5 4 3 2 1*
Y *24 23 22 21 20 19 18 17 16 15 14 13 12 11 10 09 08 07*

Contents

Figures

Tables

Acknowledgments

WE HAVE MANY TO THANK who contributed to or supported us in the process of bringing this massive project to fruition. We begin with thanking Robert Davies, former executive director of Exodus International, who urged us to execute a study that until that point had existed only as a mental exercise and unrequited grant application, and who energized the board of Exodus International and constituency to provide the initial funding for the study. Bob demonstrated at several key points his devotion to truth and high-mindedness. Our thanks are also extended for the continuing support of Alan Chambers, the current executive director, and the Exodus board.

We are each grateful for the strong support of our respective institutions. Wheaton College and Regent University have been excellent contexts in which to pursue our ideas and see this project to fruition. It is worth noting that while each of these institutions are committed to the Christian moral vision we embrace, neither institution has a position as such on change of sexual orientation or the types of methods employed by the ministries we studied.

In the initial stages of the project, Professor Gary Strauss of the Rosemead Graduate School of Psychology, Biola University, contributed to our conceptualization of our research protocol and served as our West Coast research coordinator. Dr. Strauss demonstrated his compassion and empathetic understanding of this population of individuals experiencing deep conflict between their sexual desires and ethical values. Thanks also to Dr. Edward Laumann of the University of Chicago for authorizing his research team to release to us several of their prepublication research protocols from their "gold standard" work on sexuality.

A number of individuals in the Wheaton College community contributed materially to this project. In the earliest days of the project through completion of the Time 2 assessments, doctoral students Jon Ebert and Jeffrey Eckert worked tirelessly researching our assessment options, helping to draft versions of what later became our research protocol and conducting assessment interviews. Later, doctoral students Alex Kwee and Pamela Vernace Strening filled crucial roles in data management and entry, and Alex assisted in our conceptualization and articulation of a number of conceptually difficult points. A special debt of thanks is due Professor John Vessey of Wheaton College, who filled a crucial role in data analysis and consultation; John, you helped us bring order out of chaos and always articulated sharp professional standards of analysis.

Several individuals in the Regent University community were supportive of this project from its inception. In particular we want to acknowledge the support we received from administration in the School of Psychology and Counseling, specifically Rosemarie Hughes, dean of the School of Psychology and Counseling, and William Hathaway, director of the doctoral program in clinical psychology, as well as colleagues in the School of Psychology and Counseling. In the first year of the project, when we conducted Time 1 interviews, Lori Burkett served as research coordinator and set a high bar for future coordinators. The Time 2 and Time 3 interviews were under the direction of Erica Tan, who served as research coordinator over the subsequent two years and guided the transition from face-to-face interviews to telephone interviews as the Regent team eventually took on the responsibilities for coordinating all of the follow-up interviews. Although we do not here present data on Time 4 and Time 5 interviews, we want to acknowledge the dedication, hard work and organizational skills of Heather Brooke and Veronica Johnson, who served as research coordinators for Times 4 and 5, respectively. Both of them have been on top of every facet of maintaining contact, setting up and tracking interviews for the past two years. The data from the work under their coordination will be presented in the future. Lori, Erica, Heather and Veronica each took seriously their responsibilities for coordinating the project and invested a significant amount of time and energy in addressing all of the details that go along with running a study of this magnitude. Students who have been part of the Institute for the Study of Sexual Identity have also taken on a significant amount of work to support the project over the past several years, and we wish to thank them for their hard work and dedication—most recently this includes Lisa Pawlowski, Stephen Russell, Adam Hunter, Edye Garcia, Lynette Bogey, Paula Pisano, Trista Carr and Anita Castellanos. A study of this size also requires many interviewers, some of whom have been mentioned already. We also want to acknowledge additional Time 1-3 interviewers from Regent, including Connie Borden, Christy Leong, Katherine Hawxhurst, Peggy Hauck, Kathi Michel, Timothy Tjersland, Stephanie Kemper, Kristen Grabowski, Angela Liszcz, Judy Babcock, Nathan Stephens, Melissa Pence, Christina Moler, Stephanie Dutton, Michael Franks, Paula Brown, Jami Sargeant, Stacey Scott, Mary Beth Covert, Josh Childers, Nicole Noble, Jon Denman, April Cunion, Jen Su, Mary Alice Quinlan, Sally Falwell, Melissa Jenkins, Lee Hall and DeAnna Fredrica Brooks. Each maintained the highest ethical standards in their role as interviewers.

As we began to move to a written presentation of our project and its findings, several people added considerably to the final product. Our thanks go to Dr. Dean Byrd, professor at the University of Utah School of Medicine and president of the Thrasher Research Institute, for brokering reviews by several excellent methodologists who nevertheless desired to remain anonymous because of potential career repercussions if they were associated with our project. Those reviews further sharpened our arguments and tightened our analyses.

We originally were quite intent on seeking publication by a nonreligious publishing house. David Vigliano of Vigliano and Associates in New York took our project on as our literary agent. Our thanks go out to Hilary Hinzman, consulting editor with Vigliano and Associates, for his extraordinary editing of our first manuscript draft. Hilary, you exemplified the kind of skeptical, fair-minded engagement with our material that we would desire from a skeptical reader. Though by personal conviction you were not inclined toward sympathy with our project, you treated the project with seriousness and fairness, asking hard and appropriate questions of us. This book is stronger from your input. Even with a strengthened manuscript, Vigliano found door after door slammed in his face because of the topic of study and likely fallout for a publisher committed to such a project. We are grateful for his efforts, fruitless though they were, on behalf of this project.

Special thanks go out to our friends at InterVarsity Press for publishing this work. Bob Fryling, Andy Le Peau, Gary Deddo, Jeff Crosby and others at InterVarsity Press: thanks for your courage, clarity and conviction. Thanks also to Barbara Woodburn, Erin Manuel, Dianne McCarty, Cindi Carder and Ann Gerber who offered crucial assistance to the first author in managing the practicalities of such a huge project.

We are blessed with spouses who love and support us. Each in their own way asked us early on in this project whether we were really sure we wanted to stir up this beehive, and yet each has stood with us in following our calling. For their love, forbearance, patience and care, we are eternally grateful.

We are grateful above all for the honor of looking closely into the lives of men and women grappling with considerable pain and conflict. These women and men, regardless of outcome, have borne with our project with patience and dignity, baring aspects of their lives that most of us seek to keep private and closed. Thank you for trusting us, and we hope that we have rewarded that trust by telling the truth about your lives.

1

The Controversy

THIS BOOK REPORTS OUR RESEARCH on the possibility of change of homosexuality orientation via religiously mediated means. In offering this report we anticipate that we are stepping into the very eye of a "perfect storm."

Homosexuality is controversial. The possibility of fundamental change in sexual orientation, that homosexuals can become heterosexuals or in any way cease to be homosexuals, is controversial. The question of whether the attempt to change sexual orientation is harmful is controversial. Religious conservatism, specifically what some would call Christian fundamentalism, is controversial. The social-scientific measurement of religiously mediated change ("healing") is controversial. Social-scientific research conducted from an explicit faith perspective is controversial. The possibility that a faith perspective can contribute something of value to the scientific enterprise of trying to better understand human experience is controversial.

The present study touches on all of these hot-button issues and more.

The Exodus Project reported here was directed at answering two simple questions: (1) Are the claims of a cluster of conservative religious ministries valid that homosexual orientation can be "healed"? In other words, is it *ever* possible for an individual who has a homosexual orientation to change that orientation via religious means? (2) Is the attempt to change harmful, as so many today claim?

About four decades ago and earlier, the majority wisdom of the leading professionals in the mental health community was that homosexuality was a psychological disturbance of some kind that could, though perhaps with difficulty, be treated successfully, resulting in satisfactory readjustment to heterosexual experience and satisfaction. In the 1970s and 1980s a rapid if not unanimous shift in professional opinion occurred, stimulated by events beginning in the 1950s and earlier, such that homosexuality was no longer viewed as a psychological disturbance or mental illness. Further, fundamental change in sexual orientation began to be generally viewed as unattainable, and slowly the view took hold that any attempt to produce change was necessarily harmful, perhaps profoundly so. This shift in professional opinion never reflected the unanimous view of the mental health professions. When the majority viewed homosexuality as a psychological disturbance amenable to change via therapeutic means, there was always a minority that questioned that majority opinion. And now, when the pendulum of opinion has swung decisively in favor of the view that homosexual orientation is *not* a psychological disturbance and is *not* amenable to change via therapeutic or any other means, a minority of dissent exists within and outside of the professional community, believing that change is possible. This Exodus Project reports on a scientific study of a community outside of the typical professional mental health world that claims that change in sexual orientation is possible via religious means.

This lack of unanimous perspective on the possibility of change has not deterred the American Psychological Association, our professional organization, from asserting an absolute answer to this thorny question. On their public affairs website, "Answers to Your Questions About Sexual Orientation and Homosexuality," the APA claims "Can therapy change sexual orientation? No. . . . [H]omosexuality . . . is not changeable."[1] This is an absolute claim, which leads us to philosophy of science.

From the beginning we wish to emphasize a fundamental point of logic, one expounded by Karl Popper over half a century ago and that is profoundly relevant to the present study.[2] Popper was the proponent of falsificationism as the fundamental rule of adjudicating scientific claims. The logic of falsificationism is easily grasped with the following illustration. The universal claim "All crows are black" is impossible to prove. Why? Because the discovery of a thousand black crows, of a million black crows, of a trillion black crows, can never prove the *universal* claim that *all* crows are black. A nonblack crow might be just around the next corner, no matter how many black crows we document. On the other hand the documentation of *even one case* of a crow that is *not black* disproves the universal claim that all crows are black. In other words, the universal claim "All crows are black" is easily *disproved* by one contrary instance, but that same statement can actually never be conclusively proved no matter how many confirming cases are documented. Based on this logical observation, Popper proposed that the fundamental task of scientific inquiry was the falsification, the disproving, of scientific claims by the discovery of contrary evidence. Popper proposed that science would progress by weeding out bad scientific theories by disproof, by offering evidence contrary to the theory.

Popper's approach has many flaws and has not carried the day as a *comprehensive* model for scientific adjudication, but his fundamental point about the power of contrary evidence to disprove universal claims remains indisputable. It is for this reason that *falsifiability* remains an important criterion for scientific theories. As we write, for instance, controversy swirls around the evolution versus intelligent design argument, with critics of the intelligent design hypothesis noting that its proponents have yet to advance a falsifiable experimental proposition.

The relevance of this illustration to the current study is this: We are investigating the claim, widely made today, that sexual orientation, homosexual orientation in particular, cannot be changed, that it is immutable. We are doing so by studying a group of individuals who, with varying motivations and levels of commitment and by varying means, are seeking to do what is commonly regarded today as impossible: to achieve fundamental change in their sexual orientations. If we take the fundamental principle of falsifiability seriously, then *compelling evidence that even one individual demonstrates fundamental change in sexual orientation will constitute an invalidation of the universal claim that sexual orientation change is impossible.* Compelling evidence, on the other hand, that not a single individual in this study makes this change would be consistent with the universal claim that change is impossible and would be evidence in support of this claim, but would not prove this universal claim. We will document the claims of the immutability of homosexual orientation as well as how prior claims of changes have been explained (i.e., explained away) in chapter three.

It is equally important to be clear from the beginning about what this study does not claim or establish. First, the documentation of significant change for some in this study will not establish that permanent, enduring change has occurred; only a very long-term study can demonstrate that.

Individuals who give evidence of significant change may, in fact, revert to prior patterns of sexual attraction and action five, ten or more years after this initial study. We hope to continue to follow our sample and provide such evidence. The evidence offered here looks at a significant span of time, but we could always examine a longer time frame.

Second, if some but not all of the 98 individuals who completed the initial assessment for this study demonstrate significant change, this study will provide no conclusive evidence about *what proportion* of individuals can change. Why? Because answering the question of probability of success would require a study examining a *scientifically representative* sample of all persons who experience homosexual attraction. We do not, however, have such a scientifically representative sample in this study. This is a ubiquitous problem in research on homosexuality—no one really has any idea of what such a representative sample would look like, and no study can really claim to have produced such a sample, for the simple reason that there is significant disagreement over how to define who "counts" as a "homosexual" and because there is so much controversy swirling around the subject that certain people will come forward or hang back from being studied for a variety of reasons.

Note, though, that *any* sample that includes such persons who show change is adequate to refute the universal claim that change is impossible. An unflattering analogy will show this clearly: If we start with the universal claim that All White Americans accept the full intellectual and social equality of African Americans, we can disprove this universal by interviewing the membership of an obscure Ku Klux Klan cell in rural Illinois and documenting their racist beliefs. But that study of a Klan population would not allow us to claim that all or most white Americans harbor racist beliefs. To make any such normative claim about "X% of the population thinks Y" requires that we study a representative sample of Americans. The main point? Refutation of an absolute claim (such as "sexual orientation change is impossible") does not require a demonstrably representative sample.

This study examined a group of individuals at least somewhat representative of persons taking part in their respective Exodus ministries. At the time we initiated this study, Exodus had about ninety ministries in the United States. We sought the participation of ministries based on their geographical proximity to sites where we could establish interview teams, so a subsample of Exodus ministries were contacted based on location rather than representativeness. Of the ministries contacted, a number declined to participate by referring participants to us, and this introduces further unknown variation in our sample. Of the ministries that agreed to participate, some referred all of their participants to us (as described later) while others clearly referred only a sample, again introducing unknown variation in our sample. Some of the most influential studies ever conducted on homosexuality (e.g., the iconic studies by Evelyn Hooker, Alfred Kinsey, Bell and Weinberg, and Bailey and Pillard)[3] have presented conclusions based on *convenience samples,* samples of no known representativeness. We believe that our sample is a fair representation of religiously motivated individuals seeking sexual orientation change, but of completely unknown representativeness of all homosexually oriented persons. Thus, we regard the sample in our study to be better than a mere convenience sample, but cannot argue for complete representativeness of the sample.

Why belabor these points? We do so to establish unequivocally and explicitly the core goals of this study. Our principal goal is to test the universal claim that sexual orientation is unchangeable and immutable, and secondarily to test the claim that the attempt to change is always harmful. It should be noted, though, that the very thought of attaining an "indisputable refutation" is ridiculous, as we live in an age and are investigating a topic area in which anything and everything may be disputed. We have sought to conduct a study by high professional standards, and are determined to report the results of that study honestly regardless of the outcomes. We are confident that these results will be important in understanding the question of change of sexual orientation; specifically, is change possible and is the attempt harmful?

We begin though with a discussion of the relationship of science and religion. Many would claim that religion can and should have no contact with science, and claim further that the matter of sexual orientation is a scientific topic that should be uncontaminated by connection with religion. For such a person, many aspects of the current study will stand as an offense against the supposed "wall of separation" between science and religion: the religious motivation for change of many of our participants, the religious nature (though profoundly mixed and complex) of the change mechanisms employed, the mixing of measurement of religious motivation and development with the measurement of sexual orientation and other behavioral matters, and the fact that the principal investigators are themselves evangelical Christians with sympathies toward the possibility of change, whose motivations for conducting the study are in some senses religious and who celebrate certain types of connections between religion and science in the fundamental conceptualization of the study. So it is with an examination of these issues that we begin.

THE RELATIONSHIP BETWEEN SCIENCE AND RELIGION

The study of human sexuality is a case study in the dialogue between science and religion. We believe that religion has much to say about human nature, including sexuality as one aspect of human experience. Likewise, we believe that the behavioral sciences, as applied to the study of human sexuality and sexual behavior, have much to say about those aspects of human experience that science can measure and describe. The interests of both religion and science in advancing our understanding of the fascinating and complex topic of human sexuality will be advanced, we would argue, by a sustained and rich dialogue between science and religion.[4]

As we have suggested elsewhere, there are those who argue that science and religion ought not be in any kind of dialogue.[5] The very nature of science and religion, they would claim, makes such a dialogue meaningless. These arguments take differing forms, from the more extreme claim that religion (particularly Christianity) and science have been and are necessarily at war, to the more modest claim that the shift away from a religious worldview and toward a scientific one, the movement that has often been called secularization, has benefited scientific inquiry.

We would distinguish these claims into two classes, the first being a set of historical claims that religion and science have been "at war," and a second set of claims that religion and science are by their basic natures incompatible. We will only comment briefly on this first argument and then treat the second a bit more extensively. The first argument has been thoroughly refuted by such outstanding work in the history of science as that of John Brooke and David Lindberg who have shown that science and religion, generally, have not been "at war," and that religious belief and practice have served in certain cases to facilitate the progress of science.[6] Many superb scientists in fact have been and still are conventionally and devoutly religious, and have themselves seen their religious faith facilitate their work as scientists. On the other hand, many of the claims made about the warfare of science and religion have in fact been based on shoddy historical analysis.

Are science and religion so fundamentally incompatible that in fact no dialogue between the two is even possible? It has been common to argue that religion can have no meaningful relation to science except when religion is an object of scientific scrutiny.[7] The major arguments for this view include the claim that religion and science are two very different and nonoverlapping human activities. Religion, it is claimed, is based on subjective experience and personal belief and faith, whereas science is based on observable, measurable data so that truth claims can be tested and verified. Science, particularly in its positivistic conception, is seen as resting on empirical facts that are fixed in meaning and do not need interpretation. Remnants of these positivistic roots of science remain and can be seen in the assumption that the scientific enterprise involves developing theories that are derived from empirical findings and then tested empirically, and that it is the accumulation of facts that moves scientists toward closer approximations of what is really true and knowable.

Religion and science are often said to be directed at utterly divergent purposes as well. It has been said that religion asks and attempts to answer many questions of ultimate concern, for example, about what it means to be human, about ethics and about the meaning of life and future existence. Science, in contrast, is said to be focused only on tangible explanations of physical phenomena.

But these are not accurate characterizations of either science or religion. Advances in our understanding of philosophy of science have demonstrated that data are theory-laden and thus sorted based on our own preorienting conceptions of one sort or another. Scientists do not come to the data in an utterly objective fashion, free from their own preconceived notions of what they are observing or analyzing. Rather, we classify data according to the theoretical views we bring to the scientific experiment, as when the Skinnerian behaviorist counts bar presses by a rat (because that is the behavior that her theoretical commitments tell her, with some rational justification, are data) and ignores other aspects of the behavior of the rat. In addition, theories are actually underdetermined by facts, meaning that the "shape" of the facts do not force the conclusion in favor of one theory to the exclusion of all other theories. By implication then, induction upward from the "raw data" is really not the foundation for theory development as was once asserted, but scientists tend to commit themselves to theories long before they scrutinize all of the relevant data. Finally, falsification of theories in science has also been shown to be much more difficult than positivists have claimed, because empirical assessment of a theory always addresses not just the claims of the theory itself but also an innumerable number of corollaries (that one's instruments are working properly, that the test tubes are clean, etc.).* Philosophy of science has helped us see the ways in which theorizing and analyzing theories is a much more complicated, human experience than had been thought. This is not to deny that science is a relatively more objective enterprise directed at creating theories that are tested against the data produced by scientific experimentation, but rather specifically to note that science is not the utterly objective enterprise devoid of the human influence that many wanted it to be.

If the characterization of science as thoroughly objective is incomplete, so too is the characterization of religion as only interested in subjective experience, values, the transcendent and questions of ultimate concern. Such a characterization overlooks many dimensions of the religions. One of these dimensions is the prepositional or declarative dimension of religion in that religion can make assertions or holds presuppositions about ultimate reality, anthropology, and ethics and morality. The religions generally—and Christianity as the particular religion of focus in the present study—make claims about the nature of the world and about human nature in addition to their claims about God and "ultimate reality." Further, the ethical claims of the religions about "the good" have implications for

*It would be naive of us here not to acknowledge the way that this argument will be used against our claims in this study that we are falsifying the claim that change of sexual orientation is impossible. Yes, falsification is complex, and our critics will, as we say here, claim rather loudly that our methodology was faulty or that we are dishonest. Falsification, we would reply, is complex, but not impossible, and further that we are honestly reporting our results and our methods are "good enough" for the purpose.

the scientific study of human beings, in that claims about what is (and is not) good must be considered as making assertions about optimal human functioning, claims that overlap and intersect with social scientific studies of persons. And some aspects of some religions make factual claims about historical events, as when traditional Christians claim that Jesus lived, performed miracles, died by crucifixion and rose from the dead.

It is a distortion to treat religions as noncognitive phenomena of an exclusively intuitive or experiential nature that make no claims about reality. Christianity, in particular, makes concrete claims about reality (including personhood and human sexuality). Nevertheless, such declarative aspects of religious belief can be complex, inconsistent and vague, not unlike those of scientific (and specifically psychological) paradigms.

We believe that the distinctive identities of science and religion can be respected and not conflated; we do not seek to substitute religion for psychological science nor the reverse. At the same time, we believe that a proper and rigorous understanding of both science and religion allows for the possibility of meaningful dialogue between the two.[8] We have pointed out that science and religion are often mischaracterized and that the mischaracterizations themselves present an obstacle to meaningful dialogue. An accurate understanding of both science and religion can help us see the potential for a mutually enriching relationship.

Another key to justifying the legitimacy of a dialogue between science and religion involves the recognition that a variety of metaphysical statements or commitments shape the practice of science. Two recent articles have provided support for the claim that such metaphysical statements, including religious beliefs, often are a factor in the shaping of the conceptualizations of the subject matter on which psychological research and practice are built. Sampson focused directly on the "role of religion in setting the terms" of the entire discipline of psychology for the conceptualization of a fundamental dimension of personhood, namely whether we adopt a "collectivist or an individualistic understanding of the person-other relationship."[9] Contrary to the standard account contrasting supposed Western-Judeo-Christian individualism with Eastern-Buddhist collectivism, Sampson contrasted Protestant Christian individualism with Judaic-Rabbinic collectivism. He discussed the tendency for psychologists to underestimate the impact of religion on culture, arguing that key assumptions that shape our research programs are influenced by religious conceptions and convictions. Specifically, "the very choice of the individual as the central object of psychological study and the key to unlocking the mysteries of human nature is supported by a set of assumptions that are derived in great measure from a particular configuration of religious beliefs and values, primarily Christian."[10]

An article by Redding provides a second example.[11] Redding made the provocative suggestion that political ideology can function in much the same way as religion in shaping the ways we conceive of problems in psychology. Redding suggests that background assumptions of a political nature (and his argument works for religion as well) shape what we simply assume versus what we deem as requiring explanation, what we construe as a legitimate question and a legitimate answer to that question, and what we deem to be methodology suitable for providing a valid answer: "how one defines a problem goes a long way in determining the proposed solution. . . . [S]ociopolitical biases influence the questions asked, the research methods selected, the interpretation of research results, the peer review process, judgments about research quality, and decisions about whether to use the research in policy advocacy."[12]

With Redding, Sampson and philosopher of science Mary Midgley, we would argue that we

> have a choice of what myths, what visions we will use to help us understand the physical world [i.e., the subject matter of science]. We do not have a choice of understanding it without using any myths or visions at all. Again, we have a real choice between becoming aware of these myths and ignoring them. If we ignore them, we travel blindly inside myths and visions that are largely provided by other people. This makes it much harder to know where we are going.[13]

What this means is that science, especially social science, does not advance in the way many of us presumed in our high school science experiences, that is, simply through the accumulation of bare facts that are known for certain. Rather, science starts with *ideas*, with complicated conjectures, about the way the world (or at least that slice of the world which is our subject matter) *is*. In the words of one author, we start the project of doing science with "metaphysical sentences," which are beliefs about our subject matter that are deeply embedded in our broader web of beliefs about the nature of reality about us and which beliefs are affected by evidence but not directly or immediately testable against experience.[14] The psychologist studying the mind-numbingly complex topic of human personality begins, before gathering any data, with a set of understandings that guides the questions one asks and indeed shapes what one regards as data and what one regards as irrelevant. Different background beliefs or metaphysical sentences will generate different questions as one approaches the complex subject of human sexuality.

Even so, *science is more than the debating of background beliefs*. As religious psychologists who are attempting to do science, we must recognize that the success of any such dialogue about the beliefs that are guiding our psychological work will be measured by the empirical fruitfulness of the dialogue, by the capacity of the dialogue to generate theoretical approaches that will in turn generate novel and significant hypotheses regarding measurable phenomena that yet in turn yield empirically powerful findings in comparison to competing explanatory systems. Paul Meehl, chafing about those he regards as "obscurantists" who minimize the importance of scientific accountability to data, said "[No] quotes from [philosopher of science Thomas] Kuhn can avoid the task of *proving* what one claims to have observed, and in a way that does not require the skeptic to accept one's theory, *that being what is in dispute*."[15] We concur with Meehl: dialogue that never results in empirically fertile inquiry and examination of data is dialogue that ultimately fails to engage the field of science. The point of the dialogue is to give religious traditions and resources the chance to explicitly shape the framework of metaphysical assumptions that in turn shape how we do our research and on what topics, and how it is interpreted and applied. The jury is yet out on whether this dialogue will indeed be recognized as productive by the field.

In deciding whether a dialogue with religion could enrich psychological theory, research and practice, we note that religious thought will rarely contribute unequivocal, immediately quantifiable, testable hypotheses. As McClay said, a "Christian perspective will not necessarily generate a specific or uniform agenda. Christianity is not an ideology, and it almost never leads its adherents to identical positions on questions of policy or politics. But it will profoundly shape the way questions are posed."[16] In shaping how questions are posed, though, a religious vision can generate, by extrapolation, hypotheses that can inspire research programs.[17]

That is what we believe has happened here. The conservative Christian communities that ground their comprehensive vision of sexuality in the teachings of the Bible, that regard homosexual conduct to be immoral and in crucial ways "unnatural," and who also have a view of God that trusts in and expects his intervention in daily life (with all of these explored in greater depth in chap. 2), these communities claim to be producing outcomes that most of contemporary secular psychology believes to be impossible: change in sexual orientation. The empirical exploration of this phenomena gives us an opportunity to explore a phenomenon of significant scientific interest, one that also stands at the intersection of profound metaphysical disputes about the nature of sexuality and personhood.

A Constructive Relationship Between Science and Religion

Jones has argued that psychology has historically been imperialistic toward religion.[18] This can be demonstrated in the literature about homosexuality, where the presumption often is that the "facts" modern science has produced about homosexuality should displace ancient prejudice and force change in contemporary religious belief.

Jones went on to argue that some psychologists (such as Perry London)[19] have recognized a possible role for religion in that applied psychology must be seen as always having a moral horizon, a normative dimension whenever it intervenes in human life. Hence, at least some psychologists have recognized the legitimate place of religion as a (junior?) dialogue partner about the moral and ethical dimension of intervention in human life.

But Jones went further in arguing for a "constructive" relationship between psychology and religion, proposing three facets of such a relationship:

- A "critical-evaluative mode of functioning, whereby social scientific theories and paradigms are examined and evaluated by the individual scientist for their fit with his or her religious presuppositions."[20]

- The "constructive mode of relating religious presuppositions to science should occur when religious belief contributes positively to the progress of science by suggesting new modes of thought which transform an area of study by shaping new perceptions of the data and new theories."[21]
- The "dialogical" nature of the relationship whereby "new findings in cosmology, sociobiology, philosophy, anthropology, sociology, and even psychology should infuse and affect the religious enterprise."[22]

We offer this study in the positive spirit of such a constructive relationship. This study will stand as a challenge of sorts to the field of psychology, but we offer this challenge in a constructive spirit of dialogue, one that presumes that the field and the public are searching for truth, including truth about our sexuality and sexual natures. We have been dubious since early in our professional lives about the rush to declare homosexual orientation (indeed all sexual orientations) unchangeable and the very attempt to change harmful; we have known people who claimed to have experienced such change. As we will document, there is room for dialogue, for agnosticism, for disagreement about this complex aspect of human functioning.

And so we begin this dialogue here with a brief overview of some of the complexities about sexual orientation, and then will return to our discussion of the intersection of religion and psychology.

Sexual Orientation

When people seek services to help them change their orientation, what exactly is it they are seeking to change?

To understand this issue we need a better understanding of what sexual orientation actually *is*. Sexual orientation typically refers to the directionality of a person's experiences of sexual attraction. Sexual orientation refers to a person's sexual predispositions, and these may come from a variety of sources: *nature* (biological antecedents) or *nurture* (environmental or psychological factors) or, most likely, some combination of both. The consensus today is that few people choose to have a homosexual orientation (or heterosexual, for that matter). Rather, they find themselves experiencing same-sex attraction, and when same-sex rather than opposite-sex attractions predominate, we refer to the person as having a homosexual orientation.

Several theories have emerged regarding the etiology of homosexuality.[23] Those implicating nature focus primarily on research on direct and indirect evidences of genetic influences, prenatal hormonal exposure and differences in brain structures. Research on potential genetic differences include direct evidence from gene scans (which have yet to produce replicated or significant findings) and indirect evidence from behavioral genetics studies of differences in concordance rates found in twin studies (which have produced much more equivocal results than some interpreters allege).[24] Support for the prenatal hormonal hypothesis includes studies of animal fetuses that have been injected prenatally with abnormal doses of sex hormones (which suffer from questionable relevance to natural conditions), from studies comparing anatomical brain structures among homosexual male, heterosexual male and heterosexual females (see pp. 96-97), and from research suggesting that the probabilities of homosexual orientation for males increase slightly as one has more older brothers. Studies of animal analogues to human homosexuality have produced fascinating results looking particularly at "gay fruit flies"[25] and "gay sheep,"[26] and while some researchers find such evidence suggestive, others raise concerns about the fundamental differences between animal and human sexual experience. Concerning the studies of brain structures, the studies completed to date have suffered inconsistent findings, failure to reproduce findings and poor methodology, though some consensus is emerging that one specific brain area, the interstitial nucleus of the hypothalamus, area 3 (or INAH3), may be different in homosexuals and heterosexuals, though this could be a result rather than a cause of homosexual orientation and behavior.[27]

The theories implicating nurture tend to focus on parent-child relationships, and psychodynamic theory has been the most clearly articulated theory for the etiology of homosexuality. Critics argue that there is little empirical evidence to support such theories; however, proponents point to studies implicating early childhood development, including research implicating disordered family relationships (e.g., loss of a parent through death or divorce), early homosexual behavior, and childhood sexual abuse as possible causal factors. One recent and powerful finding out of a huge national database implicates family structure as a possible causal factor in shaping homosexual orientation.[28]

This research is as of yet decidedly inconclusive. We do not know what causes sexual orientation. We can say definitively that it is not genes alone and that the causal process is undoubtedly multifactorial and complex, but beyond this firm conclusions are not responsibly drawn. But to understand causation, we should understand precisely what it is that we seek to explain. Do we know what sexual orientation is?

What Is an "Orientation"?

We often use the terms *heterosexual*, *homosexual* and *bisexual* to communicate information about a person's sexual orientation. Interestingly, there remains much debate among human sexuality experts as to what sexual orientation actually *is*. The debate is typically characterized as being between essentialists and constructionists.[29]

Essentialists generally hold that the types of sexual orientation we have been discussing, that is, heterosexual, homosexual and bisexual, represent what Stein refers to as "natural human kinds" that can be found in other cultures and throughout history.[30] Some essentialists are also nativists insofar as they assume that sexual orientation is a real thing or essence that is produced by specific genetic or prenatal hormonal influences that lead to actual differences in orientation.

Constructionists, in contrast, hold the view that sexual orientations are "social human kinds."[31] From this perspective the distinctions we make among homosexual, heterosexual and bisexual orientations reflect linguistic constructs that capture certain culturally derived meanings about sexual behavior. To the constructionist, sexual orientations are categories, linguistic constructs, not unlike the categories we use to describe political preferences such as Democrat or Republican, liberal or conservative. These categories are not universal "givens" across all cultures and time. Rather, they are constructs fashioned by and given meaning within our society.

Edward Laumann and his colleagues observe that many scientists assume that essentialism is true for the purposes of conducting research.[32] They may personally adhere to constructionism in their actual beliefs about the nature of sexual orientation, but for the purposes of conducting research they rely on essentialist categories.

Unfortunately, the debate about the nature of sexual orientation is not merely philosophical. It can have an impact on our understanding of people who seek to change their sexual orientation. In our opinion many people who implicitly adopt an essentialist perspective often lapse into a stronger form of essentialism. A strong form of essentialism begins with the premise that sexual orientations are universal, that is, sexual orientations exist across all cultures and throughout history. The second claim is that orientation is a real thing or essence. Third, this essence is presumed to be at the core of one's very self as a human being and thus defines who they are as a person. Same-sex behavior, it follows, is morally blameless behavior that is in fact prescribed for those who experience same-sex attraction: "Even disavowing homosexuality is a response to it; and the response slowly, subtly alters who you are. . . . The abandonment of intimacy and the rejection of one's emotional core are, I have come to believe, alloyed evils."[33]

The strong form of essentialism links same-sex attraction to self-identification and claims that the expression of that identity is a moral good. Same-sex behavior then is removed from the category of behaviors that can be judged to be immoral in and of themselves and is considered alongside any other morally neutral behavior that must be judged for its consequences (or some other ethical criteria rather than something intrinsic to the act). Many critics of "reorientation" therapies assume a strong form of essentialism, and in the discussions about sexual identity and change, evidence for strong forms of essentialism can be seen in concerns about gay, lesbian and bisexual persons failing to act on the attractions that reflect their orientation. Consider Troiden's unsubstantiated claim that those who experience same-sex attraction and *dis*-identify with those attractions or pursue chastity are at-risk:

> Women and men who *capitulate* avoid homosexual activity because they have internalized a stigmatizing view of homosexuality. The persistence of homosexual feelings in the absence of homosexual activity, however, may lead them to experience self-hatred and despair.[34]

Rather than formally arguing for specific metaphysical and moral claims—or providing evidence from the behavioral sciences to support implicit metaphysical assumptions—many authors and researchers merely presume them to be true.

In addition to the empirical question of whether there is research to support specific forms of essentialism, the strong form of essentialism allows people to describe their same-sex behavior as a necessary expression of an orientation that is a *given* of existence. People are able to identify with their same-sex attractions without taking responsibility for such identification or subsequent behavior, which establishes an inroad to experiencing same-sex attractions as an identity.

What is particularly important for understanding the study we have conducted is that Christianity has historically rejected a strong form of essentialism and affirmed God's intention to commune with us and to interact with us as persons who make real choices among alternatives, called to live in a manner consistent with God's revealed will for human sexual expression. Christians do not simply follow their sexual impulses; rather, they look outside themselves to evaluate their attractions and live in way that is in keeping with God's will. We will find that the individuals in view in this study—the "clients" of Exodus—mostly reject the kind of essentialism we have just been discussing. They reject that homosexual attraction and action define the core self, reject the notion that this is a given of their existence, reject that the embrace of their essential identity as gay or lesbian is the pathway to wholeness, and reject the notion that they cannot change.

"Sexual Minorities" in Contemporary American Culture

The essentialist-constructionist debate raises several questions among conservative religious persons as to how to think about what it means to identify as "gay" in our culture. The community of persons who have a homosexual orientation is now referred to as the Lesbian, Gay, Bisexual and Transgendered (LGBT) community, or "gay community" for short. They are also referred to as "sexual minorities" in contemporary American culture.

It is perhaps more accurate to make a distinction between those who report a homosexual orientation and those who take on a gay identity. In fact, it may be helpful to make a three-tier distinction among those who experience same-sex attraction, those who have a homosexual orientation, and those who identify with their attractions and integrate them into a gay identity. The most descriptive approach is to simply refer to those persons who report experiencing same-sex attraction. For example, Laumann and his colleagues found 6.2% of males and 4.4% of females reported experiencing attraction to members of the same sex.[35] Among those who experience same-sex attraction, some experience a consistent, persistent experience that we commonly refer to as a homosexual orientation. In the Laumann study 2.0% of males and 0.9% of females reported identifying themselves as having a homosexual orientation. Among these an even smaller percentage self-identifies as gay or lesbian, that is, they take on the sociocultural identity as "gay."

The tension surrounding appropriate language can be placed in a conceptual context of what it means to have a sexual identity. Sexual identity is not the same thing as sexual orientation, though people often confuse the two terms. Sexual identity has been defined in a few different ways but with significant conceptual overlap. For example, Shively and DeCecco focused on *biological sex* (as male or female), *gender identity* (sense of being masculine or feminine), *social sex role* (adherence to social expectations for one's sex) and *sexual orientation* (direction of one's sexual attraction).[36] More recently, Althof mentioned the three key distinctions of *gender* (as one's sense of being male or female), *object choice* (those people or items to whom one is sexually attracted) and *intention* (what a person actually wants to do with their desires).[37] These accounts of sexual identity point to the complexities inherent in discussions of a shift in preferred language from *homosexual* to *gay*. To use the term *gay* is to say something about sociocultural communities that have formed among those who have a shared identity.*

One of the problems with this shift in language from *homosexual* to *gay* is that it is one more way in which we blur important, meaningful distinc-

*This is how the *Publication Manual of the American Psychological Association* explained its decision to shift preferred language in APA style away from *homosexual* to *gay:* "*Lesbian* and *gay* refer primarily to identities and to culture and communities that have developed among people who share those identities." Further, "the terms lesbians and gay men are preferable to homosexual when referring to specific groups. . . . Homosexuality has been associated in the past with negative stereotypes." American Psychological Association. (2001). *Publication Manual of the American Psychological Association* (2001), Washington, DC: American Psychological Association, p. 67.

tions by treating certain words as synonymous. By treating *homosexual* or *homosexually oriented* as synonymous with *gay* is to actually leave out an important subpopulation of persons who experience same-sex attraction but do not identify with their experiences and do not wish to integrate them into a gay identity.*

The most descriptive way to speak of a person's experiences is to say that he or she has same-sex feelings or sexual attractions. It is the most descriptive account one can give because it simply means giving an account of the person's experience of erotic attraction. In the Laumann and colleagues study, 6.2% of men and 4.5% of women reported experiencing same-sex attraction.[39]

When we consider the relationship between same-sex attraction and a homosexual orientation, it is not always clear how much same-sex attraction translates into a person's subjective account that they have a homosexual or bisexual orientation. When people report same-sex attraction continually, or perhaps *persistently,* we often refer to that person as having a homosexual *orientation.* Homosexual orientation normally refers to the consistent directionality of one's experiences of sexual attraction, that is, the attractions are consistently same-sex in such a way that we think of the person's attractions as *oriented* to the same sex. It might also be said that those who identify as having a homosexual orientation and those who report having a bisexual orientation are a subpopulation of those who report experiencing same-sex attraction. In other words, many more people may have occasional experiences of same-sex attraction but they would not have so many or such a consistent experience of same-sex attraction that they would think of themselves as having a homosexual orientation. It may also be the case that even if a person experienced significantly intense same-sex attraction, they might refuse to describe themselves as having a homosexual orientation on metaphysical grounds, that is, they may believe that sexual orientation is something real, but that the category "heterosexual" is the only natural human sexual orientation, and that other experiences that are referred to as "homosexuality" and "bisexuality" are linguistic constructs fashioned by society to describe variations in sexual preference. Generally speaking, however, the language "homosexual orientation" is descriptive and not loaded with any implicit meaning; it does not necessarily communicate anything definitive about that person's sexual identity.

This is the first culture throughout history in which a substantial number of individuals have said of themselves, "I am gay."[40] A number of historical factors appear to have contributed to this point in time when the emergence of a gay community was even a possibility. In his analysis of the various forms of homosexuality, Herdt concluded that "only by disengaging sexuality from the traditions of family, reproduction, and parenthood was the evolution of the gay movement a social and historical likelihood."[41]

Although many theorists believe that the beginnings of sexual orientation are present early on in a person's life, solidification of a homosexual orientation and integration of same-sex attraction into a gay identity is something that occurs over time. In most models this occurs in later childhood through young adulthood.[42]

Also, although this subpopulation has not been studied extensively, research suggests there are a number of people who experience same-sex attraction but who dis-identify with a gay identity, that is, they choose not to integrate their experiences of same-sex attraction or a homosexual or bisexual orientation into a gay identity. For example, Yarhouse and Tan compared and contrasted the experiences of 20 individuals who identified as Christian and integrated their experiences of same-sex attraction into a gay, lesbian or bisexual identity, and 34 individuals who identified as Christian and dis-identified with a gay identity.[43] Dis-identification can also be found in studies of gay and lesbian identity development and synthesis. For example, 15% of McDonald's sample of 199 males reported not having acquired a positive gay identity but had an alternative sexual identity.[44] Also, 3 of 14 lesbians in Sophie's study reported dis-identifying with their experiences of same-sex attraction and self-identifying as heterosexual.[45]

So while we might refer to those who self-identify as "gay" as sexual minorities, there is also a group of persons who experience same-sex attraction but do not assume a gay identity. They are a minority among those who identify with the gay community, and perhaps as minorities within a sexual minority group they are particularly marginalized in society. Not all who experience same-sex attraction identify themselves as having a homosexual orientation; not all who experiences, same-sex attraction or who identify themselves as having a homosexual orientation engage in homosexual behavior; not all who experience same-sex attraction or identify themselves as having a homosexual orientation or engage in homosexual behavior in turn think of themselves as "gay."

We want to pursue one more chain of thought in this section. We would argue, on behalf of the population of individuals under study in this project, that those seeking change of sexual orientation are often the object of misunderstanding, scorn and active suppression in contemporary society. Nothing serves to demonstrate this better than the amazing and rapid transition in the relationship of sexual orientation and the diagnosis of "mental illness" in the pages of the *Diagnostic and Statistical Manual of Mental Disorders (DSM)*[46] of the American Psychiatric Association, the "diagnostic Bible" of the mental health professions, across its various editions over the last three decades.*

In the first edition of the *DSM* in 1952, the manifestation of homosexual orientation was a disorder by its very nature; in this edition, homosexuality was prima facie evidence of a "personality disorder." To be homosexual, in other words, was to be disordered.

Even in the 1960s the homosexual condition began to move away from being considered a "mental illness" in and of itself. In the second edition of the *DSM*, published in 1968, homosexuality appeared as a separate disorder under the categorization of the "neuroses," a diagnostic category whose prominent feature was anxiety, but was kept separate from the sexual deviancy classification. Specifically, the *DSM-II* added a new classification called "sexual orientation disturbance [homosexuality]," but homosexual orientation per se was no longer a disorder. Rather, this classification was for

> individuals whose sexual interests are directed primarily toward people of the same sex and who are either disturbed by, in conflict with, or wish to change their sexual orientation. This diagnostic category is distinguished from homosexuality, which by itself does not constitute a psychiatric disorder. Homosexuality per se is one form of sexual behavior, and with other forms of sexual behavior which are not by themselves psychiatric disorders, are not listed in this nomenclature.[47]

---

*Parts of the following discussion of the evolution of DSM terminology are adapted from the doctoral dissertation of Jon S. Ebert, "Toward Crisis or Communion: Questioning Psychological Distress in Religiously Mediated Change," Wheaton College, supervised by Stanton L. Jones and completed 2003.

It was no longer the case that to be homosexual was to be disordered, but rather a diagnostic category was set up for those distressed about their orientation. This foreshadows the question we sought to study here, in that the insipient implication of this conceptualization was that if there is a "disorder" present with homosexual orientation, it is tied to being distressed about the orientation.

In 1973 the American Psychiatric Association voted to remove homosexuality per se from the *DSM* as a disorder, though when one understands clearly exactly what the *DSM-II* said, this was less of the radical move than it is often represented to be. This became codified in the *DSM-III* (1980): sexual orientation disturbance [homosexuality] was removed and a new classification called "Ego-dystonic homosexuality" was added. This classification was reserved for "homosexuals for whom changing sexual orientations is a persistent concern, and should be avoided in cases where the desire to change sexual orientations may be brief, temporary manifestation of an individual's difficulty in adjusting to a new awareness of his or her homosexual impulses."[48]

This change was short lived; the *DSM-III-R* (1987) removed ego-dystonic homosexuality and any mention of homosexuality all together. The *DSM-IV* (1994) made only minor changes in the treatment of sexual orientation. The most recent edition, *DSM-IV-TR* (2000), is more explicit about the types of deviation clinicians should not pathologize, stating, "Neither deviant behavior (e.g. political, religious, or sexual) nor conflicts that are primarily between the individual and society are mental disorders unless the deviance or conflict is a symptom of a dysfunction in the individual."[49] It later mentions sexual orientation generally in a diagnosis called "sexual disorder not otherwise specified (NOS)." Within the sexual disorder NOS, one of the criteria is "persistent and marked distress about sexual orientation."[50]

With this final change the transformation in views is clear. Just over three decades before, to be homosexual was to be disordered. Now, *to be distressed about one's sexual orientation* is to be disordered. Put another way, disorder was once considered endemic to homosexual orientation, but now it is a disorder not to be fully accepting of one's "given" sexual orientation. Now, individuals who seek change to their sexual orientations are pathologized. Who is the sexual minority now in the eye of the mental health establishment?

A Case Study in Dialogue

The present study is, we hope and intend, an example of a constructive exchange between psychology and religion, one with the potential to manifest all three of these positive characteristics as articulated previously. Already we failed to resist to the temptation to leap into this dialogue, saying "some psychologists say this, but Christians have believed . . ." It is this sort of dialogue that characterizes the present study.

The hypotheses for the study came out of a fruitful interchange between the type of psychological essentialist view previously discussed and a Christian theology and ethic that regards homosexual practice as a moral violation of God's intent for human life and the "homosexual condition" as one that must be seen as disordered in comparison to God's creational intent. This religious orientation led us to question whether secular conceptualizations of sexual orientation were (1) intellectually compelling and (2) empirically sound or well established; this is "the critical-evaluative mode of functioning."

In the light of these questions, we proposed empirical research hypotheses in order to seek to advance the science of psychology. If there are trustworthy verities in modern psychology, the immutability of sexual orientation would seem to be among them. To quote Jones's 1994 study:

> Koch (1981) said "We cannot discriminate a so-called variable . . . without making strong presumptions of philosophical cast about the nature of our human subject matter" (p. 267; see also Tjeltveit, 1989). The nature of psychology, given the complexity, irreducibility and obscurity of its subject matter, is profoundly shaped by conceptual presuppositions we bring to our areas of study. This "theory-ladenness" (a term attributed to philosopher of science N. R. Hanson) of the data may be accentuated in the human or behavioral sciences.[51]

Our presumptions of a "philosophical/theological" nature led us to explore what most psychologists today would believe to be impossible: change in sexual orientation. Whereas it would seem that nonreligious psychologists have tended to look at the claims of sexual-orientation change as necessarily a false artifact of extremist religious belief, we were more open to examination of this claim. Perhaps, we pondered, contemporary science has it wrong about the immutability of sexual orientation, and perhaps even about the nature of sexual orientation itself and about the fundamental role of sexuality in human personality. Indeed, our results stand as an anomaly to the reigning paradigms.

Other anomalies have been documented, but without fundamentally challenging the reigning paradigm. Surely the most bizarre would be the study published by three respected behavioral scientists in the late 1970s of the "healing" of a transsexual through exorcism. Abel, Barlow and Blanchard were running a fairly standard evaluation protocol on transsexuals going through the (then avant-garde) surgical sex-reassignment treatment process.[52] "John," a biological male who wanted to become a female, had already been undergoing psychotherapy directed at gender-reassignment as well as hormone therapy to enlarge his breasts and to develop other secondary sex characteristics of females; he was already living as a female, and was on the verge of the final and irreversible surgical procedure to remove his male genitals and replace them with constructed female genitals. The subject, however, disappeared from the study before surgery, and only came in contact accidentally with the researchers some time later, at which time the following story emerged: Family members and friends had pleaded with John to see a faith-healer/exorcist, who had indeed "cast out" many evil spirits, leaving John feeling completely cured of his transsexualism. Abel, Barlow and Blanchard put John through the standard battery used with the rest of their patients and found to their amazement that by all scientific standards John was no longer a transsexual, but in every discernible way a healthy, functional male whose biological and psychological gender were in perfect synchrony. The authors commented, "What cannot be denied, however, is that a patient who was very clearly a transsexual by the most conservative criteria assumed a long-lasting masculine gender identity in a remarkably short period of time following an apparent exorcism."[53]

Similarly, other studies have been published claiming that homosexual orientation can be changed, some claiming the possibility of change by religious means. Perhaps the first was by respected psychiatrist E. Mansell Pattison, whose report in a premier journal of psychiatry of documented change in homosexual orientation as a result of involvement in a religious healing ministry of a Pentecostal church was discussed and generally dismissed.[54] Much more recently, respected research psychiatrist Robert Spitzer reported his study of a large number of "success cases" of religiously mediated change, but was subjected to unprecedented negative critique and his findings dismissed as post hoc.[55]

The present study of the experiences of men and women who enter a religiously affiliated ministry to help them change their sexual orientation can be treated as a case study of science examining what is purported to be a religiously grounded phenomenon and of scientific study inspired by a set of religious presuppositions alien to a good many members of the scientific community. And we would add as well that our study, though decidedly imperfect, corrects for the most glaring limitations of prior studies because it is prospective (attempts to start assessing the participants at the beginning of the change process rather than dealing with "after the fact" successes) and longitudinal (following participants over time rather than serving as a "one time snapshot" of their status). The American Psychological Association has set these standards as the necessary basis for a serious claim that change is possible; it says that the problem with research claiming to show sexual orientation change is that "treatment outcome is not followed and reported over time as would be the standard to test the validity of any mental health intervention."[56] This study meets these standards.

In other words, the often very separate worlds of behavioral sciences and religion intersect in meaningful ways in the lives of these who turn to religious resources to change their sexual orientation because of reasons grounded in their religious worldviews.

Unfortunately, the scientific worldview we have been discussing may make it difficult for some within scientific circles to understand the motivations of those who have chosen to pursue these services. Post believes that a "strong scientific ideology and world view" may contribute to the failure among some clinicians to assess religious functioning or to "consider religion or other cultural aspects of patient experience with seriousness."[57] A historical analysis also suggests that as the scientific framework emerged it challenged existing "theologies,"[58] thereby planting a seed of suspicion toward religious persons within those trained as scientists.

Bluntly, many scientists are deeply distrustful of and suspicious toward religious belief and experience.

Interestingly, the United States, though it has seen an increase in religious diversity in the past two hundred years, has remained remarkably religious in its overall composition. The U.S. population today is predominantly Judeo-Christian, with Protestants making up over 50% of the population, Catholics representing about 25% of the population, and Jews making up about 2% of the population.[59] Other religions, for example, Hindu, Muslim and Buddhist, account for less than 10% of the population; about the same percentage reports no religious preference.

But does religious affiliation translate into anything of any greater significance? Recent polls reflect that over 90% of people surveyed believe in "God or a universal spirit."[60] Nearly 90% of people identified religion as either "very important" (58%) or "fairly important" (29%), and nearly 90% pray to God at least occasionally to thank God for blessings or to talk to God, to ask for their sins to be forgiven or to ask for guidance.

Religiously Grounded Presuppositions Alien to the Scientific Community

If we are a society that is relatively religious in terms of the general population, and if there are among those who are religious a group of people who actually try to follow the prescriptive claims of their faith community, it would come as no surprise to find a subpopulation of persons who do not wish to act on their experiences of same-sex attraction in light of their religious beliefs and values.

But the risk is that some religiously grounded presuppositions are alien to the scientific community, such as the presupposition that God has preexisting claims on one's sexuality and sexual behavior. When these presuppositions are alien to those behavioral scientists providing services through the mental health professions, there is a danger of a fundamental failure on the part of the clinician to understand and enter the phenomenological world of the client. Post recognized the risk when he stated:

> No one could deny that an incorrect clinical interpretation of a religious patient would be harmful if it leads to an incorrect or distorted picture of a person's mental health. Certainly, a bias against religion would contribute to

> failing to recognize the religious patient in her or his fullest human dimension—a failure that can only compromise the therapeutic enterprise. It is difficult to estimate the extent of this bias in clinical practice, but to the extent that it may occur, it is cause for concern.[61]

One of the most relevant religiously grounded presuppositions that is alien to some within the scientific community is the moral valuation of homosexual conduct that fuels motivation to pursue change of orientation treatment.

In chapter two we will look specifically at the population we are studying and how religion plays a role in their lives, as well as ways in which religiously grounded presuppositions motivate their pursuit of treatment. As we turn our attention to the population in question, we would note that there has been considerable and intense debate in professional circles about whether people have the right to choose to seek to change their sexual reorientation. What if that decision is based on religiously grounded presuppositions?

Many within professional mental health circles recognize that we have moved from implied consent (prior to the twentieth century) to informed consent, which was established by case law and reflects a growing respect for personal autonomy in making decisions about medical procedures. Not long ago people were not given the opportunity to consent to medical procedures. Their consent was implied as patients deferred to the expertise of their physician. That was the standard in health care. But we have witnessed a shift from implied consent to informed consent. Today people have the right to choose among treatment options, as well as the right to decline treatment against the judgment of their medical provider. Informed consent is the standard today. However, we are beginning to see a movement toward what might be referred to as "ignored consent." There are those who who would keep patients from access to reorientation therapies even if they give consent; we will look more closely at such arguments in chapter ten.

Conclusion

This study is an exercise of conversation between religion and psychological science. The prevailing psychological wisdom is that sexual orientation cannot be changed and that the attempt to change is harmful. The religious perspective of traditional Christian belief offers a contrasting perspective from which to see the homosexual condition. Psychological science must finally put its emphasis on empirical data. Out of conversation with religious belief, that of the authors and of an understudied minority of those experiencing same-sex attraction, comes the empirical hypothesis that sexual orientation may not be immutable. The present study produces significant scientific evidence that sexual orientation is in fact changeable for some, and this should trigger a considerable reexamination of many of the presuppositions about sexual orientation and sexual identity that hold sway in contemporary Western culture.

2

Understanding the Population

Christian Views of Sexuality, Ethical Norms, and Views of Healing and Change

MANY PEOPLE TODAY STILL CONSIDER the United States to be a Christian nation. There is some research to support this view, or at least the view that many in this country are religiously affiliated or engage in specific religious behaviors. For example, recent Gallup Polls report that about two out of every three Americans claim to be a member of a synagogue or church and attend services at least once a month or more.* This attendance rate has remained remarkably stable for the past thirty years. Over two-thirds of Americans (68%) say that religion can answer all or most of today's problems, which suggests that significant numbers of people turn to religion during difficult times. Almost 88% of Americans say religion is either very or fairly important to them, and an astounding 90% of Americans say they believe in God. However, it has been estimated that a smaller percentage (closer to 20%) of Americans hold to the traditional or conservative Christian beliefs and live according to these religious beliefs day to day.[1]

Many psychologists and other mental health professionals, like other cultural and intellectual leaders, are profoundly unfamiliar with and unsympathetic to the religiosity of the general population. Since the events of 9/11, some key leaders in the popular media have admitted their igno-

*The Barna organization (www.barna.org) reports on their polling research suggesting that while "born agains" might represent almost half of the U.S. population, those with more conservative theological views are a considerably smaller percentage of the population. The Gallup Poll from 2001 also notes that 45% of Americans identify themselves as evangelical or "born again" Christians.

rance of and lack of respect for the large conservatively religious constituency in the United States and internationally, and have called for more empathetic engagement with religious populations and views.[2] Prior research has established that mental health professionals are substantially less traditionally religious than the general population and that graduate training programs in these fields do little to train future practitioners in the meaning and role of religion in the lives of many in the populations they will be serving.[3] Generally speaking, it simply seems to be the case that because religion is unimportant in the lives of many professors of clinical psychology, religion does not make its way onto the list of important diversity variables that developing professionals are trained to attend to and respond empathetically toward. It is a commonplace in the mental health field that a prerequisite of respectful and effective engagement with a person is a compassionate understanding of the subjective world of the other, and yet religious conservatives are often not accorded this respect, especially in connection with their views on sexuality and sexual orientation.

In this chapter we want to give readers who may be unfamiliar with the conservative Christian community an understanding of its beliefs and practices, especially as regards sexuality and sexual orientation.[4]

In explaining "the conservative Christian view of sexuality," we want to acknowledge the lack of either unanimity or uniformity among either this religious constituency or the "secular world" that fails to understand it. There is no monolithic "secular humanistic" view of sexuality against which "the conservative Christian view" is easily contrasted. Further, there are an array of less traditionalist Christian views of sexuality and of sexual ethics, the proponents of which would dispute that the family of views expressed here are deserving of the title "a conservative Christian view of sexuality."[5] Still, in contrast to the kaleidoscope of views of sexuality in the world, there is something approaching homogeneity in the views of the population under study here. We are able to articulate this view as dedicated participants in the subculture from which this population is drawn, but hopefully with some objectivity and openness to critique. We would emphasize as we begin that the view of sexuality we are about to explicate is fundamentally at variance with the most frequent views of sexuality expressed in the scientific or professional sexuality fields, and also those found in the gay advocacy world. This view provides a set of fundamentally different metaphysical assumptions, a different presumptive grid, through which to see the world of sexuality and sexual orientation, and it leads to different action choices (see chap. 1).

We will focus here on the type of conservative Christian views that predominate in the population we have studied. These views are very similar, but not identical, to the views of conservative or traditionalist Roman Catholics. The views of sexuality we will explore cannot themselves be understood apart from understanding the broader context of religious views about the nature of the body and of the person, of God and his work in the world, and of the nature of our relationship to God and his calling on our lives. It is worth noting that the views of sexuality of the conservative Christian world hold strong similarities to the views of sexuality (but *not* of the person and work of Jesus) of Orthodox and other conservative Jews and of most Muslims. This, of course, makes sense given the connection of all three religions to the God who revealed himself to and established a covenant with Abraham. Even so, our focus here is traditionalist Christianity.

Christianity holds that God is a personal being who is all-powerful, all-knowing, and perfectly loving and perfectly just. When humanity was alienated and lost due to our own willful rebellion against him (this rebellion being the root and substance of sin), this loving God revealed himself and his will to a rebellious humanity. This revelation was essentially an intrusion into history and an unprecedented breakdown in the barriers (caused by sin) that exist between God and humanity. This "break-in" began with the call of a covenant people, a people of the promise, through Abraham and the growth of the Jewish nation, continued through the more complete revelation of his will through Moses, continued through the judges, the establishment of the Jewish nation under Kings David and Solomon, and through the prophets. Jews and Christians agree that God is perfectly good, while we are not, and that our acceptance to be God's children occurs through his mercy, forgiveness and love. They agree that out of that mercy, forgiveness and love, God made a covenant with those he claimed as his people, a covenant (or everlasting and irrevocable promise) to be their God, to faithfully guide and bless those who love him and serve him, to bless the entire world through them by illuminating the darkness of the world through them, and to bring the life of this world to a culmination in which good triumphs and God is vindicated as the Lord of all. They also agree that God communicated to his people in words through his prophets, and that this communication (often called revelation) is faithfully and trustworthily recorded in the Bible.* They agree that this revelation includes a faithful history of God's dealings with his people, a truthful depiction of his character and nature, and an outline of his moral laws for human conduct, which constitute an objective standard by which we may know (though never exhaustively) good from evil.

Then, in a departure from Judaism, Christians believe that God's central and focal intrusion into history came through God's entering history himself by becoming human in the fully human and yet fully divine person of Jesus Christ. Jews had been looking (and many are still looking) for a Messiah, a Savior, and Christians believe that Jesus was that provided Savior. God became a human and yet remained God. Christians believe that Jesus lived a perfect (sinless) life and was crucified. His crucifixion, his death, was a sacrificial offering that paid the penalty for human rebellion against God, a penalty that a perfectly just God rightly demanded for the rebellion of all humanity. In this way Christians see the confluence of God's just demands for punishment with the sacrificing love of God's mercy. Christians also believe that by conquering death through rising to life again after being fully dead for three days (the resurrection), Jesus provides the way to a new life to those who believe in him and give their lives to him. Christians believe that the sacrifice of Jesus on the cross and his defeat of death through rising to new life is the full and final revelation of exactly how God's mercy is extended to those that love him and are his children.

For conservative Christians, a personal relationship with Jesus Christ and a belief in the veracity of the Bible as God's own words to guide their lives together affects how they view the way they are supposed to live, including how they are to relate to others as sexual creatures. We will now begin to focus specifically on their view of sexuality.

---

*Christians, of course, believe that that process of divine revelation continued during and past the time of Jesus resulting in what Christians call the New Testament; Jews, traditionally, demur and regard only what Christians call the Old Testament (or Hebrew Bible) as God's revelation of himself.

To begin, because God is the benevolent Creator of the natural world, Christians view physical reality as good. God did not make the world out of his own divine essence, so the physical world is not worthy of human worship, but God did speak the physical world into existence out of nothing. The physical world is not a god, but it is the good handiwork of God. Over and over again the Bible records God referring to his creation as "good," and this affirmation confirms the inherent goodness of the created world, of physical reality.

Human beings' existence as embodied persons is an aspect of this good (but not divine) physicality; we are made from the dust, and to the dust we will return. From a Christian perspective, though, people are more than bodies. We are made "in the image of God" (Genesis 1:27), including the spiritual and soulish aspects of our persons. We are nevertheless "living beings," bodies "formed . . . from the dust of the ground" into which has been breathed "the breath of life" (Genesis 2:7). A picture of complexity begins to emerge: we see that we are dust, but at the same time much more than dust.

The goodness of bodily existence is not grounded only in the doctrine of *creation* but in two additional key theological themes unique to traditional Christianity as well. The doctrine of the *incarnation*, of God becoming a human being in Jesus, is central to Christianity and is perhaps its most stark contrast with Judaism (as well as the other Abrahamic faith, Islam). Christians believe that God (God the Son, the second person of the trinitarian, or threefold, God)[6] became fully human as the man Jesus. Clearly, bodily existence must not be intrinsically evil or incompatible with the perfect good if God can assume human life. This teaching attests that the bedrock of Christian theology is incarnate, embodied love.

The other great theological theme that affirms bodily goodness is that of the *resurrection of the body*. Christians believe that the final state of humanity, when all the brokenness of this world is healed, will be as resurrected and perfected bodies, and that we will, in that state, enjoy God forever. Christians have thus, throughout most of history, held views of their own existences as fundamentally embodied (in a positive way as opposed to the negative view of embodiment from Buddhism). Caroline Bynum, for example, documents that consideration of the physical body was central to reflections about identity and personhood, and about the very nature of the soul, for a huge swath of church history.[7]

This embodiment, while not reducible to sexuality, certainly grounds and subsumes sexuality. Unlike other creation stories in surrounding Mesopotamian and Hellenistic cultures that regarded gender to have occurred as an accident or defect in the original creation, the Genesis narrative about creation declares God's creation of a gendered people to have been by divine intent, with *both* sexes declared to have been made in the "image of God" (Genesis 1:27) and both the male and female together declared "very good" (Genesis 1:31). This was a radically egalitarian declaration in the context of the ancient world.

We are given clear indications of a relational conceptualization of human character, a relationality grounded in part (but perhaps not reducible to) our sexuality. The first man, as the story unfolds in Genesis 2 before the creation of the first woman, living in a state of perfection in the perfect environment and in the context of a perfect relationship with God, is judged incomplete by his Creator. "It is not good for the man to be alone," God says (Genesis 2:18), thus establishing that even perfection in all other areas of life cannot erase the divinely created human need for "the other." God then creates the suitable partner for the man. The man himself recognizes the profound complementarity of this new creation, the first woman, and God declares that because of this reality, "a man will leave his father and mother and be united to his wife, and they will become one flesh" (Genesis 2:24). This union of husband and wife is tied to passionate love and deep communion in a number of places in the Scriptures (e.g., the Song of Songs; Proverbs 5:18-19), though the patriarchal society of the time with its arranged marriages did not always exalt this potentiality.

The foundation for the Christian rejection of homosexuality is rooted here, in the creation story and its assumption of the intentionality of God in designing one male and one female to be united in permanent union. This vision of sexuality in marriage stands in contrast to an individualistic ethos of the type that permeates contemporary secular psychology and that celebrates human autonomy and a presumed capacity to shape and form our erotic choices in the absence of transcendent and fixed meaning and purpose for our sexuality.

The declaration that the two "will become one flesh," an outcome explicitly tied to sexual union in intercourse in other parts of the Christian Scriptures, is the foundational teaching of the Christian tradition anchoring its view of marriage. Other meanings besides one-flesh union are attached to full sexual intimacy: (1) the prospect of bearing children is voiced as a blessing on the first couple (Genesis 1:28) and on other subsequent persons in Scripture; (2) Scripture itself extols the physical pleasures of sexual union (Proverbs 5) and links eroticism explicitly with romantic love and intimacy in the Song of Songs; and (3) the Christian apostle Paul even gives stern admonition to married couples that fulfillment of sexual need is a legitimate function that each spousal partner should provide for the other (and again, does so in a remarkably egalitarian fashion [1 Corinthians 7:1-6]).

Despite these other meanings, however, it is the inevitability that sexual intercourse will unite a woman and man in a one-flesh unity—some sort of transindividual reality—that anchors the prohibition on adultery and of all sexual union outside of marriage (what is commonly called sexual immorality [1 Corinthians 6:12-17]) and against divorce in the teachings of Jesus (Matthew 19:1-10). Sexual intercourse thus is seen as having a determinate or fixed meaning, regardless of the intentions of the participants in the act. Nonreligious persons today are accustomed to thinking that the meaning of their sexual actions are conferred by their intentions for those acts. What is intended as a casual sexual encounter is exactly that, casual, because only our intentions determine the meaning of the sexual act. But the Christian tradition asserts the opposite: that sexually intimate acts have fixed meanings by their very nature. In 1 Corinthians 6:12-17, the apostle Paul asserts that though both the Corinthian man and the prostitute with whom he is consorting mean their encounter to be a pleasurable, casual and transient one, nevertheless the fixed and unalterable meaning and function of the act is the establishment of a one-flesh union.

Conservative Christians are often stigmatized as having negative views of sex. The sex-therapy literature is replete with numerous examples of negative views of sexuality attributed to conservative religious upbringing. The attributional error here may be truly parallel to the complaint of gay-affirming therapists who criticize the attribution that all homosexuals are depressed (for example) because the homosexuals one happens to see in therapy are there because they are depressed. With numerous clinical examples in training texts referring to sexually repressed individuals raised in rigid, antisex, religiously conservative homes, the impression of many mental health professionals based on their training (and a complementary lack of direct exposure to the conservative religious population) is that conservative religion is typically associated with sexual pathology and repression. Interestingly, the research literature paints a clearly different picture. In empirical research on sexual satisfaction, traditional religiosity is often associated with more positive experiences of sexuality and higher sexual satisfaction.[8] When one understands the core teachings of the tradition, this is no longer mysterious.

In the context of marriage the teaching of the Christian Scriptures is unequivocal that sexual intercourse is a created good that should serve the wholly positive purposes in marriage of one-flesh union and also reproduction, pleasure and need gratification (e.g., Hebrews 13:4). The positive view of sexuality is clear upon careful study of many passages of the Bible.[9] Take, for instance, 1 Timothy 4:1-5, in which the apostle Paul declares:

> The Spirit clearly says that in later times some will abandon the faith and follow deceiving spirits and things taught by demons. Such teachings come through hypocritical liars, whose consciences have been seared as with a hot iron. They forbid people to marry and order them to abstain from certain foods, which God created to be received with thanksgiving by those who believe and who know the truth. For everything God created is good, and nothing is to be rejected if it is received with thanksgiving, because it is consecrated by the word of God and prayer.

Though this passage seems on the surface to say little directly about sexuality, in condensed form it may be the best summary of the traditional Christian view of sexuality in the Bible. In it we find the creational view of sexuality as good, but also the qualifications needed on that view. To see this, the historical background to the passage must be unpacked. The "hypocritical liars" Paul is attacking were the Gnostics. The early Christians were in a pitched battle with Gnosticism, which taught that the two essences of the world, physical reality and spiritual reality, were antithetical. According to Gnostic teaching, spiritual reality was good by its nature, while physical reality (the physical world and the physical body—marriage and sexuality in particular) was intrinsically evil or at least a substantially lower level of good. Gnosticism was becoming mixed with Christian teaching, resulting in Christ-followers who were repudiating marriage because of the sexual relations intrinsic to it. In florid terms, Paul brands such teaching as heresy, focusing on the Gnostic rejection of sex ("forbid people to marry") and of certain types of food. In contrast to Gnostic teaching, Paul teaches that these created gifts are to be "received with thanksgiving." Paul approaches the issue of sex starting from creation, declaring that "everything God created is good."

But Paul also acknowledges that the rebellion of humankind has complicated things, such that there is a qualification to just accepting marriage and sexuality as good. Because human rebellion has marred the creation, we must, in a sense, "wipe the dirt off" of God's beautiful creation; this is done when these gifts of marriage and food are "received with thanksgiving" and "consecrated by the word of God and prayer." So Paul in this passage approaches sex *first* from the viewpoint of creation, and then secondarily through the implications of our brokenness and God's redemptive work.

Sexual union is foundational to marriage, but marriage in turn serves crucial purposes, one of which might be termed iconic. An icon (most common in the various Orthodox traditions of Christianity) is a tangible object that serves as a "window" to the transcendent. The Scriptures present marriage as an instantiation of spiritual truth, an earthly model or icon of the relationship of the risen Jesus Christ to his "bride" the church (Ephesians 5:25-33).[10] Marriages are formed by sexual union and also by the public exchange of vows of fidelity. Engaging in sexual union with one's spouse functions to continually renew and reaffirm the covenant between God, husband and wife.

We paint here a rather "rosy" picture of a traditional Christian view of sexuality, but we do so in the sincere belief that it is historically accurate. Many negative distortions of this core teaching abound in conservative Christian circles, and the sources of these distortions are many. Revivalists and evangelists of this tradition often seek to instigate repentance (regret for moral wrongdoing and a resolve to turn to righteous behavior) by inducing guilt. Some churches have taught (erroneously) that the primal sin of Adam and Eve was not disobedience but rather sexual passion. When Scripture speaks of the "flesh" as being the enemy of the "spirit" in the religious life, these churches conclude that the enemy is our bodies instead of understanding properly that the term *flesh* refers to the whole person in an attitude of rebellion and rejection toward God. The list could go on and on—the perception that Christian religious conservatism is linked often with antisexuality biases is not without some foundation. Our key point here is that these are distortions or misunderstandings of the heart of the teaching of the tradition and of the Bible.

A traditional Christian view of sexuality recognizes that God provided moral boundaries for human sexuality because of the human proclivity to rebel against God and to behave in ways utterly contrary to his will for our lives (i.e., sin). Humanity is seen, in Christian theology, as retaining this creational goodness as a foundational reality, but humanity is also seen as "totally depraved." The concept of total depravity may be the most frequently misunderstood of the major doctrines of the church. It does not assert we are "as evil at every moment and in every way as it is possible to be" (a clear impossibility since we can all always imagine how to behave yet more badly than we currently are). The doctrine of total depravity instead means that there is no aspect of our human existence that does not reflect our brokenness and rebellion against God. This reality has not eradicated the primal good of human character, but it conditions or infects all of human experience.

Sexual longings of all sorts, for example, are grounded first in our commonly shared and fundamentally good capacities for union and love and pleasure, but all of our sexual desires are also tainted with such evil tendencies as selfishness, sensuality (the disconnection of physical appetites from the transcendent purposes to which they are connected) or subjugation or violence flowing from inclinations toward broken and evil domination of the other. Hence, people experience a deep conflict in their sexuality (as in all their experience) wherein they know the potential and realized good of their sexual natures, but never experience that good distilled and pure, disconnected from their sinfulness.

This brokenness also entails a loss of sure moral sensitivity through our own capabilities; we are not only twisted in our experience of our sexuality (and all other areas of life too!) but in our capacity to know what is true and good as well. This is crucial: our sinful brokenness not only impairs our ability to be as good as we should, but *also impairs our desire to be good and even our ability to see and understand what is good.* Not only do we fail to be good; we also do not fully desire good or even recognize good. It is for this reason that explicit moral boundaries are placed on sexual behavior by God's command itself. God does not leave moral guidance to our instincts or intuitions, but he rather left an objective record, his instructions, of how he desires us to live in the form of written divine revelation.

The core moral prohibition of the Hebrew and Christian Scriptures with regard to sexuality is found in the Ten Commandments: "You shall not commit adultery" (Exodus 20:14). Full sexual intimacy was to be reserved for one relationship, that of heterosexual marriage. Some have interpreted this commandment in a very constricted way, arguing that this command was a limitation only on *married* people having sex with someone to whom they are not married, or even more restrictively that the prohibition is actually only against the wife who is the sexual property of her husband and not to be possessed by another man. So, it has been argued, the adultery ban prohibits a married man from having sex with another man's wife, but does not prohibit an unmarried man from having sex with an unmarried woman, nor indeed a married man from having sex with an unmarried woman such as a prostitute.

The textual evidence argues against such a narrow reading and favors the broader interpretation we have offered of reserving sexual intercourse for the married relationship alone. Note for example the pattern of civil punishments in ancient theocratic (ruled by God) Israel for sexual violations other than adultery. While adultery itself was a capital crime punishable by death, and punishments for infractions other than adultery less serious, such acts were nevertheless seen as crimes and were punishable. For example, if a young bride was discovered by her new husband to have had sex previously, she was to be stoned, even though no punishment is mentioned for her premarital partner (Deuteronomy 22:13-21).[11] Sex with a female slave who was promised in marriage but not yet freed was punishable by the man (slave owner) having to make a sin offering of a ram (Leviticus 19:20-22). Prostitution is termed *wickedness* in Leviticus 19:29, throughout Proverbs and in other places. It is clear that Scripture condemns sexual relations by any man with a woman to whom he is not married, even though the civil penalties vary according to marital status.

All of the subsidiary moral prohibitions regarding sex were extensions of and supportive of this core restriction on sexual intercourse outside the boundaries of heterosexual marriage: rape was forbidden (e.g., Deuteronomy 22:25-27), as was incest (e.g., Leviticus 18:6), homosexual intercourse (e.g., Leviticus 18:22; 20:13), and sexual intercourse with animals (e.g., Leviticus18:23; 20:15-16). In Matthew 5:27-30, Jesus added lust as an additional moral prohibition, broadening the explicit moral concerns of the faith from behavioral acts to thought acts. These prohibitions set the boundary conditions for behavior approved by God, but the "thou shalt nots" should not overshadow the profoundly positive affirmation of sexuality generally, and of its genital expression in marriage, communicated in the Bible.

Despite these moral boundaries, adherents of the Christian faith (including leaders charged and entrusted to be exemplars of wholeness and integrity) manifest their brokenness in failing to live by these constraints. At the worst, adherents and leaders do not just "fail to live up to these standards," but manifest the most heinous enslavement to sexual brokenness, as exemplified in the tragic crisis current at the moment of sexual abuse of children and adolescents by priests of the Roman Catholic Church and of other branches of Christianity. Equally, some Christians themselves have reduced their understanding of sexuality to these prohibitions alone, resulting in a repressive and negative approach to sexuality of the type that would produce the (likely unrepresentative) negative stereotypes many people may summon up from experience when they think of religion and sexuality.

With our sexual natures we might also ask what role overt sexual gratification plays in personal happiness and well-being, as well as in relational happiness and well-being. This way of framing the question parallels another issue crucial to the topic of this empirical study, and that is the state of choice of sexual abstinence or celibacy in response to the discovery that one is only attracted to persons of one's own sex. Hence, the question, Is overt genital sex essential to happiness or wholeness? is truly crucial.

Historically, Christian theology has answered that our sexual natures can be accepted and actualized without overt genital intimacy; this possibility and pattern are attested to by the moral constraints placed on sexual intimacy (constraints which would require unmarried persons, including widows/widowers and the divorced, to remain celibate until remarriage), by the specific commendation of celibacy as a lifestyle choice by the apostle Paul (1 Corinthians 7:8-9), and by the lived models of celibate individuals (foremost in the person of Jesus) who nevertheless lived fully actualized human lives. To experience the fullness of human life, denial of the specific physical, sexual needs of the self for the sake of living faithfully with and to God can be as or more essential than gratification of those physical needs, even as such choices create pressing practical and developmental challenges for the person to meet. This issue will become central later as celibacy as a strategy for coping with unwanted homosexual behavior and inclinations comes into focus with our sample.

This general account of a traditional Christian view of human sexuality and sexual behavior lays an important foundation for understanding the population from which our sample was drawn. We turn now to the range of responses within Christianity to homosexuality before focusing specifically on the nature of religious ministries and the various ways that ministries provide services to those who struggle with homosexuality.

Christian Ethical Responses to Homosexual Behavior

We have already mentioned homosexual behavior as a moral prohibition under the more superordinate prohibition on extramarital sexual intercourse. For the conservative Protestant traditions from which the ministries studied here derive their identities, the unequivocal condemnation of such behavior in Scripture is decisive; given this, we want to take the time to unpack this treatment of homosexual behavior in the Bible.[12]

The scriptural passages of direct and critical importance to the topic of homosexual behavior include Genesis 18—19 and its related passages, Leviticus 18:22; 20:13; Romans 1:18-32; 1 Corinthians 6:9-20; and 1 Timothy 1:8-11. All of these passages address homosexual practice as sin.

The first mention of homosexual behavior in the Bible is in the story of Sodom and Gomorrah in Genesis 18—19; it is from this story that the term *sodomy* was derived as a descriptive term for homosexual intimacy. Abram's nephew Lot receives two angels in his residence at Sodom, and as they prepare to retire for the evening,

> all the men from every part of the city of Sodom—both young and old—surrounded the house. They called to Lot, "Where are the men who came to you tonight? Bring them out to us so that we can have sex with them."
>
> Lot went outside to meet them and shut the door behind him and said, "No, my friends. Don't do this wicked thing. Look, I have two daughters who have never slept with a man. Let me bring them out to you, and you can do what you like with them. But don't do anything to these men, for they have come under the protection of my roof."
>
> "Get out of our way," they replied. (Genesis 19:4-9)

The story, of course, ends badly for the residents of Sodom. The angels strike them all blind, Lot and his family flee the city, and God destroys both Sodom and Gomorrah.

Even within the corpus of the biblical text, commentary on this passage leads to complicated interpretation. On the face of it an Old Testament prophetic passage, Ezekiel 16:48-50, decries the sin of Sodom and Gomorrah, but seems to omit mention of deviant sexuality at all, focusing instead on the pride, arrogance and lack of concern for the poor of the residents. Recent scholarship, however, has documented that the type of "arrogance" described in the passage is likely to have been understood implicitly in the context of the ancient world as a reference to blatant sexual deviancy.[13] A New Testament passage, moreover, describes how "Sodom and Gomorrah and the surrounding towns gave themselves up to sexual immorality and perversion" (Jude 7). Most biblical expositors throughout history have argued that the depravity of the twin cities was compound, including but not limited to homosexual intercourse (specifically rape in this story).[14]

The second mention of homosexual behavior refers to males only and is a straight moral disapproval of behavior described with reference to its heterosexual parallel: "Do not lie with a man as one lies with a woman; that is detestable" (Leviticus 18:22).

The third mention of homosexual behavior echoes the second, but includes a civil penalty of capital punishment for such behavior: "If a man lies with a man as one lies with a woman, both of them have done what is detestable. They must be put to death; their blood will be on their own heads" (Leviticus 20:13).

The New Testament seemingly mirrors the treatment of homosexual behavior of the Old Testament. Commentators arguing against the traditional stance have commented on the silence of Jesus with regard to homosexual behavior, but inferring approval or tolerance from his silence seems to have little credibility. As argued by Gagnon and others, Jesus evidenced little tolerance for watering down the sexual ethic of the Old Testament, and in his pronouncements either reiterated the sexual ethics of the Old Testament or raised the ethical bar (for instance by declaring lust to be as sinful as the actual commission of adultery and urging, in obviously hyperbolic terms, the most extreme exertions directed at the avoidance of sexual sin in Matthew 5:27-30).[15] Further, any argument that the silence of Jesus must be interpreted as tacit approval or tolerance toward homosexual conduct would have to be consistently applied to other actions condemned in the Old Testament on which Jesus is equally silent, and would anyone argue that Jesus is accepting of rape, incest or sex with animals because we have no recorded words from him on such behavior?

Two passages written by the apostle Paul mention homosexual conduct:

> Do you not know that the wicked will not inherit the kingdom of God? Do not be deceived: Neither the sexually immoral nor idolaters nor adulterers nor male prostitutes nor *homosexual offenders* nor thieves nor the greedy nor drunkards nor slanderers nor swindlers will inherit the kingdom of God. And that is what some of you were. But you were washed, you were sanctified, you were justified in the name of the Lord Jesus Christ and by the Spirit of our God.
>
> "Everything is permissible for me"—but not everything is beneficial. "Everything is permissible for me"—but I will not be mastered by anything. "Food for the stomach and the stomach for food"—but God will destroy them both. The body is not meant for sexual immorality, but for the Lord, and the Lord for the body. By his power God raised the Lord from the dead, and he will raise us also. Do you not know that your bodies are members of Christ himself? Shall I then take the members of Christ and unite them with a prostitute? Never! Do you not know that he who unites himself with

> a prostitute is one with her in body? For it is said, "The two will become one flesh." But he who unites himself with the Lord is one with him in spirit.
>
> Flee from sexual immorality. All other sins a man commits are outside his body, but he who sins sexually sins against his own body. Do you not know that your body is a temple of the Holy Spirit, who is in you, whom you have received from God? You are not your own; you were bought at a price. Therefore honor God with your body. (1 Corinthians 6:9-20, emphasis added)

> We know that the law is good if one uses it properly. We also know that law is made not for the righteous but for lawbreakers and rebels, the ungodly and sinful, the unholy and irreligious; for those who kill their fathers or mothers, for murderers, for adulterers and *perverts*, for slave traders and liars and perjurers—and for whatever else is contrary to the sound doctrine that conforms to the glorious gospel of the blessed God, which he entrusted to me. (1 Timothy 1:8-11, emphasis added)

The two italicized terms are actually differing translations of the same Greek term, which is a compound of two words that are side by side in the ancient Greek translation (the Septuagint) of the Leviticus 18:22 passage, where God condemns men who lie with men. Paul combines the Greek words for "man" *(arsēn)* and for "one who lies with" *(koitēs)* to create a term that literally means "man-liers" or as J. I. Packer translates it, "man-bedders."[16] The precise words Paul chose seems to assume the continuing validity of the Levitical command regarding homosexual conduct. Further, Paul uses a term that, like the Old Testament passage, focuses on behavior. Some today dismiss the biblical teaching because it does not use our modern concepts of sexual orientation, but by focusing on behavior he provides the specificity needed for a truly universal guideline.

The most complex passage condemning homosexual passion and behavior (albeit incidentally and illustratively) is at the very beginning of the book of Romans. Here, homosexual behavior is presented as representing a distortion of the creational intent of God in providing sexual intercourse as a means for creating a one-flesh union, of uniting husband and wife with sexual pleasure and need gratification, and of providing a means for the provision of children. It is in this sense that homosexual practice is viewed as a distortion of what is seen as natural by the apostle Paul. In the context of a searing condemnation of the sinfulness of the entire human race (Romans

1—3), Paul stresses that the order God intended for all of creation has been overturned by human sinfulness. The creatures he made in his image neither worshiped nor obeyed him, but "exchanged the truth of God for a lie." God thus gave them over to sexual impurity, just as a human parent might allow a rebellious child to continue on a path destined to result in pain and frustration. In keeping with the comprehensive pattern of an overturning of the created order, Paul mentions one form of sexual impurity, homosexual activity on the part of both genders, as overturning the creational, the "natural," order of sexuality. The mention of female homosexual activity is remarkable, as it is the only mention of such conduct in the Bible.

> The wrath of God is being revealed from heaven against all the godlessness and wickedness of men who suppress the truth by their wickedness, since what may be known about God is plain to them, because God has made it plain to them. For since the creation of the world God's invisible qualities—his eternal power and divine nature—have been clearly seen, being understood from what has been made, so that men are without excuse.
>
> For although they knew God, they neither glorified him as God nor gave thanks to him, but their thinking became futile and their foolish hearts were darkened. Although they claimed to be wise, they became fools and exchanged the glory of the immortal God for images made to look like mortal man and birds and animals and reptiles.
>
> Therefore God gave them over in the sinful desires of their hearts to sexual impurity for the degrading of their bodies with one another. They exchanged the truth of God for a lie, and worshiped and served created things rather than the Creator—who is forever praised. Amen.
>
> Because of this, God gave them over to shameful lusts. Even their women exchanged natural relations for unnatural ones. In the same way the men also abandoned natural relations with women and were inflamed with lust for one another. Men committed indecent acts with other men, and received in themselves the due penalty for their perversion.
>
> Furthermore, since they did not think it worthwhile to retain the knowledge of God, he gave them over to a depraved mind, to do what ought not to be done. They have become filled with every kind of wickedness, evil, greed and depravity. . . . Although they know God's righteous decree that those who do such things deserve death, they not only continue to do these very things but also approve of those who practice them. (Romans 1:18-29, 32)

Historically, the church has had consensus that these biblical injunctions, which appear across a variety of genres of biblical literature, apply across chronological and cultural boundaries in universal condemnation of homosexual intercourse as immoral. No less of a respected and central figure in twentieth-century Christian theology than German systematic theologian Wolfhart Pannenberg has stated that "the biblical assessments of homosexual practice are unambiguous in their rejection." Further, he stated that "the entire biblical witness includes practicing homosexuality without exception among the kinds of behavior that give particularly striking expression to humanity's turning away from God."[17] Homosexual behavior has historically been seen as representing disobedience against the express command of the one true God. Christ himself indicated that obedience to the command of God is central to the Christian ethic (John 14:21), an emphasis echoed by his most beloved disciple (1 John 2:4).

There are, of course, many today who disagree with the historical consensus as presented here. Some of the disagreement is institutional. Most prominently in the United States, the Episcopal Church in the USA (the "mainline Episcopalians") has fully embraced acceptance of active homosexual persons as ordained ministers. Such international church bodies as the United Church of Canada, the Methodist Church of Great Britain and the Church of Sweden, among others, have offered similar acceptance. Gay-affirming churches and even a denomination, the Metropolitan Community Church, have also arisen. The rationales offered for departing from the traditional teaching are various, including (1) arguments that new understandings of textual and historical-contextual issues undermine the traditional understandings of the biblical texts prohibiting homosexuality, (2) arguments that the higher and more universal ethical demands of sincere Christian faith—particularly justice and love—supersede more parochial and primitive moral teachings, (3) arguments that the findings of science and the consensus of mental health professionals should carry weight in moral reasoning, and (4) arguments that the spiritual experience of homosexual persons demands respect and affirmation. It would be well beyond the scope of this work to further elaborate these and other arguments or to articulate the responses of traditionalists to such. Our straightforward presentation of the biblical material, however, would be congruent with the moral views of the Protestant ministries studied here, and so the disputation about the teachings of the Bible and their relevance for today is not germane. We now turn to the practical responses to homosexual persons that flow from these conservative views.

Christian Pastoral Responses to Homosexual Persons

What comes to mind when you think about traditionalist Christianity and homosexuality? Some people may think of Fred Phelps and the gay-hatred movement. Phelps, termed a pastor in his small, independent church, is perhaps best known for attending the funeral of Matthew Shepard, a young gay man who was brutally murdered, and chanting "Matt is in hell." Phelps provides a vivid example of one extreme approach a few Christians have taken to homosexuality, an approach we might term "gay hatred." It is gay hatred because his response to homosexuality is a condemnation of both the behavior and the people who identify as homosexual. Because he identifies himself as a Christian and proclaims the motivation of his actions to be "the will of God," Phelps may be a salient image in the minds of many people who think about the relationship between Christianity and homosexuality. Though salient, he is nonetheless a poor representative of conservative Christianity.

Other traditionalist Christian responses share the condemnation of homosexual behavior but not the condemnation of the person who contends with homosexual attractions. There are a range of responses that reflect this view within Christian circles, and an example of this includes the more charismatic healing approaches. Proponents of this view focus on a "cure" of homosexuality through miraculous healing. An example of this approach might be Francis MacNutt and his Christian Healing ministry. His book *Homosexuality: Can It Be Healed?* explores what it means to provide healing to a person's sexual orientation through prayer. In his section on "How to Pray for Healing of the Homosexual," MacNutt writes:

> First, you should expect that the chances of prayer changing the homosexual's orientation are extraordinarily good. I would expect that ideally, it should be close to 100%, but because of our human limitations, the results are not that perfect. Nevertheless, expect wonderful things to happen.[18]

Although MacNutt presents the healing of homosexuality through prayer as a process, one that could take several weeks, months or even years, he also states that he knows of several "instant changes."[19]

Still other approaches include tough discipleship approaches. These might focus more on resisting urges by an act of the will and bringing one's behavior patterns into conformity with God's moral direction for life. The Christian Counseling approach of Jay Adams is an example of such an approach, wherein the author emphasizes the replacement of immoral behavior patterns with godly behavior patterns.[20]

There are a number of approaches that incorporate themes from some of the approaches already mentioned. For example, Leanne Payne's Pastoral Care Ministries emphasizes inner healing prayer, but has a greater appreciation for some of the possible psychological considerations.

Pastoral Care Ministries does not offer professional or lay counseling; rather, it consists of a ministry team that conducts seminars on personal wholeness and healing prayer. In some of her written materials Payne discusses the etiology of homosexuality as related to a "sexual identity crisis" that should be understood in the context of one's "overall search for identity and personhood."[21] In her book *The Broken Image*, Payne shares case studies of healing where the etiology is tied to suppressed masculinity, problems in the parent-child relationship and childhood sexual trauma. Certain threads tie the case studies together, including struggles with masculine or feminine identity.

Similarly, Redeemed Lives was founded and is run by Mario Bergner. This ministry consists of in-depth discipleship and pastoral care. Bergner offers a detailed account of the etiology of homosexuality in his book, *Setting Love in Order.*[22] Bergner has also ministered as part of Pastoral Care Ministries and draws on the work of Leanne Payne. Bergner describes the process by which healthy sexuality develops. The two central developmental experiences are bonding to and identifying with one's same-sex parent and relating to and eventually experiencing the complementary qualities in one's opposite-sex parent. According to Bergner, gender role identity problems arise when a child fails to identify with the same-sex parent and the gender roles learned in that relationship, and when the child fails to experience gender differences learned by relating to the opposite-sex parent.

Homosexuality, then, reflects a legitimate developmental need for same-sex intimacy that can be healed through divine intervention mediated through loving relationships grounded in a wise understanding of the homosexual condition.

Many Christians and other religious persons have found a home in the National Association for Research and Therapy of Homosexuality (NARTH).[23] NARTH is not a religious organization; rather, NARTH describes itself as a scientific organization emphasizing the right to choose treatments intended to change a person's sexual orientation. But many religious people find that their beliefs and values are affirmed by NARTH and its affiliated practitioners, and that there are enough common interests that involvement in the organization provides a real benefit to them as professionals.

We turn now to explicitly religious organizations that minister to people struggling with same-sex attractions and behavior.

Christian Ministries

In this section we introduce the reader to several religion-based ministries that offer services to those who struggle with homosexuality.[24] These include Homosexuals Anonymous, Courage, a number of independent Christian ministries, and Exodus International. What these many different ministries hold in common is that they are conservative Christian organizations. They offer a place for reflecting on sexuality from a traditionalist Christian perspective. It is this traditionalist Christian *perspective*—beliefs and values about human sexuality and sexual behavior—that lays the foundation for services provided through the various ministry groups.

Traditionalist Christian ministries are not professional mental health support groups. They are *para*-professional ministries. Ministry groups may be led by pastors, licensed and nonlicensed counselors, or laypersons. Many of the leaders have themselves experienced same-sex attraction; some continue to experience same-sex attraction. It should be noted that there have been instances of sexual misconduct among some leaders of Exodus-affiliated ministry groups. Ralph Blair discussed some of the circumstances surrounding the founders of Homosexuals Anonymous (another umbrella organization of support groups for persons contending with same-sex attraction) and Exodus, specifically charging that many of the original leaders have returned to the homosexual life and repudiated their earlier claims of healing, and that several have been charged with unethical conduct toward others involved in their "ministries."[25] Although past misconduct does not discredit present ministry programs, it does offer a sober reminder of how vulnerable people are who enter ministry groups. It also suggests that accountability among leaders and staff is of utmost importance.

It is important to note that some ministry groups focus on homosexuality; others address much broader issues related to human sexuality and provide services to heterosexuals and homosexuals alike. Some offer direct services to those who are struggling with some aspect of their sexuality; others provide ministries to friends and family members seeking to support or cope with the choices of their loved ones.

Although we will review several major Christian ministry organizations, such as Homosexuals Anonymous, Courage and Exodus, it should be noted that other religions are also represented among ministry groups, including JONAH (Jewish) and Evergreen (Latter Day Saints).

Homosexuals Anonymous. Homosexuals Anonymous (HA) is a Christian, self-help ministry group for persons in conflict with homosexuality. "Colin C." originally developed a counseling program (Quest) that evolved into the HA ministry. HA is a fourteen-step program similar to Alcoholics Anonymous (AA). (Five of the fourteen steps are modified from AA, while nine others are said to be from Colin C's own experience.)[26]

The mission or vision of HA is described in their Statement on Philosophy, which covers three main points:

1. Homosexuals Anonymous, a Christian fellowship, holds the view that homosexual activity is not in harmony with the will of God and that the universal creation norm is heterosexuality. Nevertheless, the great message of righteousness by faith in Christ brings mercy and hope to all people in homosexuality.
2. Christ, the *Imago Dei* (the Image of God), is the restoration of the creation image, in whom all men and women find their identity by faith. The search for wholeness and heterosexuality within ourselves thus comes to an end. Men and women receive Christ as their image of God,

in whom is their wholeness and heterosexuality. As a trained faith grasps this awareness, there is a breaking of the power of the homosexual inclination so that freedom from the homosexual drive and activity is a real possibility.

3. H.A., however, does *not* believe that a change in homosexual inclination is a requirement for acceptance with God or entrance into the fellowship of the church. Although deliverance from homosexual activity is the call of God, the healing of the homosexual inclination will vary according to growth and is a result of our faith identity *with* Christ, rather than as a *way* to it. Nevertheless, H.A. holds that the homosexual inclination may be healed and that all who desire it may realize their inborn, though fallen, heterosexuality, thus opening the way to heterosexual marriage and family.[27]

Although each local chapter of HA is different, the primary method of intervention is small groups of five to eight members who discuss and work through the fourteen steps. Help is also offered through a "step coach" who functions similarly to an AA sponsor, because he or she is further along and able to help others follow the steps.

Meetings typically begin with prayer, introductions and a reading of the steps. The majority of the time is spent sharing (1) histories (where senior members share with new members their experience and the work that God is doing in their lives), (2) "step talk" (where a member gives a brief talk on one of the fourteen steps and offers suggestions for application), and (3) discussion (where members encourage one another in the step process or other experiences).

Some chapters also provide what they refer to as "H-anon groups." These are not official HA groups, but they are the equivalent of Al-anon groups, in which education and support are provided to family members and friends of people who experience same-sex attraction, self-identify as homosexual or are members of HA.

Courage. Courage is a Catholic group that offers support to persons who contend with same-sex attraction.[28] Courage originated in 1980 out of Archbishop Terrence Cardinal Cooke's diocese in New York under the direction of the Reverend John Harvey. There are presently over ninety

Courage chapters in the United States and more internationally.

Courage seeks to help those who experience same-sex attraction to develop "an interior life of chastity, which is the universal call to all Christians, [by which] one can move beyond the confines of the homosexual identity to a more complete one in Christ."[29] According to the Catechism of the Catholic Church, homosexual persons are called to chastity by the "virtues of self-mastery that teach them inner freedom" and the Church calls its people to accept homosexual persons with "respect, compassion and sensitivity." However, the Catholic Church makes a clear distinction between the homosexual as a person and the sexual acts of a homosexual. The Catechism of the Church specifically states that homosexual acts are "intrinsically disordered" and are "contrary to the natural law." It further states that homosexual acts "close the sexual act to the gift of life" and that "under no circumstances can they be approved."[30] Following this, persons experiencing same-sex attraction who commit themselves to the Catholic faith are encouraged to participate in Courage groups.

As people join Courage they are introduced to Courage's five goals:

1. Live chaste lives in accordance with the Roman Catholic Church's teaching on homosexuality. (Chastity)
2. Dedicate one's life to Christ through service to others, spiritual reading, prayer, meditation, individual spiritual direction, frequent attendance at Mass, and the frequent reception of the sacraments of Penance and Holy Eucharist. (Prayer and Dedication)
3. Foster a spirit of fellowship in which all may share thoughts and experiences, and so ensure that no one will have to face the problems of homosexuality alone. (Fellowship)
4. Be mindful of the truth that chaste friendships are not only possible but necessary in a chaste Christian life and in doing so provide encouragement to one another in forming and sustaining them. (Support)
5. Live lives that may serve as good examples to others. (Good Example)[31]

Like HA, Courage chapters provide ministry through support groups. The groups tend to allow time for prayer, discussion and fellowship. It is also common for meetings to follow a twelve-step format similar to HA, and for discussions to be drawn from the fourteen-steps of HA. However,

Courage groups discuss these steps within a Catholic understanding of homosexual behavior and fellowship.

Courage support groups are offered in diverse formats. The method of intervention typically consists of the director reviewing the goals of Courage and then initiating a group discussion about a relevant topic.[32] Some groups follow a more structured program. In some meetings members also hear testimonials from fellow members or guest speakers and celebrate Mass. Fellowship outside of the support groups is also encouraged (with other members and with people who do not contend with same-sex attraction). These "virtuous friendships" are based on four guidelines offered by John Harvey: (1) belief that genital sexual fulfillment is not a prerequisite to intimacy, (2) commitment to being known by others, (3) friendship with those who share the Courage member's ideals, and (4) friendship tied to God as a common bond.[33]

Additional resources include EnCourage (which is an organization for friends and family of those who contend with same-sex attraction), an annual international conference and "Days of Recollection" (miniretreats sponsored by local Courage chapters).

Independent religious ministries. Many Christian ministries are affiliated with larger, umbrella organizations. However, some Christian ministries such as Bergner's Redeemed Lives are independent ministries; that is, they are not affiliated with a larger umbrella organization.

As was the case with the HA and Courage ministries, there is a range of offerings among independent religion-based ministries. Some focus explicitly on helping people deal with homosexual feelings; others extend their ministry beyond homosexuality to a range of sexual and emotional concerns, including parenting skills, couples conflict, addictive behaviors, sexual abuse and so on.

Most independent Christian ministries provide care through a small group format. Some small groups follow a twelve-step format; others utilize the fourteen steps of HA. While some of the independent Christian ministries are open groups (i.e., they allow for "drop-in" participants), other independent Christian ministries offer closed groups.

Small groups tend to be organized around worship, education programs and speakers, small group discussion, and prayer. Some ministries sponsor conferences and offer seminars and tape ministries. Still other ministries actively reach out to evangelize the gay community.

Exodus International. Exodus International (Exodus) is a worldwide interdenominational, "Christian organization dedicated to equipping and uniting agencies and individuals to effectively communicate the message of freedom from homosexuality, as well as how to effectively convey support and understanding to individuals facing the reality of a homosexual loved one."[34] Exodus began in 1976 and is the largest umbrella organization for Christian ministries to people who are struggling with sexual behavior or sexual identity concerns. At this writing, Exodus' North American network includes over 120 ministries in the United States and Canada, and a total of over 150 ministries worldwide, with ministries in several countries in Europe and Latin America, Australia, New Zealand, the Philippines, Japan, and Singapore.

There are categories of Exodus membership. *Applicants* are those ministry groups that are working toward affiliation with Exodus. To become a *Member* of an Exodus referral ministry, a ministry must (1) agree with the doctrinal and policy statements of Exodus, (2) be in existence for a minimum of 2 years, (3) have a governing board that can change or remove a leader/director as needed, (4) have a leader/director who has not been involved in immoral sexual behavior for a minimum of 2 years, (5) have a leader/director who attends the national conference every three years, and (6) have a leader/director who is actively involved in a local church.

The vision of Exodus International is "freedom from homosexuality through the power of Jesus Christ."[35] Exodus seeks to equip and unite Christian agencies and individuals to effectively communicate the message of liberation from homosexuality, as well as support individuals facing the reality of a homosexual loved one. To this end Exodus serves as a support and accountability organization to the independent ministries that join it, serves as a referral source to those seeking help with "sexual brokenness," and hosts an annual conference, among other activities. Exodus sees itself as articulating a Christian perspective that neither rejects homosexual persons nor embraces a "gay" identity.

Although there is no one clear statement concerning what causes homosexuality embraced by the entire organization, Exodus literature points to various emotional hurts and deficits as playing a prominent role in the etiology of same-sex attraction. Thus, Exodus and its affiliates tend to view homosexuality as more of a psychological and spiritual issue, as shaped more by one's environment (nurture) rather than by one's genes or other predominantly biological variables (nature). For example, Exodus states that "if homosexuality is genetic, then that doesn't explain why we see such a similarity in personal backgrounds among the men and women who seek our help. There is a pretty uniform picture of poor family dynamics in general, a rift in the father-son or mother-daughter relationship growing up, feelings of being an outsider among one's peers during childhood and adolescence, and instances of sexual abuse/incest. These are root issues that men and women can address."[36]

In other places the literature of some Exodus affiliates appears to reject the notion of a valid homosexual "orientation" and sees redemption in Jesus as a means by which people can overcome their struggles with same-sex attraction. Keys Ministries, an Exodus-affiliate ministry in Minnesota, maintains that "homosexuality and lesbianism is not really a sexual problem, but rather a search to fulfill an unmet love need."[37] The belief that homosexuality is a consequence of legitimate needs gone awry is widely held by many of the Exodus affiliates. Homosexual behavior is depicted as a symptom of complex and deep emotional needs, for which one can find healing through an intimate relationship with Christ. First Stone Ministries, an Exodus affiliate in Oklahoma, states "we recognize homosexuality and/or any form of sexual/relational brokenness is not part of God's intent; we believe that through a personal relationship with Jesus that our hearts and lives can be transformed by the power of the Holy Spirit."[38]

Similar to the other Christian ministries we have discussed, most Exodus-affiliated ministries utilize a small group format to address the concerns and issues of individuals who seek their services. There are noted exceptions to this. For example, Love in Action, an Exodus affiliate in Tennessee, utilizes a residential program that is structured in five phases. The phase structure was implemented to provide accountability and consistency. One key component of their program curriculum is the utilization of a Christ-centered twelve-step format. Individuals desiring to enter the Love in Action Residential Program must complete a comprehensive application, a Minnesota Multiphasic Personality Inventory (MMPI), and a Myers-Briggs Type Indicator Test.[39]

Some ministries draw on any number of resources to facilitate their small groups. Others, such as Desert Stream Ministries, an Exodus-affiliated ministry in California, work from a specific curriculum. Desert Streams Ministries developed a twenty-week program called Living Waters. The Living Waters program is often provided as a closed group and is designed as an "in-depth, Christ-centered program for people seeking healing in areas of sexual and relational brokenness."[40] Living Waters is presented as a multidimensional program, containing three practical and essential elements—the worship, words and works of Jesus. According to Desert Stream ministry, worship helps focus participants on Jesus rather than ministry leaders. The words and works of Jesus are emphasized and serve to remind participants that the ministry is concerned with the power of the gospel rather than mere psychology, technical knowledge or theory. Healing is said to occur not by insight but through the incarnation.

Most Exodus-affiliated ministries offer some form of group intervention. The varied approaches utilized by these ministries include twelve-step programs, mentoring programs, "drop-in" groups (where people can participate at any time), the Living Waters program, and the New Directions program. (The last two programs are examples of programs that tend to be closed and run for a set number of weeks.) Exodus's small groups tend to begin with worship, followed by a time of education and discussion, and then end with a time of small group interaction and prayer. Each of these methods is intended to support the primary method of intervention, that is, a relationship with Jesus Christ. This personal relationship is facilitated through local ministry groups, some of which are under a specific church, while others are independent. Additional services are provided by Exodus, including an annual conference with workshops and presentations, a monthly newsletter and a speakers bureau.

Some Exodus-affiliated ministries also offer forms of support to spouses, family and friends of strugglers. Many affiliated ministries hold weekly or monthly support groups for family and friends. Most affiliates also offer educational services to both the community and the individual seeking change. For example, Mastering Life Ministries, an Exodus affiliate in

Florida, distinguishes itself as a ministry dedicated to "teaching people how to heal sexual brokenness."[41] David Foster, founder of Mastering Life Ministries, has written several books and travels extensively conducting workshops that teach others how to minister more effectively to individuals struggling with sexual sins. Other Exodus-affiliate ministries invite the community to utilize their resources. Ministry directors and staff are often called on to speak for community functions, at local high schools and in local churches. Many ministries provide resource catalogs and information that specifically address the various aspects of homosexuality.

In answer to the question "Can homosexuals change?" the Exodus literature states an emphatic yes. There is great diversity within the Exodus network ministries, and accordingly one finds a range of definitions of success. Some focus primarily on one's relationship with God and others, including freedom from dependence in relationships. Other programs define success in behavioral terms, including what it means to achieve celibacy and chastity, while others are concerned with change of thoughts, fantasies and feelings, which are seen as leading to change of orientation. It is the claims of successful change of this latter universe of ministries to homosexual persons that we sought to test in this study. The motives behind the various ministries are grounded in the traditional Christian moral condemnation of homosexual conduct. The individuals who enter these ministries for help may or may not share that motivation initially, but such religious understandings of homosexual behavior are the backdrop for their experiences in these groups. Unfortunately, few ministries explicitly define success or healing, although there are some exceptions. For example, Eagles' Wings, an Exodus affiliate in Minnesota, defines healing as "a dynamic, living thing which includes an ongoing sense of belonging to one's own gender, comfortableness with same-sex heterosexual people, and the ability to have relationships with them that are not emotionally dependent. It is furthermore the ability to relate emotionally, spiritually, and physically to the opposite sex, and to function effectively as a spouse and parent as the Lord leads."[42]

First Stone Ministries, an Exodus-affiliated ministry in Oklahoma, proclaims, "Freedom from homosexuality is not a method, but a person, Jesus Christ. . . . We minister freedom through a personal and intimate relationship with Jesus Christ as Lord."[43] Similarly, Living Hope Ministries, an Exodus-affiliated ministry in Texas, states that "we offer hope and healing to persons seeking freedom from homosexuality and lesbianism. In a world where homosexuality is either unconditionally accepted or condemned as a sin greater than all others, Living Hope Ministries presents an alternative. While holding to God's biblical standards for sexuality, we offer the power of God's forgiveness and grace to heal the deep pain of homosexual struggles."[44]

To summarize, many Exodus-affiliated, Christian ministries emphasize freedom from homosexuality. This is important because it is a different impression than what one might get from the public debates about whether people can change their sexual orientation. Apparently, while change of orientation from homosexual to heterosexual is the focus in some ministry groups, it is not the primary concern in many groups. Most Exodus-affiliated ministry programs appear to view homosexuality as the result of experiential factors (such as dysfunctional family dynamics, childhood sexual exploitation or even spiritual oppression). *Conversion* to heterosexuality may in fact be an experience that occurs as a result of ministry involvement, but "freedom from homosexuality" may not involve a full experience of such conversion.

Exodus is a fluid and changing organization. Independent ministries associated with Exodus come and go, leaders change, and programs morph. There can be no static picture of this dynamic and loose confederation of ministries. Not all the changes are consistent with the philosophy or theology of Exodus. In reviewing our manuscript copy and checking our sources, we discovered that the website of an Exodus-affiliated ministry in Minnesota was inoperative, but that a Google search of the name of the ministry led us to a press release on a GLBT site that proclaimed the return to homosexual identity of a former leader of the ministry, a release that contained an unqualified condemnation of the practice of attempting to change sexual orientation and a personal testimony of the harm from the attempt to change that is regarded as of such concern by mental health professionals.[45] This was one more reminder that the claims we have investigated are deeply contested and controversial.

3

Rationale for the Study

IS IT EVER POSSIBLE FOR PEOPLE TO CHANGE their sexual orientation? Is the attempt to change potentially harmful? These are two of the most controversial and contested questions of our day. Why address such questions when the complexities of answering them are substantial, absolute answers likely elusive and the attempt puts our professional reputations at risk?

The short answer is simply that these are fascinating questions for a variety of reasons. They are fascinating questions *empirically,* in that the common professional opinion today is that change is impossible and the attempt likely harmful. Given the ongoing scientific debate about the nature of sexual orientation, the absolute claim that change is impossible and the probabilistic claim that the attempt is harmful both invite empirical inquiry. Further, these are fascinating questions *theoretically,* particularly in that evidence that sexual orientation may change (however frequently or infrequently), especially if the method of change is a religious one, opens up questions both about the nature of sexual orientation and about the array of change processes that may affect seemingly permanent and deep facets of human experience and character. These are fascinating questions *theologically and morally,* in that the possibilities of change in sexual orientation are relevant to theological conceptions of human persons and their sexuality, and to the nature of virtue and the good in the realm of sexuality.

Our interest in these questions was aroused originally by the contradiction between the growing tide of professional opinion that homosexual orientation is unchangeable and the change attempt likely harmful, and the experience of meeting persons in conservative Christian contexts who claimed to have been "healed by God" of their homosexual orientation in favor of heterosexual experience.

On the former point, it is important to understand the forcefulness of contemporary professional opinion. The following material appears on the official website of the American Psychological Association, where we find closely linked the claimed impossibility of change and the potential harm of attempting to change:

> **Can Therapy Change Sexual Orientation?**
> No. Even though most homosexuals live successful, happy lives, some homosexual or bisexual people may seek to change their sexual orientation through therapy, sometimes pressured by the influence of family members or religious groups to try and do so. The reality is that homosexuality is not an illness. It does not require treatment and *is not changeable.*
>
> **What About So-Called "Conversion Therapies"?**
> Some therapists who undertake so-called conversion therapy report that they have been able to change their clients' sexual orientation from homosexual to heterosexual. Close scrutiny of these reports however show several factors that cast doubt on their claims. For example, many of the claims come from organizations with an ideological perspective which condemns homosexuality. Furthermore, their claims are poorly documented. For example, treatment outcome is not followed and reported over time as would be the standard to test the validity of any mental health intervention.
>
> The American Psychological Association is concerned about such therapies and their *potential harm to patients.* In 1997 the Association's Council of Representatives passed a resolution reaffirming psychology's opposition to homophobia in treatment and spelling out a client's right to unbiased treatment and self-determination. Any person who enters into therapy to deal with issues of sexual orientation has a right to expect that such therapy would take place in a professionally neutral environment absent of any social bias.[1]

For its part, the American Psychiatric Association's website states:

> [T]here is no published scientific evidence supporting the efficacy of "reparative therapy" as a treatment to change one's sexual orientation. The potential risks of "reparative therapy" are great, including depression, anxiety and self-destructive behavior.[2]

Absolute claims ("always," "never," "all," "none") are unusual in the behavioral sciences, and so it is notable to find them being made in relation to homosexual orientation. Professional organizations in social work, pediatrics and various other fields have taken similarly strong stands, often responding to the initiatives of their subdisciplinary organizations dedicated to advancing the perspectives of their gay and lesbian members. (The American Psychological Association's resolution originated with and was strongly advanced by its Division 44, the Society for the Study of Gay and Lesbian Concerns, and the American Psychiatric Association's motion was originally proposed by its Committee on Gay, Lesbian, and Bisexual Issues.) Similarly, a growing chorus of voices within the Christian church echoes the professional societies' claim that change is not possible.

The statements previously cited are from the late 1990s, but the sentiments expressed were rumbling about the various professional organizations for years before. The discord between these professional opinions and the testimonies of change we heard led us to embark on our own reading of the existing research literature on attempts to change homosexual orientation. What we read surprised us. We found, contrary to the claim that there is no evidence that change is even possible, that there is in fact a substantial body of research suggesting that change happened for some. As we have said elsewhere, the quality of these studies was not impressive by present-day standards, although it was adequate to merit publication in respected professional journals and comparable to that of other studies of the time that are still held in good repute.[3] The "success rates" reported in this research were modest, but comparable then and today to those attained, for example, with therapy for marital issues and for complex and recalcitrant human conditions, such as the personality disorders. In short, the claimed successes reported in these studies do not appear to merit dismissal out of hand. But that was precisely what they had received.

We were struck also that serious research on the possibility of changing homosexual orientation began to disappear from the professional literature at about the time that homosexuality was removed from the *Diagnostic and Statistical Manual* of the American Psychiatric Association in the late 1970s.* At one level, this made perfect sense: why study change attempts directed at a condition that was no longer regarded as a "mental illness"? The growing societal acceptance of homosexual orientation as a natural

---

*We previously summarized this series of changes in the *DSM* in Chapter one.

and acceptable variant of the human condition undermined motivation for such research. This social change inevitably had an impact on the politics of research funding and publication, as the make-up of institutional research committees, academic and government funding bodies, and journal editorial boards came to reflect the new consensus that homosexuality was to heterosexuality not as disease is to health but as one taste is to another. Broad acceptance of the claim that sexual-orientation change is impossible effectively closed off psychological research into possible change of sexual orientation.

All of these factors, in turn, were surfacing in the moral debates within the Christian churches about the full acceptance of homosexual persons that had been growing in seriousness since the mid-1970s. The churches had widely different responses to this issue, and in some of them it remains unsettled and potentially divisive, as discussed in chapter two.

Out of the aggregate of these influences, Stan Jones wrote a grant proposal in the early 1990s to fund an attempt at a rigorous examination of whether profound and lasting change of sexual orientation occurred as claimed in the religious ministries under the Exodus umbrella. All of the broad motivations we have mentioned figured into this research proposal. In the process of writing that grant proposal, he obtained the commitment of the governing board of Exodus, if the grant proposal received funding, that they would support his attempts to gain access to the populations undergoing the change attempt in Exodus groups.

The grant proposal was not funded, however. The granting agency gave very positive feedback on the design of the study but communicated indirectly to Jones that it did not want to be associated with research on such a controversial topic. A quick survey of other potential funding sources produced similar feedback. On this basis, Jones shelved any thoughts of conducting such a study.

Several years later, Exodus came under withering criticism. In response to the growing belief among mental health professionals that homosexual orientation is not changeable, Exodus International had taken out a series of full-page advertisements in major newspapers around the country proclaiming that homosexual orientation is changeable. They were criticized severely for making claims that they could not substantiate with acceptable scientific evidence. Indeed, the chief criticism leveled against the Exodus ads was that their claims were absurd in light of scientific evidence that allegedly proved that sexual orientation is immutable.

In the midst of this media firestorm Exodus International's executive director at the time, Robert Davies, found a copy of Jones's prior grant proposal while cleaning out old files. Davies called Jones, asking if he would still be willing to lead the proposed research study if funding could be obtained. Davies clearly wanted to document that change did occur through the medium of the Exodus ministries; he was himself a product of such efforts. Jones's motivation, as well as that of Mark Yarhouse, was that of tackling an interesting, important and controversial subject.

The first focus of our study was, Is it ever possible for homosexual persons to change their sexual orientation? The second focus was, Is the attempt to change potentially harmful? In this chapter we examine several key issues related to the first question, beginning with a review of the research on change of homosexual orientation, both within the psychotherapeutic literature and the religious-ministry literature, and moving then to reaction to this literature and a discussion of the issues it raises. These bodies of literature form the conceptual background for the design of the current study. We then more briefly consider the claims that the attempt to change sexual orientation are likely to be harmful, and reexamine the core issues of the study.

Sexual Orientation Is Immutable: Review of the Psychotherapeutic Change Literature

The claim that sexual orientation is immutable is an absolute claim, and yet there exists a substantial research base of studies reporting success at such change, as well as anecdotal reports of such changes and of reversions back from them. Several dozen such studies on change of homosexual orientation were published in the 1950s, 1960s and 1970s, with a few surveys conducted since that time and a resurgence of interest in change in the past ten years or so.

A review of the older studies on change reveals many varied interventions, ranging from depth psychology approaches, such as classical psychoanalysis directed at developing insight into resolving the relational fixa-

Table 3.1. Individual Treatments for Homosexuality (1950s-1990s)

Study	Theoretical Orientation	N	PO	IP	NC	UC	%PO
*†Bieber et al. (1962)	Psychoanalytic	106	29	4	58	15	27
Cantom-Dutari (1974)	Behavioral	49	19				39
*Freeman & Meyer (1975)	Behavioral	11	9		2		82
*Hadfield (1958)	Psychoanalytic	9	6			3	67
*Hatterer (1970)	Psychoanalytic	143	49	18	76		34
*†‡Kaye et al. (1967)	Psychoanalytic	24	6			18	25
McConaghy (1970)	Aversion	40	10				25
*†MacIntosh (1994)	Psychoanalysis	1215	276				23
MacCulloch & Feldman (1967)	Aversion	35	10				29
*Masters & Johnson (1979)	Behavioral	67	29				43
Mayerson & Lief (1965)	Unspecified	19	9		10		47
Schwartz & Masters (1984)	Behavioral	54	35				65
*Socarides (1978)	Psychoanalytic	45	20			25	44
*van den Aardweg (1986)	Adlerian	101	37	11	9	43	37

N = total number of patients in study. PO = Positive Outcome. IP = In Progress. NC = No change. UC = Unclear. %PO = Percentage with Positive Outcome (x = 41.92%). *See Goetze for a detailed review of methodology, definition of change, and summary of results with special emphasis on change from exclusively homosexual to exclusively heterosexual. **Utilized a control group. †Figures based on psychoanalysts' responses to survey questionnaire. ‡Study of females exclusively.

tions seen as giving rise to homoerotic responses, to cognitive-behavioral and behavioral approaches that aimed among other goals to develop heterosexual and heterosocial interpersonal skills and diminish anxiety, aversion treatment that attempted to establish a conditioned aversion to "deviant" homosexual attraction, and experiential therapy. Interventions were conducted in individual or group treatment format or some combination.[4] We present a brief summary of most of these past studies in highly condensed tabular form, with studies reporting individual interventions in table 3.1[5] and studies reporting group interventions in table 3.2.[6]

Nearly every study ever conducted on change of orientation found some evidence of change. That is, the vast majority of studies conducted found that some participants experienced meaningful change. Unfortunately, the early research on change was often of poor methodological quality by to-

Table 3.2. Group Treatments for Homosexuality (1950s-1970s)

Study	Theoretical Orientation	N	PO	IP	NC	UN	%PO
Eliasberg (1954)	psychoanalytic	6	3	1	1	1	50
Hadden (1958)	psychoanalytic	3	1	2			33
Hadden (1966)	psychoanalytic	32	12	20			38
Singer & Fischer (1967)	psychoanalytic	8	4				50
Litman (1961)	psychoanalytic	1		1			----
*Truax et al. (1970)	psychoanalytic	20		20			----
*Truax & Tourney (1971)	psychoanalytic	30	20	5	5		67
Birk (1974)	social learning	66	15	15			23
Beukenkamp (1960)	experiential	1	1				100
Mintz (1966)	unknown	10	3	3	1	3	30
Johnsgard & Schumacher (1970)	unknown	5			5		----
Stone et al. (1966)	unknown	1		1			----
Pittman & DeYoung (1971)	unknown	6	3	1	2		50
Munzer (1965)	unknown	18	5	2	1	10	28
Finney (1960)	unknown	3	2			1	67
Covi (1972)	unknown	30		8			----

N = total number of clients in study. PO = Positive Outcome. IP = In Progress. NC = No Change. UN = Unknown. %PO = Percentage with positive outcome as measured by therapist or self-report (x = 33.5%). *Utilized a control group.

day's standards, though it is important to note that these studies were of sufficient rigor in their contemporary context to merit publication in respected, mainstream professional journals and met the prevailing professional standards of the day for research sophistication and integrity. Of particular concern by today's standards are the methods used for measurement of sexual orientation and its change, and the definitions of success used.

For example, the most common measure of change in these earlier studies was either the therapist or analyst's perception of the matter or the client's or patient's perception. These therapist and client reports of change rarely used standardized questions or scales, but rather each new study used its own idiosyncratic rating scale of "satisfaction" or "significance of change." Also, the object that was reported to have "changed" varied from orientation to attraction, fantasy and behavior. In some studies "change" meant that a client discontinued same-sex behavior; in others that a client initiated opposite-sex behavior. Rigorous examinations of indexes of sexual orientation were rarely if ever used.

The reliance on therapists' ratings is particularly problematic by today's standards, based on concern that therapists have a vested interest in reporting their own success and are not truly objective or reliable reporters of client success. It is widely believed that absent objective constraints, most of us will, in any area, rate ourselves through a positive halo. Widespread evidence for this type of bias has been compiled.

Self-reports by persons attempting to undergo change can be equally problematic. The same sort of positive bias that can be operative in therapist rating can affect self-rating, as individuals may feel that it reflects poorly on them if they do not report success after an extensive investment of time, money and energy in a change process.* At its worst, this method can involve people providing subjective ratings of the degree of change from some prior condition, leaving open the possibility of biased recall of those prior conditions.

Only a few studies used physiological measures of change, such as physiological measures of sexual arousal to various visual stimuli. The studies that used these types of measures of change often attempted to change sexual behavior and reduce anxiety about heterosexual sex. We discuss such measures, and why we did not use them in this study, in chapter four.

We can certainly lament the lack of sophisticated methodology in these studies. They cannot be cited as incontrovertible evidence that homosexual orientation can change to heterosexual orientation. However, some people who pursue change of behavior, thoughts or orientation will be encouraged to see evidence that change of same-sex behavior and impulses, and possibly of sexual orientation, was reported to have occurred for a significant percentage of people undergoing such treatment. The average positive outcome across these studies is about 30%, with another 30% or so "in process." While this is surely not a stunningly high rate of success, it is in line

*The same problem likely afflicts reports of the failure to obtain change. Individuals who have attempted change and failed and who now have embraced the homosexual condition may be no more neutral than any other persons when providing ratings of their prior experiences. Negative reflections on their change attempts may serve to justify current decisions and lifestyles.

with the reported success rates for change attempts dealing with complex relational issues that are often faced in marital or family therapy, or the more difficult and stable psychological conditions. Also, the lack of sophisticated methodology does not prove the treatments failed; rather, it challenges researchers to provide more sophisticated program evaluations and outcome studies to clarify what clients can expect from various programs.

Although the publication of research on the topic of change of homosexual orientation dramatically decreased in the late 1970s, occasional studies have continued to appear, and these more recent studies deserve closer examination. Most of the research conducted recently has employed surveys of therapists or patients. For example, psychoanalyst Houston MacIntosh published data based on a semi-random survey of psychoanalysts, which had an unusually high response rate of 67.5%.[7] Among respondents, 274 analysts reported working with 1,215 homosexual patients. Of the homosexual patients treated, analysts reported that 276 patients (22.7% total, or 23.9% of the males and 20.2% of females) changed their sexual orientation from homosexual to heterosexual, and 84.0% obtained "significant therapeutic benefit" (again, the sexes were nearly identical, with 85.3% of males and 81.3% of females achieving "significant therapeutic benefit").[8] Both male and female patients spent an average of about four years in analysis. Remember, these are the ratings of the psychoanalysts, not of the patients themselves.

An additional interesting finding was that the vast majority of analysts surveyed (97.6%) did *not* agree with the statement that a "homosexual patient 'can and should' change to heterosexuality." This counters the charges that analysts are prejudiced by society's negative view of homosexuality, or that analysts are unable to muster the neutrality needed to provide analysis. In fact, MacIntosh stated that these very assertions by Richard Isay, the chair of the American Psychiatric Association's Committee on Gay, Lesbian, and Bisexual Issues, are what motivated him to conduct the survey. Moreover, although most analysts (62.3%) reported believing that homosexual patients "sometimes" change their sexual orientation, only 4.2% reported believing that change of orientation happens "frequently."[9]

In a follow-up report, MacIntosh examined some of the factors related to change of sexual orientation in his previous survey.[10] Factors associated with change of orientation included analysts' expectation of change (positive expectancy was related to greater likelihood to report change). Factors associated with significant therapeutic benefit were length of treatment (especially for males), change of sexual orientation (less so for females) and gender of analyst ("Female analysts report a significantly higher rate of significant therapeutic benefit for their female patients than male analysts report for their female patients").[11] The gender of the analyst is complicated by length of treatment, because female analysts reported seeing female patients longer than did male analysts.

Before we move on from the MacIntosh study, we want to highlight the limitations inherent in this type of survey. Robert Goetze identifies several limitations to this type of therapist survey research, including the possibility that psychoanalysts misapplied the labels "homosexual" and "heterosexual."[12] It is conceivable that some of the analysts mislabeled bisexuals as homosexuals and then mistook heterosexual adaptation by the bisexuals as true heterosexuality. Also, the reports of the psychoanalysts were not corroborated by reports from patients themselves or other objective measures of sexual identity or behavior. The standard practice in the evaluation of psychotherapy is not to rely on therapist reports of change but rather to study patient experience directly; the MacIntosh study is quite deficient by this standard.

A recent major study of the effectiveness of reparative and conversion therapies was conducted by the National Association for Research and Treatment of Homosexuality (NARTH). NARTH formed a number of years ago to challenge the increasing acceptance of homosexuality in the mental health professions and the growing rejection of the idea that homosexuality can be changed.[13] NARTH recently produced a study of the change experience for a large number of persons seeking change and of therapists who try to help individuals change.[14] Through advertising in newsletters of change-support groups and announcements at conferences, NARTH sought research participants of two sorts: individuals "who had experienced 'some degree of change' " and counselors who attempt to facilitate such change. The study explicitly attempted to document that change can happen and sought a subject pool that would support this claim.

Eight hundred eighty-two persons responded to the survey who had changed from homosexual to heterosexual orientation or who were seeking such change. As a group they tended to be well-educated, male, white and devoutly religious. The average age of awareness that they had "homosexual tendencies" was age 12.4. Interestingly, 520 (almost 60%) reported having had a childhood homosexual contact at an average age of 10.9 years, with the person initiating that contact being an average age of 17.2 years. Survey respondents rated their sexual orientation before treatment began and at the time of the survey. Before the change process, 36.6% reported being exclusively homosexual ("6" on the Kinsey scale), 31% reported being a Kinsey "5," 22.1% were Kinsey "4," and 9% ranged down through the rest of the scale. After the change effort, 16.2% reported being exclusively heterosexual (Kinsey "0"), 18.1% reported being almost exclusively heterosexual (Kinsey "1"), 19.7% reported being more heterosexual than homosexual (Kinsey "2"), 10.9% equally homosexual and heterosexual (Kinsey "3"), 22.3% more homosexual than heterosexual (Kinsey "4"), 8.2% almost entirely homosexual (Kinsey "5"), and 4.6% exclusively homosexual (Kinsey "6").[15] The participants reported substantial decreases in "homosexual thoughts," masturbation to gay pornography and overt homosexual behavior. Seven hundred twenty-six participants of the 882 total had undergone some sort of reorientation therapy, either by a professional therapist or a pastoral counselor (over an average span of 3.3 years); 156 had not obtained such therapy. The researchers compiled separate statistics for those who reported being exclusively homosexual before treatment began to see if these individuals obtained less help from the therapeutic process; the results suggested that the success rates in this group were similar to the whole group. The responses to the therapist survey, perhaps predictably, indicated that the therapists were confident that homosexual orientation can be changed and that they are capable of facilitating that process of change. This study has several significant methodological limitations. To its credit, the Kinsey scale it used was a widely respected measure of sexual orientation. The major problems with the study were first that its ratings of change were retrospective, asking those surveyed years after the fact to remember the nature of their earlier sexual orientation, and second that the sample was recruited to represent "success stories." By simply tabulating scaled ratings by NARTH member therapists and their selected clients, the NARTH study failed to meet scientific standards of using validated outcome measures with something approximating a representative sample of individuals under study.

In 2002, psychologists Ariel Shidlo and Michael Schroeder, explicit opponents of the offering of reparative therapy, published the article "Changing Sexual Orientation: A Consumer's Report" on their study of 202 "consumers" of reorientation therapy.[16] Sponsored by the National Lesbian and Gay Health Association, the study was originally presented at a conference and was titled "Homophobic Therapies: Documenting the Damage."

Shidlo and Schroeder describe a developmental model of their sample's experience with reorientation therapy. The first period is referred to as the *pre-entry period*, characterized by a variety of motivations for pursuing reorientation therapy (e.g., a desire "to belong to a community," "religious guilt" and "fear of social stigma").[17] Next comes what Shidlo and Schroeder call the *honeymoon period*, characterized by many participants as a time of hope: "a sense of relief in telling their story, a sense of hope for change, and the adoption of a model that explains their difficulties and offers ways of changing." The major split that occurred for this sample was that people either went down a pathway of *self-perceived failure* (n = 176 or 87%) or a pathway of *self-perceived success* (n = 26 or 13%). Since all of the sample had at one time participated in reorientation therapy, these results might be taken by some as evidence that sexual orientation cannot be changed, or that it can only rarely be changed.

However, as with the NARTH study, Shidlo and Schroeder obtained a convenience sample of people who at one time had participated in reorientation therapy, so no conclusions can be drawn about how likely it is that people can experience reorientation. Just as NARTH recruited in venues and by methods likely to solicit "success stories," this study was likely to solicit failure stories. Also, given that the design of the study relies on retrospective participant recall, which is susceptible to influence based on one's present life circumstances, the results must be interpreted with caution. In particular, individuals who have embraced a gay identity may be prone to interpret their experience of their reorientation attempt negatively through their current gay identity. The reverse is obviously equally plausible; there is no neutral vantage point on this conflicted issue.

These three studies, with all their limitations, represent the major studies published since the early 1980s on this controversial topic. We turn now to the existing research on Christian support groups and religion-based healing ministries.

Review of the Religiously Mediated Change Literature

In chapter two we discussed the array of Christian religious ministries that seek to help persons change their experience of their sexual orientations. The most prominent are those that affiliate under the umbrella organization Exodus International, those affiliated with Homosexuals Anonymous and those that are part of the Roman Catholic organization Courage. There are also many other independent religion-based ministries, including Redeemed Life and Pastoral Care Ministries, for example.[18] Some of these groups state or suggest that a person can change from homosexual to heterosexual orientation, but they also applaud moves away from homosexual behavior and self-identification into celibacy, which they regard as an experience of freedom and a good in and of itself. Other faith-based support groups, such as the Catholic group Courage, do not attempt change of orientation at all; rather, they singularly encourage and support efforts at celibacy.

Although anecdotal reports of change abound on the websites and in the published literature of these groups, there have been few published outcome studies of such groups. The first notable scientific study of the effectiveness of a change ministry was performed with an independent Pentecostal church ministry unaffiliated with any of the previously mentioned groups. In the late 1970s, respected research psychiatrist E. Mansell Pattison and Myrna L. Pattison came into contact with a Christian Pentecostal "hot-line crisis program" that sought to help homosexuals change to heterosexuality via "religiously mediated" means.[19] The Pattisons reviewed with the church staff three hundred cases in search of individuals who had, in the estimation of the staff, "changed sexual orientation." Thirty such cases were identified and contacted for extensive interviewing; of the thirty contacted, eleven agreed to cooperate fully with the evaluation.[20]

As in the NARTH study previously discussed, the Pattison study used the widely respected Kinsey scale of sexual orientation in gathering data, and its 11 subjects provided retrospective ratings of their pretreatment sexual orientations. Nine of the 11 had been exclusively homosexual ("6" on the Kinsey scale) before their work with the ministry. After that work, 5 reported being exclusively heterosexual (Kinsey "0"), 3 reported some incidental homosexual feeling or behavior (Kinsey "1"), and 3 reported "definite same-sex response but strong and predominant reaction to the opposite sex" (Kinsey "2").[21]

The Pattisons asked commendably precise additional questions. The group averaged having self-identified as heterosexual for four years at the time of the evaluations. Six of the 11 were married, with most reporting their marriages to be "very happy." Most of the men reported some continuing occurrence of homosexual dreams, fantasies or impulses. And most reported fairly low incidence of negative psychological/emotional symptoms. The Pattisons sought objective external verification of the self-reports of the subjects and obtained concurring reports from church staff and spouses for some of the subjects in the study.

This study does appear to provide definitive evidence that change is possible for some individuals, but it raises significant concerns. First, the retrospective reports of pretreatment sexual orientation are problematic. Further, the fact that the sample pool was 11 out of an initial potential pool of 300 reviewed suggests that radical change is seldom likely to occur. Third, the small scale of the subject sample undermined the impact of the study.

When presenting the results of the Pattison study, we have frequently encountered the emphatic claim on the basis of widely shared anecdotes that the conversions reported in this study are fraudulent. The usual form of this claim is that "someone" has reported that those subjects who are reported to have changed merely told the researchers what they wanted to hear but never really changed at all.

Stan Jones has experienced this directly. While serving as a scientific advisor to a theologically conservative group at the national General Convention of the Episcopal Church in July 1991, he spoke of the evidence for the possibility of change, mentioning the Pattison study specifically. After the presentation, an individual in the audience identified himself as one of Pattison's "success cases," and then claimed that he "came out of the closet" soon after participating in that study and that his testimony to the Pattisons was untrue.

There is little a researcher can do with such anecdotes. First, there is no way to verify that this individual was telling the truth. Scientific authors protect the anonymity and confidentiality of their participants and typically do not identify study participants under any circumstances. This creates a curious imbalance of power, allowing anyone to claim to be a participant while the authors of the study have to remain mute and refuse to confirm or deny participation.* Second, if this person was telling the truth, this simply reduced the number of Pattison's successful cases from 11 to 10; it did not establish that change was impossible. Third, if the testimony of this individual was true, it is also logically possible that others in the Pattison sample had the opposite experience: perhaps they were reported as "failures" only to later experience the type of change that qualified as success in this study. Or perhaps some of the 19 out of 30 identified successes who refused to participate in the Pattisons' study did so not because they had failed to experience change but because they no longer wanted to be identified with a past from which they were now disconnected (a common sentiment in our sample), or because they feared the controversy the study would generate. Finally and at the most general level applicable to this entire subject of study, one has to question why the negative anecdotes—"I was a participant in that research project (or I underwent precisely that therapeutic technique) and my apparent success disappeared over time"—are given credence while the positive anecdotes—"I made the change attempt and it worked"—are not.

---

*To pursue this a bit further, note that scientific authors cannot risk hurting participants, and identifying one person in the study, even with that person's permission or insistence, can in turn risk hurting others. To understand this, imagine the following: If a participant in this study were to approach us to renounce her confidentiality and seeking verification of her identity as a study participant, we would be in unprecedented territory but would have to prioritize potential harm to this and other participants. If we were to verify the identity of this participant, that individual, for any of a variety of motives, could in turn hurtfully "out" others. Even the individual confirmation of one participant's identity can have unexpected consequences, and the researcher's ethical obligation is to prevent harm from study participation.

Although its limitations are considerable, we do not concur that the Pattisons' study can be dismissed.

A second attempt to measure successful religiously based change of orientation has produced interesting results. Psychologist Kim Schaeffer and his colleagues report findings on 184 males and 64 females from Exodus-affiliated ministries.[22] They found on measures of both feeling and behavior that "participants rated their current sexual orientation [i.e., after involvement in the attempt to change sexual orientation] as significantly more heterosexual than when they were 18 years of age."[23] Another finding was that the more heterosexuality that was reported, the better the self-reported mental health, including higher levels of happiness, positive outlook on life and self-acceptance, and lower levels of tension, depression, and level of paranoia.* Many participants had also been involved in psychotherapy to change sexual orientation in addition to their involvement with an Exodus ministry, and results from this study did not find evidence for the effectiveness of these experiences in psychotherapy for changing sexual orientation. Involvement in professional therapy *in addition to* Exodus group involvement, in other words, did not appear to increase the likelihood of change occurring based on Exodus involvement in itself.

This research team also reported that religious motivation predicted a person's current sexual orientation; that is, those who were highly motivated religiously reported experiencing more heterosexuality.† A follow-up study one year later suggests that religious motivation is also associated with efforts to abstain from physical homosexual contact (referred to as "behavioral success," which was reported at a rate of 60.8% of the 102

---

*These findings are particularly interesting in light of claims from some mental health professionals that efforts to change are harmful to gay and lesbian persons. This is an especially complicated issue. The findings from this study show an association between more heterosexuality and various measures of mental health; however, another study by Lynde Nottebaum, Kim Schaeffer, Julie Rood and Deborah Leffler reported that, when compared to a those who rejected their homosexuality and were involved in Exodus-affiliated ministries, those who accepted their homosexuality reported experiencing better mental health on measures of happiness, self-acceptance, paranoia, and loneliness. (See Nottebaum, L. J., Schaeffer, K. W., Rood, J., & Leffler, D. [1998]. Sexual orientation: A comparison study. Unpublished manuscript.)

†Kim Schaeffer and his colleagues are right in pointing out that this finding should be interpreted with caution. We would not want to send the message that those who do not experience change are simply not motivated to change. At the same time, religious motivation may be an important factor in deciding whether to pursue change.

males in the follow-up study and 71.1% of the 38 females in the follow-up study).[24] The major limitations of this study are again the use of retrospective measures to judge degree of change, and also the use of nonstandard measures of orientation itself.

Do the Schaeffer studies support the claim made by Exodus and other ministries that people can change their sexual orientation? The Schaeffer studies certainly support the claim that people can change their behavior and abstain from same-sex conduct. The studies also demonstrate that participants' subjective sense of sexual orientation changes, although critics are right to point out that this subjective report may reflect a person's sexual identity more so than their sexual orientation. Sexual identity has been defined a number of different ways, but a recent definition focuses on three key dimensions: gender identity (a person's sense of being either male or female), object choice (what we are referring to as sexual orientation) and intention (what a person chooses to do with their attractions).[25] It is possible then that these subjects were reporting a change in their sexual identity through greater identification with their sex (as male or female) and their gender (masculinity or femininity), while refraining from same-sex behavior. Although the Schaeffer studies support the claim that sexual orientation can change, a more in-depth analysis of a person's experiences of sexual attraction is needed to distinguish between sexual orientation change and sexual identity change (of which sexual orientation is but one dimension).

Perhaps the most highly publicized recent study in which participants reported successful change of sexual orientation was authored by research psychiatrist Robert L. Spitzer.[26] Spitzer could be construed to be the most qualified person in the world to conduct this sort of research; in addition to a distinguished research career, he was the lead scientist responsible for revision of the *Diagnostic and Statistical Manual* of the American Psychiatric Association through the 1970s and 1980s when the various diagnostic categories related to homosexuality were modified as advocates for acceptance of homosexuality desired.

Spitzer reported on interviews he conducted of a convenience sample of 200 persons (143 males, 57 females) who reported experiencing change of sexual orientation from homosexuality to heterosexuality. The sample was a mixed one, including those recruited through NARTH (and hence the product of psychotherapeutic change attempts) and those recruited through religiously mediated change groups such as Exodus. The unique characteristics of the sample must be emphasized: Spitzer explicitly recruited success cases—men and women who believed that they had experienced dramatic change.

A majority of participants reported a shift from predominantly or exclusively homosexual orientation before therapy to a predominantly or exclusively heterosexual orientation at least one year prior to their interview. Of direct relevance to the present study, Spitzer reported that the subjects typically reported the change process to have spanned a five-year period or even longer. Most significant, change was reported for variables that are considered fairly static dimensions of sexual orientation, including sexual attraction, arousal, fantasy and yearning. Sixty-six percent of males and 44% of females reported "good heterosexual functioning" one year following what they identified as their successful change attempt. Good heterosexual functioning included a current heterosexual relationship, emotional satisfaction in that relationship rated a 7 or higher on a 1-10 scale, heterosexual sex at least "a few times a month," physical satisfaction from heterosexual sex rated at least 7 on a 1-10 scale, and never or rarely having homosexual thoughts during heterosexual sex.

Spitzer also deliberately looked for those within his sample who had experienced what we might call a "total cure." Based on his strictest criteria (no homosexual orientation at all), Spitzer reported that 10% of males and 40% of females reported the lowest scores possible on indicators of same-sex attraction—daydreams, lust, yearning for intimacy, masturbatory fantasies, thoughts and so on—following what they viewed as their successful change effort.

From the degree of change and marital satisfaction reported, Spitzer concluded with reasonable confidence that his participants had neither lied about nor exaggerated their claims of change. Mindful of the methodological limitations of his study, Spitzer called for further empirical research, ideally prospective in design, to examine the effectiveness of reorientation therapies.

Spitzer conducted his study following, as he explicitly noted, the call of the American Psychiatric Association for research "to further determine 'reparative' therapy's risks versus its benefits."[27] Spitzer was not conducting a prospective treatment efficacy study, and his study should not be criticized for failing to achieve ends it was never designed to accomplish. Like the present study, it was targeted at answering the question, Is change of sexual orientation ever possible?

The Spitzer study might well be compared to the groundbreaking study by Evelyn Hooker, who in the late 1950s looked at whether all homosexuals are psychologically maladjusted such that a panel of mental health professionals could distinguish them from heterosexuals.[28] She studied 30 homosexual men and thirty heterosexual men who were matched in IQs, age and educational attainments. These were small convenience samples that were not necessarily representative of either homosexuals or heterosexuals. Indeed, the samples did not need to be representative. The failure of the panel to distinguish between the two groups did not prove that homosexuals are on average as psychologically well-adjusted as heterosexuals, as is commonly thought, but it did show that the homosexual participants in her study—representative or not—were indistinguishable from the heterosexual participants on various measures of mental health functioning.

The limitations of Spitzer's methodology are easily summarized and were explicitly noted by the author: (1) the study was retrospective rather than prospective, (2) it was a cross-sectional "snapshot" of functioning at one moment in time rather than longitudinal, (3) it relied on retrospective reports of sexual attraction and other variables rather than using assessments in the present, and (4) it examined a self-selected sample that cannot be regarded as representative. But as we have already argued about our own study, the sample was adequate to the question, which was whether or not it is ever possible for any homosexual to change. If the accepted wisdom is that change is *never* possible, then even one documented case of change refutes the absolute negative.

The unprecedented forty-nine pages of peer commentaries to Spitzer's study, which were published in the same journal issue, exhaustively discussed the study's methodological limitations.[29] But the discussion went much further than to challenge the methodology. The most reasonable voices among Spitzer's peers lauded his attempt to address an important research question. One of these commentators, Fritz Klein, also noted, "Some claim that they know that the mere publication of this report will cause grievous social, political, and personal harms. This amounts to a call for censorship, rather than meeting the issues on factual and logical grounds."[30] Klein effectively captured the tone of some other commentators whose reaction to the study was to attack Spitzer's ethics and professional credibility, even to the point of accusing him of violating the Nuremberg Code of medical ethics for reinforcing the stigmatization and mental suffering of gays and lesbians.[31]

We agree with Klein that such unmerited accusations are borne of an unscientific mindset and have the effect of suppressing research potentially supportive of politically unpopular positions. What sets science apart from politics is the heuristic capacity for self-examination and the willingness to revise one's conclusions in the face of new evidence. Spitzer is a rare exemplar of this mindset in the field of sexual orientation research.

LESSONS FROM EXISTING RESEARCH

We have noted a number of substantive problems with the existing research. First, many studies have failed to use standard measures for sexual orientation, leaving the meanings of their findings in doubt. Where possible, standard measures should be utilized, and ideally there should be multiple measures. Second, many studies have been single-time, cross-sectional "snapshots" of a population where change is only documented through having the research participants compare their experience in the present with their *memories* of how they were at some point in the past. A superior methodology would be longitudinal, that is, it would follow the participants over time and focus on change in their current reported experience. Third, therapist (or in our case, ministry-leader) ratings should be avoided as unhelpful; the most valid measure is one that directly accesses the experience of the person him- or herself. Finally, the attempt should be made to get a sample that has not been filtered or selected for likely success (or failure). The ideal would be to come as close to a representative sample as possible.

The studies of change we have cited have been the target of withering criticism from gay-affirming scholars. Douglas Haldeman's analysis, a standard in this field, is a wide-ranging and negative critique of the "conversion" literature.[32] In addition to the sorts of criticisms we have just summarized, Haldeman ventures others as well. He demeans the conversion literature in an ad hominem fashion (e.g., describing various studies as "founded on heterosexist bias")[33] or implies that reported "conversions" (such as those in the Pattison study) are fraudulent. The lack of substance to these criticisms has not stopped others from echoing them. Haldeman's critique has been cited by many who question the ethics of even providing change of orientation therapies, and these criticisms reflect a kind of bias against those who seek professional help for their experiences of same-sex attraction. For example, according to Kathleen J. Bieschke and her associates, "inherent in conversion therapy is the premise that same-sex orientations are pathological, an arrest in normal development, or (less stigmatizing but still homophobic and harmful in nature) not as well accommodated in society as a heterosexual orientation."[34]

More substantively, however, Haldeman criticizes the conversion literature as based on naive and dichotomous views of "gays and straights," without proper understanding of the complex realities of sexual attraction and orientation. Haldeman seems to have in mind the therapist or researcher who naively assumes that any indication of heterosexual functioning on the part of a person undergoing change means that the person has become heterosexual. But this criticism cuts both ways, as the same naiveté seems operative in reverse when reports of therapeutic successes are dismissed because the subjects continue to report some level of continuing homosexual arousal or attraction. If subjects are not to be declared heterosexual on the basis of the presence of minimal heterosexual arousal, then neither should they be declared homosexual on the basis of the mere presence of some homosexual arousal.

Second, Haldeman attributes the supposed successes of conversion efforts to the researchers having actually worked with mixed samples of bisexuals and homosexuals, with resultant alterations in the behavior and perhaps inclinations of the bisexuals but not the homosexuals. Again, this could truly be a complicating problem, because what brings individuals to Exodus ministries typically is the presence of unwanted homosexual attraction, and if the person also experiences significant heterosexual attraction, this person may indeed fit the classic definition of a bisexual. Even so, there is no clear reason to consider bisexual orientation any more amenable to fundamental change than homosexual orientation, and so the real issue becomes whether there is actual movement in the fundamental orientation as opposed to mere behavioral change.

More important, Haldeman and others sometimes seem to slip into a circularity of reasoning wherein no matter what the subject's report of preintervention sexual arousal or behavior, any movement toward heterosexual function is assumed to be clear evidence of preexisting bisexual orientation. In other words, anyone who moves toward heterosexuality could not have been homosexual to start with, because homosexuals cannot become heterosexual. Still, the legitimate point here is that the most honest and complete description of the baseline sexual orientations of the research sample will be crucial.

Finally, Haldeman criticizes as trivial what might be described as the grafting of heterosexual action over a homosexual orientation, without more basic change in desire or attraction. We agree that this could be a problem, especially if the absence of homosexual action is taken as conclusive proof of the success of an intervention. From this we conclude that various measures of attraction and arousal apart from behavior are crucial.

From "Research Limitations" to "Immutability"

We summarize this review simply by saying that the dozens of studies that have been published to date all indicate that change from homosexual orientation to full or substantial heterosexual orientation is attainable by some individuals by a variety of means. There is no indication that such change is easy (in fact there are numerous indications that the change process is challenging and substantial), or that a high percentage of individuals attain this change. There is also no indication that change or modification of sexual orientation is possible for everyone who attempts such change. But there is no positive empirical evidence whatsoever that change is impossible. All of the studies in this research literature have limitations, and some have significant flaws, just as much of the older social scientific research does.

Given this state of the scientific research literature, how have we moved from statements about the limitations of the research ("this research is not convincing for the following reasons") to absolute statements of immutability and their often associated call for a ban on reorientation and related therapies?[35]

At a conceptual level, perhaps the resistance that many commentators have to the possibility of change of homosexual orientation and the resulting tendency to (wrongly) interpret past empirical literature as somehow proving that orientation is not changeable, is that such a possibility of change raises questions about the stability of any sexual orientation, whether it be heterosexual, homosexual or bisexual. Stability seems to play two key roles in contemporary discourse. First, stability or immutability would seem to strengthen an argument for moral acceptance of the homosexual condition on the argument that if change is impossible then it would be cruel to deny people the opportunity to live according to their desires for sexual intimacy. Second, many people are uncomfortable with the notion that something they take as fundamental to their identities, their sexual orientation, may be subject to change under the influence of a range of biological and environmental forces, including their own moral choices.

Thus claims that homosexual orientation can change threaten the very core of a gay-affirming understanding of morality and of personhood. It comes as no surprise then that such claims are fiercely disputed.

The claim of immutability is being made frequently and emphatically today. We have already explored the American Psychological Association's assertion that sexual orientation is immutable.[36] The APA's claim was predated by many arguments, but none more important than that of Richard Green, who helped provide a conceptual foundation for the later stand by the APA. Green, a psychiatrist and lawyer, made his claim in the title of his influential article "The Immutability of (Homo)Sexual Orientation: Behavioral Science Implications for a Constitutional (Legal) Analysis."[37] Interestingly, Green argued little from the actual evidence on change attempts, dismissing them as simply unconvincing, but he rather centered his argument on the putative persuasiveness of the evidence for biological causation of sexual orientation.

The implicit logic of Green's argument was that if homosexual orientation is solely biological in origin, any claim of orientation change through psychosocial means is ludicrous. Yet the case for biological causation of homosexual orientation remains inconclusive almost two decades after the publication of Green's analysis, and current medical practice provides psychosocial interventions for biologically based conditions such as when, for example, we use various forms of cognitive retraining to speed recovery from stroke and other types of loss of brain function.

In an influential article in the *Atlantic Monthly* in March 1993, journalist Chandler Burr claimed, "Five decades of psychiatric evidence demonstrates that homosexuality is immutable."[38] This is a curious inversion of the facts; the research evidence for decades established that homosexual orientation could sometimes be changed and there is still not a shred of evidence against this finding. The claim of immutability nonetheless was clear and forceful. The claim that homosexual orientation is immutable also began to become standard fare in the beginning education of students of psychology. The bestselling introductory psychology text in the world, by David G. Myers, says that sexual orientation is "something we . . . seemingly cannot change."[39]

Attempts to establish the immutability of homosexuality have proceeded along two paths, as we have already hinted. The first path, represented by such figures as Richard Green and neuroscientist Simon LeVay, focuses on the causes of sexual orientation and seeks to establish immutability by showing that homosexuality is set very early in life by irreversible biological means.[40] Such claims about the origin of homosexuality can be contested, and may not have the conceptual power or implications claimed.[41] For example, LeVay claimed to have found conclusive proof for brain structure differences between gay and straight men, specifically that a small area of the hypothalamus was smaller in gay men than in straight men and similar in size to that of women. From this he argued that the only reasonable conclusion from these findings was that these brain differences were the biological causes of sexual orientation.

Recent research has weakened the force of LeVay's conclusions. First, a more methodologically sophisticated study by research psychiatrist and neuroscientist William Byne only partially replicated LeVay's findings, thus reducing the force of LeVay's conclusions.[42] More important, Byne rightly notes that brain differences may be the effects (rather than the causes) of behavioral or psychological differences between persons. The brain is a remarkably malleable organ that changes in response to how we use it. Thus people may have different sexual orientations because their brains were different from the start, or people's brains may be different upon autopsy because of the biological effects of the life-long impact of how they lived out their sexual orientations (however those orientations came about).[43] So in short, documentation of possible biological factors associated with homosexual orientation may not prove that that orientation cannot change.

The second path for establishing immutability involves attacking the research literature with the aim of trying to establish that change is impossible. As we discussed in chapter one, this is a difficult undertaking logically, because even one instance of such change disproves the absolute claim that the condition is immutable. Despite this logical difficulty, the claim is still often made as if it is based on empirical evidence. The most important step to such a claim involves a curious logical progression. Consider three statements:

1. The research evidence in support of fundamental change in sexual orientation for homosexual persons is suggestive of such change, but is not of adequate quality to provide indisputable proof that change is possible for any homosexual persons.
2. The research evidence in support of fundamental change in sexual orientation for homosexual persons is of such poor quality that it provides no persuasive evidence that such change is ever possible for homosexual persons; without such supportive evidence we must remain agnostic as to whether such change is possible.
3. The research evidence in support of fundamental change in sexual orientation for homosexual persons is of such poor quality that its findings must be utterly discounted, and the absence of such positive evidence stands as a powerful indictment against the notion that such change is possible. In other words, the conclusion to be drawn from this pattern of evidence is that sexual orientation cannot be changed.

We acknowledge that the research background to this question that we have reviewed in this chapter has some noted limitations and is not utterly convincing. Thus we do not agree with statement 1 but recognize it as a reasonable conclusion to draw.

Those voicing statement 2, however, seem to us to take too strong a step into agnosticism. This could be a reasonable position *if* the skeptics voicing it were consistent in their skepticism. To adopt the position of agnosticism without compelling empirical evidence would be paralyzing, especially to the applied psychologist. For example, the vast majority of the clinical work done by practicing psychologists is done with patients who do not fit the pristine diagnostic parameters of the research studies that provide some partial support for the therapeutic efforts. Further, few practicing psychologists limit themselves to techniques that have conclusive empirical support. In other words, were psychologists to limit themselves only to using well-established therapeutic techniques applied to clients who fit the clear diagnostic standards on which the techniques were validated, the mental health field of clinical and counseling psychology would be reduced to a tiny fraction of its size today. So we would challenge the application of such selective skepticism and its resulting agnosticism. We would argue that the vast majority of those voicing this view from within the field of psychology are not consistent in applying this agnosticism to other aspects of the field.

Statement 3 is utterly illogical. It is perverse to draw from a consistent pattern of empirical evidence suggesting that change is possible for some, however limited that evidence might be, the *opposite* conclusion that change is impossible.

We believe, even before reviewing our results from this study, that to argue for the immutability of sexual orientation is ill-founded. Further, we would argue that embracing such an illogical stance has had unfortunate consequences for the field. In a discussion of how therapists might deny services to those who seek change of sexual orientation, Erinn Tozer and Mary McClanahan state that if "the therapist continues to refuse to provide conversion therapy, and the client continues to insist that he or she desires reorientation, the possibility of termination emerges. . . . If the client remains steadfast in her or his desire to reorient to heterosexuality . . . termination becomes a very real possibility."[44] In other words, clients who insist on reorientation are to be punished for their intransigence by denial of care. Of course the professional and ethical concern with recommending this response to the client is that clients are being denied the right to seek a certain treatment outcome under the coercive threat of the withdrawal of a psychotherapeutic relationship because the client disagrees with integrating their same-sex feelings into a gay, lesbian or bisexual identity.

Is this a hypothetical concern? No. An example of this kind of bias appeared recently in an otherwise highly regarded sex-therapy textbook. Margaret Nichols discusses the case of a forty-four-year-old white male who suffered from depression and sexual identity confusion. He reported same-sex fantasies during masturbation, but no experience with same-sex behavior. He stated that he could not "imagine being gay."[45] (This individual might well be typical of the population served by Exodus.) Nichols says that the patient's sexual identity confusions were "highly unusual" in this day and "therefore" the treatment team "concluded [his] struggle with sexual identity [was] symptomatic of a deeper, entrenched problem and diagnosed him with avoidant personality disorder."[46] The treatment team determined that the goal for treatment was "to help him accept his gay orientation."[47] This kind of presenting concern may be rare in the treatment center where Nichols works, but it is not uncommon in a variety of other settings and practices. It is certainly not uncommon for therapists and pastoral-care providers and ministry leaders who work with conservative Christians who contend with same-sex attraction. The fact that it is uncommon in Nichols's experience to see someone who is struggling with his sexual identity is no justification for diagnosing that person with a psychopathology. Many people pursue change of same-sex behavior, identity or orientation for a variety of reasons related to personal, cultural, or religious beliefs and values.

The skepticism about change of sexual orientation also seems to be applied selectively: skepticism about change from homosexual to heterosexual is applauded, but other options may be celebrated. It is interesting to read published accounts of changes from heterosexual to bisexual, at least with respect to a person's capacity to expand his or her sexual orientation to accommodate same-sex behavior. For example, Nichols presents the case of "Mike" and "Jenny," a couple in a nontraditional, polyamorous (or open) relationship. After they worked through a number of issues not uncommon in the polyamorous community, the therapist worked with Mike on his capacity to respond sexually to other men:

> More recently, Mike has become close with a bisexual man. Mike very much wants to have sex with this man, primarily because he feels it would enhance the relationship [with Jenny]. Although Mike is at most only incidentally attracted to men, he feels he can develop the ability to enjoy male-male sex because his sexuality is so flexible. Treatment interventions have included bibliotherapy and helping Mike identify ways he might find a "tutor" in the gay male community.[48]

The logical implications of the formulation seems to escape Nichols entirely. If change in the direction of bisexuality and homosexuality is possible, then change in the other direction should also be possible.

Our primary hypothesis. We take as our main hypothesis for the present study that change of sexual orientation is impossible. That is the prevailing professional wisdom, and such a conclusive, clear and absolute prediction makes an ideal hypothesis for a scientific study because even one case of change will refute the absolute claim.

IS THE ATTEMPT TO CHANGE HARMFUL?

We have been grappling so far with the question of whether change of sexual orientation is ever possible. Now we turn to the claim that attempts to change sexual orientation are harmful.

Early in this chapter we quoted the official websites of the American Psychological Association and the American Psychiatric Association on the potential harm of the attempt to change sexual orientation (see p. 74). The American Psychological Association's website references as the source or justification for its concern about harm the "Policy Statement on Appropriate Therapeutic Responses to Sexual Orientation"[49] adopted by its Council of Representatives on August 14, 1997. That statement is difficult to interpret, laden as it is with confusing qualifiers and probabilistic statements. In the midst of multiple "whereas" statements, the following two statements come closest to being substantive premises for the resolutions to follow:

> WHEREAS some mental health professionals advocate treatments of lesbian, gay, and bisexual people based on the premise that homosexuality is a mental disorder (e.g., Socarides et al., 1997)
>
> WHEREAS the ethics, efficacy, benefits, and potential for harm of therapies that seek to reduce or eliminate same-gender sexual orientation are under extensive debate in the professional literature and the popular media (Davison, 1991; Haldeman, 1994; Wall Street Journal, 1997)

In the resolutions that are supposed to be based on the "whereas" premises, the reader is reminded that "homosexuality is not a mental disorder," that "psychologists 'do not knowingly participate in or condone unfair discriminatory practices,' " that they "respect the rights of individuals to privacy, confidentiality, self-determination and autonomy," that they "try to eliminate the effect on their work of biases," that they "do not make false or deceptive statements concerning . . . the scientific or clinical basis for . . . their services," and that they "attempt to identify situations in which particular interventions . . . may not be applicable . . . because of factors such as . . . sexual orientation."

The actual evidential basis for putative harm from such therapies, however, is not directly asserted. The invocation of discriminatory practices, bias, falsehood and the like certainly raises a negative cloud of concern and doubt, but it is not a cloud from which clear assertions can be distilled. The references embedded in the resolution ("Davison, 1991; Haldeman, 1994; Wall Street Journal, 1997")[50] refer to conceptual or opinion articles where individual authors express their rationale for concluding that such therapies cause harm, or reference anecdotes about individuals they know or have heard of who claim to have been harmed by such interventions. No scientific evidence whatsoever of such harm, however, is produced to support the claim that these interventions cause harm.

Helpfully, the American Psychological Association's website points out that the concerns are based, in part, on the reality that "treatment outcome [for these therapies] is not followed and reported over time as would be the standard to test the validity of any mental health intervention."[51] In other words, the website is saying that prospective and longitudinal documentation of treatment outcomes and their collateral impact on psychological well-being would help to alleviate concern about potential harm, but that proponents of these treatment methods have failed to provide this data. This claim is mostly true, and we have conducted the present study to fill this void.

But we would point out the opposite application of this rule. Those claiming that these interventions cause harm also have failed to follow this professional recommendation on how to determine if a therapy helps or harms clients. Those claiming harm have never followed actual persons attempting to change to measure the impact of the change attempt; they have produced no scientific evidence justifying their claim.

In this study we explore the question of whether involvement in this change process has been harmful on average. Our second scientific hypothesis for the purposes of this study was that the change attempt *would* be harmful to the individuals participating. This was not our personal supposition at the start of the study; in this area, we had no clear hypothesis. We expected that some would experience positive mental health outcomes as a result of their involvement in the attempt to change, that others might well experience negative outcomes, especially if they experienced no change, and finally, that many would likely find the experience difficult as they went through a long and challenging process with little societal understanding or support.

Why then did we make the formal hypothesis of this study that the change attempt would be harmful? First, the weight of professional opinion at this moment in time is that the effort to change one's sexual orientation will probably harm emotional health. Hence, we hypothesized that we should observe a decrement in emotional well-being as a result of involvement in the change process. Those attempting to change sexual orientation should report more negative psychological symptomatology, more distress, as a result of their involvement in Exodus ministries.

We extended this hypothesis to spiritual functioning as well, assuming that there is a necessary connection between emotional and spiritual well-being and growth. Further, if the APA is right and change is impossible, we hypothesized that people would be negatively affected spiritually by attempting what must ultimately be utterly frustrating. Thus we hypothesized that the change attempt would produce a decrement in spiritual well-being and faith maturity as a result of involvement in the change process. The ways we measure psychological distress, spiritual well-being and faith maturity are all discussed in chapter nine.

Our secondary hypothesis: We take as our secondary hypothesis for the present study that the attempt to change sexual orientation will create psychological distress for these individuals. That such change attempts are harmful is the prevailing professional wisdom, and thus this makes a reasonable hypothesis. Rather than an absolute claim ("every change-attempter will be harmed"), this claim seems more probabilistic in nature ("the attempt to change is intrinsically harmful, so clear indications of harm to change-attempters overall should be noted"), requiring us to look at average trends in our data. We extend this hypothesis to spiritual well-being and faith maturation as well.

The Present Study

Controversy continues to swirl around attempts to convert homosexuals into heterosexuals. It is likely that even the most well-established evidence of change would become the target of withering criticism, as has been the case for both therapeutically mediated and religiously mediated change toward heterosexuality. Nevertheless, it is the purpose of this study to produce well-grounded evidence of what people can experience when they participate in religiously mediated change processes.

What stood out to us at the outset of this project was the immensity of the task. We were taking on a study of "ex-gays" in a contentious, politicized climate characterized by "us"-versus-"them" thinking. The debates about "change" needed to be informed by science and not by inflammatory rhetoric; a spirit of discussion and common ground is more beneficial than a spirit of debate and criticism from entrenched positions.

This has actually begun to occur in some mental health circles. For example, in 2000, the American Psychological Association held a symposium on the topic of *Gay, Ex-Gay, and Ex-Ex-Gays* that brought together professionals from the gay and conservative religious communities to discuss the needs of clients who experience same-sex attraction.[52] When the discussion moves away from rhetoric and toward a common ground of what is in the best interest of a client population, there seems to be much more room for discussion of both science and worldview assumptions, including religious and other orienting systems for understanding morality and ethics.

One of the participants in this symposium was someone that we have cited frequently (and in a few instances quite critically), Douglas Haldeman, who presented from a gay-affirmative perspective. Haldeman readily acknowledged in this 2000 symposium the problems with the sociopolitical and religious contexts within which reorientation therapies are offered. He expressed concern that the existence of such programs runs the risk of sending what seems to him the wrong message about homosexuality. However, Haldeman also recognized that in a diverse and pluralistic society, there is a need to respect the rights of those who make choices that he and others would not make:

> For some, it is easier and less emotionally disruptive to contemplate changing sexual orientation than to disengage from a religious way of life that is seen as completely central to the individual's sense of self and purpose. However we may view this choice, or the psychological underpinnings thereof, do we have the right to deny such an individual treatment that may help him to adapt in the way he has decided is right for him? I would say that we do not. This is why the mental health organizations have adopted advisory policies about conversion therapy that . . . do not . . . ban the practice of conversion therapy outright out of concern for the individual whose personal spiritual or religious diversity may supersede his concerns about sexual orientation.[53]

It is in this spirit that we decided to undertake this study. We wanted to know more about the experiences of those who are distressed by their experiences of same-sex attraction and enter a Christian ministry to help them change their sexual orientation. In this book we introduce the reader to the population of persons who report being distressed by their experiences of same-sex attraction and pursue change through involvement in a Christian-based ministry. We recognize that this work is not merely a scientific study but a study entrenched in cultural debates about human nature, sexual identity and sexual ethics.

The past thirty years have witnessed a proliferation of research on lesbian, gay and bisexual (LGB) issues, including studies of sexual identity development and synthesis, issues in LGB relationships, sex therapy, discrimination and stereotyping behaviors, AIDS education and prevention efforts, and so on. Some of the research has been tied directly and indirectly to political movements, such as legitimizing or opposing same-sex marriage or civil unions, adoption of children by homosexual couples and so on. This study will no doubt be applied to multiple ends that we cannot foresee. We want to stay focused, nevertheless, on our two key questions: Is it ever possible for homosexual persons to change their sexual orientation? Is the attempt to change harmful?

4

Methodology for This Study

"Greene's Law: . . . [T]he more susceptible an inquiry is to precise formulation, the more likely it is to produce trivial results."
W. M. McClay, in *Public Morality, Civic Virtue and the Problem of Modern Liberalism*

"Research design is never just a theoretical exercise. It is a set of practical solutions to a multitude of problems and considerations that are chosen under the constraints of limited resources of money, time, and prior knowledge."
E. O. Laumann, J. H. Gagnon, R. T. Michael & S. Michaels, *The Social Organization of Sexuality*

In chapter three we discussed our rationale for this study, and in reviewing the existing research we made note of the limitations of that research and of how a better research design might avoid such limitations. The following are the core characteristics we have developed so far and which should be fairly noncontroversial:

- A strong study will be *longitudinal*, following participants over time and gathering their current reported experience of sexual orientation and other variables in an ongoing and dynamic way.* (This is in contrast to single-time, cross-sectional "snapshots" of a population.)
- A strong study will be *prospective*, starting with participants who are initiating the change process and observing the change process as it

*One of our models both in terms of prospective and longitudinal research characteristics was the series of studies of the impact of divorce on children conducted by Judith S. Wallerstein, Julia M. Lewis, and Sandra Blakeslee, *The Unexpected Legacy of Divorce* (New York: Hyperion, 2000).

happens (or fails to happen). (This is in contrast to a retrospective study that depends on memory of how the subjects used to feel, think or behave.)

- A strong study will examine the experience of a *representative sample* (or an approximation thereof) of those seeking change. (This is in contrast to a convenience sample gathered because it is already judged to be successful or to have failed.)
- A strong study will gather data *directly* from the persons experiencing the change process (i.e., use self-report) and do so with the best existing *standard measures* (multiple measures where possible) of sexual orientation and other variables for the sake of comparability to other studies and samples. (This is in contrast to the use of solitary, idiosyncratic or unique measures, and particularly in contrast to ratings by ministry leaders, counselors and other intermediaries.)
- A strong study will examine a *large* sample.

We will describe our research methodology in this chapter, and return at the end to a self-analysis of the quality of this study. Briefly, though, we would judge this study to have met the established standards. This is the first report of a prospective and longitudinal study (reporting on assessments at Times 1, 2 and 3) of a respectably large and arguably representative sample of those seeking to undergo change in sexual orientation via religiously mediated means, one that utilizes a compound array of established and validated self-report measures of sexual orientation, psychological distress and other variables to measure the outcomes of interest with data supplied from the research participants themselves. We sought to follow participants seeking change through a number of different Exodus ministries in different areas across the United States so that we might gather results representative of the Exodus change process in general. This was also a pragmatic choice. Since most Exodus ministry groups are small, we did not believe that we had much of a chance of gathering a significant population of people going through the change process if we limited ourselves to one or a small group of Exodus ministries. We have been successful at this: we have gathered information from participants from sixteen different Exodus ministries from across the nation. But as is often the case, every choice creates limitations. These Exodus ministries do not, as we discussed in chapter two, employ a standardized intervention protocol. By working with individuals involved in a diverse group of Exodus ministries, we diminished our ability to attribute any changes documented to any particular intervention method, since apart from prayer and Bible study there were few methods that all ministries held in common.

There were several points where we chose not to implement what some would regard as ideal methods. These issues require more extended discussion.

Why didn't we implement a "true experiment" design using random treatment assignment to experimental and control conditions? The "gold standard" for psychological research is the true experiment. The true experiment in psychology is defined by several characteristics, the most important being random assignment of research volunteers to multiple intervention conditions, with information kept from subjects as to whether they are receiving the experimental intervention that is the focus of the study or one of the control interventions against which the experimental condition is being measured.

This ideal design is simply illustrated by the prototypical drug study: Subjects with a certain medical concern are recruited for an experimental trial of a new medication. They are randomly assigned to one of three conditions, the experimental condition and two "controls": Group A receives the new experimental medication. Group B, the first control group, receives the "standard" treatment in the field which is presumed to be the "treatment to beat." Group C, the second control group, receives a placebo (inert) medication, which is the equivalent of no treatment. In cases where there is a very well-established standard treatment or where it would be judged unethical to withhold treatment from the subjects, the placebo control is not used.

In the psychological parallel to the ideal experiment study design, subjects with a certain psychological concern are recruited for an experimental trial of a new psychological intervention method. They are randomly assigned to an experimental condition and to appropriate control conditions. The experimental group receives the new experimental intervention. This experimental group is compared against an appropriate control. Often, and especially when the psychological intervention is projected to work rapidly, a "waiting list control" is the chosen control condition. The randomly assigned control subjects are told that the experimental study is full, but that they will be assigned to treatment as soon as possible and that while they wait for treatment, the researchers would like to monitor their functioning. Then, the difference in the psychological functioning of the waiting list control and experimental groups becomes the test of the effectiveness of the experimental method.

If a waiting list control is not appropriate, either because it is unethical to withhold treatment (for example, with suicidal persons) or because the experimental intervention takes longer to implement than is reasonable to ask people to wait for treatment, an active control group of some kind must be utilized. One approach would be to offer a standard intervention against which to compare the experimental intervention (as when a new form of psychotherapeutic intervention with depression is pitted against the appropriate standard treatment). Another is to create a seeming "placebo." What has been called "non-directive listening" has been used in many studies as a presumed placebo in the past.

There are several key issues, however, that would have made such a true experiment difficult to undertake in this subject area. First, such a study would have been pragmatically impossible for us. By definition, such a true experiment would either have doubled the size of our study in order to match our experimental sample with a control sample, or would have required us to divide the sample we had into halves, thus diminishing the size of the sample we were able to study.

Second, the background logic for establishing a control condition against which to compare an experimental treatment contains at least two key assumptions that are invalid with respect to sexual orientation change. These assumptions are (1) that there is some level of spontaneous remission of the condition being treated, and/or (2) that the question being answered by the study is not whether change occurs but whether it occurs faster or better through the experimental treatment than through spontaneous remission or other existing treatments.[1]

Consider depression, the "common cold" of mental health. It is well known that if people who are experiencing depression go without treatment, then after a given duration of time (during which they presumably experience new life circumstances and also draw on the resources around them—caring family and friends, the wisdom of a pastor or bartender, and so forth), a certain percentage of the original sample will spontaneously (i.e., without professional treatment of any kind) experience a remission of symptoms and recover. Further, there are lots of existing professional treatments for depression, so a new treatment, to establish its worth, must be shown not just to work, but to work better than existing alternatives.

None of this logic has much hold on our study if the reality is that homosexual orientation is in fact impossible to change. As we have already belabored, the mental-health-care establishment has spoken clearly: homosexuality is immutable. Hence, our primary research hypothesis was that change would not occur at all. This greatly simplified our methodology, as we did not have to worry about spontaneous remission, nor about proving that Exodus treatment is better than existing alternatives. Sexual orientation change is supposed to be impossible, and so any demonstration of change stands against a presumed backdrop of impossibility. These logical arguments mitigate against the need for a control group of any kind.

Third, if we take Robert L. Spitzer's study, which we discussed in chapter three, as any indication, the change process, when it is successful, takes a long time.[2] Spitzer reported that it took an average of two years for participants to begin to experience change, and that it took an average of five years for 79% of participants to report a change of sexual orientation. This is far too long to ask a wait list control group to wait for professional services. A "wait list control" design works very well for interventions that target immediate and rapid symptom reduction, such as a program designed to alleviate panic attacks among those diagnosed with an anxiety disorder. Such a study looking at rapid treatment of panic symptoms has been run by David Barlow and others over the course of twelve to fourteen weeks, and the rapid treatment program has been demonstrated to be successful for 60 to 80% of participants.

But there is consensus among the few mental health professionals who believe that change of sexual orientation is possible that such change is a complicated clinical concern that likely requires a significant commitment on the part of participants over the course of several years. To make persons seeking change wait such a long time would be questionable ethically.[3]

On this basis, we decided to implement what is best called a "quasi-experimental design." Such a design does not solicit volunteers but rather gathers information on those naturally pursuing an existing intervention method (Exodus).

In the current highly politicized cultural wars surrounding homosexuality, it would be very difficult to solicit volunteers who critics on either side of the change debate did not believe were participating to prove or disprove claims of change. The typical controlled experiment testing a new treatment of depression might appropriately place an advertisement on TV and radio or in newspapers stating, baldly, "We are recruiting volunteer subjects to study an unvalidated treatment for depression. Subjects who volunteer may be assigned to this treatment, or to a placebo treatment. Please volunteer."

Imagine the response, however, if a similar ad was placed stating, "We are recruiting volunteer subjects to study an unvalidated religious treatment for homosexual orientation. Subjects who volunteer may be assigned to this treatment or to a placebo treatment. Please volunteer." Advocates against such treatment might flood the volunteer rolls merely to "prove" that it does not work, advocates for such treatment similarly might volunteer to "prove" it does work, and it is quite possible that individuals who sincerely desired change would avoid such a study in order not to risk being assigned to a "placebo" treatment and thus waste months or years with methods that do not produce success.*

Fourth, control conditions such as placebo-attention conditions (with perhaps lots of active listening but no active treatment) or competing treatments must truly be credible alternatives to the experimental treatments being studied. Given the long time spans needed for change of sexual orientation to occur even in the most optimistic projections and the lack of

---

*This is no longer a hypothetical example as we finish the first draft of this chapter. In October 2005, word flashed around the Internet that "Dr. Phil" was taping a television episode in Los Angeles on gay teens seeking healing of homosexuality. Friends on *both* sides of this contentious issue forwarded us e-mails urging the rallying of troops to flood the studios and create the impression that all the support was on one side or another—pro-gay advocates to protest and shout down the oppressive religious conservatives, and religious conservatives to cheer on testimonies of change and silence the sinful homosexual lobby. That would be the precise fate of a publicly announced study.

credible alternative treatments (our subjects were typically aware that it was "Exodus or nothing," so to speak), there was simply no opportunity to create a credible control or comparison condition.

Finally, we should note that in the mental health field so-called true experiments are undertaken typically in contexts where treatments are rigidly defined and controlled. Handbooks to define and govern the interventions are created, and interventions are conducted by therapists working under the direction of those conducting the research. Because of our limited funding and our commitment to studying established intervention programs in the "real world," and because the ministries we were working with would not condone putting those who wanted their help on a "no treatment waiting list" for three to five years, we decided that use of a true experiment research design with random subject assignment was impractical.

Why didn't we use psychophysiological (biological) measurement of sexual orientation? "Behavioral" or psychophysiological measurement of sexual response would appear to be a truly scientific, utterly objective measure of sexual orientation superior to putatively subjective self-report measures of sexual response. If such methods are available and respected, why didn't we use them in this study? There were three reasons we had for not using them: (1) the use of the methods posed insurmountable practical challenges for our study, (2) the methods would have been morally unacceptable to our study participants, and (3) these methods are not the indisputable scientific measures that many imagine them to be. This presentation of these issues is a condensation of our original discussion of this issue; that original discussion is available on the website where we are archiving materials related to this project for public access at <www.ivpress.com>.

A commonsense explanation of this method is in order before we unpack these three reasons. Both men and women respond with a variety of whole-body responses during sexual arousal. Men and women breathe faster, their nipples harden, their pulses quicken. And the genitals undergo a process called vasocongestion ("congestion by or with blood") as blood flows to and enriches the genital area to facilitate sexual pleasure.

For men, the primary result of vasocongestion is erection of the penis. The penis is composed of a spongy tissue that can hold blood, and a man's penis becomes erect simply because more blood gets pumped in than gets out when he is aroused. An erect and aroused penis, as a result, gets warmer, longer, thicker (of greater diameter and circumference) and harder when it is erect than when unaroused or flaccid. For women, vasocongestion results in a reddening or darkening of the vagina and the tissues of the labia, swelling or thickening of these tissues, a tightening or narrowing of the outer third of the vaginal opening but an opening up (or "tenting," after the image of a tent being lifted up from the ground to create a space within) of the inner portion of the vagina, and perhaps most obvious, lubrication of the vagina.

All of these physiological reactions can be measured and quantified. Various measures have been developed and standardized to measure how sexually aroused a person is. A vaginal plethysmograph is inserted like a tampon into a woman's vagina, where it bounces light off her vaginal walls to measure changes in their redness, a direct correlate of vasocongestion and arousal. Penile plethysmography measures the physical changes in the penis in a variety of ways, either through measuring temperature or change in size or both. In the classic paradigm for such measurement, individuals are fitted with the appropriate plethysmographs and then are exposed to a variety of sexual stimuli while being urged to relax and simply respond normally. The sexual stimuli are usually a variety of pornography (or "erotica," as it is commonly called).

If we were attempting to assess whether a person who was a pedophiliac had overcome his sexual attraction to children, that person might be shown a series of video clips or photographs mixing sexual scenes involving children and those involving only adults of various ages and sexes, with the resulting responses carefully measured. Obviously, the expectation would be that if the person had not changed, exposure to the depictions of sex with children would elicit a response of sexual arousal.

Experimental use of this method requires a fairly sophisticated and stable lab environment with facilities for computer measurement, changing facilities where subjects can undress enough to put the plethysmograph on or in, video capabilities for the delivery of erotic stimulus materials (pornography of some kind), separate rooms where the subject can experience the stimuli without the experimenter intruding and so forth. Our subjects were spread all over the country, requiring at Time 1 that our interviewing teams travel widely to interview subjects and by Time 3 to resort to phone assessments because subjects were too dispersed for face-to-face interviews. This made it impossible to establish a central and accessible psychophysiological laboratory. Further, the substantial demands in time and energy we were already planning to make on our subject population to complete hours of interview questions and survey instruments, together with the personal intrusiveness of our questionnaires, led us to conclude that it was simply impractical to include such psychophysiological measurement among our dependent variables.

The moral unacceptability of psychophysiological measurement of sexual response to our population should also be fairly obvious. The moral and ethical acceptability of these psychophysiological measures of sexual arousal, as with all methods of intervention (whether for the purposes of research or therapy), must be assessed from the perspective of the professional and from the perspective of the recipient of the professional's intervention (the research participant or therapeutic client). Exodus seeks to provide support for change from a biblical perspective for those who are struggling with homosexuality, lesbianism or bisexuality. The vast majority of our participants, as we shall see in chapter five, reported themselves to be born-again Christians at the start of our study, and the methods used by Exodus are all directed toward helping the individual understand who he or she is as a sexual person created by God and how to live in a way that honors the biblical principles of sexuality.

One of the most important goals for any participant in an Exodus ministry is sexual purity. Such purity includes, at the minimum, desisting from overtly immoral sexual behavioral patterns, but desired change toward sexual purity does not stop there. Participants are urged to purge their thought lives of immoral sexual images. The scriptural basis for this stance comes from the words of Jesus in Matthew 5:27-30:

> You have heard that it was said, "Do not commit adultery." But I tell you that anyone who looks at a woman lustfully has already committed adultery with her in his heart. If your right eye causes you to sin, gouge it out and throw it away. It is better for you to lose one part of your body than for your whole body to be thrown into hell. And if your right hand causes you to sin, cut it off and throw it away. It is better for you to lose one part of your body than for your whole body to go into hell.

This passage is viewed by traditionalist Christians as embodying both a morally normative judgment that lust is wrong and a moral imperative to avoid such responses and to discipline oneself to avoid the occasion of such responses. On this basis, the following sorts of practices are viewed as morally undesirable: sexual fantasy about immoral actions, masturbation (because of its typical incorporation of sexual fantasy), and consumption of erotic sexual images whether in the form of literary pornography, photographic or video pornography, Internet pornography and other forms.

Any method of assessment or change that itself embodied practices judged incongruent with biblical principles of sexuality would be unacceptable in these groups. Psychophysiological assessment of sexual response involves, at a minimum, having the research subject fantasize about a variety of sexual action possibilities that are specifically designed to be arousing to the viewer, and often utilizes the subject's active consumption of a variety of pornographic materials as an aid to fantasy. Accessing pornography in any form would be in direct discord with the stated goals of most participants and their sponsoring groups. Had we attempted to use such methods, we would not have received referrals from participating Exodus groups and would have had high, if not total, refusal rates from participants.

That brings us to the remaining issue, the scientific validity of psychophysiological measurement of sexual response. Many studying sexual response scientifically would argue that the best measure of sexual arousal in the male is penile tumescence. Geary Alford, Daniel Wedding and Stanton Jones stated that "clinicians and researchers have generally assumed (at least implicitly) that penile tumescence is more difficult to control subjectively or to fake than are self-reports. Hence it is considered a more valid indicator of subjects' true levels of sexual arousal in response to clinically or experimentally administered sexual stimulus materials."[4] There is reason to doubt this presumption, however. We will only highlight the major confounding findings here:

- Alford, Wedding and Jones reported conclusive evidence using an elegant single-case design that their homosexual research subject (who had sought treatment to eradicate unwanted homosexual arousal) could under one set of instructions "fake" being a treatment success by producing heterosexual arousal when he was "supposed to" and completely mask homosexual arousal to feign its eradication.[5] Under different instructions the subject demonstrated (truthfully) that the treatment had actually been a complete failure. In the words of Alford, Wedding and Jones, "this patient was able to suppress or generate arousal with almost perfect reliability, parallel to instructions."[6] On an autobiographical note, Stan Jones was the third author in this study, which was a sobering introduction to the "scientific measurement" of sexual arousal and orientation.

- Laws and Holmen[7] similarly established that clients were capable of producing penile responses to stimuli that were not erotic to them, and able to inhibit their erectile response to stimuli that they normally found sexually arousing.
- Recent research has challenged the validity of plethysmography by demonstrating that sexual arousal can be conditioned or learned, thus potentially distorting assessment regarding which stimuli are or are not "naturally" arousing.[8]
- Kaine, Crim and Mersereau found in a mixed group of sex offenders and non–sex offenders that subjects had "a clear ability to suppress penile response to preferred stimuli, both as determined by the subject's choice and by measurement of tumescence."[9]
- A study completed by Wilson confirmed that the penile tumescence test has the potential to be faked.[10] Subjects were able to control their penile response under conditions of instructed faking, with subjects showing a pattern that it was easier to suppress a response to arousing stimuli than it is to fake an arousal response to nonarousing stimuli.
- McAnulty and Adams found one-third of their study participants were capable of complete suppression of undesired arousal, while another third exhibited no significant ability to suppress genital arousal.[11] The researchers suggested that the use of plethysmography as a "lie detector" regarding sexual arousal patterns would be invalid and unethical.

This pattern of findings has led to a reexamination of the idea of measurement of penile tumescence as the "true" index of arousal. According to one prominent research report, the mere presence of physical arousal (as measured by the instrument) does not automatically and univocally equate to physical or mental feelings of sexual arousal.[12] Other components of sexual arousal, particularly the subjective psychological, emotional and relational dimensions of sexual attraction, appear to be at least as important as genital response in conceptualizing and explaining sexual arousal. No objective measure comparable to genital vasocongestion has been developed for assessing the level of one's psychological sexual desire.[13] It would appear that self-report techniques are the best option to investigate this crucial realm.

So it was that we considered and rejected the use of psychophysiological measurement of sexual response as practically impossible, morally unacceptable and of insufficient value empirically to override the prior two reasons.

A Methodological Self-Critique

We will soon explain our methodology in considerable detail. First, though, we want to engage in an exercise of self-criticism. How does our research design measure up to high professional standards?

Although some might have preferred or insisted that a valid study of this controversial subject utilize a "true experiment" design and psychophysiological measurement of sexual arousal as the ideal critical measure of sexual orientation change, we have offered what we take as convincing reasons for not using such methods. Will our study receive more criticism for not using these methods? Undoubtedly. But our decision not to use these methods was deliberate and defensible.

This brings our key criteria for empirical respectability to six. Our research design should

- be longitudinal
- use the best contemporary self-report measures of sexual orientation, and use multiple measures
- sample subjects in different Exodus groups
- study a large subject population
- be prospective

- study a sample representative of the population relevant to the methods studied

How did the actual study we conducted measure up against these aspirations?

Longitudinal design. We feel confident that we achieved great success in launching a study that is longitudinal (covering here our findings for Times 1, 2 and 3) and ongoing (we have at this writing gathered, but not analyzed, data at both Time 4 and Time 5, and are preparing to gather our Time 6 data).*

Quality and breadth of self-report assessment instruments. We are proud of the rigor of the self-report assessment instruments we used. The central question of our study was whether or not it is possible for sexual orientation to change, and this naturally made it crucial to obtain as accurate an assessment of the study participants' sexual orientation as possible. There are several measures of sexual orientation in use by researchers. Because none has secured unequivocal approval from a majority of researchers and each one has its critics, we simply used every established sexual-orientation measure with our sample (see chap. 6). On other variables, particularly psychological distress and religious maturity, we tried where possible to use "industry standard" measures (see chap. 9).

Sample an array of Exodus ministries. We attained great success in gathering information from participants in a variety of Exodus ministries, sixteen to be exact.

We are confident as well about the representative nature of our sample, the size of our sample and the prospective nature of our sample. But in these three key areas, hard choices had to be made. Edward Laumann, J. H. Gagnon, R. T. Michael and S. Michaels, the authors of the "gold standard" of all studies of sexuality in America, commented about their own superb research design, "Research design is never just a theoretical exercise. It is a set of practical solutions to a multitude of problems and considerations that are chosen under the constraints of limited resources of money, time, and prior knowledge."[14] In creating practical solutions to in-

*A good longitudinal study will retain a high percentage of its subjects as it moves forward in time; we discuss our very respectable retention rates in chap. 5.

numerable problems, we had to make compromises with the ideal, and these issues are best discussed more fully.

Large sample size. The first compromise with reality was in the size of the sample studied. We originally hoped to recruit 300 to 400 subjects in the study, but in the end we stopped data collection with 98 subjects at Time 1. Our final participant tally brings our sample size to respectable and scientifically significant, but not impressive, size. Why the smaller-than-intended sample? We were deeply disappointed by an unexplained lack of cooperation by specific Exodus ministries that, despite the pleas of Exodus International's leadership, would not refer their ministry participants to us. The least cooperative ministries were actually the largest and the ones widely regarded as among the most successful in Exodus. These ministries could have referred many dozens of research participants to us, but actually failed to refer even one subject to us and failed to return our phone calls or answer our pleading letters.

A first step to understanding this lack of response is appreciating that Exodus and its affiliated ministries are activist organizations. Their resources, which have been in chronic undersupply, have accordingly gone to other worthwhile projects that provide tangible services to their target population.

Second, it has been the general sense of those involved in Exodus ministries that science has been used against them as a rhetorical tool. Many of the ministry leaders remain deeply suspicious as to whether they would be treated fairly, even in a study conducted by researchers with our "evangelical credentials."

Third, as we discovered in making contacts for this study, a number of individual ministries that affiliate with Exodus have been subjected to "drive-by research." Quite a few reported having been approached about having their unique population studied in some form (usually as the subject population for a doctoral dissertation project for an aspiring clinical psychologist in training), only to (1) have the researcher enter the organization and in some way disturb the conduct of the ministry through cynicism/skepticism or undermining the leaders, (2) fail to abide by promises made (most often failing to actually study the variables agreed upon or to provide empirical feedback of some kind to the ministry), and (3) have the researcher embarrass or demean the host organization in some way, often quite publicly, after the project was over.

Although we did not attain the 300-subject study we had aspired to, we are proud of an initial sample of 98 that must be seen as meaningful. This sample size has other implications, however. We had originally hoped to answer a variety of questions, such as what variables predicted how well people responded to the change process. For example, were younger subjects more successful than older? Men than women? Those with no homosexual experience than those with experience? Married as opposed to single subjects?

We had hoped also that with a large enough sample, we might be able to responsibly search our data set for signs of differential effectiveness of different Exodus intervention methods, for evidence, in other words, that certain intervention techniques were more effective than others in producing change. To have any chance to answer these types of questions, we would need to study a large sample. The importance of size is fairly obvious. To be able to answer the question about which variables predict success, you need a large array of research participants demonstrating a wide variety of the variables studied in order to produce statistically significant results of group differences.

For example, suppose that it is true that change is possible for some, and that those who are younger when they begin the change process (or who are involved in psychoanalytic therapy in addition to attending Exodus ministry meetings, or who were sexually abused as children, or who had never had any homosexual behavioral experience, or who had had a great deal of homosexual behavioral experience, or who had had dramatic and intense religious conversion experiences, or who had close relationships with their parents) are much more likely to experience this change when they go through an Exodus group than those without such characteristics. For such a finding to emerge as statistically significant, we would have to have a solid number of subjects with and without this variable. Sample size matters. And in the end, because of the size of our sample, we chose not to attempt to study which variables predicted differential outcome. Our sample size made it unwise to search our data on these sorts of questions because there simply are not enough cases in the groups to justify such "data-mining."

Prospective design. This disappointment in sample size led to our second compromise with reality, and here we return to the prospective nature of the study. Initially, we wanted our study to be composed entirely of subjects entering "fresh" into the change process; this is the basic definition of a "pure prospective" study. We had hoped to pick up only volunteers who had been involved in the change process for less than three months. The roadblocks we encountered in getting subjects at all led us to broaden the parameters for inclusion in the study. We designated the persons who were new to the change process as "Phase 1" subjects and *extended the period of prior involvement to less than one year,* and then *added* "Phase 2" subjects, those who had been involved in a change ministry *for between one and three years.* In the final breakdown of the total 98 subjects, we have 57 who are Phase 1 participants (involved in the change process for one year or less at Time 1) and 41 who are Phase 2 participants (involved in the change process for between one and three years at Time 1).

Is the inclusion of our "Phase 2" group a fatal compromise? We do not think so; we believe, rather, that inclusion of these subjects is justifiable. Earlier, we discussed one small but crucial finding of the Spitzer study. He reported that the change process, when it was successful, took a long time, reporting an average of two years for participants to begin to experience change, and an average of five years for a meaningful change of sexual orientation to occur. We sought to study people who were still deeply into the change process rather than those reflecting on change after the fact, and generally speaking, studying those who have been in this change process less than three years is unlikely to constitute an "after the change" analysis.

But because the Phase 1 group more closely matches our original research plan, because inclusion of the Phase 2 group is truly a compromise, and in case differences between these two groups emerge, we will always present separate analyses of our findings on these two groups in case there are significant differences in their experiences in the change process.

Representativeness of sample. Representativeness of one's sample is a crucial and ubiquitous problem in research on homosexual persons. Evelyn Hooker, author of one of the earliest and most influential studies of the psychological health of homosexual persons, utilized convenience samples of only thirty heterosexual men and thirty homosexual men. In introducing the study she said, "It should also be stated at the outset that no assumptions are made about the random selection of either group [homosexual or heterosexual]. No one knows what a random sample of the homosexual population would be like; and even if one knew, it would be extremely difficult, if not impossible, to obtain one."[15] The fact that our sample is composed of persons experiencing same-sex attraction but who are among the least likely to be out, proud, vocal or identified publicly with their sexual attractions—and hence completely unlikely to be sampled in any explicit study of the LGBT population—is yet one more example of the nature of this problem.

Let us give one tangential but instructive empirical example of the way a gay and lesbian sample can misrepresent the population it is supposed to represent. It is popularly believed that there is a scientific consensus that behavioral genetics studies have established that there is a strong genetic component to the causation of homosexual orientation (i.e., that people are "born gay").[16] No studies were more central to establishing this public perception than the two studies of J. Michael Bailey, Richard Pillard and their colleagues.[17] These studies looked at patterns of "concordance," or matching of the sexual orientations of siblings, to see if there was increasing sexual orientation concordance as genetic similarity of the siblings increased.

Capitalizing on the fact that monozygotic (or identical) twins are genetically identical, dizygotic (or fraternal) twins and full siblings share fewer of their genes, half siblings share even less of their genes, and adopted siblings share no more than the general population, Bailey and colleagues looked for and found in their original study increasing concordance in homosexual orientation as genetic similarity increased, exactly the pattern one would expect if there is a genetic component in the causation of homosexual orientation. Supposedly, these studies showed that about 50% of the time, if one identical twin is homosexual (for both males and females) then the other twin is too, with the concordances falling to the 15 to 20% ranges for fraternal twins and siblings, and even lower for the other categories. So this key study supposedly found that as siblings shared less genetic similarity they also manifested less sexual orientation similarity, thus suggesting genetic causation.

The 50% finding, however, is truly a "supposed" finding, a confusion created by two factors, the first being a common misunderstanding, even among professional researchers, of what a "Probandwise Concordance" is, how it is calculated and what it represents.[18] Simply put, a "proband" is a research subject who manifests the condition or characteristic of interest in the research (in this case, homosexual orientation). If there are two identical twin pairs, one of which "matches" for homosexual orientation (call these Gay-A and Gay-B) and the other of which does not (call these Gay-C and Straight-D), there are three probands (the 3 gay subjects A, B and C) and a Probandwise Concordance of 67% (the number of probands that match—2, since Gay-A and Gay-B each have a match in their twin—divided by all probands whether they match or not—3 for each of the 3 gay subjects A, B and C; 2/3 = 67%).

Bailey and Pillard reported Probandwise Concordances of 52% (29/56) for male identical twins,[19] but this finding should not be understood as "50% of the time, if one identical twin is homosexual then the other twin also is." What they actually found in this study was thirteen identical twin pairs where both twin brothers were gay, one triplet trio where all three brothers were gay, and twenty-seven identical twin pairs where one brother was gay and the other twin was not.

But the vastly more important point is that these findings appear to be unrepresentative of the homosexual population in general due to the studies being conducted with a biased sample. The importance of a representative sample is easily illustrated. If we want to understand what the American public thinks about a controversial question, on average, then we must gather the opinions of a representative sample. It would present a grossly inaccurate portrait of public opinion to ask either the national membership of the organization Parents and Friends of Lesbians and Gays or the national membership of the Southern Baptist Convention their opinion on the question of homosexual marriage, and then present those findings as representative of the American public, regardless of the size of the sample.

Similarly, for Bailey's studies to be able to provide normative estimates of levels of genetic influence in the causation of homosexual orientation, his sample would have to be truly representative of the population of homosexual persons. We expressed concern early on about the representativeness of Bailey's samples.[20] Bailey recruited his samples by advertising in popular homosexual media outlets in the greater Chicago area. If such advertising were assured to produce a representative sample of homosexual persons, this would not be a problem. But if there were any chance that such advertisements for a scientific study would produce a biased sample through this form of recruitment (biased, for example, by an increased volunteer rate for those who have higher concordances and higher genetic similarity), then these findings would prove unfounded. Given the enthusiasm of the gay community for a genetic explanation of the origins of homosexuality, we were concerned that there was in fact a volunteer bias in this study, with identical twins who matched for homosexual orientation being more likely to volunteer than those who did not match.

Our concerns have proven well-grounded. Recognizing this limitation in his own sampling, Bailey and his colleagues got access to a population that would not have such a bias, the Australian Twin Registry.[21] With a more representative sample of every twin born in Australia, the genetic effect essentially disappeared as a statistically significant variable affecting causation of homosexual orientation. They found twenty-seven identical male twin pairs where at least one of the twin brothers was gay, but in only three of the pairs was the second twin brother gay as well.* This study "did not provide statistically significant support for the importance of genetic factors" in causing homosexual orientation.[22]

To his credit, Bailey recognized this and stated, "This suggests that concordances from prior studies [i.e., his own two prior studies] were inflated due to concordance dependent ascertainment bias" (or, in other words, sample bias).[23] Other studies have also produced lower heritability estimates, but none is more important than the recent study by P. S. Bearman and H. Brückner who, using a truly nationally representative sample, failed to find a significant genetic component to sexual orientation causation and

*Here the Probandwise Concordance is calculated by the following method: The six gay twins in the three matching pairs count as six successful probands with matches (six for the numerator), which is then divided by all of the probands, which here would be the six that matched plus the twenty-four that did not. Six probands that match divided by thirty probands total = 20% Probandwise Concordance.

who reiterated emphatically the chronic problem of nonrepresentative samples in research about homosexuality.[24]

How representative your sample should be depends on the questions you are asking. You seek a different population when you ask, What do all openly GLBT people think? versus What do all people who experience same-sex attraction think? versus What do all devoutly religious people who experience same-sex attraction think? It would be an interesting research question to ask, Is it possible for *every* person who experiences same-sex attraction to change his or her sexual orientation? Interesting, but that was not our question. It would also be an interesting research question to ask, Is it possible for devoutly religious *and explicitly nonreligious persons* who experience same-sex attraction to change their sexual orientation? Interesting, but that also was not our question.

Our primary research question was, Is it possible for *anyone* to change his or her sexual orientation? To get at that question we chose to focus on a specific subpopulation of those who might seek to change their sexual orientation by asking, Is it possible for *those persons who experience same-sex attraction and seek to change their sexual orientation through the Christian ministry group Exodus to change?* This more-focused research question allows us to answer our primary research question, because anyone who experiences change through Exodus becomes a case study that change is possible for some.

We want to disabuse all readers of the idea that our sample somehow is representative of the gay, lesbian and bisexual community. Exodus ministries are distinctively Christian groups, largely Protestant and conservative in orientation, that, while not restricting their ministry to those who share all their views, certainly draw and retain those who resonate with the distinctive principles and goals of the ministry. Individuals with no religious affiliations who might nevertheless desire sexual orientation change would likely feel no connection with such groups. And further there are many areas of the country where such groups are not active or are unknown. Exodus draws a unique crowd.

Did we get a representative sample of those who populate Exodus? We just quoted Hooker, who said, "No one knows what a random sample of the homosexual population would be like; and even if one knew, it would be extremely difficult, if not impossible, to obtain one."[25] We believe that our sample is somewhat representative of the Exodus population seeking help, but we have to remain somewhat cautious in making claims here. We had no access to all individuals seeking help from Exodus. Rather, we sought subjects from those ministries that were geographically accessible to our research teams, and this eliminated many ministries around the country. Further, we did not have direct access to participating Exodus ministries' records and thus could not contact all individuals who sought help from them.

Our instructions to and agreement with the ministries we studied were that they would refer to us every participant in their ministry that met our minimal criteria. Those criteria for involvement in the study were simply that all subjects had to be at least eighteen years old; same-sex attraction had to be a significant part of their motivation for their involvement with this Exodus ministry; and they had to have been involved in the change process for less than three years.1 Nevertheless, we were then dependent on referrals from the ministries for interviews, and although it is not impossible that some sort of bias could have entered into that referral process, we have no suspicion that it did.

In the end, then, we are convinced that we got a reasonably representative cross section of those seeking change through Exodus. Here is our candid summary assessment of how we did on the key dimensions of study quality:

- *Prospective design.* Achieved, with the compromise of recruiting a minority of Phase 2 subjects who were in the change process one to three years.
- *Longitudinal design.* Achieved.
- *Study a sample representative of the population relevant to the methods studied.* Achieved, but without complete control of subject enrollment.

1Many Exodus groups seek to help people with a range of sexual issues, including heterosexual acting-out behavior, sex addictions, transvestism (with and without significant homosexual inclination) and other sexual concerns. Their common concern is "sexual brokenness" and not only or purely homosexual orientation. Hence, at the Time 1 interview, one of the first questions we asked referred subjects was, "Is concern about homosexuality, same-sex attraction, a significant part of your motivation for your involvement with this Exodus ministry?" Subjects had to answer yes for inclusion in the study. We recognized that this could introduce into the study bisexuals and other individuals; see our discussion of how we dealt with this in the construction of our Truly Gay subsample in chap. 7.

- *Use the best contemporary self-report measures of sexual orientation, and use multiple measures.* Achieved.
- *Study a large subject population.* Achieved (large, but not as large a population as originally projected).
- *Sample subjects in different Exodus groups.* Achieved.

Development of the Study

At the beginning of chapter three we discussed how our study evolved from a grant proposal Stan Jones wrote in the early 1990s. Shelved for lack of funding on account of its controversial subject matter, the study proceeded when Exodus International offered to provide funds to support it, on the understanding that we would have complete scholarly freedom in conducting the study and publishing its findings.

The Exodus board approved the proposal for the study in the winter of 1999, and the search for funding through Exodus began. During the spring of 1999 the research team began preparation of a pilot assessment instrument. In late spring 1999 when the Exodus board made a funding commitment and raised an initial $30,000, we began planning formally for the pilot study. Mark Yarhouse (Regent University) and Gary Strauss (Biola University) agreed to serve as (respectively) East and West Coast coordinators and research collaborators for this project, with Jones supervising a Wheaton College-based Midwest team. A research team was assembled, a research plan developed and assessment materials gathered.

The Exodus International annual conference was held in July 1999, and at that conference a pilot interview instrument was administered to approximately eight "ministry veteran" volunteers from whom we also solicited feedback. This pilot experience showed us significant holes in the way we were conceptualizing the project, differing perceptions of the wording of research questions given the outlook of Exodus participants, and also the tremendous sacrifice research participants would be making to participate in the study. It took these eight volunteers an average of approximately 4.5 hours to complete all of the pilot interview and survey questions and standardized questionnaires we asked them to complete, and this was clearly asking too much.

In the fall of 1999 we refined further the research instrument, developed detailed procedural instructions and interviewer training materials, and established standardization of research interview procedures. By this time it was clear that the original commitment from Exodus to provide $100,000 in funding for the study was not going to be realized. In the end they provided approximately $65,000 in funding for direct costs related to the execution of this study.

As we entered 2000 we trained interview teams and began to recruit subjects. We assessed the first subjects in February of 2000, focusing on those individuals who had entered involvement in their ministries since September 1999. Within two months we were concerned at the modest numbers of subjects we had been able to recruit. Our original plan had been to enroll all subjects in the spring of 2000, but it became clear that we were going to have to extend enrollment in the study many more months to have a significant sample. We made repeated appeals for cooperation with the study to ministries that we had counted on to provide referrals but from whom we had received no cooperation, but to no avail. In May 2000 we decided to enroll "Phase 2" subjects who had been in the change process for one to three years in addition to the subjects newer to the change process. We extended enrollment in the study and broadened the subject population we were enrolling, extending our Time 1 interviewing. We interviewed the last subject for the study in April 2001.

Wanting to conduct the Time 2 follow-up interview approximately one year after enrollment in the study, we began developing the Time 2 assessment instrument in the fall of 2000. Subjects first assessed in February were first interviewed for Time 2 in December 2000 (about ten months after the Time 1 assessment, and as new Time 1 subjects continued to be enrolled). Almost all of our Time 2 interviews were completed between December 2000 and December 2001, though one Time 2 interview took place as late as September 2003. The vast majority of subjects experienced a nine- to fifteen-month gap between their initial Time 1 assessment and the Time 2 follow-up, but there was one subject that was interviewed at Time 2 just five months after Time 1, while another extreme subject went two years and four months between Time 1 and 2, both of these due to extraordinary contact and scheduling problems.

We knew that we could not sustain interviewing spread across such a wide span of time, and at Time 3 we consolidated schedules. All Time 3 interviewing took place between February and December 2003, but mostly between February and June 2003. We had intentionally sought to hold the timing gap between Time 1 and 2 assessments between nine and fifteen months but knew that we would have to let some subjects interviewed early for Times 1 and 2 go a very long time before Time 3. Indeed, although the average gap between Times 2 and 3 was about eighteen months, one subject went almost three years between Times 2 and 3.

The Question of Bias in Research and Biased Researchers

Funding for this study was provided through grants and gifts to Exodus International. This funding source raises the serious question of whether objective and credible outcomes are possible from this study. But our funding source is not the only issue. Some might allege preexisting bias on the part of the research team based on the fact that the principle investigators are evangelical Christians who have published extensively about homosexuality, espousing and defending the traditional view of the Christian church through two millennia that homosexual behavior (i.e., full homosexual erotic and physical intimacy) is immoral. How, it might be asked, can ideologically committed researchers funded by Exodus conduct a fair study?

These concerns are points of legitimate discussion. Any reasonable person would be wise to ponder the implications of lung cancer research being funded by the tobacco industry and conducted by a person who has "declared his allegiances" before the study is conducted. These concerns must be balanced, however, by the realization that there seem to be few neutral parties in the debate over homosexuality to fund the research or conduct the proposed study. Let us focus first on bias introduced by the preexisting views of the researchers.

This is a field of study in which few come with no preconceived notions or strongly held ideas. Much of the most-cited research in the area is published by gay, lesbian and bisexual individuals who write from a perspective of passionate commitment in their critiques of existing research, development of new lines of empirical inquiry and advocacy for their views.

Further, we have each expressed in print the belief that while change may be possible for some, it may occur less frequently and in a more fragmentary fashion than many conservative Christians would like to believe. We have also expressed our belief that the scientific evidence is not decisive in the moral debates about homosexuality, including arguing specifically that the moral debate does not hinge on whether or not homosexual orientation can be changed. Specifically, we have argued that in the end the Christian moral argument about homosexuality does not stand or fall on the possibility of "conversion" of sexual orientation, because in the end the Christian moral demand is not orientation change but rather, at a minimum, "chaste behavior."[26]

On this view the homosexual person pleases God by ceasing to engage in homosexual sex. Although we might suppose that God would "heal" some homosexual persons to experience heterosexual desire and fulfillment in the context of marriage, we would not presume this to be necessary to the Christian sexual ethic.

Our views have placed us in opposition to several prominent leaders of the "healing of homosexuality" movement outside of Exodus, one of whom has chided us publicly and privately for dishonoring God by not believing that all homosexual persons can and will be healed completely (to heterosexual normalcy) if they simply submit their lives to God. We have been criticized, in other words, for not believing strongly or unequivocally enough in sexual-orientation change for the homosexual.

Ultimately, the issue of researchers' bias must boil down to one of scientific integrity, to whether scholars are willing and able to "bracket" their beliefs and to report honestly the results they garner. We confronted this issue of our integrity with the Exodus administration and board of directors, because we were not sure that our construal of the moral situation was in perfect alignment with that of Exodus. When finalizing the agreements about the research with the Exodus International organization, Jones presented the following statement to the Exodus board of directors:

> Since it [i.e., this research project] will be sponsored by Exodus and funded through Exodus contacts, the proposed study will be subject to severe criticism that it is hopelessly contaminated with bias and proprietary interests. The only possible counters to such criticisms are a clean and rigorous methodology, and absolute intellectual and academic integrity on the part of the

research team. To be perfectly clear: Once a commitment is made to this study, *it is my unalterable intent as Principal Investigator to publish our findings regardless of what they are.* This commitment rests on a conviction that the God of the Christian faith is glorified by truth, and that more harm than good would be created by any avoidance of or suppression of whatever findings this study unearths.

What about Exodus's funding our research? Concern about such proprietary funding is growing as governmental funds for research dwindle and corporate funding expands. Of particular concern is the growing pattern of pharmaceutical companies' funding their own clinical trials documenting the efficacy of new drugs. Often here, the issue is much deeper than that of the pharmaceutical companies' providing core research funding, but more broadly a pattern of vested financial interests of researchers in the profits of the company, direct or indirect.[27]

Ultimately, the only defense against research bias is solid methodological design executed by honest researchers with the results reported honestly and completely. Much of the research on which we depend in the Western world is conducted under circumstances similar to that of the present study, as when pharmaceutical companies fund studies of the effectiveness of experimental drugs they have produced or when an environmentalist foundation funds research on new approaches to recycling. We have been committed since the outset to publish honestly all of our findings regardless of the outcomes. Exodus International funded our research but was not allowed to exercise any control over our methods or the reporting of outcomes. Our funding has gone solely toward the practical challenges of running this study, and no funds have gone to the personal enrichment of the researchers. Outcome studies such as this one are often funded by governmental agencies for many multiples of the types of funding supplied here; in contrast, our research has been conducted on a shoestring budget.

One way to bring these issues together is to assess whether research is done by "interested" or "disinterested" parties. Recently, the Academic Senate of the University of California system, representing the thousands of faculty of that massive university system, voted to change the academic freedom policy of the system.[28] In the words of the resolution, the original policy "associated academic freedom with scholarship that gave 'play to intellect rather than to passion.' It conceived scholarship as 'dispassionate' and as concerned only with 'the logic of the facts.'" In contrast, according to the resolution,

> The revised version of [APM-010, the Academic Freedom statement] supersedes this standpoint. It holds that academic freedom depends on the quality of scholarship, which is to be assessed by the content of the scholarship, not by the motivation that led to its production. The revision of [APM-010] therefore does not distinguish between "interested" and "disinterested" scholarship; it differentiates instead between competent and incompetent scholarship. Although competent scholarship requires an open mind, this does not mean that faculty are unprofessional if they reach definite conclusions. It means rather that faculty must always stand ready to revise their conclusions in light of new evidence or further discussion. Although competent scholarship requires the exercise of reason, this does not mean that faculty are unprofessional if they are urgently committed to a definite point of view. It means rather that faculty must form their point of view by applying professional standards of inquiry rather than by succumbing to external and illegitimate incentives such as monetary gain or political coercion. Competent scholarship can and frequently does communicate definite and politically salient viewpoints about important and controversial questions.

This is an apt statement of the approach to which we aspired in conducting this study. We came to this study with convictions, but these convictions were neither blind nor naive; they were forged through engagement with our religious tradition, but also through a professional, critical and fair engagement with the empirical literature evaluated by exacting standards. Our views, though deeply held, were open to revision based on the data.

THE CONSTRUCTION AND ADMINISTRATION OF THE QUESTIONNAIRE

In constructing our assessment instrument we discovered why it is so easy to criticize how questions are asked in other studies: there are infinite ways to formulate questions, with pros and cons to every possible formulation.

Our final assessment instrument was a complex combination of interview questions and what we termed self-administered questionnaires (or SAQs), with the SAQs being a mixture of standardized survey instruments with preexisting research support, and new measures constructed for the purposes of this study (and often adapted from other studies). The flow of the formatting had to be carefully monitored so that the interviewers could gather all of the necessary information without putting the participants through unnecessary or inapplicable questioning (such as asking a participant about their experience of sexual abuse when none had occurred).

We benefited greatly from the then recently published research by E. O. Laumann and his colleagues, who developed and administered extensive standardized questionnaires examining sexuality and sexual behavior. The aim of these studies was to understand the causes and consequences of human sexual behavior. They conducted the National Health and Social Life Survey (NHSLS), which was a survey of a 3,432 person 1992 U.S. national sample, with a wide range of questions asked about adult sexual behavior and attitudes. This study, widely considered the gold standard of sexuality studies, was published as a book, *The Social Organization of Sexuality,* which contains a complete version of their questionnaire in an extended appendix.[29]

Laumann and his colleagues were kind enough to furnish us with a copy of their more recent, then ongoing Chicago Health and Social Life Survey (CHSLS), which they considered a methodological improvement over the NHSLS.[30] Both the NHSLS and the CHSLS surveys served as methodological models for many of our questions, and where possible we followed their question wording exactly to facilitate possible comparison of the answers of our research participants to the norms from these samples. In chapter five, we compare some of our details about our sample with the reports of national norms in Laumann's *The Social Organization of Sexuality.*

When it came to our inquiries both about the subjective experience of sexual orientation and about sexual experiences related to the cause of homosexual orientation, we also consulted interview protocols used in several of the major interview studies of homosexuality.[31] We also relied on input from those deeply involved in Exodus ministries. We gathered suggestions from other experts in the field as well and often adapted questions from other surveys, especially if those questions were related to major criticisms of the possibility of change or to major theories of the origin of homosexuality. The process of putting together the questionnaire was a complicated and lengthy one. Among the goals that we sought to attain were

- to use standardized questions wherever possible (such as using the same questions Laumann et al. had used in their study) in order to facilitate comparison of the answers of our population with national norms
- to use well-validated and normed inventory instruments to facilitate comparisons across samples
- to minimize biases, particularly any biases that presumed that the participants were attaining success in their efforts to achieve change
- to get essential information in a reasonable period of time
- to minimize emotional distress for our population
- to use clear language to insure precision of meaning of the responses (such as defining what it would mean for two people to "have sex")
- to minimize the influence of social desirability, the tendency of people to give the answers they think their questioners want, a concern that has come up as a criticism in many of the studies of orientation change.2

After our piloting of a draft instrument at the July 1999 Exodus conference, we finalized the instrument. We sought to create an instrument that followed logical and natural transitions during the course of the interview as we moved from topic to topic. We included not just standardized quantitative questions, but in several areas of key importance we added qualitative (or more open-ended) questions which were tape-recorded and later transcribed. Where we used such qualitative questions, we typically began the respective section of the interview with those qualitative ("Tell us

---

2Social desirability" refers to the tendency of individuals to answer questions in ways that make them look good in the eyes of others rather than reflecting an honest response. People are likely to overestimate the degree to which they report anything desirable (as when 80% of people say they are "above average" on some trait) and underestimate anything undesirable. Researchers try to minimize the impact of social desirability through a variety of techniques, but the most important in this study were to avoid any language that communicated judgment of any kind (e.g., asking "Have you ever engaged in anal sex?" rather than "Have you ever engaged in abnormal acts such as anal sex?") and to ask the most threatening or undesirable questions in the SAQs so that responses were private from the interviewer.

about _______") questions, because we reasoned that asking the qualitative questions after administration of the standardized questions would risk "contaminating" the responses to the open-ended questions with the categories and vocabulary of the standardized questions. Such qualitative questions were asked in an open-ended way.

The standardized and more quantitative questions were asked in the form of verbal questions from the interviewers, but also in the form of self-administered questionnaires (SAQs). Prior research has established that respondents are much more likely, especially in response to invasive or highly sensitive questions, to give honest responses when they can privately and anonymously report their responses without observation by the interviewer.[32] Accordingly, we followed the methodological pattern of Laumann and associates (1994) in interspersing face-to-face interview questions with administration of SAQs. When the interviewer reached the time for administration of an SAQ, the subject was instructed to fill out the instrument without showing it to the interviewer, and when finished to put it in a "privacy envelope." All of the standardized inventories mentioned on pages 136-138 were administered as SAQs. At the end of the interview the interviewer invited the subject to seal the privacy envelope containing the SAQs for mailing, and gave the subject the option, in case of extreme privacy concerns, of mailing the SAQ privacy envelope him- or herself after the interview (none of our subjects chose this option).

The full interview instrument involved the following major components. Certain specific questions and discussion of the standardized instruments are reserved for the separate topical chapters where the findings from those instruments are discussed. A copy of the entire interview protocol and of the SAQs as administered is available on the website where we are archiving materials related to this project for public access at <www.ivpress.com>.

Here we summarize the major sections of the interview assessment:

- *Introduction and informed consent.* This section established that the participant fit the eligibility requirements for the study, introduced the subject to the confidentiality standards for the study and surveyed the purposes of the research, gave an overview of the topics to be covered and various methods to be used in gathering data, and culminated with having the participant sign an Informed Consent document and fill out a "contact information" sheet to enable the research team to contact the subject again later for follow-up. This latter sensitive information, the only information gathered that contained the subject's identifying information, was sealed in a separate envelope for mailing before the rest of the interview continued; subjects were instructed not to report any further personal identifying information in the rest of the interview.

- *General demographic information.* This section of the interview included many questions that followed the Laumann CHSLS. Since we were gathering information about families of origins, we included several questions relevant to the origin of sexual orientation, including a qualitative question about "family atmosphere," a probe about birth order and an inventory called the "Parental Bonding Instrument."[33]
- *Concerns leading to Exodus involvement and previous change attempts.* This section asked a number of quantifiable and qualitative questions about past and current involvement in attempts to change sexual orientation, including probes about motivations for change attempts, nature of the involvement in Exodus ministries and concurrent involvement in psychotherapy.
- *Description of religious experience.* We began here with a qualitative probe about the person's religious experience, and followed it with demographic probes based on the work of Laumann on denominational affiliation and frequency of church involvement. We finished this section with the administration of two standardized inventories of religious experience suitable for a largely Christian population, the Spiritual Well-Being Scale and the Faith Maturity Scale. After this section, subjects and interviewers took a brief break.
- *Description of sexual orientation.* We began here with qualitative questions about the person's experience of sexual orientation and personal hypotheses about the origins of their sexual orientation. A series of historical questions were then presented about such topics as the age at which and manner by which the subject began to feel he or she was

"different," and questions about gender conformity and nonconformity, and then a Gender Conformity Scale was administered as an SAQ. The interviewer then continued with several verbal questions about sexual orientation; these questions were the source of the categorical ratings of sexual orientation, the Kinsey ratings, and of the Shively and DeCecco orientation ratings. Our interviewers then administered three sexual orientation scales as two SAQs, the Klein Sexual Orientation Grid and a sexual orientation inventory, the former being a stand-alone inventory and the latter being a composite document containing the Sell Sexual Orientation inventory and the Sexual Orientation Thermometer instrument developed by Yarhouse and loosely based on the work of Shively and DeCecco. Finally, the interviewer returned to a body of questions asking about the degree of openness (or "out-ness") of the person's homosexual experience. All of the scales used are discussed more fully in chapter six.

- *Examination of emotional well-being, part 1.* We were very interested in the issue of psychological distress in this population, both at entry into the change process and over time. We administered the Millon Clinical Multiaxial Inventory at this point in the interview to break up the inquiry into the sexual behavior and experiences of the subjects.3

3Originally, we had hoped to administer the MMPI (the most thoroughly validated and widely respected measure of psychological functioning) to our subjects, but chose to go with the shorter MCMI. We have not, however, analyzed these data. The MMPI is the better validated instrument, and one that is normed on the general population and hence optimal, for a technical perspective, for our study, but the MMPI was simply too long to include in our study. The major problem with the MCMI in respect to its use with our population is that it is normed on a clinical population, and hence has the reputation for "pathologizing" those who take it who are not really clinical cases. The MCMI is understood informally as helping clinicians to generate diagnostic hypotheses for persons in treatment, so if the general public takes the instrument, they are likely to receive results that depict them as suitably receiving various DSM diagnoses. With ambivalence we justified the initial administration of the MCMI on the rationale that our subjects, having committed to the process of sexual-orientation change, were at least in some ways like those starting outpatient counseling. By Time 2, though, we chose to drop the MCMI as an ongoing assessment instrument because it was too time-consuming and we had to trim back what we were demanding of our subjects. In the end we chose not to analyze the data from the MCMI because we had no Time 2 data or beyond on which to demonstrate change. The question of whether our population was a suitable one for administration of the MCMI is probably further complicated by our findings for the SCL-90-R in this study, because our empirical results (presented in chap. 9) for the SCL-90-R show that our subjects are on average as much *unlike* a clinical outpatient population in terms of psychological distress as they are like such a population. There may be some useful role for analysis of this data at some point in the future.

After this section, subjects and interviewers took a second brief break.

- *History of sexual behavior and experiences*. After two brief questions about the sources of the subject's sexual knowledge and the general atmosphere toward sexuality in the person's family of origin, we administered another SAQ, the Survey of Sexual Behaviors and Experiences. This was a composite instrument that focused not narrowly on matters of sexual orientation but more broadly on current and lifetime sexual experience, asking questions about the number and gender of sexual partners, relational circumstances of sexual acts, childhood and adolescent sexual experiences, and the occurrence of a variety of specific experiences. Much of this data is presented in chapter five.
- *Examination of emotional well-being, part 2*. We then returned to the topic of emotional distress, which began with our own Quality of Life Inventory administered as an SAQ, followed by several interview questions about current, recent (last year) and lifetime experience with anxiety, depression, alcohol and drug abuse, major mental illness, and suicidality. We administered a Religious Coping Activities Survey and then concluded the substantive portion of the interview by administering the Symptom Check List-90-Revised as an SAQ.
- *Debriefing*. The interview concluded with some evaluative questions about the interview and an attempt to deal with any distress created by the process.

The interview process lasted approximately 3 to 3.5 hours on average the first time we interviewed subjects. The interviews were audiotaped to facilitate analysis of the qualitative items and to allow excerpts from them to be used in the final report of the study.

We departed from the methods used by Laumann and his colleagues in defining sex or sexual activity. They defined sex or sexual activity as "any mutually voluntary activity with another person that involves genital contact and sexual excitement or arousal, that is, feeling really turned on, even if intercourse or orgasm did not occur."[34] We defined sex or sexual activity in our interview when we first asked about sexual orientation using the Kinsey scale. We asked (interview section 4, question 20), "Have you ever been sexually intimate with another person?" and then followed that question with the following explanation: "Our term 'sexually intimate' means sexual intercourse between you and another person, whether your partner was a man or a woman, where there was genital contact between the partners such that at least one of you had an orgasm." We then provided instructions to the interviewers that "If queried, [they should respond to the participants that] this definition would include such activities as mutual erotic touching or 'mutual masturbation,' one-way erotic touching, oral sex, vaginal sex, and anal sex."

The most significant difference between our questions and those of Laumann and colleagues was the presence or absence of orgasm. By requiring orgasm to be present for an episode to be defined as "sex" in our study, we took a more conservative or stringent definitional stance toward the occurrence of episodes of sex than Laumann and his colleagues. We made this departure from Laumann's methods reluctantly, but did so because we found in our pilot efforts that our subject pool found the broader definition of sex confusing. The idea from Laumann that a sexual event had occurred on the basis of "feeling really turned on" seemed too broad to our pilot subjects, and so we settled on the more restrictive definition, knowing that this would cloud to some extent our comparisons with the Laumann data.

A word about the language we used to ask about sex is also in order. Following Laumann, we avoided the use of highly technical terms (such as "penile-vaginal intromission"). At the other extreme, we also avoided the use of slang because of its vagueness and the potential negative connotations (i.e., offensiveness) of such language to our mostly religiously conservative interviewees. Our goal was for the interview to be a neutral, professional experience.[35] Pursuant to that goal, we also avoided sensationalistic language as well as language that suggested social desirability for the "direction" subjects might think we would want them to report. We tried to use language that made treatment dropout or failure as easy to report as continuation and success.

We began to realize early in our Time 1 interviews that we were asking a great deal of our subjects. Even though we used incentives to help offset the inconvenience of participating in this very personal interview (giving

$30 to each participant for each interview), we knew that we had to shorten the interview process. We chose first and most obviously to drop historical questions that requested reporting from the past and which were unlikely to change. Most substantively, after conceptual and practical review, we dropped the Millon Clinical Multiaxial Inventory for reasons discussed in the footnote on page 137. Few changes in the interview materials were made for the Time 3 assessment.

Another major change as we moved through assessments at Time 1, 2 and 3 was the mode of assessment. We began this study intent on conducting face-to-face interviews with our subjects at all points of assessment. Face-to-face interviewing is more costly since it involves travel of the interviewing team, arrangements for interview locations and so forth. We felt that it strengthened the study to choose this mode of administration. Most studies conducted to date had been survey studies, some had involved primarily phone interviews, but none had primarily involved face-to-face interviews. Phone interviews might cost less, but given the nature of the questions we were asking, the telephone did not lend itself to the development of rapport with our research participants, nor was it optimal given the length of the overall interview or the complexities inherent in the many ways in which we were asking questions.

To our disappointment, however, and perhaps due to our inexperience at administering a complex longitudinal study, our intention of continuing only face-to-face interviews had to evolve with the realities we faced with the sample. All 98 Time 1 interviews were conducted face to face. Already at Time 2 we were beginning to see our funds depleted, but more important we were beginning to see the geographical dispersion of our sample. A total of 12 Time 2 interviews were done by phone due to the subjects having moved or having been otherwise inaccessible to face-to-face interviewing. As we drew our Time 2 assessments to a close, we began to realize that our subject base was mobile and going to present impossible challenges for continued in-person interviewing. Thus we switched to all telephone and SAQ assessment at Time 3.

PROCEDURES

Selection and training of interviewers. We selected and trained graduate-level students in psychology as interviewers. These research associates did the actual work of contacting participants and conducting the interviews, and were paid $40 per completed interview. To facilitate a standardized training program, we developed a videotape of a model interview that was used as the foundation of the standardized training method and shown to all potential interviewers. As part of their training, interviewers also gave practice administrations and received feedback from the research team. Each interviewer read and signed a Code of Ethics and Practice for Research Associates form in which they affirmed their responsibility to protect the confidentiality of the interviewee.[36]

Gender of interviewers. We decided at the outset that male or female interviewees could interview male participants, but that only females could interview female participants. This decision was prompted by our pilot research, where ministry veterans told us of their perception of a high rate of sexual abuse in the past of many female participants, and of their likely discomfort in disclosing matters of sexuality to male interviewers.

Informed consent. It was important that interviewees understand what they were agreeing to. In the phone contacts setting up the interviews, potential subjects were given an explicit description of the nature of the research and told that the interview was long and intrusive. At the beginning of the interview itself, each interviewee read and signed a Description of Research Methods form that explained the purposes of the study, how confidentiality would be protected, and the research procedures.[37] We placed great emphasis on asking participants to tell us their experience and assuring them that we were not looking for any one particular outcome. We also assured participants that we would keep the information from the interview confidential. Finally, we informed participants that we would be asking "detailed and blunt questions about the most personal aspects" of their lives and we noted that the experience itself might lead to feelings of "discomfort, embarrassment, or other negative feelings."

Those who chose to participate in the interview then read and signed a Voluntary Consent and Agreement for Project Exodus Research Participation form.[38] Participants were also asked to provide follow-up contact information for themselves and for three or four others who could be contacted if the person were unreachable by the research team.[39] At the end of the interview participants received $30 to compensate them for their time, and they signed a receipt acknowledging payment.[40] We also asked participants to sign a Limits of Confidentiality form. This form specifically addressed issues that would, by law, require us to break confidentiality.[41]

Privacy, confidentiality and security concerns. Privacy, confidentiality and security concerns, as discussed by Laumann and his colleagues and other researchers, were of utmost importance to us and to our interviewees. The right to *privacy* belongs to the participant and it has to do with that person's ability to control what others know about him or her. *Confidentiality* refers to the assumption that what is shared will not be disclosed to a third party. *Security* refers to the actual, physical structures that are in place to protect participants with respect to their disclosures and involvement in the study.

Privacy, confidentiality and security are important issues in ethical research, all the more given the nature and sensitivity of the topic. There is stigma attached to experiences of same-sex attraction in some religiously conservative circles, and respecting the subjects' privacy and confidentiality was at the forefront of our attention. Many of our subjects, though, were more concerned about disclosure of their identities and information to the gay community.

We took several practical steps to scrupulously protect the identity of the interviewees. Interviewers kept no records of the identities of those they interviewed after completing the interviews. Interviewees actually sealed the envelopes with their identifying information themselves and were invited to walk with the interviewer to the nearest mailbox to insure that the letter was being sent to the main research headquarters. Each interview was audiotaped, but no identifying data were included on the audiotape; taping started after the identifying data were gathered and the consent forms signed.

Recruitment, screening and retention of subjects. We began the recruitment of subjects by soliciting involvement of ministry leaders and getting an estimated number of persons known by the ministry leader to have participated in at least one group meeting since September 1, 1999. We then asked the ministry leader to contact all persons from this list, most of whom were contacted through their current participation in the ministry group. Then we received a list of all persons who agreed to be contacted by our research team and attempted to make interview appointments with all subjects.

One issue we had to address at the beginning was that of building a climate of trust with participants. Participants had to see the potential purpose behind the study and to be assured not only of their anonymity but also that we had not been dispatched by Exodus to prove the effectiveness of the Exodus ministries, nor were we attempting to disprove the claims of success. Rather, we were documenting the experiences of those who enter Exodus-affiliated ministries, first and foremost to see if such a ministry can have an effect on sexual orientation and, second, to give an account of the experiences of those who walk such a difficult path.

Conclusion

This study is the best designed and implemented study to date on religiously mediated change of sexual orientation. The official website of the American Psychological Association criticizes existing evidence regarding therapeutic change of sexual orientation, stating "treatment outcome is not followed and reported over time as would be the standard to test the validity of any mental health intervention."[42] This study is prospective and longitudinal, studies a large and representative sample of individuals seeking sexual-orientation change via religiously mediated means through a broad sample of religious ministries seeking to support such change, and uses a wide range of the best available psychological measures of sexual orientation and of psychological distress to examine the resulting outcomes. The study, although not above criticism, is significantly stronger than any other existing study. Our results demand careful attention.

5

Our Sample

THIS CHAPTER SUMMARIZES THE DEMOGRAPHIC and descriptive data, mostly gathered at the initial or Time 1 assessment, that describe the participants in our study of individuals attempting to change their sexual orientation. We begin with a quick portrait of our retention in this study, that is to say, the number of participants who dropped out of the study and those who remained in it, and then move to an overview of the quantitative demographic and behavioral data. After this extensive quantitative section, we close the chapter with a qualitative portrait of the responses of our participants to some of our open-ended questions.

There are many important findings reported in this chapter, all of which inform our understanding of the population for this study. The retention statistics for this study are excellent, comparing favorably to several "gold standard" studies. Roughly one-fourth of our sample was female. In contrast to the caricature of Exodus working with homogenous samples of young, confused, naive, sexually inexperienced individuals, the sample was quite diverse. The majority of the sample had extensive sexual experiences and involvement in the gay community. Many had early sexual experiences, including nonvoluntary experiences. Perhaps most notably, our sample is older than we had anticipated, with an average age in the late thirties. Overall the portrait that emerges is of a sample for whom change of sexual orientation would not be given an optimistic prognosis under any construal.

RETENTION/SAMPLE EROSION

Longitudinal studies—studies that follow groups of subjects over a period of time—can be difficult to interpret if large numbers of subjects are lost from the study. To give a simple example, in studying the effects of a drug over time, loss of 50% of the sample creates huge problems for interpretation. These individuals may be missing because they disproportionately experienced negative drug side-effects, because they experienced elevated rates of morbidity (i.e., many of them died between assessments), because they experienced dramatic improvement and lost interest in the study because of their improved health, and so forth. On the other hand, it is harder than it might seem to keep research participants connected to a study and motivated to continue to participate. People move, lose interest, experience life circumstances that complicate giving time to a study, die or decide they no longer want to participate because of various negative reactions to the content of the study.

We lost subjects over time for a number of reasons of which we are aware. We know from direct conversation that at least one subject dropped out of the study because he had decided to accept his gay sexual orientation and did not believe that we would honestly report data on his experiences, because to do so would reflect negatively on the Exodus ministries. On the other hand, we also learned that a woman dropped out of the study because she believed herself cured or healed of all of her homosexual inclinations, had married and was enjoying "normal heterosexual life," and found continued participation in the study odious because she no longer wanted to be reminded of the very negative experiences she had had as a lesbian. No amount of coaxing on our part would persuade either of these subjects to stay in the study. But these two were exceptions: generally speaking, when we lost subjects we gained little or no insight as to why they dropped out.

Over time, our sample eroded from 98 subjects at our initial Time 1 assessment to 85 at Time 2 and 73 at Time 3. The only information we can offer for our sample erosion of thirteen subjects from Time 1 (sample of 98) to Time 2 (sample of 85) is the following:

- Five subjects directly refused further participation in the study. (The two examples already mentioned fit in this category.)
- Eight subjects were lost (by which we mean that none of our efforts to contact them gave evidence that we had the right contact information anymore) or were unresponsive to any of our attempts at contact despite our presumption that we had the right contact information

for them (letters and phone calls went unanswered; this latter group might be considered passive refusers).

For our sample erosion from Time 2 (sample of 85) to Time 3 (sample of 73, for a total loss of 12 subjects):

- Five subjects refused further participation in the study.
- Four subjects were lost or were unresponsive to any of our attempts at contact.
- Two agreed to participate, failed to be available at the time of the scheduled telephone interview and then were unresponsive to further contact.
- One subject voiced a desire to continue in the study but was unwilling to be assessed at Time 3 due to life circumstances that made assessment at that time impossible.

How does our retention rate compare to that of the best "gold standard" studies? One answer comes from a standard text on psychotherapy research, where it is "estimated that most researchers can expect nearly 20% of their sample to withdraw or be necessarily removed from the study before it is complete."[1] This would be the expected erosion factor for completion of the treatment, which for many treatment studies would be a time span of fifteen to twenty-five weeks, a span much shorter than our Time 1 to Time 2 period. By this standard, our retention in our study is quite strong.

But we have an even better standard against which to compare our results. There are not many studies that actually attempt to assess their subjects for more than one follow-up (in our language, past a Time 2 assessment), but one recent major study offers an example against which we can gain a comparison: the widely respected and amply funded National Longitudinal Study of Adolescent Health (or *Add Health*) study has conducted several follow-up assessments of their enormous sample, and in reporting their retention state that "of the original *Add Health* wave 1 respondents (n = 20,745), 15,170 individuals, or 73%, participated in wave 3."[2] Our retention results suggest a favorable comparison to the 73% retention in this respected study; our 73 subjects retained from an original sample of 98 converts to a respectable 74.5% retention rate.

Who are the people that make up this research population?

A Quantitative Portrait of our Sample

In chapter four we mentioned that subjects were either designated as "Phase 1" subjects (57 subjects were new to the change process, having been involved in it for less than one year) or "Phase 2" subjects (41 subjects had been involved in a change ministry for between one and three years). In all of the data to follow, reported responses may not add up to 98 because of missing data. We do not typically report percentages here, because with 98 subjects, the percentages are essentially identical to the actual number of participants (for example, 72 men out of 98 total participants means that 73.5% of the sample is male) and thus would be redundant to report the percentage. Where data exists, allowing us to compare our sample to that in other well-known studies of sexuality, we will report the comparison data.

Basic demographics. *Gender and age.* Our sample was composed of 72 men and 26 women. Subjects were required to be at least eighteen years old, but we had no subjects that young; our youngest was twenty-one at the initial or Time 1 assessment. The age data are best presented in bands: 8 subjects were twenty-one to twenty-five years old, 15 subjects were twenty-six to thirty, 19 subjects were thirty-one to thirty-five, 20 subjects were thirty-six to forty, 22 subjects were forty-one to forty-five, 5 subjects were forty-six to fifty, 6 subjects were fifty-one to fifty-five, and 3 subjects were over fifty-six years old. The average age was 37.5 at the initial or Time 1 assessment. This average age was older than we had expected. This age also would suggest more pessimistic expectations for change for this sample, as increasing age would normally be associated with sexual orientation being more "set."

Country of origin, educational attainment and race. Ninety-four subjects were born in the United States of America (USA); the 4 born outside the USA were born in Turkey, Venezuela, China and Puerto Rico. Our sample was surprisingly well-educated, especially against the casual caricature or stereotype of the conservatively religious as undereducated or unsophisticated: 2 had completed some high school, 7 had finished high school, 2 had completed vocational or trade school, 22 had completed some college or a two-year associate's degree, 39 had completed college, 21 had completed a master's degree or its equivalent, and 5 had completed another advanced/

graduate degree. Regarding race, 86 self-reported as white, 7 as black or African American, 1 as Asian, 2 as Hispanic, and 2 reported themselves as biracial. This sample's education attainment is substantially higher on average than that reported in the national study of sexuality completed by Laumann and his colleagues, in which 14.5% had less than a high school education, 63% had completed high school or the equivalent, 15.6% had completed college, and 6.9% had completed an advanced degree.[3]

Information about the family of origin. We asked subjects to describe the place they were living at age 14, with the following options (and number of responses): open country (14), farm (3), town (23), medium city (25), suburb (20) and large city (13). When asked to describe their relationship with the woman who "mostly raised" them, 90 subjects reported being raised by their biological mother, with other responses being stepmother (1), adoptive mother (3), grandmother (1), stepgrandmother (1), older sister (1) and foster home mother surrogate (1). The educational attainment of the woman most like a mother was given as eighth grade or less (5), some high school (5), completed high school (34), vocational or trade school (7), some college or two-year degree (26), completed college (18) and master's degree (3).

When asked to describe their relationship with the man who "mostly raised" them, 89 subjects reported being raised by their biological father, with other responses being stepfather (7), adoptive father (4), and 6 reporting "don't know" (a response likely reflecting the absence of any stable male figure that could be described as a father). The educational attainment of the man most like a father was given as eighth grade or less (8), some high school (5), completed high school (30), vocational or trade school (5), some college or two-year degree (15), completed college (21), master's degree (7) and other advanced degree (2).

We asked our subjects to report the degree of closeness they felt with their mothers and fathers when they were children and at the present (table 5.1); the results reflect the frequently noted lack of perceived closeness with fathers.

Subjects also reported on their sense of the perceived degree of closeness between the adults who mostly raised them or were most like parents, with the following results: not at all close (9), not very close (26), somewhat close

Table 5.1. Perceived Closeness to Parents

	Not at all close	Not very close	Somewhat close	Very close
Mother as child	3	19	32	44
Mother at present	5	15	41	36
Father as child	24	37	23	10
Father at present	14	21	43	15

(39) and very close (23). In terms of family stability the subjects reported that until the respondent left home, his or her parents lived together: all of the time (71), most of the time (12), some of the time (12) or never (3). If participants reported any response other than that their parents had lived together all of the time, they were asked for the reasons for their parents' separation, and reported: death of father (2), legal marital separation (4), divorce (15), separation due to job or migration (3), that the parents had never married or lived together (1), and 3 answered "other." Those whose parents had separated were also asked their age at the time of separation; aggregating their responses into bands, one to five years (5), six to ten years (9), eleven to fifteen years (7) and sixteen to twenty years (3).

Marital status and living situation in the present. For current (Time 1) marital status, 64 reported being never married, 27 as currently legally married, 6 as divorced, and 1 as legally married but separated. Those who were not legally married were asked if they were cohabiting with a non-marital sexual or romantic partner at that time, and 65 (of the 70 total—64 never married and 6 divorced) reported that they were not currently co-habiting. Those who were not legally married also were asked if they were dating; 61 reported they were not dating and 6 that they were dating. Our sample had a much higher number of never-married persons and a lower number of married compared to the nationally representative sample in the Laumann study, where 27.8% of the national sample were never married, 58.6% were married, 9.3% were divorced, 2.9% were separated, and 1.4% were widowed.[4]

Subjects were asked who they lived with (these numbers add up to more than 98 because subjects were to note all that applied, with the most common overlap being a spouse and children): 30 reported nobody, 25 a spouse or partner, 18 with their children, 7 with mother, 5 with father, 3 with their spouse or partner's mother, 1 with their spouse or partner's father, 4 with some other relative, 25 with a roommate or roommates, 2 with a landlady or landlord, 4 with a boarder or tenant, and 3 with "someone else." Asked specifically about how many of their children lived with them (for those that had children), 8 reported living with one child, 4 with two children, 5 with three children and 1 with four children. Reported ages of the youngest child living with the respondents were ages one to four (5), ages five to seven (3), ages eight to ten (4), ages eleven to thirteen (3) and over age fourteen (2). Reported ages of the oldest child living with the respondents were ages eight to ten (4), ages eleven to thirteen (2) and ages fourteen to seventeen (4).

RESPONSES TO QUESTIONS ABOUT "PRESENTING CONCERNS AND CHANGE ATTEMPTS"

We present these summary responses to questions in the second section of our Time 1 interview protocol by quoting the question as it was asked in the interview with the corresponding responses by subjects.

How many months or years ago was it that you first began thinking about seeking to change your sexual orientation? Answers: zero to two years (17), two to four years (12), five to eight years (19), nine to twelve years (11), thirteen to sixteen years (12), seventeen to twenty years (12), twenty-one to twenty-five years (5), more than twenty-five years (7), and 3 subjects simply said "my whole life."

How many months or years ago was it that you actually began to take concrete steps in seeking to change your sexual orientation? Answers: zero to one year (28), one to three years (16), three to five years (21), five-and-a-half to seven years (10), eight to twelve years (8), thirteen to twenty years (10) and more than twenty years (5).

In the past, have you ever utilized any forms of* professional *therapy or counseling to attempt to change your sexual orientation or feelings? Fifty-six reported having used professional therapy, while 42 reported that they had not used professional therapy. Those who had reported using professional therapy were asked the number of different types of therapy tried: only one type (25), two types (23), three types (3) and four types (5). Given the opportunity to describe those types of therapy without categories being provided, the following types of therapy were listed: support group (3), Living Waters (3—this is a structured Exodus program), psychiatrist (8), church, Christian or other pastoral counseling (15), "professional counselor" (with examples given such as licensed family-and-marriage therapist, psychologist, and licensed professional counselor) (41), unspecified counselor (19), campus counseling center (4), scream therapy (1), sexual addictions therapy (1), and aversion therapy (1).

We also queried our participants about attempts to change their sexual orientation via religious-ministry organizations other than their current Exodus effort; overall, our sample was divided down the middle on this issue, with 49 having tried ministries other than Exodus, and 49 not having tried any form of ministry other than Exodus. Fifteen had tried one other type of ministry organization, 5 had tried two others, 3 had tried three others, and 1 had tried four others. This finding, in combination with the immediately preceding one on professional therapy, is interesting, in that it depicts a high degree of tenacity in seeking change on the part of this sample.

Responses to the following question about their motivation in seeking change are displayed in table 5.2; subjects could affirm more than one response. These findings are notable for the emphasis placed on religious and ethical reasons and their de-emphasis on practical concerns. We asked: ***Now let me ask about some specific motivations for change that may or may not have been a motivation for you to seek help for change. I will state a possible reason, and you tell me how important this was to you on this five-point scale.***

The subjects at Time 1 approached the change process with considerable optimism.

Do you believe that the attempt to change homosexual orientation or feelings can be successful? Eighty-nine said yes, 8 were uncertain, and 1 did not respond.

Responses to Questions About "Religious Experience"

Religion as a child. In response to a query on the major religion in which they were raised, the subjects reported being raised in none (4), Christian (15), Protestant Christian (56), Roman Catholic (19), Muslim (1), and 3 as other (one each of Christian Science, Mormon and pagan). Those who responded that they were raised either Christian (15) or Protestant Christian (56) were queried for more specifics on their denominational heritage, with the following results: nondenominational (4), Baptist (22), Methodist (8), Lutheran (8), Congregational (1), Presbyterian (9), Episcopalian (2), and under the category of "other" (15), the following denominations were reported: Pentecostal/Assembly of God (6), Church of God (2), Unitarian (1), evangelical (2), Southern Baptist (2), Church of Christ (1) and Reformed (1).

Forty-three subjects reported their current religious preference to be the same as when they were growing up; 55 reported it to be different. Those reporting that their current religious preference was different from that when they were growing up were queried further on their current religious preference, with the following responses: 36 said they were now Protestant Christian, 17 Christian, and one each said "other" or refused

Table 5.2. Self-Reported Motivation for Seeking Change

	1 Not important	2	3 Somewhat important	4	5 Very important
Feel homosexuality is unnatural	7	7	8	17	59
Personal conscience	3	2	7	15	71
Fear of AIDS	45	11	17	10	15
Teaching of the Bible	0	1	9	17	70
Disapproval of the church	22	13	22	17	24
Wanting to be married and have children	21	5	14	22	36
Unhappy with gay lifestyle	25	6	18	13	36
Feel very unhappy as a homosexual	12	8	15	16	47
Peer group disapproval	30	10	18	17	23
Job discrimination against homosexuals	65	9	9	8	7
Concern over societal disapproval	36	13	19	17	13
Other	0	0	0	2	35

to provide further specification. Once again, those who responded either Christian (17) or Protestant Christian (36) for their current religious preference were queried for more specifics on their denominational heritage: nondenominational (30), Baptist (3), Methodist (1), Presbyterian (2), Episcopalian (4), and under the category of "other" (13), the following denominations were reported: Pentecostal/Assembly of God (8), Open Bible Standard (1), Covenant (1), Church of God (1), Calvary Chapel (1) and evangelical (1).

To get a portrait of the current (at the initial Time 1 assessment) religious preferences of our sample, we combined those who had stayed with their family religious heritage and those who had moved to a new religious practice for the following portrait of our 98 Time 1 subjects: The largest religious preference was nondenominational Protestant Christian, with a total of 31 individuals who had initially described themselves as Protestant Christian (17) or Christian (14), then going on to specify nondenominational as their current religious preference. The other religious affiliations in descending order of frequency were Baptist (16, including the various types of Baptist denominations, if identified); charismatic/Pentecostal/Assembly of God (9); Episcopalian (6 unspecified, and an additional 2 specifying charismatic Episcopalian); Presbyterian (5 unspecified, and an additional 1 specifying Presbyterian Church of America); Roman Catholic (5); Lutheran (4); Methodist (4); Christian evangelical (2); Latter-day Saints/Mormon (2); Evangelical Free (2); Church of God (2); African Methodist Episcopal (2); Calvary Chapel (1); Reformed (1); Open Bible Standard (1); Church of Christ (1); Covenant (1).

Our respondents reported a fairly high level of current religious involvement, with 3 reporting they attend religious services several times a year, 4 reporting about once a month, 6 reporting two to three times a month, 49 reporting attending weekly or nearly every week, and 36 reporting attending more than once a week.

To compare these rates of religious attendance to a national sample, we can look at the Laumann study of sexuality, in which 15.0% reported never attending religious services, 8.6% attended less than once per year, 16.7% reported attending one or two times a year, 14.1% reported attending several times per year, 6.9% reported attending once per month, 9.7% reported two to three times per month, 4.1% reported attending nearly weekly, 16.8% reported attending weekly, and 8.1% reported attending several times per week.[5] Whereas less than one-third of Laumann's national sample attended church weekly or more, over 80% of our sample attended church weekly or more.

Would you say you have been "born again" or have had a "born again" experience—that is, a turning point in your life when you committed yourself to Christ? Yes (90), no (8). The 90 who said yes were asked at what age they had had this experience: Before the age of ten years (17), eleven to fifteen years (17), sixteen to twenty years (21), twenty-one to twenty-five years (11), twenty-six to thirty years (10), thirty-one to forty years (10) and over age forty (4).

Clearly, our sample was much more religious than a typical sample of the American public.

RESPONSES TO QUESTIONS ABOUT "SEXUAL ORIENTATION"

We asked a series of questions related to the process of growing up that are often thought of as related to the development of sexual orientation.

Our first question, about the age when the subject reached puberty, was actually asked among the questions about family of origin: ten years old or younger (8), eleven years old (14), twelve years old (34), thirteen years old (26), fourteen years old (7), fifteen years old (3), sixteen years old (4), and seventeen years old or later (2). Now to the other questions asked in this section on "sexual orientation."

Did you feel different from other children of the same gender growing up? No (23), yes (75).

Questions about the perceptions of the males as they were growing up. *As a child between about ages 6 and 12, did you feel you were as "boyish" or "masculine" as the other boys your age?* More masculine than others (0), about as masculine (15) and less masculine (56).

As a boy between about 6 and 12, were you considered a "sissy" more than other boys your age? No (21), yes (48), don't know (3).

As a child or adolescent, were you ever called a "fag" or "queer" or other term related to homosexuality? No (23), yes (46), don't know (3). *If yes, how often did this happen?* Rarely (6), occasionally (17), often (9), very often (14).

Did you ever think you would prefer to be a girl rather than a boy? No (39), yes (28), don't know (2).

Questions about the perceptions of the females as they were growing up. *As a child between about ages 6 and 12, did you feel you were as "girlish" or "feminine" as the other girls your age?* More feminine than others (0), about as feminine (4), less feminine (21), don't know (1).

As a girl between about 6 and 12, were you considered a "tomboy" more than other girls your age? No (6), yes (20).

As a child or adolescent, were you ever called a "butch" or "dyke" or other term related to homosexuality? No (19), yes (5), don't know (2). *If yes, how often did this happen?* Rarely (4), occasionally (1), often (0), very often (0).

Did you ever think you would prefer to be a boy rather than a girl? No (11), yes (15).

Other questions about sexual orientation. After administration of a number of scales on sexual orientation, we returned to questions asked of all subjects.

Were you raised in a home where being Gay or Homosexual was considered morally wrong? No (6), yes (78), refused (3), don't know (11).

At what age did you first consider yourself to be homosexual? Subjects could state any age to this query; we report the responses in categories: Never (11), ages seven to ten (11), ages eleven to fifteen (30), ages sixteen to twenty (28), ages twenty-one to twenty-five (8), ages twenty-six to thirty (4) and over age thirty (6). Clearly, the majority of our sample came to a stable sense of sexual orientation between puberty and age twenty.

When asked which family members currently (at Time 1) knew about the sexual orientation of the respondent, the following were reported: spouse (27), children (6), mother (50), father (47), sister (36), brother (29), other relatives (22) and none (22). Asked how many of their friends know of their sexual orientation, the following were reported: all (11), most (22), some (60) and none (5).

Subjects were also asked, *From whom have you received the most support in your quest to change your sexual orientation/feelings?* The following were reported: mother (9), father (7), sister (6), brother (4), spouse (16), other relatives (2), friends (41), church (14), other (29) and no one (1).

In section six of the interview protocol, subjects were asked about the

Table 5.3. Report of Atmosphere in Family of Origin Toward Sexuality

1	2	3	4	5
1 (66) Closed/secretive. "Sex never talked about"	2 (17)	3 (7)	4 (6)	5 (2) Open/accepting. "Sex is normal; let's talk"
1 (31) Negative. "Sex is bad"	2 (21)	3 (31) Neutral.	4 (6)	5 (9) Positive. "Sex is good/gift"
1 (52) Rigid rules. "Closed, punitive"	2 (19)	3 (16) Balanced.	4 (7)	5 (2) Permissive. "Liberal; free sex; do it"
1 (44) Hypermodest. "Secrecy, keep hidden"	2 (24)	3 (21) Appropriate.	4 (5)	5 (4) Immodest. "Open nudity; exposure is fine"

general atmosphere in their family of origin on the topic of sexuality. The specific question was, *How would you describe the atmosphere or attitudes toward sexuality in the home in which you grew up?* Subjects were given four scales on which to rate their family; each of these allowed for a rating on a five-point scale with definite "anchors" at the extremes (points 1 and 5). In table 5.3, we present the array of responses. In each cell the top number is the rating, the number in parentheses is the number of subjects who endorsed that rating, and then the actual words that described that rating are presented as well.

It is obvious that most of our participants reported their families of origin to be closed, secretive, negative, rigid and overly modest when it came to sexuality.

In chapter two we discussed how conservative Christians are often stigmatized as having and suffering under negative views of sex that they inherit from their families. The vast majority of our participants reported such pervasively negative views of sexuality in their families. It is reasonable to suppose that these negative views may contribute causally to the various sexual difficulties and distress these individuals experienced, but this would be nothing more than a supposition because we did not gather evidence that would substantiate such a causal connection. We also did not collect evidence to indicate that these reported negative environments regarding sexuality had any tie to the religious environment of these families (i.e., that the negative views about sexuality had anything to do with religious faith).

The Sexual Experiences of Our Sample

In addition to the already discussed questions, we asked our sample a series of quantifiable questions about their sexual behavior and experiences. Our method was derived directly from an extremely well-regarded national survey of adult sexual behavior, the National Health and Social Life Survey (NHSLS),[6] and from a subsequent study of sexual behavior in the urban environment that was underway as we were preparing our research methodology.[7] Participants completed our survey in the form of a self-administered questionnaire (SAQ), which gave them assurance that the interviewer was unaware of their responses. We report here on these findings from this SAQ, the Sexual Behavior and Experiences Survey, at Time 1.

Results from the Time 1 SAQ on number of sexual partners in the last year and in the last five years are indicated in table 5.4. The specific question asked was, *How many sex partners have you had in the last 12 months (5 years)?* The sex of the participant's partner was not specified, so this question sums together male and female sex partners (and so it includes both homosexual and heterosexual experiences). The results suggest that about one-third of male and over half of female interviewees reported no sexual partners in the past twelve months. Among females, one-third reported one sexual partner in the past twelve months, and fewer than 10% reported two sexual partners in the past twelve months.

Males reported a greater range of numbers of sexual partners than the females in the last year and in the last five years. Nearly 10% reported between twenty-one and one hundred sexual partners in the previous year, and almost 20% of the sample reported that same range of sexual partners in the five-year time frame. This is in keeping with some of the literature on gay male sexual behavior, as gay males are generally thought to have more sexual partners than females who report experiencing same-sex attractions and behavior.

Rather than ask in categories about adult lifetime sexual partners, we simply and directly asked for a best estimate, specifically, *Now thinking about the time since your 18th birthday (again, including the recent past that you have already told us about), how many female [and in a separate question, male] partners have you ever had sex with?* We report these categorically, and you can see in table 5.5 that nearly one-third of male participants reported having over thirty lifetime male partners. Among these, 2 males indicated having approximately 1,500 lifetime male sexual partners, while 1 participant estimated 3,000 lifetime male sexual partners.

These seemingly extreme estimates are not to be regarded as lacking in credibility given the estimates of some of the major surveys of the extremes

Table 5.4. Number of Sexual Partners in the Last Twelve Months

		Male participants		Female participants	
		N	%	N	%
Last 12 months	None	24	33.3	16	64.0
	1 partner	16	22.2	7	28.0
	2 partners	7	9.7	2	8.0
	3 partners	3	4.2		
	4 partners	4	5.6		
	5-10 partners	5	6.9		
	11-20 partners	6	8.4		
	21-100 partners	7	9.7		
	More than 100 partners	0	0		
Last 5 years	None	15	21.1	4	16.0
	1 partner	9	12.7	9	36.0
	2 partners	5	7.0	4	16.0
	3 partners	4	5.6	3	12.0
	4 partners	2	2.8	1	4.0
	5-10 partners	7	9.9	3	12.0
	11-20 partners	9	12.7	1	4.0
	21-100 partners	13	18.3		
	More than 100 partners	7	9.9		

of sexual activity in aspects of the gay community. For example, a nonrandom but large sample of gay men (taken in San Francisco in the late 1970s) reported that 28% of white homosexual males reported having had 1,000 or more lifetime homosexual partners by the time they were interviewed, while only 17% reported having had sexual relations with fewer than 50 homosexual partners (thus 83% of white homosexual males had sexual relations with 50 or more partners in their lifetimes).[8] Such numbers are not lacking in credibility in comparison to heterosexual or general populations either. In the NHSLS study, one male reported 1,016 lifetime sexual partners, and one female reported 1,009 lifetime partners (sex of the partner was unspecified).[9] Heterosexual men "living the playboy lifestyle" or who value sexual conquest

Table 5.5. Adult Lifetime (Since Age 18) Sexual Partners

Number	Male participants				Female participants			
	Male partners		Female partners		Male partners		Female partners	
	N	%	N	%	N	%	N	%
0	12	16.8	32	44.4	7	28.0	2	8.0
1	7	9.7	20	27.8	6	24.0	4	16.0
2	2	2.8	8	11.1	6	24.0	3	12.0
3	4	5.6	3	4.2	1	4.0	3	12.0
4	1	1.4	2	2.8	1	4.0	1	4.0
5	2	2.8	2	2.8	0	-	3	12.0
6	3	4.2	2	2.8	0	-	4	16.0
7	0	-	0	-	0	-	1	4.0
8	0	-	0	-	1	4.0	0	-
9	2	2.8	0	-	1	4.0	1	4.0
10-15	6	8.3	1	1.4	0	-	1	4.0
16-20	2	2.8	2	2.8	1	4.0	1	4.0
21-30	7	9.7	0	-	0	-	0	-
31-100	15	13.9	0	-	1	4.0	1	4.0
101-200	3	4.2						
201-500	2	2.8						
501+	4	5.6						

often claim many sexual partners, as do some heterosexual women.

Male Exodus participants reported an average of 1.74 lifetime (since age eighteen) female sexual partners, and an average of 131.26 lifetime (since age eighteen) male sexual partners. This extraordinary reported number of male sexual partners is pulled upward by the four participants that reported the highest numbers of partners, respectively 600; 1,500; 1,500 and 3,000. If we remove these four extremely high reports from the average, the average of (since age eighteen) male sexual partners drops to 41.93. To some, this may still seem like an extraordinarily (even incredibly) high number, but it actually compares favorably to the report of the NHSLS study for homosexual men. They report that heterosexual males reported an average of 16.5 lifetime sexual partners, while homosexual men (those who reported any "same-gender identity," bisexual or homosexual) reported an average of 42.8 lifetime partners.[10]

For comparison purposes, we re-sorted our data on lifetime sexual partners for this Exodus sample, without regard to the sex of the partner, in the format reported by the NHSLS study. The percentage comparisons are reported in table 5.6. Generally speaking, our Exodus males reported a higher percentage of those who were completely sexually inexperienced (33% versus 9.9% in the last year; 11% versus 3% lifetime), but also a very significantly higher number of those with many sexual partners (for instance, for lifetime partners, reporting over 45% with over twenty-one partners versus over 16% for the national sample). Females were significantly less sexually active, in terms of numbers of partners, in the last year but had many more partners than the national sample of women in their lifetimes. Note that the NHSLS numbers are a report of a nationally representative sample that includes heterosexuals, homosexuals and others; these two samples have very different characteristics. We would note also that we naively assumed that our Exodus sample would be dominated by younger, less sexually experienced individuals. Finding that the sample is older and *much* more sexually experienced than expected drives home that many in our sample must be regarded as "truly homosexual." This sample is not dominated by confused, sexually inexperienced bisexual or heterosexual individuals.

We now turn from one-year, five-year and lifetime partners to try to un-

Table 5.6. Comparison of Exodus Sample and NHSLS National Sample for Sexual Partners Since Age 18

		Male participants (%)		Female participants (%)	
		Exodus	**Laumann***	**Exodus**	**Laumann**
Last 12 months	None	33.3	9.9	64.0	13.6
	1 partner	22.2	66.7	28.0	74.7
	2-4 partners	19.5	18.3	8.0	10.0
	5+ partners	25.0	5.1		1.7
Last 5 years	None	21.1	7.1	16.0	8.7
	1 partner	12.7	45.7	36.0	59.4
	2-4 partners	15.4	27.7	32.0	24.3
	5-10 partners	9.9	12.0	12.0	5.9
	11-20 partners	12.7	4.2	4.0	1.4
	21+ partners	28.2	3.3		0.4
Since age 18	None	11.1	3.4	0.0	2.5
	1 partner	5.5	19.5	20.0	31.5
	2-4 partners	15.3	20.9	16.0	36.4
	5-10 partners	13.9	23.3	32.0	20.4
	11-20 partners	8.3	16.3	20.0	6.0
	21+ partners	45.8	16.6	12.0	3.2

*From Laumann, E. O., Gagnon, J. H., Michael, R. T., & Michaels, S. (1994). *The social organization of sexuality.* Chicago: University of Chicago Press, pp. 177-179, tables 5.1A, 5.1B, 5.1C.

derstand who their sexual partners were. First, note that a fairly high percentage of respondents indicated that they did not have a sexual partner in the past year. This was not surprising, given that our sample is of a population that is seeking religiously mediated change of sexual orientation. Though it should be noted that the decision not to have a sex partner can be for any number of reasons, including poor health, lack of available partners, personal beliefs and values, and so forth, it is our clear understanding that sexual chastity is a clear and urgent teaching of Exodus groups, and further that such chastity is congruent with the beliefs and teaching of born-again Christians (a label that fits 90 of our 98 subjects).

We recognized too that some participants in the study may be married, and interviewees who reported at least one sexual partner were asked if one of their sexual partners (in the one- or five-year time frame) was their spouse or regular partner. Exactly half of those who answered this question indicated yes, while half indicated no. These percentages were generally consistent whether we asked male or female participants this question. For example, among women, 5 of the 11 who answered this question (or 45.5%) indicated yes while 6 (54.5%) indicated no. A response of no could mean the person was married and not having sex with their spouse (though he or she was having sex outside the marriage).

We asked interviewees about the partner(s) they had in addition to their spouse or regular partner. Three women indicated that a close personal friend was a sexual partner, and one woman indicated that someone other than a close personal friend was a sexual partner. In each of these four cases the sexual partner was a female. Among men, 28 identified a casual date or pick-up as a sexual partner, and 2 indicated that a close personal friend was a sexual partner. In 23 of these instances the sex partner was exclusively male, while in 8 instances interviewees indicated having both male and female sex partners.

We also asked if—in the past twelve months—interviewees had ever had sex with someone other than their spouse while married. Four female interviewees and 11 male interviewees indicated having had sex with someone other than their spouse.

When we asked similar questions with reference to the last five years, we found that 9 female interviewees reported having sex exclusively with women in the past five years, while 9 additional female interviewees reported having sex with both males and females, and 2 reported having sex exclusively with men in the past five years. Among male interviewees, 29 reported having sex exclusively with men in the past five years, while 21 reported having sex with both males and females, and 6 reported having sex exclusively with females in the past five years.

We also asked if interviewees ever paid or were paid to have sex since their eighteenth birthday. Eighteen (24.7%) male interviewees answered yes to this question, as did 2 (8.3%) of the female interviewees.

We asked about past experiences with pregnancies and abortions. Three

(4.1%) of the male interviewees indicated that they had a sex partner who became pregnant and had an abortion. Among female interviewees, 2 (8.3%) indicated having had an abortion. In another question we asked about number of abortions, and 4 interviewees indicated having had one abortion, and 1 interviewee indicated she had had two abortions. Two (8.3%) of the female interviewees reported ever paying a man to have sex, and none of the male interviewees indicated that they paid a woman to have sex.

Three men (4.1%) reported ever forcing a woman to do something sexual, and 11 (45.8%) female interviewees reported ever being forced by a man to do something sexual. One female interviewee indicated that she had forced a woman to do something sexual.

Because base-rate information suggests that a disproportionate percentage of persons who have sex with same-sex partners are at risk of HIV/AIDS, we asked whether interviewees had been tested for HIV. Sixty-six percent (N = 16) of the female interviewees and 74% (N = 54) of the male interviewees indicated having been tested for HIV. Among the males, 5.5% (N = 4) tested positive for HIV, and none of the female interviewees indicated testing positive for HIV.

With respect to additional sexual practices with the opposite sex, 35 male interviewees (47.9%) indicated that they have had a woman perform oral sex on them, and 28 (38.4%) reported having performed oral sex on a woman. Among female interviewees, 17 (70.8%) indicated having performed oral sex on a man, and 19 (79.2%) indicated having had a man perform oral sex on them.

Six (8.2%) male interviewees indicated having had anal sex with a woman, and 8 (33.3%) female interviewees indicated having had anal sex.

Additional sexual practices with the same sex. When we asked about sexual practices with the same sex, 59 (80.8%) of male interviewees indicated that they had performed oral sex on a man and 55 (75.3%) indicated having had a man perform oral sex on them. Among female interviewees, 17 (70.8%) reported having ever performed oral sex on a woman, and 19 (79.2%) reported ever having a woman perform oral sex on them. Forty-one (56.2%) male interviewees indicated that they had anal sex with a man where the interviewee inserted, and 43 (58.9%) reported having been the recipient of anal sex. Fifty-six (76.7%) males also indicated having done "anything else" sexual with a man. Twenty-two (91.7%) female interviewees indicated having done "anything else" sexual with a woman.

Ten (13.7%) male interviewees and none of the female interviewees reported having paid someone of the same sex to have sex. Twelve (16.4%) male interviewees and none of the female interviewees reported having been paid to have sex with the same sex.

In terms of forced sexual behavior with someone of the same sex, 24 (32.9%) males and 2 (8.3%) females reported having been forced by someone of the same sex to do something sexual. Nine (12.3%) males and 3 (12.5%) females reported having forced someone of the same sex to do something sexual.

Thirty (41.1%) male interviewees and 5 (20.8%) female interviewees reported having participated in group sex or sex with more than one person at a time.

Sexual Experiences in Childhood

First childhood sexual experiences. We asked detailed questions about sexual experiences that may have happened in childhood, which we defined as prior to age thirteen, or puberty. The first question was worded as follows: *Before you were 13 years old, did anyone touch you sexually?* About two-thirds of all male interviewees indicated that they had been touched sexually prior to age thirteen. Age of sexual touch prior to age thirteen is indicated in table 5.7. This is a much higher rate of childhood sexual contact than was reported in the Laumann and colleagues' national study of sexuality, in which about 12% of men reported childhood sexual contact.[11]

We followed this question with a series of questions about that first childhood experience, asking participants to *think ONLY of the first relationship in which you as a child experienced sexual touching or some other sort of sexual relations.* Among male participants, 47 (65.2%) of the sample reported such sexual touching before age thirteen, and the majority of the time (40 out of 47 cases or 85.1%) the experience of being touched sexually prior to age thirteen was by another male. In 7 cases (14.9%) males reported having been touched sexually prior to age thirteen by a female. The age of the person who touched them sexually ranged across the continuum of prepubertal ages; reporting an average is likely not meaningful given the flat distribution of the reported ages.

Male interviewees indicated the relationship with the person with whom they had their *first relationship in which they as a child experienced sexual touching or some sort of sexual relations.* This was most frequently a friend (N = 11, 15.1%), someone else (unspecified) (N = 7, 9.6%), neighbor (N = 5, 6.8%), cousin (N = 5, 6.8%) or other relative (N = 5, 6.8%).

Among female participants, 18 (69.2%) indicated having been touched sexually before age thirteen. Again, this is a much higher rate compared to the national sexuality study by Laumann and his colleagues, in which about 17% of females reported childhood sexual contact.[12] We asked follow-up questions about the first relationship in which they as a child experienced *sexual touching or some sort of sexual relations.* Ten (41.7%) participants indicated that the person who touched them sexually was male; fewer than one-third (N = 7 or 29.2%) indicated that the person who touched them was female.

Female interviewees indicated that the relationship with the person

Table 5.7. Age of Sexual Touch (Prior to Age 13)

Age	Male participants		Female participants	
	N	%	N	%
1	1	1.4	-	-
2	-	-	2	8.3
3	-	-	2	8.3
4	6	8.2	2	8.3
5	4	5.5	2	8.3
6	5	6.8	2	8.3
7	7	9.6	2	8.3
8	8	11.0	1	4.2
9	-	-	2	8.3
10	8	11.0	3	12.5
11	2	2.7	-	-
12	7	9.6	-	-

who touched them was most frequently a friend (N = 5, 20.8%), with the next most frequently cited persons being a cousin (N = 3, 12.5%), father (N = 3, 12.5%), neighbor (N = 2, 8.3%), family friend (N = 1, 4.2%) or other relative (N = 1, 4.2%).

We asked participants about the types of sexual behaviors that went on in the relationship in which they as a child experienced sexual touching or some other sort of sexual relations prior to age thirteen. These data are recorded in table 5.8; the percentages add up to more than 100% because subjects can report more than one type of behavioral experience. Among male participants, the most frequently identified sexual touch was having one's genitals touched, followed by touching the other person's genitals. Other first childhood sexual experiences included giving and receiving oral sex, kissing, receiving anal sex (and 4 males [5.5%] indicated having had their anus penetrated with something other than a penis), and vaginal intercourse.

Table 5.8. First Childhood Sexual Experience

Sexual Experience	Male participants		Female participants	
	N	%	N	%
Having genitals touched	41	56.2	13	54.2
Touching other person's genitals	32	43.8	9	37.5
Giving oral sex	14	19.2	4	16.7
Receiving oral sex	14	19.2	3	12.5
Giving anal sex	-	-	-	-
Vaginal intercourse	5	6.8	1	4.2

When we asked females about the types of sexual behaviors that went on in the relationship in which they as a child experienced sexual touching or some other sort of sexual relations prior to age thirteen, the most frequently identified sexual touch was having one's genitals touched, followed by touching the other person's genitals. Other first childhood sexual experiences included kissing, giving and receiving oral sex, anal sex, and vaginal intercourse (and having one's vagina/anus penetrated by something other than a penis, which was reported by 4 or 16.7% of female respondents who had indicated first childhood sexual experiences).

Other childhood sexual experiences. For the next series of questions we asked participants to think of all of the other relationships other than their very first experience of sexual touching in which they as a child experienced *sexual touching or some other sort of sexual relations.* Participants who only had childhood sexual experiences with one person (which was addressed in the preceding set of questions) skipped this section and continued with the next item from the SAQ. Among those who had other relationships in which they experienced childhood sexual touch or other sorts of sexual relations, we first asked about number of sexual "partners" or those who had engaged in these sexual acts prior to age thirteen. The number of "partners" by gender is listed in table 5.9.

Based on these findings, a higher percentage of male participants reported having had male sexual "partners" in childhood (in contrast to males who reported having female sexual "partners"), and this is in keeping with the literature that suggests that sexual perpetrators tend to be male. A sim-

Table 5.9. Number of Male and Female "Partners" in Early Childhood

Number	Male participants				Female participants			
	Male "partners"		Female "partners"		Male "partners"		Female "partners"	
	N	%	N	%	N	%	N	%
1	6	8.2	6	8.2	4	16.7	1	4.2
2	6	8.2	-	-	2	8.3	-	-
3	3	4.1	-	-	1	4.2	-	-
4	2	2.7	4	5.5	-	-	-	-
5	5	6.8	-	-	-	-	1	4.2
6	-	-	-	-	1	4.2	-	-
7	1	1.4	-	-	-	-	-	-
8	1	1.4	-	-	1	4.2	-	-
9	-	-	1	1.4	-	-	-	-
10-15	1	1.4	-	-	1	4.2	2	8.3
16-20	1	1.4	1	1.4	1	4.2	-	-
21-30	1	1.4	-	-	-	-	-	-
30+	1	1.4	-	-	-	-	-	-

ilar pattern emerges from the responses of female participants, wherein the majority of those who reported childhood sexual experiences reported that the "partner" was male.

Participants were asked to indicate their relationships with all the persons with whom they had these childhood sexual experiences, with the relationships specified in the survey (they could choose from father, stepfather, mother's boyfriend, stepbrother, uncle, brother/half-brother, mother, cousin, other relative, neighbor, teacher, stranger, family friend, your friend or someone else). Participant responses are listed in table 5.10. The Laumann national sample was asked about the relationship to the respondent of the adult who had sex with the respondent as a child (a narrower category than that which was used in our study). The most frequently identified relationship reported by women was a family friend (29%) or other relative (29%), followed by "other" (19%), an older brother (9%), stranger (7%), stepfather (7%), or father (7%). The most frequently reported relationship among male respondents was a family friend (40%),

Table 5.10. Relationship to "Partners" in Early Childhood

Relationship	Male participants		Female participants	
	N	%	N	%
Your friend	19	26.0	4	16.7
Family friend	7	9.6	4	16.7
Neighbor	1	1.4	5	20.8
Father	-	-	-	-
Mother	1	1.4	1	4.2
Stepbrother	1	1.4	-	-
Mother's boyfriend	19	26.0	-	-
Brother/half-brother	2	2.7	1	4.2
Cousin	7	9.6	3	12.4
Other relative	4	5.5	2	8.3
Teacher	1	1.4	-	-
Stranger	6	8.2	1	4.2
Someone else	9	12.3	3	12.5

"other" (17%), other relative (13%), stranger (4%), teacher (4%) and older friend (4%).[13]

Interviewees indicated all of the types of sexual behaviors that they experienced in any of the relationships, even if the sexual behavior occurred only once. They were asked, *Please check all types of sexual behaviors that you experienced in any of these relationships (even if only once).* When we asked males about the types of sexual behaviors that went on in any of the relationships prior to age thirteen, the most frequently identified sexual touch was touching the other person's genitals and having one's genitals touched,

Table 5.11. Sexual Experiences Prior to Age 13

Sexual Experience	Male participants		Female participants	
	N	%	N	%
Having genitals touched	32	43.8	9	37.5
Touching other person's genitals	34	46.6	5	20.8
Giving oral sex	19	26.0	3	12.5
Receiving oral sex	16	21.9	3	12.5
Kissing	21	28.8	7	29.5
Receiving anal sex	10	13.7	2	8.3
Giving anal sex	5	6.8	-	-
Vaginal intercourse	8	11.0	2	8.3

both of which were indicated by over 40% of males (see table 5.11). The next most frequently indicated sexual experiences prior to age thirteen were kissing, giving oral sex, receiving oral sex, receiving anal sex, vaginal intercourse and giving anal sex (and 9 males or 12.3% indicated having their anus penetrated with something other than a penis).

When we asked females about the types of sexual behaviors that went on in any of the relationships prior to age thirteen, the most frequently identified sexual touch was having one's genitals touched, followed by kissing. These sexual experiences were followed by touching the other person's genitals, giving and receiving oral sex, vaginal intercourse and receiving anal sex.

In Laumann and his colleagues' national study of sexuality, about 12% of men reported childhood sexual contact. Boys were more often touched by females than by other males, and were more likely to have had contact with an adolescent (between the ages of 14 and 17) than an adult. The most frequently reported sexual contacts with females were touching genitals (82% of those who reported childhood sexual contact), kissing (64%), vaginal intercourse (42%) and oral sex (10%).[14]

About 17% of women in the Laumann study reported childhood sexual contact. In that national sample the most frequently reported sexual contact in childhood was by males over the age of eighteen, and the most common form of sexual touching was touching genitals (90% of those who reported childhood sexual contact), followed by kissing (32%) and vaginal intercourse (14%).[15]

FORCED SEXUAL EXPERIENCES AFTER AGE THIRTEEN

We also asked interviewees detailed questions about forced sexual experiences that may have happened to them after age thirteen. Sixteen (21.9%) males and 11 (42.3%) females reported having a forced sexual experience. Again, this is higher than the prevalence of forced sex reported by Laumann and his colleagues. In the national sample about 4% of males and 22% of females reported forced sexual experiences.[16]

We asked those who had had a forced sexual experience to think of the *first* relationship in which they had experienced some sort of forced sexual relations and to identify the biological sex of the person. Among male interviewees, 15 of 16 (93.8%) indicated that the sex of the person was male. We also asked interviewees to identify their relationship to the person who forced them to have this sexual experience, and males reported that the most frequently identified person was someone they just met (N = 6 of 16, 37.5%), followed by a stranger (N = 3, 18.8%), a date (not serious) (N = 2, 12.5%), a relative (N = 1, 6.3%) and a friend (not dating) (N = 1, 6.3%). Three males indicated that another person ("other") forced them to have this sexual experience.

When we asked males about the types of sexual behaviors that went on in this first forced sexual experience, the most frequently identified sexual behavior was having one's genitals touched and receiving oral sex (see table

5.12). These experiences were followed by touching the other person's genitals, giving oral sex, kissing, receiving anal sex and giving anal sex (and 3 males or 18.8% indicated having their anus penetrated with something other than a penis). None of the male interviewees reported experiencing vaginal intercourse in this forced sexual experience.

Among female interviewees, 10 of 11 (90.9%) who provided a response to this item indicated that the sex of the person who forced them to have this sexual experience was male. When asked to identify their relationship to the person who forced them to have this sexual experience, females reported that the most frequently identified person was an acquaintance or a relative, both of which were indicated by 3 of 11 interviewees (27.3%) who answered this item. These were followed by someone they just met (N = 2, 18.2%), a stranger (N = 1, 9.1%), a date (not serious) (N = 1, 9.1%) and their spouse (N = 1, 9.1%). In the Laumann national study, females reported that the most frequently identified person with whom they had a forced sexual experience was someone with whom they were in love (46%), followed by someone they knew well (22%), an acquaintance (17%), their spouse (9%) and a stranger (4%).[17]

When we asked female interviewees about the types of sexual behaviors that went on in this forced sexual experience, the most frequently identified sexual behavior was having one's genitals touched, followed by vaginal

Table 5.12. First Forced Sexual Experience After Age 13

Sexual Experience	Male participants		Female participants	
	N	%	N	%
Having genitals touched	11	68.8	8	72.7
Touching other person's genitals	7	43.8	5	45.5
Giving oral sex	6	37.5	3	27.3
Receiving oral sex	8	50.0	3	27.3
Kissing	6	37.5	6	54.5
Receiving anal sex	6	37.5	1	9.1
Giving anal sex	2	12.5	-	-
Vaginal intercourse	0	0	7	63.6

intercourse and kissing. Other sexual experiences included touching the other person's genitals, giving and receiving oral sex, anal sex, and vaginal or anus penetration by something other than a penis, which was reported by 4 (36.4%) interviewees who had indicated having a forced sexual experience.

Other forced sexual experiences after age thirteen. In addition to this first forced sexual experience, we asked interviewees to think of all other relationships in which they experienced some sort of forced sexual relations. Nine male interviewees reported experiencing other forced sexual experiences with males. One interviewee reported 6 such male "partners," while 8 others reported 1 forced-sex male "partner" each. Interestingly, 10 male interviewees reported 1 forced sexual experience each with a female "partner."

Three male interviewees reported that the forced sexual experience was with a stranger, while 1 reported it was with someone they just met; 1 with an acquaintance; 1 with someone they were seeing or going out with (but not seriously); and 1 with a person with whom they were in some other relationship.

Among male interviewees the most frequently cited forced sexual behaviors were kissing (N = 3), having one's own genitals touched (N = 3), touching the person's genitals (N = 3), giving oral sex (N = 3), receiving oral sex (N = 1), receiving anal sex (N = 4) and having one's anus penetrated by something other than a penis (N = 1).

We asked female interviewees the same question: In addition to the first forced sexual experience, could they think of all other relationships in which they experienced some sort of forced sexual relations? Two female interviewees reported experiencing other forced sexual experiences with males. One interviewee reported one forced sexual experience with a female "partner." One female interviewee reported that the forced sexual experience was with a relative, while 1 reported it was with a stranger.

Among female interviewees, the most frequently cited forced sexual behaviors were kissing (N = 1), touching the other person's genitals (N = 1), having one's own genitals touched (N = 2), vaginal intercourse (N = 1), giving oral sex (N = 1), receiving oral sex (N = 1), anal sex (N = 1), and having one's vagina or anus penetrated with an object other than a penis (N = 1).

First unforced sexual intercourse with the opposite sex after age thirteen.

Excluding forced sexual experiences that had already been discussed, we asked about first sexual experience with the opposite sex. Forty of 72 (55.6%) males indicated that they had had sexual intercourse with a woman after age thirteen, excluding forced sexual experiences. The average age of first sexual intercourse with a woman was 21.3, with a range of 7 to 51.

We asked male interviewees to identify the relationship with the woman with whom they had their first experience of sexual intercourse. The most frequently identified person was a marital partner (N = 9 of 40, 22.5%) or date (not serious) (N = 9, 22.5%), followed by a serious relationship (N = 6, 15.0%), a friend (not dating) (N = 5, 12.5%), an acquaintance (N = 3, 7.5%), a relative (N = 3, 7.5%), their fiancée (N = 1, 2.5%), and someone they just met (N = 1, 2.5%).

We asked about the types of sexual behaviors that went on in the relationship with the woman with whom they had their first experience of sexual intercourse. Of the 40 male interviewees who indicated that they had had sexual intercourse with a woman, 37 (92.5%) reported that kissing was involved. Thirty-eight (95.0%) reported having their genitals touched by the woman; 36 (90.0%) reported touching the woman's genitals; 34 (85.0%) reported vaginal intercourse; 15 (37.5%) reported giving oral sex; 18 (45.0%) reported receiving oral sex. Laumann and his colleagues, in their national study of sexuality, included questions about techniques used in the context of one's first vaginal intercourse, and among males 85% reported kissing, 79% reported touching genitals and 16% reported oral sex.[18]

Eighteen of 26 (69.2%) females interviewed indicated having had sexual intercourse with a man after age thirteen, excluding forced sexual experiences. The average age of first sexual intercourse with a man was 20.0, with a range of 13 to 28.

We asked female interviewees to identify the relationship with the man with whom they had their first experience of sexual intercourse. The most frequently identified person was a friend (not dating) (N = 4 of 17, 23.5%), followed by a serious relationship (N = 3, 17.6%) and a date (not serious) (N = 3, 17.6%), an acquaintance (N = 2, 11.8%), someone they just met (N = 2, 11.8%), their marital partner (N = 1, 5.9%), and their fiancé (N = 1, 5.9%). In the Laumann study, women reported the following relationships with their first sex partner: someone with whom they were in love (53%), spouse (22%), someone they knew well but were not in love with (17%), someone they knew but not well (5%), someone they just met (1.0%) and a stranger (0.7%).[19]

We asked about the types of sexual behaviors that went on in the relationship with the man with whom they had their first experience of sexual intercourse. Of the 17 female interviewees who indicated that they had had sexual intercourse with a man, 16 (94.1%) reported that kissing was involved. Fourteen (82.4%) reported having their genitals touched by the man; 12 (70.6%) reported touching the man's genitals; 15 (88.2%) reported vaginal intercourse; 8 (47.1%) reported giving oral sex; 7 (41.2%) reported receiving oral sex; and 1 (5.9%) reported engaging in anal sex (and 2 of 17 or 11.8% reported vaginal or anal penetration with something other than a penis). In the national study of sexuality the most commonly identified sexual behaviors reported by females in the context of first intercourse experience included kissing (87%), touching genitals (74%) and oral sex (8.5%).[20]

First unforced sexual (homosexual) experience with the same sex after age thirteen. Excluding forced sexual experiences that had already been discussed, we asked about first sexual (homosexual) experience with the same sex. Sixty-one of 72 (84.7%) males indicated that they had had sexual intimacy with a man after age thirteen, excluding forced sexual experiences. The average age of first sexual intimacy with a man was 18.66, with a range of 12 to 36.

We asked about the types of sexual behaviors that went on in the relationship with the man with whom they had their first experience of sexual intimacy (see table 5.13). Of the 61 male interviewees who indicated that they had been sexually intimate with a man, 52 (75.4%) reported having their genitals touched by the man; 53 (86.9%) reported touching the man's genitals; 39 (63.9%) reported giving oral sex; 37 (60.7%) reported receiving oral sex; 31 (44.9%) reported kissing; 6 (9.8%) reported giving anal sex; 14 (23.0%) reported receiving anal sex; 3 (4.9%) reported having their anus penetrated with an object that was not a penis.

Twenty-one of 24 (87.5%) females interviewed indicated having been sexually intimate with a woman after age thirteen, excluding forced sexual

Table 5.13. First Homosexual Sexual Experience After Age Thirteen

Sexual Experience	Male participants		Female participants	
	N	%	N	%
Having genitals touched	52	75.4	19	100.0
Touching other person's genitals	53	86.9	15	78.9
Giving oral sex	39	63.9	10	52.6
Receiving oral sex	37	60.7	13	68.4
Kissing	31	44.9	19	100.0
Receiving anal sex	14	23.0	2	10.5
Giving anal sex	6	9.8	-	-
Vaginal intercourse	-	-	-	-

experiences. The average age of first sexual intimacy with a woman was 23.3, with a range of 14 to 37.

We asked female interviewees to identify the relationship with the woman with whom they had their first sexually intimate experience. The most frequently identified person was a serious relationship (N = 8 of 19, 42.1%), followed by a friend (not dating) (N = 5, 26.3%), a date (not serious) (N = 3, 15.8%), their fiancée (N = 2, 10.5%), someone they just met (N = 1, 5.3%) and another relationship not listed (N = 1, 5.3%).

We asked about the types of sexual behaviors that went on in the relationship with the woman with whom they had their first sexually intimate experience. Each of the 19 female interviewees who indicated that they had experienced sexual intimacy with a woman reported that kissing was involved and that their genitals were touched. The next most frequently indicated sexual experiences with the same sex were touching the other woman's genitals, receiving oral sex, giving oral sex and engaging in anal sex (and 5 of 19 or 25.3% reported having their vagina penetrated by an object).

A *Qualitative* Portrait of Our Sample on Selected Dimensions

The following reports the types of responses subjects gave at Time 1 to a variety of qualitative (open-ended, unstructured) questions in the interview. These responses are taken from the typed transcripts of the interviews. We have not attempted here to be systematic; these snippets are meant to be illustrative. We report on the major concerns that brought the participants to Exodus, responses to the question of why they are trying Exodus, statements as to their goals and how they would define complete success, additional concerns they have other than their concern about homosexual orientation, their degree of motivation, how strongly they believe success is possible, and the nature of their religious experience and any description of major phases in their faith journeys. Participant quotes are presented as bulleted material, with our introductory comments either presented as introductory prose or bracketed. Responses from Phase 1 (early change, up to one year in Exodus) and Phase 2 (longer change, from one to three years) are presented separately. Responses from males are denoted with an (M); females with an (F).

Question 1. "In your own words, what is the major concern that led you to seek help from this ministry?"

Response from Phase 1 participants:

- "Same-sex attraction. Having erotic feelings toward the same sex. Having emotional needs met by the same sex." (M)
- "If I could be free of anything in my life, I would be free of this, the bondage. I use about 10 to 20% of my energy to suppress the guilt and the bondage and the shame. Every day it's like I get on the carousel and I take my place on the carousel and I ride in a circle. And at the end of the day I get off. Nothing ever changes." (F)

Response from Phase 2 participants:

- "It was the conflict I had with a homosexual lifestyle and my beliefs in God. I needed somewhere where I could know that I could be honest about where I was in life and try to bring God back into my life. I know I had kept him out for too long. I was looking for a safe place with God." (F)
- "There was one specific event where I was arrested and charged with loitering and prowling. I was in an automobile with another man,

and the police came and put the floodlights on. That police officer called my boss. I was teaching at a religious institution, and I lost my job. It became quite public within my church body, and so that was a really big event." (M)

Question 2. "What is it about [your major concern] that brought you to seek change through this Exodus ministry?"

Response from Phase 1 participants:

- "I think, I know that I realize that that type of life is not ever going to meet what I see to be my emotional, physical and spiritual needs in any appropriate manner. To really achieve the highest that God has for me, I believe that living in a healthy sexual relationship with the opposite sex is to my best interest spiritually, emotionally, physically and mentally." (M)
- "Lack of being a complete person. Lack of wholeness. Self-esteem is an issue. I am a very suspicious person, and I feel that people are suspicious about me because they wonder why I don't have any family or anything. The most damaging aspect of it is since I could never trust my earthly father; because the Bible says even though you're evil, you would give your children something to eat. Well, my father wasn't like that. He was evil, and that interferes with my trust in my heavenly father. When I go through a trial, I feel like I'm being punished instead of that it's just a trial. What that causes is a distortion in relationships and the way that I deal with people. Whenever you're introverted, you don't have reality on your side because you don't have other people to use as a sounding board." (F)
- "My main concern was isolation. Trying to hide my sexual problems. I was going kinda well. I had been in counseling before, a few years ago, and made a lot of progress. I felt like once I finished counseling I didn't seek any further help or friendship as far as discussing the issues. I just kinda let it go. That was about five years ago. Four years before I came to this ministry, I was at a point where I could see myself involving myself more in pornography and homosexual activity and wanted to change. I wanted to get back on the path that I had

been on before. I felt one of the main ingredients for that was sharing that with other people where I could deal with it and talk about it with other people. That's why I brought that up. I've been dealing with it alone, and that's virtually impossible." (M)

- "Well, first of all, it was a group that didn't promise instant healing which I think is . . . [I] wouldn't get involved with a group like that [which promised instant healing] because I don't think that's realistic. Second of all, it was a Christian group that sought help from God to work through the issues rather than just . . . it wasn't just other people to talk to. It involved prayer and invoking God for guidance and for help and forgiveness and dealing with shame, things like that. So those are the two main things. It was a very realistic . . . and also when I met the leaders they were very understanding. They weren't judgmental. They definitely had a conviction, and I'm sure their conviction was that this behavior is wrong. But at the same time, they weren't passing judgment . . . they were understanding." (M)

Response from Phase 2 participants:

- "It has always been a problem and always been something that I struggled with, but I just felt that it wasn't something I could share with anybody. I felt that within my church body that, well, it was going to be a problem with my job. There wasn't going to be anywhere to go or any understanding or help or whatever. . . . Someone had once told me about Exodus about a year ago, but I didn't really understand what it was. Also with the whole secrecy thing, I couldn't take the chance of even being associated with an Exodus group for fear that it would come out." (M)
- "I didn't believe that homosexuality was the right thing to do. It was a sin. I was trying to find someone to deal with the emotional pressure that I felt inside, to alleviate that. And to seek change so that I could have heterosexual feelings or at least so that there wouldn't be so much pressure on myself." (F)
- "I know a friend had referred me. To expand on that, I had said to her that I'm feeling like a woman with no country. I want God in my

life, and I also have the gay lifestyle to deal with. And where do you go? The gay lifestyle has nothing to do with religion. In church, it's just really hard to be open about where you are. Where do you go? I felt like I had nowhere to go." (F)

Question 3. "What goal would you like to achieve in dealing with this concern?"

Response from Phase 1 participants:

- "I would like to come to the point where I'm comfortable thinking about being a sexual partner with the opposite sex. Resolving just a lot of, I guess, irrational fears and insecurities concerning the opposite sex." (M)
- "I would like to be a whole person so that I can be there for somebody else. The irony is that most women say that they've never been treated as well by anyone as they are by me. But when a lady is intimate with me, that worries me because I can't go beyond, you know. . . . My feeling toward other men is usually jealousy. I'm jealous of what they have. I can be jealous of their family, physical attributes, that type of thing that I wish that I possessed." (M)
- "My goal is to understand what makes me think this way and have this inclination. Maybe not necessarily. I mean, I would like to know the root, the very root cause of it, whatever it is. But, realistically, I would like to know what makes me . . . when these desires come up, what triggers these desires. And then to have . . . to know that about myself and have those desires under control to the point that I don't turn to pornography or sexual outlets with other people, or looking for sex or pornography. To deal with whatever problems they are causing." (M)

Response from Phase 2 participants:

- "My biggest thing has been gaining a better understanding of what happened, of how I got to this point, especially from a religious context. I would read Scripture and I was convicted of the fact that to have same-sex attractions or that type of relationship was wrong, yet it was there. I couldn't mesh everything. I understand this is wrong, but I also don't know where it came from. To me everybody was always saying it was a choice, and I didn't really feel it was so much a choice. That was very natural to me. As far as I was concerned, that was just the way that things were. I could agree that the behavior was a choice, but the whole issue didn't seem to be a choice. That always just tormented me growing up and reading Scripture and not understanding how this could all fit together. I think I was really looking for that kind of help from Exodus. I wanted something that was spiritually based." (M)

- "It would be nice if I didn't have to struggle with temptation sometimes. It's not a sexual temptation, it's an emotional one. It would be nice to be strong enough to not have to do that. To just stand on my own and, you know, walk with God. To not have that need. To have close friendships but not have the dependencies and things like that." (F)
- "The goal, I guess, would be to continue to allow God to show me what he wants in my life." (F)

Question 4. "Let me ask about your goal in a different way. How would your life look different if you met with complete success in this ministry?"

Response from Phase 1 participants:

- "I think that I would be married. I would be forming a family. I would have a very warm, secure, equal relationship with somebody of the opposite sex." (M)
- "I would have a family. I'd have a wife that loved me, someone that understood me. Married couples live longer than single people. The sheer fact of it is that then you have someone to help you through life's troubles. The other thing about this is an underlying lack of maturity. I see myself as a child. When I was a child, I had to live like an adult because my father wasn't an adult. He was an escapist. He was a Peter Pan personality. What that did was when I moved out so young . . . I worked since I was 14, very independent, very angry. I was always upset when I was unkind to people, because the virtue that I seek especially in other men that I think is attractive is kindness

when somebody is strong. The immaturity is a problem because it was like I was trapped. Now I have an older body, but I'm still that child that never went past and got developed. I would also be confident. I've noticed that in other people, and I would like to possess what God has for me and have a life while there's still a chance." (M)

- "I would be less captivated by my homosexual desires. I wouldn't be looking at pornography. I would call a friend to deal with my issues in prayer, and I would pray more when I see things that trigger my homosexual desires. I can't say that that's myself; I don't want to hear it or admit it or share it. I would be more likely to reach out." (M)

Response from Phase 2 participants:

- "I would be a lot closer to God. I wouldn't have emotional tendencies to reach out for other women friends in an unhealthy way. I don't think that I would be involved with a man because I'm not sure about being married. I have some really negative viewpoints about marriage. I think that I would just be closer to God and doing things, the goals in my life." (F)
- "My success may not be a husband and all of that. I don't know. And I'm not going to push that if that's not where God is pushing me. Probably knowing God more than I do today. I'm sure what he wants from me and who he really is so good and huge." (F)
- "My self-esteem would be a lot greater. I would really have a confidence about myself that I was always lacking no matter how much schooling or how many degrees I got. I never felt good about myself because I was always struggling with this. Secondarily, the possibility of marriage and children. I don't know if that's exactly a goal, but I guess if I really had complete enough change, that might be an option." (M)

Question 5. "What other concerns are there with which you hope this group will help you?"

Response from Phase 1 participants:

- "Not being so . . . I've always allowed the same-sex attraction in my life to be a big poison in my life. So it's something that I've separated and compartmentalized and never wanted to take out and look at. So I hope discussing it and being with other people who are dealing with the same issues can make me not feel like such a monster and so poorly about myself." (M)

- "I think physically I would feel better if I were free of this bondage." (F)

Response from Phase 2 participants:

- "Just a source of encouragement too. It's been nice that you can go and be with a group of people who are on the same page, by and large, theologically. We have some differences. Yet you can just talk, and then everybody understands each other. When you talk with other people, by and large, they just can't really comprehend what you're talking about. It's just comfortable to be with a group of people that does understand what you're talking about." (M)
- "Well, I have a real issue with self-acceptance. I have a lot of anger inside and I would like to deal with that so I can be more loving." (F)

Question 6. "How would you describe your degree or intensity of motivation to change at the point at which you began your involvement in this ministry?" (Interviewers were urged to probe responses by asking further, "What would you say has fueled this motivation of yours?")

Response from Phase 1 participants:

- "Intense. And the reason is to overcome the shame and the embarrassment. Just by going to the meetings I'm confirming suspicions that people have already. Also that was a yielding to God for me because I always had a wall around my emotions. To yield and to trust a God that, like I said, I didn't feel I could trust was a big step." (F)
- "Very high. Let's see . . . I would say being forty years old and not wanting to be the old one." (M)
- "My degree of motivation on a scale of 1 to 10 is probably around 7. Because of the hold that that lifestyle has on you, it still seems really, you know, seems really pleasing. So at the time it is probably about 7." (M)

- "I would say very high. I have a strong desire for change. I don't think that my desire is strong enough that I've cut out everything that I need to, that I consider my own power to change. So, I wouldn't say the desire is extremely high, because there's a big part of me that holds that back. I don't think . . . I didn't come here because I thought they could change me. I came because it was a way that I could get in the process of changing. And I knew, I thought, that this ministry could help me do that. So, in that sense I wanted help. <*probe*> Well, my first motivation would be that I think homosexuality is wrong. Homosexual behavior and the homosexual lusting are wrong. I think a big desire is to make other people happy too. . . . I think a lot of it is because I need people . . . I think the people in my life that I'm close to. I think that's a big motivator. Personal happiness. I wouldn't have said that a year ago, but now I see much more happiness in starting to deal with the issue of homosexual activity." (M)

Response from Phase 2 participants:

- "I would say that it was a little higher when I started. I am still wanting to change, but I don't have the desperation I had. I think that's a good thing. But the desire to change is still very strong. I feel like my attractions to women are a little less than what they were when I started. But they are not completely gone." (F)
- "In one sense, it was very intense because of the fact that I lost my job and it became known in my church. It was very shameful. But I don't know, even though there was an intensity to change, I don't think there was the belief that change was possible. I naively wanted it to go away. Like if I came to group and I learned a little bit, then all of a sudden everything would be OK. Then I went through a long period of being upset again because it's long and involved. And that's been hard to deal with. <*probe: current motivation?*> Lately, I went to the Exodus conference, and I've been reading another round of books. I almost feel like I'm getting to the point of saying OK, I am ready to deal with change even if it really takes a long time. I don't know if I'm 100% there but I feel a difference. When I came in I was committed to change if it was going to be instant, but if it wasn't going to be in-

stant, then I wasn't so sure. I was still kind of holding on to the orientation, very ambivalent. Now it seems like it's truly possible if I'm willing to put myself through whatever it's going to take, realizing that it could be a life-long process. . . . Finally I felt like it was time if I was really going to get anywhere. It's difficult to go." (M)

- "In the beginning was very intense. I don't know that I was looking for change, I just needed God somewhere. That was very intense. It was obviously to change. If that's implied to change sexuality, I just wanted to let God into my life. I figured that the rest will follow. <*probe*> I care to continue to change how I do any kind of relationship. That is itself hugely different than when I first started going to [Exodus group]. I look at relationships very differently. I would like to continue to improve relationship and see it more like God does than the world does. It's not as intense, but it's consistent." (F)

Question 7. "Do you believe that the attempt to change homosexual orientation or feelings can be successful?" <Yes or No> "Do you have particular reasons for believing this?"

Response from Phase 1 participants:

- "Yes. I believe on a natural level that, whereas I think that sexuality is innate, I feel like sexual behavior is learned. So I feel that anything that can be learned can be unlearned. There's another aspect that can be learned. On a spiritual level I believe that God is able to intervene in every level of our lives and bring healing in every level of our life." (M)
- "Yes. I believe that it's mostly psychological. I'm ashamed to say it. I don't know how to say it. There have been times when, for example, I saw someone at a distance and they were attractive and it was a lady. So I know that if I can overcome the bias, that I can have normal feelings. I know that the feelings from my childhood filter out and distort normal emotions. It was odd that my father always touted himself as being so sexually active and indiscriminate with having so many children but not raising them properly. It was another irony that he was so dirty with women. That was brought to bear in that." (M)

- "Yes, but I don't think it's like an on-or-off switch. I think that it's a process. I think a lot of it has to do with personal choices, discipline and the intervention of God. I don't think necessarily for every person that the feelings will just go away. I think that they can be . . . I think that . . . for me it's just more of an issue of having them under control than having them gone. I don't have a whole lot of hope that they'll just go away, I think under control and not interfering with my life. I think that's more possible than them just going away. Although for some people it does work out that way. Although I think that's for a very few people." (M)

Response from Phase 2 participants:

- "Yes, I am becoming more convinced of that. I was somewhat unsure. I have been reading Alan Medinger's book about resuming the journey. It's really pulled a lot of it together. I've read so many books that I feel like I could write my own book. His is really good; it really speaks to my experience. It's pulling a lot of things together and striking a chord with me. He's being real and honest, and he is sincerely convinced that it's possible." (M)
- "Uncertain. I'm not sure that the feelings will go entirely away. I think a person can change their lifestyle and the feelings will follow it up to a point. I wouldn't say that I would ever be in love with a man." (F)

Question 8. "We want to ask some questions to help us understand your religious faith and journey. We want to begin by asking you to describe your religious life in your own words. Could you begin by describing, in about three or four minutes, your current religious beliefs or spiritual life? Another way of asking this question would be to ask how, in a few brief minutes, you would describe yourself to me, someone who really does not know you, if you wanted me to understand who you are as a person of faith."

Response from Phase 1 participants:

- "I believe that we are all separated from God, and the only way to be reconciled to God is by Jesus Christ. Christ suffered for me on the cross. By faith in Christ, and not by anything that we do. I guess one of the biggest obstacles in one of the prior counseling and stuff was that I couldn't get past the fact that God would forgive me for what I had done. But, during the course of my time with [specific Exodus ministry], . . . God answered that prayer. I realized then that he did love me enough to forgive me. That's been a big turning point." (M)

- "I think right now I'm in a crisis of faith. For the greatest part of my life I have been a professing Christian. Actually, as a Pentecostal I was raised. Over the past year I would say that I see myself as a very spiritual person who loves the Lord. But, it's just, I'm just dealing with a lot of stuff, blaming towards God. I'm still very much a believer in who he is and what he is capable of doing." (M)
- "I'm a Christian in recovery from sexual addictions. I've been a believer most of my life and struggling with a battle. I firmly believe that the Bible is God's inerrant Word. I believe that I'm forgiven and that God is in control. I believe that he knows the desires of my heart. I believe that he's capable of making those changes." (M)

Response from Phase 2 participants:

- "I am a Christian. I believe that Christ is my Savior and that nothing that I can do is going to gain me salvation—it's only by my faith in Christ. I grew up in a religious family, conservative Lutheran background. I went to parochial grade school in the sixth grade, went to parochial high school. I have always been a member of a Lutheran church, and not just a member but active. I've always been a part of things. Once I got done with law school, I was kind of debating what to do, and I had the opportunity to teach at a religious, faith-based institution—a small liberal arts college. I thought that was very attractive because I thought with the struggle it was not likely I would ever get married. It didn't seem like that would be a reasonable thing to do. I thought that would be my life. I would devote myself to God by serving in that type of capacity. I was very active there. I gave chapel. I took students on evangelism trips and taught evangelism. From that standpoint, I would say I was very active in my religious life." (M)

- "I would say that I am committed to following Jesus and walking with God. I would say I'm not very successful at it for whatever reason. I'm not sure what the reason really is. But he is very important to me. If it wasn't, I would still be in the lifestyle. I'm not sure. I might have stopped anyway. I've had experiences with God that are very real, and I know that Christianity is very real and the truth. I could even say that just based on the experiences I've had. I get real satisfaction when God answers prayer, even the little things he does. Little prayers he answers. Just, I don't know. It really touches my heart. I still have a lot of things to work through." (F)
- "Still learning. There's that part that is big. We'll never learn it all. But very much a seeker. When I grew up, my mom didn't join church for a while. I was probably twelve or thirteen when my mom started going to church. So did I, with her. Got very involved in the church then. I'd go to Sunday school and junior Sunday school and youth group, and all that kind of stuff. Very involved. Which was more of an exposure to religion, because I hadn't had that. And then as I grew up and went to college, I went to a religious college. Because I appreciated the values that people have. I'm always had ahold of some set of values. People that just bounce through life, I don't have a lot in common with. Through the end of college, I guess, out came the rebellious teenager. Of course, that's when I started to stray from the beliefs that I'd been learning. You start drinking, you start whatever. And that's the last place that I should have started, but that was where I started. A whole different environment. I wanted to be different. For whatever reason, I said subconsciously that I don't like this huge group of sameness. So I probably strayed and rebelled from that. And then as I let church go and pursued after the gay lifestyle and bouncing around on my own. And then I started seeking God again. My spiritual beliefs have stuck with me. The things that I grew up with and had learned were missing. And I know that there's a ton of different perspectives on different religions and everything else. I was always taught take it to God. Question everything if you want to, but question God. Don't just take people's intellectual thoughts

and whatever. Maybe something is for you, and maybe something isn't for you. That doesn't mean that it's right or wrong. The only person who is accountable for my life is me. I have had that belief all of the way through. Accountability is huge. So, I still am pursuing seeking all of those things in my spiritual life because I'm accountable, not anybody else. And I don't want to just follow this person or this person. I want to know for me. That's more of my religious life in a nutshell." (F)

Question 9. "Could you now describe, again in about three or four minutes, the major phases you have been through in your life as your religious experience has changed? In other words, please tell us in your own words the major stops along the path of your faith journey."

Response from Phase 1 participants:

- "Let's see, I remember when I was about six or seven years old, giving my life to the Lord. The sister who was being sexually abused by my father was eight years older than I was. She began to do to me what he did to her, so . . . [d]uring that time I was very mixed-up in the sense of spirituality. I felt like if something sexual happened between her and I that I would lose my salvation. So, I got saved a million times when I was a kid. There I was still very committed, very faithful in prayers as early as thirteen, fourteen, fifteen. And then sixteen, seventeen drifting somewhat, wanting to experience more of a wild life. And, in my twenties, being very committed. Mid-twenties, being committed, or being still committed to my spirituality but not living as I should. And from there on, for the most part, I've been very committed to my faith." (M)
- "From the time I was born, I was in church. My grandfather was a pastor. I was in church from birth up until . . . I got saved when I was ten years old. Then, we were in church about another year, and then we moved. And when we moved, we quit going. My parents never did go to church, they always sent us, but themselves never went. After we moved, they didn't send us to church anymore. From eleven until up to 1988, which then I was about twenty-six or twenty-seven

years old, I was out of a church. Been going regularly with the exception of two months a couple of years ago when I dropped out because of things again. I had a fall and had given up. There was a period of about four or five months when I didn't go." (M)

- "I was raised in the church. Had some major setbacks in the church too. I was molested by the youth group leader in the fellowship hall of the church when I was ten. There's been a tug-of-war sometimes with God. I recommitted my life at the age of fourteen at a Billy Graham crusade. . . . I don't claim to understand all of God's way or God's timing. I prayed for twenty-five years for my issue, but the answer didn't come until I could practice James 5:16, "therefore confess your sins one to each other and pray for each other that you may be healed." (M)

Response from Phase 2 participants:

- "When I was in . . . school, I was involved with a campus ministry. That had an impact on my life because we did some small-group Bible studies. There was some real fellowship there, and people had dinners together. It was a close-knit bond. That had a real impact on me. I remember thinking at that time, it made the New Testament and the New Testament church and what was going on there seem more real. It didn't seem real to me as a member of a large, established congregation. That was one time when I think I really saw Scripture and I felt that I experienced something that I could really relate Scripture to. Then I would also say one time was at the college and teaching there too. I really grew and had a lot of opportunities for growth. We had daily chapel. I needed to have a certification, so I took a number of different theology classes and actually became active doing things that were spiritual in nature, especially doing some of the evangelism trips that I did. We would go help a small congregation that was just starting out. I would take a group of students and we would do canvassing and follow up with people who came to church. That had an impact on me. It really helped me to grow." (M)
- "I was brought up to believe, because of the influence of my mother.

When I was in junior high and high school, I felt like I was close to God. I didn't have really any knowledge of anything. I just thought I knew what the Bible said and what it was all about. When I was around twenty-two or twenty-three, I decided I wanted to pursue a gay lifestyle. I had real trouble reconciling that with my faith. I read a lot of books! I finally decided that it was okay and I was going to do it, you know. I found enough justification to go ahead with it. I think my relationship with God still stayed strong, maybe for about a year after that. Then I became more and more involved in having relationships, which that didn't happen first. The first two years I was in the gay lifestyle, but I didn't have a lover. I began to get further and further away from God. And I started to do other things that I would never have done before, like stealing and lying. I just didn't care . . . everything went. I started to realize after a while that I wasn't walking with God. And then I didn't believe in God, like I didn't have any faith. I became anti-Christian. When the people were passing Amendment 2 in 1992, that was when I was most against Christians. It was two years after that that I came back. But I had to struggle through to regain faith. Because I didn't have any, I didn't know if Jesus was God, a man. I had to search through all of that for the first time. And I must have read more books then and seen more things than any point in my life. The only thing that I could base my faith on was that Jesus actually did miracles and there was no disputing that. All of the books I read they could dispute everything else but that. God did things too that helped." (F)

CONCLUSION

Based on the findings in this chapter, it is evident that we are reporting on a diverse sample. There are those who have little or no sexual experience, as well as individuals who have had significant sexual experiences with the same sex. We also see in our sample a range of sexual experiences, from voluntary experiences to forced-sex experiences that are spread across the age range.

We interviewed both males and females. This is important to note because much of the research published to date has been on males who identify as gay, and scientists simply know less about the experiences of females who experience same-sex attractions.

Some of our more remarkable findings include the fact that our sample is a fairly old group with an average age in the late thirties. Even those who believe in sexual-orientation change would probably suspect that this would be associated with a more pessimistic prognosis for change. The sample is very well educated as well. While a good number of our subjects have refrained from overt sexual activity as adults, this percentage was smaller than what we had originally expected and was a minority of our population. A high percentage of our sample had experienced sexual contact, both voluntary and forced, in childhood.

6

Understanding and Measuring Change of Sexual Orientation

IN THIS CHAPTER WE

- review the major conceptual challenges to understanding what sexual orientation is, doing so in part by reviewing how the scientific community's understanding of sexual orientation has evolved over the years
- review the major psychological assessment instruments that are commonly used to assess sexual orientation, their strengths and limitations, and the scientific evidence (or lack thereof) for the validity of those methods
- describe in detail the specific instruments we used in this study and how, in a few cases, we adapted those instruments to the specific demands of this study

This study examines the question of whether anyone can change their sexual orientation. But to know if this is possible, we must understand with some reasonable clarity what sexual orientation is. This is not as simple as it might seem. The major conceptual obstacle to the execution of this project is the ambiguity of what we mean by sexual orientation and hence what it would mean to change it.

Human sexuality is at once obvious and self-interpreting, but at the same time diffuse and mysterious. On the one hand, certain people may be able to state with utter confidence, "I am gay" or "I am straight," but on the other hand, we have no indisputable markers outside of the declarations of those persons of these distinct states, nor have we complete clarity that these are distinct and mutually exclusive states. Kinsey revolutionized our thinking about sexual orientation by reconceptualizing it as a continuum between exclusively homosexual and exclusively heterosexual; this was perhaps the first forceful recognition of some of the complexity of this matter. But others soon recognized that Kinsey's reliance on behavior as the definer of orientation was too narrow, and there followed a shifting from behavioral markers for sexual orientation to an emphasis on psychological attraction.

We see these complexities reflected in the types of criticisms of the existing "change" literature that we noted in chapter three. For example, Douglas Haldeman criticized the reorientation or conversion literature as based on naive and dichotomous views of "gays and straights" that do not do justice to the complex realities of sexual attraction and orientation.[1] What he had in view was the tendency to take the presence of any homosexual attraction as diagnostic proof that the individual is "homosexual." It is too simplistic at the start of a conversion study to say that the presence of any homosexual attraction makes a subject homosexual, when in fact they might be anywhere between the extremes of the Kinsey continuum, as if no homosexual attraction at all equals heterosexuality while *any* homosexual attraction equals homosexuality. Haldeman rightly argues that this is a simplistic conceptual scheme, and we avoided such absurdities in this study.

Haldeman expressed a related concern at the other end of the research process, the matter of defining what constitutes success. Haldeman speculated that when change interventions work, they do so by grafting heterosexual action over a homosexual orientation without a more basic change in desire or attraction. What is right about this criticism, it seems to us, is the claim that teaching or helping a lesbian woman who has no attraction to men at all to endure sex with her husband without complaint should not be presented as a therapeutic success at the level of a basic change of orientation. What is profoundly wrong about this type of criticism, though, is the way that critics of the reorientation literature often level this charge when those undergoing reorientation report *any* degree of continuing homosexual attraction. This is wrong at two levels. First, if Haldeman's criticism in the previous paragraph is valid, then it must be equally true for "reoriented" persons who have moved from homosexual to heterosexual: the presence of some continuing level of homosexual attraction in a "reoriented person" whose dominant orientation has moved from gay to straight cannot be taken to deny the change in their dominant orientation. Second, those who claim that any acknowledgment of continuing homosexual attraction by reoriented persons is clear proof that no change has really taken place at all have implicitly taken as a definition of successful conversion to heterosexuality the standard that the convert must *never again* experience homosexual attraction. That this is an unreasonable standard is proven by the test of generalization to other psychological conditions. We would never demand that successfully treated depressed people never again feel blue or that successfully treated married couples never again experience discouraging arguments or breakdowns in communication.

The most sophisticated assessment tools for sexual orientation continue to expand the complexity of the definition of sexual orientation and, most important, consistently refuse to introduce cut-off scores that categorize people into certain fixed orientations. Instead, we are presented with an expanded group of multidimensional continua relating to sexual orientation, on which individuals can be plotted in various ways, resulting in unique constellations of sexual interest, but which do not result in dichotomous (either gay or straight) or trichotomous (either gay or straight or bisexual) categorizations. Further clouding the question of what constitutes sexual orientation is the confusing, complex and inconclusive evidence about etiology or causes of sexual orientation, with evidence existing for genetic, prenatal hormonal, birth order, brain structure, parental, cultural and other experiential variables. No one variable or cluster of variables stands forth as possessing dominant explanatory power.

A recent content analysis of nearly 150 studies on homosexuality revealed five methods used to assess sexual orientation: *self-identification* (participants self-identify as heterosexual, homosexual or bisexual), *sexual preference* (participants indicate being attracted to the same sex, the opposite sex or both sexes), *sexual behavior* (involvement in same- or opposite-sex activities), *single dimensions* (use of a bipolar scale, such as the Kinsey scale, with "exclusively homosexual" on one end and "exclusively heterosexual" on the other), and *multiple dimensions* (utilizing more than one of the methods noted).[2] Also it should be noted that many of the studies reviewed (nearly one-third) actually fell into an additional category—

unsure—meaning no assessment was done or no assessment method was indicated. If we use these five categories to help us understand how sexual orientation is often assessed, it will help us see the potential limitations in each approach and the potential value in using multiple methods for assessing sexual orientation.

- *Self-identification.* Many studies simply ask participants to identify themselves by their sexual orientation. Participants are often given three choices, for instance, to check a box marked "heterosexual," "homosexual" or "bisexual." This is by far the easiest and most convenient measure, and it is an improvement on failing to use an assessment at all. However, there are problems with relying on these categories. The most damaging criticism is that this method of assessment may not tap into sexual orientation at all, particularly if the options listed are "gay," "lesbian" "bi" or "straight," because these categories are, to many participants, reflective of a sociocultural self-identify and may merely reflect one's sexual identity rather than one's sexual orientation as such.
- *Sexual preference.* Researchers who determine sexual orientation based on sexual preference are essentially interpreting people's/individual's self-reports of their attractions as indicative of sexual orientation. This global and rather simplistic measure of sexual orientation does not reflect the degree of attraction to one or the other or both sexes. It simply draws conclusions based on the direction of people's attractions.
- *Sexual behavior.* Perhaps the most widely criticized measure of sexual orientation is to conclude that a person has a homosexual or heterosexual orientation because they engage in same- or opposite-sex behavior.
- *Single dimensions.* Another common measure of sexual orientation is to use the Kinsey scale or another scale like it to get a sense of the direction and degree of sexual attraction. The common factor among these scales is that they are bipolar, typically having the extremes of "exclusively homosexual" on one end and "exclusively heterosexual" on the other end. The major criticism for the ongoing use of this

measure alone is that it assumes a necessary relationship between same- and opposite-sex orientation, such that changes in one are reflected in changes of the same degree in the other.

- *Multiple dimensions*. In an attempt to correct for the limitations inherent in a single-dimension approach, most researchers today recognize the value of assessing sexual orientation across multiple dimensions. A researcher might use the Kinsey scale, for example, and then add two unipolar scales to measure self-reports of homosexual and heterosexual attraction and orientation.

From the beginning we realized that the claim that homosexuals can change is complicated by the uncertainty, at least in scientific terms, of defining who is homosexual and who is not, and of defining what homosexuality is. This in turn radically complicates the definition of success for change attempts. If there are no tightly defined dichotomous categories of gay and straight, then the reorientation of a person moving from one place to another in a multidimensional space defined by an array of variables related to sexual orientation can always be disputed. In its simplest form, we see this when someone who self-identifies as ex-gay admits to continuing homosexual temptation (i.e., attraction of some sort), with that person then quickly labeled by some as really not having changed at all. Behind this is a presumption that the experience of any homosexual attraction is an indication of an enduring orientation, a presumption put into doubt by the huge definitional questions we have just discussed.

The focus of our research has been to attempt to document whether sexual orientation changes over course of involvement with an Exodus-affiliated ministry. In this chapter we (1) discuss the conceptual debates about the nature of sexual orientation, (2) review existing methods for measuring the construct of sexual orientation and (3) describe the methods chosen in this study to measure sexual orientation. As we begin this chapter, we draw the reader's attention to the fact that we have relied in this study almost exclusively on the reviews and assessment methods that have garnered support in the gay and lesbian academic community; for instance, the principle methods of assessment we use have been published and discussed in the widely respected *Journal of Homosexuality*.

DEFINITION AND MEASUREMENT OF SEXUAL ORIENTATION

Ronald Sell has capably outlined the troubled conceptual and empirical history of modern efforts to define and measure sexual orientation.[3] Drawing largely upon his work, we begin with a conceptual introduction to this thorny matter of definition of sexual orientation. To the person who has not thought hard about this matter or who does not know people with a variety of sexual desires and appetites, defining sexual orientation might seem a simple matter. Alfred Kinsey stated:

> It is characteristic of the human mind that it tries to dichotomize in its classification of phenomena. Things are either so, or they are not so. Sexual behavior is either normal or abnormal, socially acceptable or unacceptable, heterosexual or homosexual, and many persons do not want to believe that there are gradations in these matters from one to the other extreme.[4]

While ethically we would maintain the dichotomy of normal and abnormal, Kinsey's point about our bias toward discrete categorization is nevertheless basically true. Discrete categorization into tidy, exclusive pigeon holes seems to be a basic human cognitive strategy, even in areas of life where it is more appropriate to recognize gradations and complexities than to categorize into tight, exclusive categories.

A quick thought experiment illuminates this. Human beings recognize certain categories that reflect enduring, true categories that exist in the "real world," categories that exist independently of our perceptions and indeed outside of human choice. Take, for example, the existence of dogs and cats. Despite the breadth of each of these categories (think of the range of difference from Chihuahuas to Great Danes), there exist real limits to these broad categories such that there is not a continuum between the two. There are not gradations of catness and dogness, and there are no animals that are at a middle point on a continuum between the two types.1 Further, there are no choices that can be made or actions that can be taken by humans that change the fundamental realities of these categorizations, at least not at the present stage of genetic engineering. Certain human characteristics fit this same pattern, with biological sex serving as a good exam-

1Whether or not there ever were animals that embodied elements of both at some point in the history of the origins of contemporary species is another matter; there are no such creatures now.

ple. Independent of our perceptions, humans are categorizable as biological males or females. But we begin to see complexity building when we realize, unlike our dog and cat example, that there *are* intermediate examples for sex, most notably the extremely rare occurrences of true hermaphrodites (also called intersexuals) with mixed male and female anatomies and physiologies. These are estimated to occur between 0.1% and 0.01% of all live births. Such intermediate entities, though, reinforce rather than disprove the validity of our underlying dichotomous categorization as they are demonstrably aberrations to the general rule.

But many of our categorizations of human characteristics differ profoundly from this simple example. The concept of race is a wonderful contemporary example. Once widely accepted as an intuitively obvious reality, modern science has eroded our confidence that we can clearly and definitively sort the races. Consider further our categorization of political types in contemporary American society. Is the human world categorizable into two clean, clear groups, Democrats and Republicans? We first easily note that while there may be classic exemplars or prototypes of each of these types, many Americans take political positions that are compromises between the pure types and thus share characteristics of both and can be understood to exist on some sort of continuum of views between the pure types. Add to this the complexity of the multiple dimensions on which the pure types differ: a person can share the core social conservatism of the classic Republican while embracing the governmental activism toward the underprivileged of the classic Democrat and also be a middle-of-the-roader on governmental regulation of big business. Thus the continua that define people in terms of their political views are multiple, not singular, continua. Further, this categorization of Democrat or Republican only makes sense in a particular culture at a particular moment and place in history, and would have made no sense at other moments in human history (such as in Nazi Germany or ancient Babylonia), and indeed makes no sense in other places in the world even today. These political categories, to the extent that they exist, are human creations and are the product of human choices that can be remade in other forms. The categorization of Americans today into Democrats and Republicans is real, but real in a way different from the way the categorization of cats and dogs, males and females, is real.

So, are the distinctions between homosexuals and heterosexuals real, and in what way are they real? Recognition of the reality of homosexual acts, and of the predisposition of certain individuals to engage in these acts, has been around basically for as long as recorded human history.[5] But how these acts and the persons who engage in them have been understood has differed dramatically in human history. A summary of that history is beyond the scope of this chapter. We will focus rather within the context of modern psychology and its immediate predecessors.

Early conceptualizations of relevance to contemporary psychology occurred first in medical contexts; it is early in the professionalization of medicine in Europe that we begin to see an elaboration of the complexity of the concept of sexual orientation.[6] In the 1860s, Karl Ulrichs, who is known as the founder of the modern study of homosexuality, proposed three basic categories of persons with regard to their sexual orientation: dionings, urnings and uranodionings (category names derived from a speech in Plato's *Symposium* and basically corresponding, respectively, to modern notions of heterosexuals, homosexuals and bisexuals). His categorization for bisexuals was in fact complex, involving subcategories based on degrees of effeminacy and types of behavioral preference. Though Ulrichs did not actually approve of the terms *homosexuality* and *heterosexuality*, they were inspired by his work and first introduced in 1868 in a letter from Benkert, a German physician, to Ulrichs. In a later pamphlet Karl Maria Benkert wrote that "Nature has endowed at birth certain male and female individuals with the homosexual urge. This urge creates in advance a direct horror of the opposite sex."[7] For future reference note that this definition focuses on biological urges and psychological attraction and repulsion, foreshadowing the focus on psychological attraction and impulses (in contrast to behavior) that would be followed by later researchers.

While Ulrichs's scheme goes beyond simple dichotomization (two categories, straight or gay), it still *categorizes* people into discrete classes or groups. It was Alfred Kinsey who championed the move away from categorization in favor of the use of a true *continuum* of sexual attraction.[8] Kinsey led a team that interviewed thousands of individuals (a sample that despite its size, it must be noted, did *not* constitute a representative sample of the population)[9] regarding their sexual behavior and experiences. When it came to sexual orientation, rather than asking about their behavior and then placing them in one of two (heterosexual or homosexual) or three (heterosexual, homosexual or bisexual) discrete categories, Kinsey's team rated his subjects on a true numerical continuum based on their behavior, one that presumed gradations even between the discrete numerical ratings and hence eschewed categories for a true continuum. His seven-point rating scale for behavior was

0—exclusively heterosexual

1—largely heterosexual, but incidental homosexual

2—largely heterosexual, but more than incidental homosexual

3—equal amounts of heterosexual and homosexual

4—largely homosexual, but more than incidental heterosexual

5—largely homosexual, but incidental heterosexual

6—exclusively homosexual

But concerns with Kinsey's scheme were inevitable. First, Kinsey categorized according to behavior, but this was recognized as unsatisfactory in terms of understanding sexual orientation because of the recognized role of the situation or context in shaping and driving behavior. One needed to look no further than the fact that a good number of the persons rated as "6—exclusively homosexual" were prison inmates whose only interpersonal sexual behavior for a number of years had been with persons of the same gender. Even so, it is worth note that categorization by behavior alone continues to be deemed useful by some researchers, as seen for instance in the recent epidemiological study of Theo Sandfort and his colleagues.[10]

Second, conceptual dissatisfaction has developed toward using a bipolar scale (a single line anchored by extreme points at either end) that implies that having more homosexual impulse necessarily means less heterosexual impulse. This way of rating sexual orientation, it is argued, fails to capture the challenge of bisexuality, making these people look like they had 50% of the sexual attraction intensity of exclusive homosexuals and heterosexuals. The next conceptual elaboration of the definition of sexual orientation was inspired by the development of the concept of androgyny in social psychology that was championed by Sandra Bem.[11] Basically, Bem challenged the conceptualization of masculinity-femininity as existing on a single continuum where more of one necessarily meant less of the other. Rather, Bem proposed, masculinity and femininity might be independent, such that one could have more or less of either characteristic *independently.* Figure 6.1 graphically depicts how this might look:

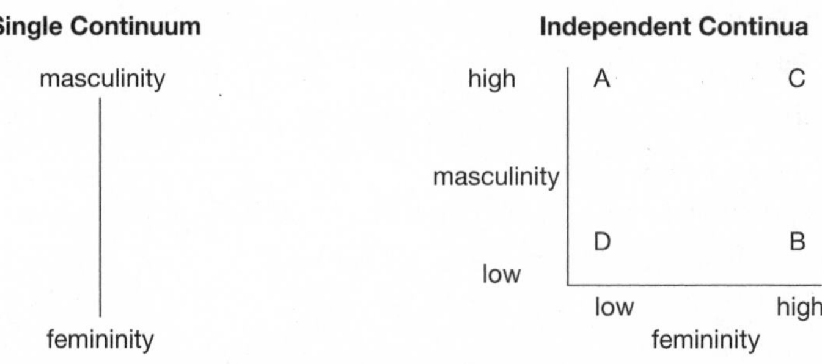

Figure 6.1. Two Conceptualizations of Masculinity and Femininity

The model on the left, which places masculinity and femininity on a single continuum, forces us to think that the more masculine person is necessarily less feminine (and vice versa). In contrast, the conceptualization of Bem allows us to consider masculinity and femininity independently, with the result that you can conceive of a person who is high on masculinity and low on femininity (person A), high on femininity and low on masculinity (person B), or high on both (person C, perhaps a woman who is stereotypically feminine—caring, loving, nurturing, sensitive—and also stereotypically masculine—emotionally controlled, aggressive and so forth). The model even allows for individuals who are low on both characteristics (person D), whose personalities simply fail to demonstrate clear indications of either type of characteristic.

The strengths of Kinsey's single continuum can be best appreciated when we realize that Kinsey focused largely on behavior. It makes intuitive sense that if we are categorizing people according to their behavior, some people's *behavior* may be exclusively homosexual, others exclusively heterosexual, and yet others existing in some combination between those extremes. The limitations of Kinsey's single continuum can easily be seen when we switch the focus from behavior to *intensity of attraction*. Does the person in the middle of the continuum experience 50% of the level or intensity of heterosexual arousal of the "exclusive heterosexual" type and 50% of the level or intensity of homosexual arousal of the "exclusive homosexual" type? Perhaps not; perhaps the person in the middle is aroused with equal intensity and frequency by persons of both genders.

It was with these concerns in mind, and inspired by Bem's concept of androgyny, that Michael Shively and John DeCecco argued that Kinsey's single continuum for measuring sexual orientation by behavior needed to be replaced by the separate measurement of heterosexual and homosexual arousal and behavior.[12] When heterosexual and homosexual arousal are measured independently, the following combinations are possible:

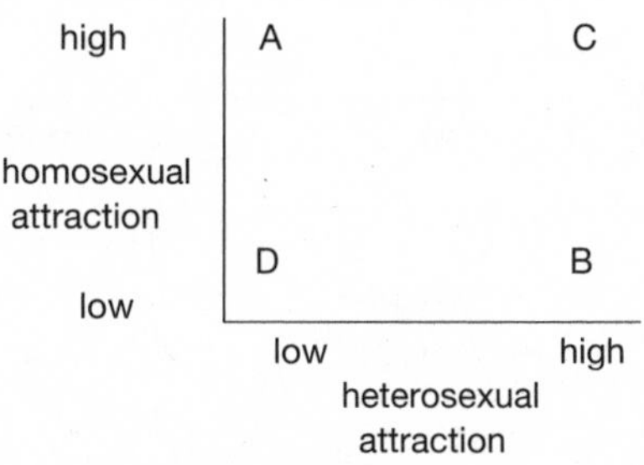

Figure 6.2. Heterosexual and Homosexual Attraction

As with androgyny, we can conceive of a person who is high on homosexual attraction and low on heterosexual attraction (person A; the "pure homosexual"), a person high on heterosexual attraction and low on homosexual attraction (person B; the "pure heterosexual"), and a person who is high on both (person C, the classic bisexual who responds intensely to both genders). The model even allows for individuals who are low on both characteristics (person D), often termed the asexual or hyposexual person.

But another complexity has crept in already, and that is the question of *which* indexes are crucial in ascertaining sexual orientation. Kinsey looked at behavior, but even a moment's reflection establishes that behavior is often influenced by external circumstance as well as by "internal nature." Homosexual intercourse in sexually homogeneous prison populations may be indicative of the enduring sexual appetites of some in that population, but certainly many others who engage in that behavior would choose to avail themselves of heterosexual outlets if they had that opportunity. Even out in the "real world," people behave as they do for a variety of motivations and in a variety of contexts (the homosexually oriented person who marries in hopes of furthering change, the confused adolescent who experiments, the emotionally distraught gay man who has a heterosexual affair). So behavior may not be an unequivocal index of orientation.

But if not behavior alone, what else should be assessed? The most obvious answer, one embraced by Shively and DeCecco, is *sexual attraction or arousal.* Surely sexual orientation is, at its most fundamental level, a matter of our sexual desires. Sell discusses the interesting point that prior to Kinsey, Ulrichs and others defined sexual orientation almost purely in terms of desire and with little or no reference to behavior per se.[13] Sell further documents the wide array of terms applied to the "psychological component" of sexual orientation as opposed to the behavioral dimension: *sexual passion, sexual urge, sexual feelings, sexual drive, sexual attraction, sexual interest, sexual arousal, sexual desire, sexual instinct, sexual identity* and *affectional preference*. But with these latter two terms, we see a further complexity in defining sexual orientation.

By "sexual arousal," we often mean something rather narrow that is well-captured by such terms as *urge, instinct* or *desire:* certain types of stimuli cause a person to become sexually excited, with that sexual arousal or excitement being fairly reliably manifested in heart-rate elevations and other indexes of physiological arousal in both genders, and also in more focal genital reactions of penile erection in males and vaginal lubrication in females. The sexual stimuli that elicit such reactions, stimuli often associated with one gender or the other, indicate some sort of directionality of orientation. But "sexual identity" and "affectional preference" transcend narrow sexual arousal. Speaking crudely, a certain man may be regularly aroused by the sight of ample female breasts (or some other specific sexual stimulus), but that person likely does not base a sexual identity on that sexual response alone or manifest an "affectional preference" for breasts. That man may be "turned on" by breasts, but is unlikely to "fall in love" with breasts.

It is immediately clear also that affectional preference does not exhaust the array of other concerns that we might be interested in when defining sexual orientation. In response to such complications Fritz Klein developed an assessment instrument, the Klein Sexual Orientation Grid (or KSOG), that looks at seven different possible dimensions of sexual orientation, which are sexual attraction, sexual behavior, sexual fantasies, emotional preference, social preference, self-identification and heterosexual/homosexual lifestyle.[14] We have already discussed attraction and behavior. Klein added fantasies out of a concern that sexual attraction is often confounded by nonsexual variables, such as in the common observation that some aspects of sexual attraction are linked with such variables as social status (e.g., women who find attractive men with high perceived wealth and power), and so the most pure measure of what we are sexually aroused by may be reflected most basically in what a person fantasizes about sexually. Emotional preference refers to romantic attraction or infatuation, who we tend to "fall in love with," and such infatuations are usually—but not necessarily—linked with sexual attraction per se. Social preference refers to patterns of affiliation that may be influenced by sexual orientation; Klein chose to include this measure despite its unclear linkage to sexual arousal per se. Self-identification refers to the person's embrace of the personal identity of homosexual or heterosexual (or gradations between). Finally, heterosexual/homosexual lifestyle refers to the immersion into the prototypical life patterns that Klein associates with the prototypical heterosexual or homosexual orientations (the heterosexual "family man or woman," the "fully out" gay man or lesbian).

Klein's dimensions, on the one hand, expand our awareness of the array of variables that can go into the composite we think of as sexual orientation. But the exact formulation of these specific dimensions is debatable. For example, is attraction really separate from fantasy? And what does social preference have to do with sexual orientation; is a heterosexual man who works with and pals with women somehow less (or more) heterosexual because of certain friendship patterns? To complicate the matter further, Klein did not assume that these seven areas remain static, and so assessed each of these in the past, the present and as the person would like to experience them in some "ideal" sense.

The enormous complexity of defining or understanding sexual orientation now confronts us. The "pure" type of the homosexual by Klein's criteria would be the person whose experience past, present and in the ideal is only and exclusively homosexual attraction, behavior, fantasy, romantic infatuation, social networking, identity and lifestyle, with no element of heterosexual response. But what about that same person considered *the instant after* a dramatic conversion to conservative Christianity, who remains exactly the same in terms of the past and the present on each of the seven variables, but now switches his or her ideal to the heterosexual norms for all seven variables because he or she has become convinced that homosexual conduct is immoral and thus wants to be healed and become heterosexual? What about the young adult raised in a conservative Christian family whose conscious experiences of sexual attraction and fantasy, and whose experiences of romantic infatuation as well, are strongly and exclusively homosexual, but who has never acted (behavior) on those attractions, who is repulsed by the idea of embracing homosexual identity, and who has never lived openly (or covertly) as a member of the gay community? All three of these individuals in the past and present would experience the same levels of and exclusivity of homosexual arousal and desire, but would score very differently on a measure of sexual orientation, like the KSOG, that measures not just desire but also behavior, identification, lifestyle and so forth. Are all three equally homosexual?

Before we conclude our discussion of the definitional issues involved in thinking clearly about sexual orientation, let us come full circle back to the issue of categorization. Kinsey and others have challenged and even derided the idea of categorization in favor of viewing sexual orientation as a continuum (or a wide array of continua) of sexual interest. But the idea of categorization has not been vanquished. Two continuing intellectual debates indicate that this issue is still open to review and reformulation.

The first is the conceptual debate between essentialists and social constructionists. The basic debate boils down to the issue of whether or not homosexuality is a "real" thing (like the biological species Homo sapiens) or a category that exists only at this moment in time because of our shared understanding in society (like the description "Republican" in twenty-first-century America). Essentialists argue that the term *homosexual* accurately defines an aspect of a person's self or inner core or nature that is a given or enduring and nonarbitrary characteristic, so that sexual orientation is intimately intertwined with one's true identity as a human being. As researcher Edward Laumann and his colleagues described essentialism, "The category *homosexual* describes an aspect of the person that corresponds to some objective core or inner essence of the person."[15] We might say that the essentialist argues that "homosexual" is a real and critically important description of a person in some manner parallel to that individual being a "female" or a "human being," a description which is assumed to be of a real, enduring and universal categorization. If the essentialists are right, there always have been and always will be homosexuals as a distinct class of persons, parallel to the existence of males and females. The failure of some cultures to recognize this enduring category represents ignorance, a failure to acknowledge what is ultimately a fact that exists independent of our perceptions of it.

Social constructionists do not deny the existence of same-sex behaviors, attractions and so forth. But in contrast to the essentialists, they argue that as a culture we have *constructed* categories of heterosexual and homosexual people on the basis of these behaviors and attractions. These categories are historical and cultural artifacts, like our political categorization in contemporary America of Democrats and Republicans. These categorizations may not be enduring. In support of their position, social constructionists point to the incredible array of ways that people in different cultures construe sexual orientation and desire. Indeed, in many societies today, homosexual attraction and behavior are recognized *without* the categorization of "the homosexual" existing.[16] The example of the New Guinea tribe described by Gilbert Herdt is instructive here: The tribe systematically exposes its unmarried male children to extensive homosexual experience from about the age of six to the age of marriage in the late teens or early twenties, and then expects them to function heterosexually in marriage with no further experience of homosexual activity for the rest of their lives.[17] In this tribe, where oral sex between unmarried males is prescribed and celebrated (with prepubescent boys as the fellators and postpubescent young men the fellatees, on the belief that without ingesting the "milk of men" the boys will not mature into men), no concept of "homosexual orientation" exists. How is this possible unless the concept of "homosexual orientation" only exists as a cultural creation in a given culture in a given moment in time?

The core debate between these two ideologies is not about whether the class "homosexuals" exists in contemporary Western culture; it is rather about whether that category of persons exists beyond (one could even say in spite of) our human recognition of it, or whether that category of persons exists because we as a culture have created it to make sense of the fluid pattern of same-sex attraction and sexual behavior we see.

That leads to the second continuing intellectual debate. The categorization debate is also still alive as an empirical scientific question. One example of this debate will have to suffice. Using similar complex statistical techniques for the detection of underlying categories or taxa ("nonarbitrary classes whose existence is an empirical question and not a matter of mere semantic convenience"),[18] two different research teams came up with two very different answers to the question of whether discrete classes of heterosexual and homosexual people exist. Nick Haslam analyzed the responses of over 1,000 men on the Masculinity-Femininity Scale of the Minnesota Multiphasic Personality Inventory-2, and reported that the results suggested "the latent variable underlying male sexual orientation is not discrete."[19] Sexual orientation for males, in other words, is better described by a series of continua and not by discrete categories. In contrast, Steven Gangestad and his colleagues reported that they found evidence of two "latent taxa," heterosexual and homosexual, in their measures, which were more directly targeted at sexual orientation.[20] Curiously, though, the latter study reported that the taxa associated with homosexual preference applied to 12 to 15% of the males in their sample and 5 to 10% of the women, when the percentages in the sample that reported homosexual behavior, arousal or identification was much smaller; this finding calls into question the meaning of the findings. This debate is alive and well.

The complexity and ambiguity of the very concept of sexual orientation challenge any work in this area. Even so, for research to occur in any area related to homosexuality, *one must embrace a definition of sexual orientation and then live with its shortcomings*. This is exemplified by Susan D. Cochran, a research clinical psychologist and epidemiologist who is also a lesbian, in her work studying the mental health of the homosexual community. As recipient of the 2001 Award for Distinguished Contributions to Research in Public Policy of the American Psychological Association, she noted in her award address that the study of the mental health of the homosexual community cannot proceed without a definition of what makes a person appropriately categorizable as a homosexual. Cochran wrote:

> Sexual orientation is a multidimensional concept including intercorrelated dimensions of sexual attraction, behavior, and fantasies, as well as emotional, social, and lifestyle preferences. . . . Some of the research reviewed here used inclusion criteria that relied on respondents' self-identification as lesbian, gay, or bisexual, as determined by various measurement strategies that do not always precisely agree with each other. Other studies used reports of a history of same-gender sexual partners, using different time frames, to classify individuals. Still others used sampling location, such as recruitment from a venue frequented by lesbians or gay men, paired with reports of sexual minority identity or same-gender sexual behavior or desire, to determine eligibility. Many researchers put lesbians or gay men in the same category as bisexuals, whether determined by self-identification or sexual behavior, generally to improve statistical power in examining differences from heterosexuals. Although currently much debate exists in the field over both essentialist and social constructionist views of sexual orientation, . . . in the present work I refer to those individuals who experience same-gender sexual desire or behavior or who label themselves with any of a number of terms (e.g., lesbian, homosexual, gay, bisexual, questioning) that reflect a sense of possessing, at least in part, a same-gender sexual orientation. Given the current state of the field, it would be premature to imply greater specificity.[21]

To repeat for emphasis, Cochran bases her work on the definition of *homosexual* as "those individuals who experience same-gender sexual desire *or* behavior *or* who label themselves with any of a number of terms (e.g., lesbian, homosexual, gay, bisexual, questioning) that reflect a sense of possessing, at least in part, a same-gender sexual orientation" (emphasis added). We must look carefully at this definition. Its use of the inclusive "or" is crucial, as this allows a person to be categorized as homosexual on the basis of desire alone, behavior alone or identity label alone, or by any of the three in combination.

Such a definition, while perhaps justifiable for the kinds of questions Cochran is pursuing and the populations she is working with, will not suffice here. We find it necessary, as argued by Sell, to recognize that the two most basic definitional components of homosexuality are the psychological component and the behavioral component. Further, based on our own understanding both of sexual orientation and of the unique individuals and unique life circumstances of the individuals in this study, we must put priority in our definition of sexual orientation on the *psychological component* of attraction, desire or arousal. The individuals in our study, as discussed in chapter two, have religious and moral reasons for both refraining from homosexual behavior and from embracing self-identification as a gay man or lesbian woman, and thus to insist on same-sex behavior as a defining characteristic of homosexual orientation would be unreasonable.

We are in good company in our emphasis on the psychological component. J. Michael Bailey and his colleagues, in their most recent exploration of the possible genetic contributors to the causation of sexual orientation, stated:

> Most current researchers, including us, define sexual orientation psychologically rather than behaviorally. . . . Sexual orientation is one's degree of sexual attraction to men or women. Of course, sexual orientation should be closely related to sexual experiences with one sex or the other, though many factors, especially social ones, could cause sexual orientation and sexual behavior to correlate less than perfectly. . . . [W]e focus more on psychological rather than behavioral sexual orientation because we suspect that the former is more stable than the latter and, furthermore, because psychological sexual orientation can typically be measured for individuals who have not had sex.[22]

Thus we will define same-gender or homosexual sexual orientation by the experience of same-gender sexual desire; the corollary experiences of same-gender sexual behavior or of self-identification with such terms as lesbian, homosexual or gay will be supportive of such categorization but not necessary for it. If this definition seems unsatisfactory, welcome to the conceptual morass of research on sexual orientation!

Review of Existing Measurement Options

Once one has a conceptual definition of what Cochran calls same-gender sexual orientation, the next step is to operationalize that definition. In empirical research, every concept in play in the empirical study must be defined operationally, that is, defined by the specific operations and actions used to measure it. While we have embraced a definition of same-gender sexual orientation that focuses on the psychological component of sexual attraction and desire, we will use a variety of operational measures of it that have been published in the scholarly literature.

One of the earliest decisions we made in structuring the current research project was to use a multiplicity of measures of sexual orientation. This strategy was deliberate, based on our observation that one of the primary grounds on which prior research of change of sexual orientation was dismissed was the way orientation was measured and "change" was defined. We concur with the criticism leveled against such methods as a simple five-point rating scale of "improvement" (undefined) or "satisfaction with treatment" (again, undefined). Similarly, a simple rating of agreement on a five-point rating scale to the stem "I am homosexual" is a crude measure of change.

It is important to point out, nonetheless, that almost every critical review of the change literature dismisses the evidence presented for change based on the dissatisfaction of the reviewer with the method used to measure change of sexual orientation, this *when there appears to be no satisfactory measure of sexual orientation (or its change) in the literature*. In other words, older literature suggesting that change is possible for some has come under withering criticism for not using valid, well-researched measures of sexual orientation, *when in fact no such measures exist*. We will soon document this, with a review of specific measures of sexual orientation. It seems questionable to dismiss prior research by saying, "The study should have used valid measures," when no method exists that meets the standard of validity invoked. But before we interact with that literature, we want to be explicit that the only way we could conceive of addressing such anticipated criticism of our own study was to *use every measure with a significant research support in the literature* to measure sexual orientation change in our study. The only exception to this rule was psychophysiological measurement, which we did not use at all; we documented in chapter four the questionable validity, the insurmountable pragmatic problems, and the moral and ethical objections involved in such psychophysiological measurement, and for these reasons chose not to use it.

We turn now to our review of the options for measurement of sexual orientation that were available at the time this study began in the late 1990s. No new well-validated measures have appeared in the literature since that time, so as of this writing, we can still claim to have used all of the available measures that exist in the literature today.

We begin with Ronald Sell's overall assessment of existing options for measuring sexual orientation: *"None of these [existing measures] is completely satisfactory."*[23] Summarizing his review by saying none of the measures was "completely satisfactory" is something of an understatement given his specific conclusions about specific psychological scales. According to Sell:

- "the Kinsey scale is unsatisfactory"
- "the Shiveley and DeCecco scale is unsatisfactory"
- "the Klein scale is unsatisfactory"

"Unsatisfactory" is significantly stronger than "not completely satisfactory." By the same standards applied by Sell in this analysis to other measures, the measure that Sell himself proposed for measuring sexual orientation is unsatisfactory.

Next, let us briefly review what goes into making a measure of sexual orientation, or indeed any important psychological trait, satisfactory. The two essential characteristics of high quality psychological assessment are reliability and validity. Reliability refers to the stability of the measurement technique, to its tendency to produce the same measure of a stable trait as it is measured over multiple assessments. Think, for instance, of the measurement of intelligence, a trait that (like sexual orientation) we assume to be relatively stable. A measure of intelligence that produces an IQ estimate of 85 one day and 115 the next for the same person is, regardless of its other qualities, unreliable and hence of questionable utility. The demonstration of measurement reliability requires repeated measurement of a stable population.

Validity is not the same thing as reliability. Reliability is a necessary but not sufficient condition for validity; a measure that is reliable may not be valid, but a measure that is not reliable is certain not to be valid. A broken digital thermometer that reads "62°" in a hot oven and in the freezer is reliable (producing the same measurement) but not valid; the fact that measurement of skull circumference is reliable does not make it a valid measure of intelligence. Validity is the concept we invoke to explore the question of whether we have solid reasons for believing that our psychological measure is measuring what we intend it to, whether the measurement technique mirrors the essential characteristics of the real human phenomenon we are trying to capture in numbers. And there are different concepts that researchers have in mind when they discuss validity:

- *Face validity* refers to a certain commonsense evaluation of the congruence between the questions asked and the concepts being measured. A measure of introversion-extroversion should ask questions about whether a person likes to be around people or to be alone, and probably not ask questions about political opinions or tastes in music.
- *Construct validity* refers to the tendency of a valid measure to be grounded in a conceptually established or justified set of distinctions. The "construct" is the theoretical entity you are trying to measure. If we are going to measure "sexual orientation" then a rigorous intellectual background to the concept should exist, a background which we trust we have already established.
- *Convergent* or *concurrent validity* refers to the tendency of a valid instrument to demonstrate that it generates similar results when compared to other measures of the same or related constructs. It is for this reason that many new psychological measures report their correlations with other existing and respected measures of similar constructs. For example, a new "brief" measure of intelligence might be "validated" by reporting its correlations with a respected and longer measure of intelligence.
- *Discriminant validity* refers to the tendency of a valid instrument to demonstrate a pattern of discriminating or distinguishing the construct being measured from others with which it is *not* related. A measure of introversion-extroversion should not demonstrate a significant statistical overlap with a measure of intelligence or of political opinion, and if it does correlate with such measures, it is not demonstrating discriminant validity, which indicates that something is wrong with the measure.

- *Criterion validity* is perhaps the most crucial and most challenging of the types of validity, referring to rigorous empirical demonstration that the measurement approach is supported by a clear pattern of evidence that relates scores on the assessment measure with *measurable criteria apart from the measure itself.* Intelligence measures should be shown to predict real-life behaviors that are conceptually tied to intelligence, such as later success in life or ability to solve problems; measures predictive of psychosis should be associated with diagnosis with a psychotic disorder by skilled professionals who have directly interviewed the patient and who have no knowledge of the patient's scores on the assessment instrument.

Generally speaking, the measures of sexual orientation reviewed here (and this means all available measures) have only modest evidence of reliability, the most basic requirement of valid assessment, demonstrate some measure of face validity (after all, they all ask direct questions about the directionality of sexual interest or desire), have construct validity of some sort (though they conceptualize sexual orientation differently as previously discussed), and have minimal or no demonstrable discriminant criterion validity since there have been so few empirical studies that have utilized them.

We turn now to a review of the actual instruments used to measure sexual orientation in this study, reminding the reader that we have attempted to use all of the measures available in the scholarly literature on sexual orientation. The following, then, is *both* a review of all of the existing assessment options *and* of all the measures used in this study. In this review we rely less on our own review of the evidence and more on that of Ronald Sell, in whose writing full documentation of the specific research base for this review can be found.

Kinsey Scale

The most well-known scale is the Kinsey seven-point scale of sexual orientation (see p. 200). Kinsey is known for introducing the idea that sexual orientation might be better understood as existing on a continuum, and the scale he developed to measure sexual orientation remains foundational for many of the sexual orientation scales used today. Further, it is still often used as the basic measure of sexual orientation, as in the famous studies of Dean

Hamer and his colleagues of a possible genetic locus for sexual orientation.[24]

When used in practice, there is some variability in how the Kinsey scale is utilized. In the original Kinsey studies the scale was applied by the researchers to rate the sexual orientations of the participants interviewed for his studies after the interviewers had gathered the details of the sexual histories of the participants. The Kinsey scale, in other words, was a rating by researchers based on the behavioral patterns reported by subjects in an interview. Contemporary uses of the Kinsey scale depart from this original methodology in several ways. First, contemporary researchers are more likely to use the Kinsey scale as a self-report of the subject than as a rating assigned by a researcher. Second, Kinsey scales are as often constructed with reference to sexual attraction or arousal as they are for behavior, or often with neither focus clarified.

Sell judges the Kinsey scale unsatisfactory for two reasons. First, he argues that the Kinsey scale "forces the artificial combination of psychological and behavioral components,"[25] referring to the sort of usage we just discussed; that is, when individuals are asked to rate their sexual orientation on the scale without clarification of whether they are to judge based on their behavior, attractions or both. Second, Sell argues that the scale "perhaps incorrectly requires individuals to make tradeoffs between homosexuality and heterosexuality."[26] This second criticism is precisely the sort already discussed that gave rise to the Shively and DeCecco scale, which is discussed next.

Although the Kinsey scale is widely used, information about its reliability and validity is largely absent.

Shively and DeCecco Scale

Shively and DeCecco proposed that measurement of sexual orientation be expanded to four five-point scales on which dimensions of sexual orientation can be independently determined.[27] Two scales measure heterosexuality and the other two measure homosexuality. The same two ratings, one of physical preference and one of affectional preference, are required separately for homosexual inclination and heterosexual inclination. Shively and DeCecco viewed it as essential for homosexuality and heterosexuality (homosexual attraction and behavior, and heterosexual attraction and behavior) to be measured *independently* rather than as a continuum, because a bipolar model requires an individual to express one orientation at the expense of the other. In other words, it requires conceptually that as one preference increases, the other must decrease, and that those in the middle of the continuum must experience diminished attraction in comparison to those at the ends of the continuum. Shively and DeCecco argued that their theory allows for more variety in the expression of sexual orientation, due to its independent ratings of homosexuality and heterosexuality, as well as its focus on both the physical and affectional expressions of sexual orientation.

Shively and DeCecco modeled their scale after the sex-role inventory developed by Bem to measure androgyny (see p. 201).[28] Shively and DeCecco viewed this independent measurement of homosexual and heterosexual arousal as essential to the measurement of sexual orientation as well. This scale was set up as a contrast to scales such as Kinsey's, in which a higher level of homosexuality indicated a lower level of heterosexuality or vice versa.

While its use of independently determined measures of degrees of sexuality may help researchers understand some aspects of an individual's sexuality more clearly, the Shively and DeCecco scale is "unsatisfactory," according to Sell, because "its properties have not been thoroughly investigated and its consideration of physical and affectional preferences may be oversimplified or even inappropriate."[29] At the same time, Shively and DeCecco added to our understanding of sexual orientation by articulating the importance of considering the multidimensional nature of sexual orientation.

Sell Assessment of Sexual Orientation

Ronald Sell sought to improve on the work of Shively and DeCecco, following their rejection of the idea of measuring homosexuality and heterosexuality on the same scale and embracing their methodology of measuring homosexuality and heterosexuality on separate scales.[30] Sell claimed to have improved on their measure by expanding the assessment focus from just behavior and attraction to behavior, attraction and identity, and by adding more questions about a wider array of specific dimensions of physical and emotional preference. The Sell Assessment asks six specific questions about sexual attractions (three each about same and opposite gender attraction), four questions about sexual contact/behavior (two each about same and opposite gender behavior), and two questions about sexual identity (one each about homosexual and heterosexual identity).

The six questions on intensity of sexual attraction are set up in groups of three basic questions, targeting sexual attraction to each sex in separate questions. Sell views the questions concerning sexual attractions as most important, because he defines sexual orientation as the "extent of sexual attractions toward members of the other, same, both sexes, or neither." Sell compared his results to the Kinsey scale by classifying groupings of responses with corresponding Kinsey classifications in order to determine the construct validity of the scale.

While the Sell scale provides a comprehensive view of sexual orientation, its properties are untested, as yet, in the context of empirical research. Sell himself provided no empirical data on administration of the scale; indeed, he gave no indication that it had ever been administered to anyone. We could find no instances after the initial publication of the scale when it has actually been used in research.

In practical application we found the Sell Assessment to be unworkably complex in some respects and at points counterintuitive (or arguably ill-conceived). The typical psychological inventory simply sums responses to separate items, whether the items score dichotomously (true-false, yes-no) or on a continuum (three-, five- or seven-point scales). In contrast, to determine its ratings for homosexual attraction, the Sell Assessment requires examination of a cluster of three items where attraction is rated (the number of persons the subject was attracted to, the frequency of such attraction and the maximal intensity of such attraction).[31] The numerical scores, which range over either seven or eight-point continua, are converted then to four ordinal categorizations by letter. (The first problem with the Sell is detected immediately at this point, as figure 3 governing the conversion from numerical to ordinal alphabetic scores reports only conversions for seven-point scales when several of the questions involve eight-point scales). Then the scorer takes the highest of the three ordinal categorizations, which determines the rating of homosexual attraction.[32]

Establishing the rating of bisexuality is even more complex procedurally and at points conceptually ill-conceived. To focus only on attraction, Sell requires that pairs of scores that contrast the number of persons the subject was attracted to for males and females be entered on the X and Y axes of a grid, with a resulting ordinal score (in this case numeric rather than alphabetic) to then be read from the figure where the X and Y coordinates intersect. The grid itself was constructed rationally/conceptually and not empirically. This reduces the six attraction scales (three each for attraction to males and females) to three ratings, from which we are instructed to take the highest as the summary rating for attraction. The ordinal scores Sell creates for the grid, however, do not always make sense. It does make sense to categorize a person reporting that she is "Extremely Attracted" to both men and women as "4-Very Bisexual," but we cannot understand Sell's rationale for assigning a male who reports being "Slightly Attracted" to males and "Extremely Attracted" to females a bisexuality score of "3-Moderately Bisexual" as opposed to "0, 1-Not at all Bisexual" or "2-Slightly Bisexual." Sell's bisexuality ratings are suspect.

For these reasons, in the end we decided not to analyze the results obtained from the Sell instrument.

KLEIN SEXUAL ORIENTATION GRID

Earlier in this chapter (p. 204) we discussed the way that Fritz Klein conceptualized sexual-orientation measurement around seven hypothesized dimensions of orientation. Klein began developing his ideas about measurement of sexual orientation in a popular book about bisexuality,[33] then began formalizing his ideas about a scale[34] with the eventual result being a formal publication of his scale as the Klein Sexual Orientation Grid (KSOG)[35] with reliability and validity documentation reported in an unpublished doctoral dissertation.[36]

Though Shively and DeCecco and Sell each abandoned the Kinsey approach of placing homosexuality and heterosexuality at opposite ends of a continuum, Klein accepted Kinsey's basic methodological premise of a bipolar scale, but in two other ways he elaborated on Kinsey's comparatively simple method of assessing sexual orientation. First, he added in assessment of not just behavior and attraction but a total of seven dimensions of sexual orientation, including behavior and attraction (specifically, sexual attraction, sexual behavior, sexual fantasies, emotional preference, social preference, self-identification and heterosexual-homosexual lifestyle). In addition, the scale is presented without the presumption that sexual orientation is fixed. Klein's scale highlighted the importance of examining the malleability and complexity of sexual orientation in developing a comprehensive measure by asking those using the scale to rate each of the seven dimensions of sexual orientation in the past, at the present and in the ideal.

There are a number of possible advantages to the KSOG. Assessing multiple dimensions provides the opportunity to obtain a more exhaustive view of an individual's sexual orientation, especially when the dimensions are measured at a number of different time periods in the individual's life. At the same time, problems can arise from assessing multiple dimensions, because as each item is added, the overall scale becomes more burdensome and less practical for research purposes.[37] Measuring sexual orientation on a number of separate dimensions will provide more data than other measures, but may be less meaningful because of the difficulty of examining the volumes of data that it produces. *This is especially so since Klein argued that no overall score of sexual orientation should be derived from his scale.* Following Klein on this leads to real problems in using the scale; without some sort of summary score or scores, one is simply left with twenty-one separate scales without any guidance on how to aggregate or summarize the information they contain.

Weinrich and his research team conducted an empirical analysis of the Klein Sexual Orientation Grid.[38] They performed a factor analysis of the KSOG in order to better understand the Klein scale. The authors utilized two samples for this analysis, the first of which included 90 men recruited for a fat metabolism study, and an HIV sample of 78 gay and bisexual men who were enrolled in a large AIDS research center. Both of these groups of men had the Klein administered to them as part of their participation in two moderate-size studies. Generally speaking, these are extraordinarily small sample sizes on which to run factor analyses, which generally require samples many multiples of this size to derive meaningful results. Still, the researchers claimed that their analysis indicated that the results on the KSOG reflect a single underlying statistical factor, which they called Sexual Orientation. If the findings are valid despite the small sample sizes, this general factor would indicate that most of the variables hang together and point toward an overall sexual orientation (heterosexual or homosexual). Analyses of both samples indicated that the Klein items represent, as desired, a homogeneous collection of variables. At the same time, the analysis indicated that differences do exist among individuals and groups within these respective orientations. Because of the small sample size utilized in this factor analysis, these results must be examined with caution and viewed as possible properties of the measure. A later study by Weinrich and Klein found that the KSOG had the capacity to produce at least somewhat stable distinctions between groups of bisexuals, specifically showing differential patterns of fluidity in sexual orientation among the identified subgroups and among men and women.[39] This study also showed Klein's social preference measure to be uniformly unreliable. The KSOG is, on the one hand, more thoroughly conceptualized and researched than most other measures, but on the other hand, compared to most other psychological assessment instruments has a thin layer of empirical support for its utility.

Sell judges the Klein Sexual Orientation Grid unsatisfactory on two additional points. First, Sell objected to the lack of clear theoretical merit to each of the seven putative dimensions of sexual orientation, saying "the relative importance of each dimension in measuring sexual orientation has not been thoroughly investigated or grounded in theory." Second, and as with the Kinsey scale, "Klein required subjects to make tradeoffs between heterosexuality and homosexuality on his scale."[40]

Conclusion on measurement methods. If we insisted that research on sexual orientation or its change requires a respected and well-validated measurement measure of sexual orientation around which professional consensus had emerged, we would not do research in this area at all. Given the difficulties of even finding a "representative sample" of people who are homosexual, the prospects of *ever* having such a validated instrument are bleak. Our choice was either to give up on doing research or to plow ahead using *all instruments for which any substantive research base at all existed.* That is the strategy we chose.

THE SPECIFIC FORM OF OUR MEASUREMENT

The overriding conceptual approach we took to the measurement of sexual orientation was that of simply using all contemporary measures that had any modicum of empirical support behind them. Though we administered the Sell instrument, we did not analyze it for the reasons discussed earlier (see pp. 216-217), reasons which only became obvious when the nightmarish task of scoring and interpreting the Sell was before us. Now we present the specific methods we used to assess sexual orientation:

1. *Categorical "self" and "orientation" ratings variables.* When surveys assess sexual orientation, they frequently rely on a single question: "Do you think of yourself as gay, straight, bisexual or other?" We included such a question in our survey, but also realized we faced a dilemma in using this question. All of our participants were, at the time of the Time 1 assessment, active in an Exodus ministry, and these ministries often (though not always) strongly urge that their participants not build their identity around their sexual attractions, with the particular implication that they not describe their *selves* as homosexual. So persons of strong and stable homosexual *attraction* might well, under the influence of their Exodus ministry, answer the question "Do you think of yourself as gay, straight, bisexual or other?" with the answer "straight" even though they experience homosexual attractions exclusively and powerfully.

To address this problem, we created a second version of the question, a version stating that "Some people would use a different word to describe their sexual orientation than they would use to describe 'themselves.' " In the analyses that follow we will distinguish these two questions, respectively, as the "Self Rating" and the "Orientation Rating." These questions were asked of our participants *verbally* as part of the person-to-person interview protocol.

18. Do you think of yourself as . . .
    ___heterosexual (straight)
    ___homosexual (gay, lesbian)
    ___bisexual
    ___something else (specify)________________________
    ___DON'T KNOW

19. Some people would use a different word to describe their sexual orientation than they would use to describe "themselves." How would you describe your sexual orientation? We mean here not what you desire to become through change, but the sexual orientation you were before you began to attempt to change.
___heterosexual (straight)
___homosexual (gay, lesbian)
___bisexual
___something else (specify)___________________
___DON'T KNOW2

2. *Kinsey one-item, two-item and expanded ratings variables.* The Kinsey scale was used as a self-administered set of ratings in the interview portion of our study; these questions are located in the Time 1 interview protocol, section 4, questions 21-24 in both the Phase 1 and 2 forms. By "self-administered" we mean that subjects assigned themselves a value on the scale as opposed to the original Kinsey methodology of an interviewer assigning a rating. As with the Klein, for Phase 2 subjects (who had been in the change process for over one year) we asked for Kinsey ratings for their sexual attractions before they began the change process.

These questions were (in accord with Kinsey's original methodology) asked of our participants *verbally* as part of the person-to-person interview protocol. For the three versions of the Kinsey ratings that follow, participants were shown a hand card that had the seven-point Kinsey scale reproduced for them for reference as they answered.

Kinsey one-item rating. Given that some of our population had never been "sexually intimate" with a person, and because the most basic aspect of sexual orientation is the directionality of attraction (which seems much more stable and enduring) and not behavior (which is much more subject to a wide range of determinants), we made the Kinsey rating of sexual attraction our single measure of sexual orientation:

22. How would you describe the gender of the persons to whom you are sexually attracted (meaning the gender of the people who you tend to

2These questions are from section 4, items 18 and 19 of the Time 1, Phase 1 interview protocol.

find arousing or who tend to "turn you on sexually")?
____Exclusively heterosexual.
____Largely heterosexual, but incidental homosexual.
____Largely heterosexual, but more than incidental homosexual.
____Equal amounts of heterosexual and homosexual.
____Largely homosexual, but more than incidental heterosexual.
____Largely homosexual, but incidental heterosexual.
____Exclusively homosexual.3

Kinsey two-item rating. The original Kinsey ratings assessed both the directionality of attraction and of sexual behavior choice. Therefore we created a two-item Kinsey rating that averaged these two measures.

21. How would you describe the gender of the persons with whom you have been sexually intimate physically? [Repeat if needed: Our term *sexually intimate* means sexual intercourse between you and another person, whether your partner was a man or a woman, where there was genital contact between the partners such that at least one of you had an orgasm.]
____Exclusively heterosexual.
____Largely heterosexual, but incidental homosexual.
____Largely heterosexual, but more than incidental homosexual.
____Equal amounts of heterosexual and homosexual.
____Largely homosexual, but more than incidental heterosexual.
____Largely homosexual, but incidental heterosexual.
____Exclusively homosexual.

22. How would you describe the gender of the persons to whom you are sexually attracted (meaning the gender of the people who you tend to find arousing or who tend to "turn you on sexually")?
____Exclusively heterosexual.
____Largely heterosexual, but incidental homosexual.
____Largely heterosexual, but more than incidental homosexual.
____Equal amounts of heterosexual and homosexual.
____Largely homosexual, but more than incidental heterosexual.

3This questions is from section 4, item 22 of the Time 1, Phase 1 interview protocol.

____Largely homosexual, but incidental heterosexual.
____Exclusively homosexual.4

For both the two-item Kinsey and the expanded Kinsey rating to follow, if a subject reported in question 20 that they had never been "sexually intimate" with a person, then the two-item and expanded Kinsey ratings were calculated with question 21 omitted. This affected a small number of subjects in our population, because for this religiously conservative population where chastity is valued, some of our participants had never been sexually active.

Expanded Kinsey rating. In the extensive literature discussing sexual orientation and its assessment, one set of complaints lodged against the Kinsey ratings has been their tendency to delimit sexual orientation to raw physical/sexual desire. Feminist critiques in particular have pointed to the importance of emotional and romantic attraction, to infatuation, to the experience of "falling in love." There has also been some discussion of the importance of fantasy in reflecting sexual orientation. Therefore, we created an "expanded" Kinsey rating composed of four measures: the measures of attraction and behavior already quoted, and two further items assessing emotional and romantic attraction and assessing fantasy. The expanded Kinsey rating is the average of these four measures (with behavior omitted for those participants who had never been sexually active). While these two added questions are similar to those asked in other assessment instruments used in this study and for which validation research is available (such as the Klein and Shively-and-DeCecco scales), we recognize that the specific way in which we ask these questions has not been validated and so these results must be interpreted cautiously.

23. How would you describe the gender of the persons with whom you have tended to be infatuated with or have a "crush" on or to "fall in love" with? By these terms, we mean the people with whom you have tended to develop intense emotional attachments.
____Exclusively heterosexual.
____Largely heterosexual, but incidental homosexual.
____Largely heterosexual, but more than incidental homosexual.

4These questions are from section 4, items 21 and 22 of the Time 1, Phase 1 interview protocol.

____Equal amounts of heterosexual and homosexual.
____Largely homosexual, but more than incidental heterosexual.
____Largely homosexual, but incidental heterosexual.
____Exclusively homosexual.

24. How would you describe the gender of the persons about whom you have tended to fantasize sexually or to have sexual dreams about? In your unguarded moments, what is the gender of the people who come to mind involuntarily as the ones you are sexually attracted to?
____Exclusively heterosexual.
____Largely heterosexual, but incidental homosexual.
____Largely heterosexual, but more than incidental homosexual.
____Equal amounts of heterosexual and homosexual.
____Largely homosexual, but more than incidental heterosexual.
____Largely homosexual, but incidental heterosexual.
____Exclusively homosexual.5

3. ***Shively and DeCecco ratings variables.*** Shively and DeCecco and others have suggested, following the androgyny literature on masculinity and femininity of the last several decades, that sexual orientation is best conceived not on a single bipolar scale (like the Kinsey) where more of homosexuality necessarily means less of heterosexuality. Rather, they argued, homosexual and heterosexual attraction may be relatively orthogonal or independent from each other, and lumping them together on a single bipolar scale may mask important aspects of the person's sexual orientation. Shively and DeCecco also distinguished between sexual attraction and emotional attraction.

We included two variants of the Shively and DeCecco approach to measuring sexual orientation. The Shively and DeCecco scale published in the literature is composed of four questions (items 25-28 in our interview) that ask for a rating of the sexual attraction and emotional attraction the person experiences *separately* to men and women. Thus we report a Shively and DeCecco rating for homosexual orientation that is an average of the person's reported sexual attraction and emotional attraction to persons of

5These questions are from section 4, items 23 and 24 of the Time 1, Phase 1 interview protocol.

the same sex (items 26 and 28), and report a Shively and DeCecco rating for heterosexual orientation that is an average of the person's reported sexual attraction and emotional attraction to persons of the other sex (items 25 and 27).

We also created an "Expanded" Shively and DeCecco rating. In our pilot research, participants complained that rating "how attracted" they were conflated issues of intensity of attraction and frequency of attraction. We found the same concerns reflected in scattered places in the literature discussing measurement and conceptualization of sexual orientation. Thus we created four additional questions that asked about intensity of attraction and frequency of attraction to persons of the same sex and to persons of the other sex. We report an expanded Shively and DeCecco rating for a male's homosexual orientation that is an average of the person's reported sexual attraction, emotional attraction, intensity of attraction and frequency of attraction to persons of the same sex (items 26, 28, 29, 31), and report a Shively and DeCecco rating for a male's heterosexual orientation that is an average of the person's reported sexual attraction, emotional attraction, intensity of attraction and frequency of attraction to persons of the other sex (items 25, 27, 30, 32). We reversed the last four items for women to create their expanded Shively and DeCecco rating for women. For Phase 2 subjects at Time 1, we used the questions that asked about orientation before they began the change process, and the numbering of specific items varied slightly from what we present here. We note that these expanded Shively and DeCecco ratings must be regarded with caution because validation work was not done on them beyond pretesting with our pilot subjects.

These Shively and DeCecco questions were asked of our participants *verbally* as part of the person-to-person interview protocol.

25. Please rate the degree to which you are *sexually attracted at a physical level* to the opposite sex:

1	2	3	4	5
Not at all Attracted Heterosexually		Somewhat Attracted Heterosexually		Very Attracted Heterosexually

26. Please rate the degree to which you are *sexually attracted at a physical level* to the same sex:

1	2	3	4	5
Not at all Attracted Homosexually		Somewhat Attracted Homosexually		Very Attracted Homosexually

27. Please rate the degree to which you are *emotionally attracted* to the opposite sex; the degree to which you tend to become infatuated with or "fall in love" with people of the opposite sex:

1	2	3	4	5
Not at all Attracted Heterosexually		Somewhat Attracted Heterosexually		Very Attracted Heterosexually

28. Please rate the degree to which you are *emotionally attracted* to the same sex; the degree to which you tend to become infatuated with or "fall in love" with people of the same sex:

1	2	3	4	5
Not at all Attracted Homosexually		Somewhat Attracted Homosexually		Very Attracted Homosexually

29. Please rate the *frequency* with which you feel sexually attracted to men.

1	2	3	4	5
Never		Sometimes		Daily or More Very Often

30. Using the same scale, please rate the frequency with which you feel sexually attracted to women.

1	2	3	4	5
Never		Sometimes		Daily or More Very Often

31. Please rate the intensity with which you can be sexually attracted to a man. Think of the time when you felt the strongest sexual attraction to a man in the last several years, and rate that experience:

1	2	3	4	5
Completely Unaroused "Cold"		Somewhat Aroused "Excited"		Totally Aroused "Consumed"

32. Please rate the intensity with which you can be sexually attracted to a woman. Think of the time when you felt the strongest sexual attraction to a woman in the last several years, and rate that experience:

1	2	3	4	5
Completely Unaroused "Cold"		Somewhat Aroused "Excited"		Totally Aroused "Consumed"6

4. *Klein Sexual Orientation Grid ratings variables.* The Klein Sexual Orientation Grid decomposes sexual orientation into seven dimensions (sexual attraction, sexual behavior, sexual fantasies, emotional preference, social preference, self-identification, homosexual-heterosexual lifestyle), each of which is rated in the past, present and in the ideal. Thus the Klein generates twenty-one ratings relevant to sexual orientation. Klein himself argued against creating any sort of composite score but rather called for looking at the twenty-one scores as a sort of profile. The KSOG (or Klein) was administered as a self-administered questionnaire (or SAQ).

One adaptation of the Klein that we made deserves comment. In Klein's original scale, *past* was undefined; the instructions provided no specification of the time frame to be considered "past." However, when defining *present,* Klein and his colleagues gave the following instructions: "select a number that describes your present sexual attraction using one year as the time period you examine."[41] To leave *past* undefined, or to always specify one year would have been problematic in our study given that we were measuring change from a baseline, and that baseline differed for Phase 1 (short-term) subjects and Phase 2 (longer-term) subjects. To that end, the SAQ form of the Klein for Phase 1 subjects being assessed at Time 1 used the seeming intent of the original Klein language in defining the past as being up until one year prior, but for Phase 2 subjects at Time 1, we defined past as "up to when you began the change process." Since these Phase 2 subjects had been in the change process with Exodus for one to three years, we felt that defining their past sexual orientation over a period when change should (according to Exodus) have been occurring would mask real findings of change. Thus the past was defined as the period before they be-

6These questions are from section 4, items 25 to 32 of the Time 1, Phase 1 interview protocol.

gan the change process for Phase 2 subjects. In all subsequent administrations of the Klein with all parts of our population, we left the definition of "the past" as before they began the change process, but we have never used these ratings in our analyses since "the past" being rated keeps retreating further from memory.

For our purposes it was not reasonable to use the Klein as a twenty-one-item profile of single items. We chose to create a composite score constructed from four items: sexual attraction, sexual fantasies, emotional preference and social preference. We omitted sexual behavior because some of our participants had limited or no sexual experience. We chose not to use self-identification because, as discussed earlier under Dichotomous ratings (see pp. 220-221), the Exodus ministries often strongly urge that their participants not build their identity around their sexual attractions, with the particular implication that they not describe their *selves* as homosexual. It thus seemed that Klein's measure of identity would have little relevance to the measurement of sexual orientation for our population and could introduce error variance. Finally, we excluded Klein's measure of homosexual-heterosexual lifestyle because few of our subjects at the start of the study were actively engaged in the homosexual lifestyle.

The Klein four-item rating we created was a simple numerical average of the four ratings: sexual attraction, sexual fantasies, emotional preference and social preference. Each of these Klein scores ranges potentially from 1 to 7 (just like the Kinsey, on which they are based), with a score of 1 indicating exclusive heterosexuality and a 7 exclusive homosexuality. The full Klein Sexual Orientation Grid as we used it can be reviewed on the website where we are archiving materials related to this project for public access at <www.ivpress.com>.

5. *Sell assessment of sexual orientation.* The Sell sexual orientation survey was administered as part of self-administered questionnaire 6 (or SAQ6), which was titled the "Sexual Orientation Survey" and which comprised the Sell instrument and the Yarhouse Sexual Orientation Thermometers. The complete Sell instrument as we used it can be reviewed on the website where we are archiving materials related to this project for public access at <www.ivpress.com>

6. *Yarhouse Sexual Orientation Thermometers variables.* Mark Yarhouse developed an experimental measure for this study, one that roughly followed the assumptions of Shively and DeCecco that sexual orientation is best conceived and measured by assessing homosexual and heterosexual attraction on separate scales, and further that "orientation" needs to be broken up into its constituent parts. Yarhouse accomplished the latter by assessing separately behavior, orientation, attraction and fantasy. We report on average scores on the Yarhouse Sexual Orientation Thermometer (YSOT) measures, which are simple averages of the four ratings, presented separately for homosexual and heterosexual experience. The YSOT heterosexual score, for example, is simply the average of the four questions querying heterosexual behavior, heterosexual orientation, heterosexual attraction and heterosexual fantasy. The YSOT was administered as part of self-administered questionnaire 6 (or SAQ6), which was titled the "Sexual Orientation Survey" and which comprised the Sell instrument and the YSOT.

The Yarhouse Sexual Orientation Thermometer instrument as we used it can be reviewed on the website where we are archiving materials related to this project for public access at <www.ivpress.com>.

7

Can Sexual Orientation Change?

Report of the Quantitative Analysis

"[Science produced by Christian persons would have to be] perfectly honest. Science twisted in the interests of apologetics would be sin and folly."

C. S. LEWIS, "Christian Apologetics," in *God in the Dock*

"[Qazi] Rahman says that his view of corrective therapies designed to turn gay men straight is simple—they will never work: 'You just can't do it. If people suggest they can, I ask them, "Can you turn someone from straight to gay? Show me the evidence." But it's never going to happen, is it?' "

QAZI RAHMAN, in "Born Gay or Made Gay: Which Camp Are You In?" *London Times*

"[The problem with research claiming to show sexual orientation change is that] treatment outcome is not followed and reported over time as would be the standard to test the validity of any mental health intervention."

AMERICAN PSYCHOLOGICAL ASSOCIATION WEBSITE

WHAT WERE OUR RESULTS? We briefly cover a few preparatory issues and then consider in sequence the results reported by subjects over time on our objective scales of sexual orientation. We report results on the following measures:

- categorical self-ratings of "self"
- categorical self-ratings of "sexual orientation"

- Kinsey scale ratings for single item, two item and expanded versions of the Kinsey scale
- Shively and DeCecco scale ratings
- Klein Sexual Orientation Grid scores
- an experimental measure, the Yarhouse Sexual Orientation Thermometer

On each of these measures, we report findings for three distinct populations (or more accurately, for the whole population and two distinct subpopulations). So we turn first to a description of those populations.

Analyses for the Whole Population and Two Subpopulations

In the following we will be presenting our analyses of outcomes on each of the major instruments for *three different populations* of research participants: the Whole Population, Phase 1 subjects, and for the Truly Gay subpopulation of the study.

The Whole Population. The presentation of the outcome results for the Whole Population for which we have data hardly needs explanation, but what may need some explanation is the way "whole population" can have different meanings. We began the study with 98 subjects, experienced erosion of our sample to 85 subjects at the Time 2 assessment, and then some further erosion to 73 cases at the Time 3 assessment. In the following presentation of our findings, we will always report first on the results from the initial (baseline) assessment at Time 1 compared to the results at Time 3 ("Time 1 to 3"), and since there were 73 cases on which we gathered data at Time 3, we can present comparisons only on those 73 cases for which we have data at both Times 1 and 3. Then we will present the same analyses, but comparing Time 1 to Time 2 (instead of Time 3), including only the 73 cases that were also available at Time 3. This allows us to look at change from Time 1 to Time 2, but with the exact same population as in the preceding Time 1 to 3 analysis. Finally, we will repeat the same Time 1 to Time 2 analysis, but on a slightly different population, that being all 85 cases for which we have data both at Time 1 and 2, regardless of their availability at the Time 3 assessment. In other words, the last two analyses are both Time 1 to Time 2 comparisons, but are either on only those for which we have Time 3 data as well (73), or on *all* those subjects for whom we have Time 2 data (85). Of course, missing data may result in our presenting Ns that are lower than the maximum possible in certain cells. This method of presentation will be repeated for each of the following two subpopulations.

Phase 1 ("early changers") subpopulation. Phase 1 participants (i.e., those who had at Time 1 been in the Exodus change process for less than one year) are analyzed separately because these were the subjects for whom we began measurement earlier in the change process. At Time 1, 57 (58.2%) of the total of 98 subjects were classified as Phase 1 subjects. Phase 2 subjects (those for whom we began assessment after they had been in the Exodus process for one to three years) must be seen as a less representative sample of those who begin the Exodus process; they are those who have "stuck it out" through the first year or more of a change process and thus likely are those who are experiencing more success in the change process. Phase 2 subjects were deemed likely to present a more optimistic picture of outcomes, and so we chose to analyze only Phase 1 results separately because those are more likely to represent the outcomes for the "average" person initiating this change process.

The Truly Gay subpopulation. We created the Truly Gay subpopulation out of an awareness that it has been a common rhetorical stance in the literature critical of any possibility of change to argue that anyone who has achieved change must not have been really gay to start off with. This is obviously both plausible and potentially circular (Why did the person fail to change? Because he was truly gay. Why did the person succeed in changing? Because he was not truly gay. How do you know that the person who changed was not truly gay? Because a truly gay person cannot change). We wanted to address this question empirically and so decided to create a subpopulation within our study of those who met fairly rigorous standards of "homosexualness."

In contrast, we note the remarkably lax standards for categorization as "homosexual" in many empirical studies. Two major sets of behavior genetics studies of the etiology of sexual orientation can serve as quick examples. The two famous studies by Michael Bailey and his colleagues that did so much to advance the erroneous notion that there was a gay gene classified as homosexual anyone who reported any rating on the Kinsey scale other than a 0 (Exclusively heterosexual) or 1 (Largely heterosexual, but incidentally homosexual).[1] The parallel study by Kenneth Kendler and his colleagues took the same standard.[2] We chose to adopt a much more rigorous standard of the subject scoring above the midpoint of bisexuality on a Kinsey-type scale. For graphic clarity see figure 7.1.

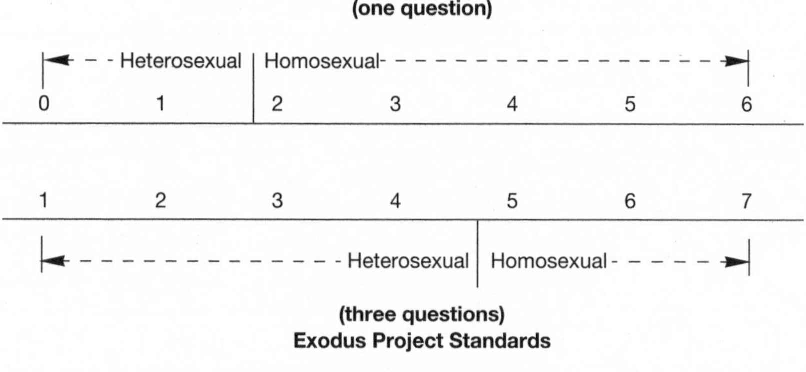

Figure 7.1. Comparison of Standards

Further, to meet our empirical criteria for assigning a subject a categorization of "truly gay," a subject had to score above the midpoint of bisexuality on a Kinsey-type scale on multiple (three) measures. In contrast to the very lenient scores leading to homosexual classification in the Bailey and Kendler studies, which used only one score and were all below the midpoint of bisexuality, we required multiple scores above the midpoint of the scale, a much more rigorous standard. Whereas a single score of 2, 3, 4, 5 or 6 on the solitary 0 to 6 Kinsey scale used in the Bailey and Kendler studies was enough for them to label the subject as homosexual, we required *three concurrent scores* of 5, 6 or 7 on either a set of seven-point Klein scales or a separate set of two Kinsey scales and one Klein scale for our classification of "truly gay." Specifically, to meet our criteria as Truly Gay, subjects had to meet one of two standards:

1. The first standard uses three scores from the Klein Sexual Orientation Grid. The Klein is a 1 to 7 set of Kinsey-style scales. Our first set of standards was
   - score a 5, 6 or 7 on the Klein for either sexual attraction or sexual fantasies, *and*
   - score a 5, 6 or 7 on the Klein for sexual behavior, *and*
   - score a 5, 6 or 7 on the Klein for either past self-identification or past homosexual-heterosexual lifestyle
2. Our second set of standards was
   - score a 5, 6 or 7 on the Kinsey scale for sexual attraction (this was section 4, item 22 of the Time 1, Phase 1 interview protocol; see these items when they are discussed under the section on the "Kinsey Two-Item Rating"), *and*
   - score a 5, 6 or 7 on the Kinsey scale for sexual behavior (this was section 4, item 21 of the Time 1, Phase 1 interview protocol; see these items when they are discussed under the section on the "Kinsey Two-Item Rating"), *and*
   - Score a 5, 6 or 7 on the Klein for either past self-identification or past homosexual-heterosexual lifestyle

It is worth noting that these standards were not only rigorous in requiring predominant homosexual attraction but particularly requiring predominantly homosexual behavior in the past for inclusion as Truly Gay. This means that none of our sexually inexperienced participants made it into the Truly Gay subsample. This likely then represents an underestimation of strong, stable homosexual orientation in our sample, since individuals from strongly traditionalist religious backgrounds and with stable, unequivocal homosexual orientation who had not yet acted on their orientation would not by this method be classified as Truly Gay.

In summary, our participants who were classified as Truly Gay reported high levels of homosexual sexual attraction/fantasy and exclusive or highly disproportionate levels of homosexual behavior and strong self-identification as gay or lesbian. At Time 1, 55 of the original total of 98 (56.1%) were classified as Truly Gay subjects.

A quick word about the participants *not* classified as Truly Gay. Remember from our discussion in chapter four that the inclusion criteria for the study included the self-identification by the participant that homosexual desire or orientation be a significant concern motivating Exodus involvement. Clearly, this standard would allow a bisexual person to join our study as a participant, since that person could easily feel that it is the homosexual aspect of his or her experience that motivates his or her Exodus participation. Thus it is likely that some of the "nontruly gay" participants are more bisexual than homosexual. On the other hand, a sexually inexperienced person who nevertheless experiences exclusive and intense homosexual attraction (i.e., who by all reasonable standards would be defined as having an exclusive homosexual orientation) would *not* be classified as Truly Gay in this study because he or she was missing the behavioral component of our empirical definition. We know that a good number of our participants fall in this latter condition. Thus we reject the argument that all of our subjects who were not classified as Truly Gay should be understood to be bisexual.

Discussion of Standard of Success

Before we turn to our findings, a final concern is the matter of setting definitional standards of what could constitute success in this study. Let us return to another of Haldeman's criticisms, that change interventions work, when they do, by grafting heterosexual action over a homosexual orientation without a more basic change in desire or attraction. Haldeman claims, in other words, that what is often claimed as success is training a person whose homosexual orientation is unchanged to learn to endure heterosexual functioning. What is right about this criticism, it seems to us, is the claim that teaching or helping a lesbian woman who has no attraction to men at all to endure sex with her husband without complaint—while it might be construed as a "successful adaptation" if that client remains utterly steadfast that toleration of heterosexual sex is her goal for change (failing other more thorough change)—should not be presented as a therapeutic success at the level of a basic change of orientation.

What is profoundly wrong about this type of criticism is the way that any acknowledgment by those who claim to have changed that they still episodically experience homosexual attraction is taken as clear proof that no change has really taken place at all. The critics have implicitly taken as a definition of successful conversion to heterosexuality the standard that the convert must never again experience homosexual attraction. That this is an unreasonable standard is proven by the test of generalization to other psychological disorders: We would never demand that successfully treated depressed people never again feel blue, that couples treated for relational discord never fight or feel frustrated with each other, that ex-smokers, alcoholics or drug addicts never again crave the substance to which they were addicted, or that athletes who consult sports psychologists never again experience performance anxiety.

It should be noted additionally that the apparent successes of the types of interventions documented in chapter three are often dismissed simply because they are less frequent (because the success rates are lower) than those reported with some other problems. Such an argument ignores the fact that many pernicious psychological maladies are difficult to treat and result in low success rates, including all of the addictions and the personality disorders. Psychologists and other mental health professionals are able to report extremely high success rates in treating certain simple and straightforward maladies such as the simple phobias, have lower yet still impressive treatment results with uncomplicated depression, but have meaningful if much lower success rates with the addictions and the personality disorders. Given the common testimony that sexual orientation is *impossible* to change, any successes at all will be highly significant. Our task in this study is to look for the possibility of change without much concern for the success rates.

Defining the baseline against which to measure change. We note that because some of our subjects had been in the Exodus change process for more than a year (i.e., our Phase 2 subjects), these subjects were asked to rate their past sexual orientation separately from their current orientation in the Time 1 assessment. In all of our analyses, we use these "past" ratings from the Time 1 assessment as our baseline against which we measure change for Phase 2 subjects; "present" ratings are used for all Phase 1 participants. This raises some of the same concerns or objections that were raised about the Robert Spitzer study about the reliability of retrospective estimations of sexual attraction (see responses to that study published with it in the same issue of *Archives of Sexual Behavior*).[3] We share Spitzer's sense that estimates of past sexual orientation are reasonably reliable, but also point out that our participants were estimating or recollecting their experience of sexual attraction and related phenomena in the *recent* past (no more than two or three years previous) rather than in the distant past (as was sometimes the case for Spitzer's study).

In all of our follow-up assessments, "current" measures of sexual orientation at Time 2 and Time 3 are used as the index against which change is estimated. So for Phase 1 subjects we look at change as differences between "current" measures of sexual orientation at Time 1, 2 and/or 3. For Phase 2 subjects, the "past" ratings of sexual orientation at Time 1 are contrasted against the "current" measures of sexual orientation at Time 2 and/or 3.

Results

In the following presentation of our results on change of sexual orientation, we rely on the discussion of the variables and scales we analyze in chapter six. Here we present the results themselves.

Categorical "self" and "orientation" ratings variables. On the next few pages, we present in tables 1-6 the responses to the two versions of the "self-identification" questions (as discussed in chap. 6). The first question asked, "Do you think of yourself as heterosexual (straight), homosexual (gay, lesbian), bisexual or something else (specify)," while the second asked for the same categorizations of the person's sexual orientation (rather than that of the "self"). In the analyses that follow we will distinguish these two questions, respectively, as the "Self Rating" and the "Orientation Rating." For each of these two questions, we present three analyses, which we have just discussed: an analysis of the results for the Whole Population, of the Phase 1 (or "early change") subpopulation and of the Truly Gay subpopulation.

Categorical ratings for "self."

"Self" ratings for the Whole Population (all discussion in this section refers to table 7.1). Table 7.1 presents a simple tabular summary of responses to the

Tables 7.1—7.3. Reporting Categorical Ratings for "Self"
Legend

1. "Other" combines responses of "something else" and "don't know," as well as any other uncategorizable responses given by subjects.
2. In each cell the first number is the number of subjects reporting for both Time 1 and Time 3 from among the 73 cases available at Time 3. So, for example, in table 7.1, 10 subjects reported themselves to be "heterosexual" at Time 1 and also reported themselves to be "heterosexual" at Time 3. The second and third numbers in parentheses are, respectively, the number of subjects reporting for both Time 1 and Time 2 among the 73 cases available at Time 3, and then the number of subjects reporting for both Time 1 and Time 2 among the 85 cases available at Time 2.
3. x = no change; x = negative change; x = uncertain change; x = positive change. Sums for these four respective change categories are presented beneath each table. The pattern of outcomes for these four categories in tables 7.1-7.6 is consistent, following the pattern in the following template table.

Time 1: Do you think of *yourself* as	Time 3 (or 2): "do you think of *your sexual orientation* as				
	heterosexual?	**homosexual?**	**bisexual?**	**other?**	**Total**
heterosexual?	No Change	Negative Change	Negative Change	Negative Change	
homosexual?	Positive Change	No Change	Positive Change	Positive Change	
bisexual?	Positive Change	Negative Change	No Change	Uncertain Change	
other?	Positive Change	Negative Change	Uncertain Change	No Change	
Total					

Result summary, Whole Population:
positive change = W; no change = X; negative change = Y; uncertain change = Z

Table 7.1. Categorical "Self" Ratings for Whole Population, Time 3 (or 2)

Time 1: Do you think of *yourself* as	Time 3 (or 2): "Do you think of *yourself* as				
	heterosexual?	**homosexual?**	**bisexual?**	**other?**	**Total**
heterosexual?	**10** (8, 11)	1 (1, 1)	1 (1, 1)	2 (4, 4)	**14** (14, 17)
homosexual?	14 (17, 19)	**10** (9, 10)	4 (1, 1)	5 (6, 6)	**33** (33, 36)
bisexual?	3 (2, 5)	2 (1, 1)	**4** (4, 6)	2 (4, 4)	**11** (11, 16)
other?	7 (7, 7)	2 (2, 2)	1 (1, 1)	**5** (5, 6)	**15** (15, 16)
Total	**34** (34, 42)	**15** (13, 14)	**10** (7, 9)	**14** (19, 20)	**73** (73, 85)

Result summary, Whole Population:
positive change = 33; no change = 29; negative change = 8; uncertain change = 3

Table 7.2. Categorical "Self" Ratings for Phase 1 Population, Time 3 (or 2)

Time 1: Do you think of *yourself* as	Time 3 (or 2): "Do you think of *yourself* as				Total
	heterosexual?	homosexual?	bisexual?	other?	
heterosexual?	5 (5, 7)	0 (0, 0)	1 (0, 0)	1 (2, 2)	7 (7, 9)
homosexual?	1 (2, 2)	5 (5, 6)	2 (0, 0)	1 (2, 2)	9 (9, 10)
bisexual?	2 (1, 2)	2 (1, 1)	3 (2, 4)	1 (4, 4)	8 (8, 11)
other?	6 (6, 6)	2 (2, 2)	1 (1, 1)	5 (5, 5)	14 (14, 9)
Total	14 (14, 17)	9 (8, 9)	7 (3, 5)	8 (13, 13)	38 (38, 44)

Result summary, Phase 1 Population:
positive change = 12; no change = 18; negative change = 6; uncertain change = 2

Table 7.3. Categorical "Self" Ratings for Truly Gay Population, Time 3 (or 2)

Time 1: Do you think of *yourself* as	Time 3 (or 2): "Do you think of *yourself* as				Total
	heterosexual?	homosexual?	bisexual?	other?	
heterosexual?	3 (3, 3)	0 (0, 0)	1 (0, 0)	0 (1, 1)	4 (4, 4)
homosexual?	11 (12, 14)	9 (9, 10)	4 (1, 1)	3 (5, 5)	27 (27, 30)
bisexual?	1 (1, 1)	2 (1, 1)	1 (2, 2)	1 (1, 1)	5 (5, 5)
other?	3 (3, 3)	2 (1, 1)	1 (0, 0)	1 (3, 4)	7 (7, 8)
Total	18 (19, 21)	13 (11, 12)	7 (3, 3)	5 (10, 11)	43 (43, 47)

Result summary, Truly Gay Population:
positive change = 22; no change = 14; negative change = 5; uncertain change = 2

Table 7.4. Categorical Orientation Ratings for Whole Population, Time 3 (or 2)

Time 1: Do you think of your *sexual orientation* as	Time 3 (or 2): "Do you think of *yourself* as				Total
	heterosexual?	homosexual?	bisexual?	other?	
heterosexual?	3 (2, 3)	5 (4, 4)	1 (2, 2)	0 (0, 0)	9 (8, 9)
homosexual?	6 (5, 5)	39 (34, 38)	2 (5, 6)	4 (7, 7)	51 (51, 56)
bisexual?	0 (1, 2)	6 (3, 3)	4 (3, 6)	1 (4, 4)	11 (11, 15)
other?	0 (0, 0)	1 (0, 1)	0 (1, 1)	1 (1, 1)	2 (2, 3)
Total	9 (8, 10)	51 (41, 46)	7 (11, 15)	6 (12, 12)	73 (72, 83)

Result summary, Whole Population:
positive change = 12; no change = 47; negative change = 13; uncertain change = 1

Table 7.5. Categorical Orientation Ratings for Phase 1 Population, Time 3 (or 2)

Time 1: Do you think of your *sexual orientation* as	Time 3 (or 2): "Do you think of *yourself* as				
	heterosexual?	**homosexual?**	**bisexual?**	**other?**	**Total**
heterosexual?	3 (2, 2)	2 (2, 2)	0 (1, 1)	0 (0, 0)	**5** (5, 5)
homosexual?	1 (0, 0)	19 (17, 18)	1 (3, 3)	4 (5, 5)	**25** (25, 26)
bisexual?	0 (0, 1)	2 (1, 1)	4 (3, 5)	0 (2, 2)	**6** (6, 9)
other?	0 (0, 0)	1 (0, 0)	0 (1, 1)	1 (1, 1)	**2** (2, 3)
Total	**4** (2, 3)	**24** (20, 22)	**5** (8, 10)	**5** (8, 8)	**38** (38, 43)

Result summary, Phase 1 Population
positive change = 6; no change = 27; negative change = 5; uncertain change = 0

Table 7.6. Categorical Orientation Ratings for Truly Gay Population, Time 3 (or 2)

Time 1: Do you think of your *sexual orientation* as	Time 3 (or 2): "Do you think of *yourself* as				
	heterosexual?	**homosexual?**	**bisexual?**	**other?**	**Total**
heterosexual?	1 (1, 1)	2 (2, 2)	0 (0, 0)	0 (0, 0)	3 (3, 3)
homosexual?	4 (4, 4)	28 (24, 28)	2 (4, 4)	2 (4, 4)	36 (36, 40)
bisexual?	0 (0, 0)	0 (0, 0)	2 (1, 1)	0 (1, 1)	2 (2, 2)
other?	0 (0, 0)	1 (0, 0)	0 (1, 1)	1 (1, 1)	2 (2, 2)
Total	5 (5, 5)	31 (26, 30)	4 (6, 6)	3 (6, 6)	43 (43, 47)

Result summary, Truly Gay Population:
positive change = 8; no change = 32; negative change = 3; uncertain change = 0

"self" ratings at Times 1, 2 and 3. Under the "Total" column on the right, we can see that at Time 1, 14 participants reported themselves to be heterosexual, 33 homosexual, 11 bisexual and 15 "other." At Time 3, reported in the "Total" row at the bottom, 34 participants reported themselves to be heterosexual, 15 homosexual, 10 bisexual and 14 "other." This would appear to document a trajectory of "progress" (in the terms understood by Exodus). On average, participants are migrating out of the homosexual category and into other classifications.

A more fine-grained examination of the findings within the table presents a cautiously optimistic picture as well. We will present these findings in terms of those that report *no change* (light gray box with black font), those that report *negative change* (black box with white font; those subjects in a number of cells that must be understood as reporting changes that Exodus would take as negative outcomes), those that report *change of uncertain meaning* (white box with black font) and those that report *positive change* (dark gray box with white font; those subjects that must be understood as reporting changes that Exodus would take as positive outcomes). These cells are graphically highlighted in the tables.

- *No change.* The diagonal from top left to bottom right in the table represents those individuals who at Time 1 and Time 3 reported the same categorization for themselves (i.e., no change). In that diagonal (focusing only on Time 1 to Time 3 self-reports) 10 persons said they were heterosexual at both times, 10 persons said they were homosexual at both times, 4 were bisexual at both times and 5 said they were "other" at both times, for a total of 29 of our 73 who reported no change in self-rating.
- *Negative change.* The subjects in a number of cells must be understood as reporting changes that Exodus would take as negative outcomes: (1) people who at Time 1 said they were heterosexual but at Time 3 were something else (1 homosexual, 1 bisexual and 2 "other" for a total of 4), and (2) people who were bisexual or "other" at Time 1 who are now self-reporting as homosexual at Time 3 (2 of each for a total of 4), for a total of 8 subjects reporting negative outcomes.
- *Change of uncertain meaning.* The movement of two subjects from bi-

sexual at Time 1 to "other" at Time 3, and of 1 subject in the opposite direction, constitutes 3 subjects who reported change of no clear valence.

- *Positive change.* From Time 1 to 3, 14 subjects reported moving to heterosexuality from homosexuality, 3 to heterosexuality from bisexuality, and 7 to heterosexuality from "other" (for a total of 24). Further, 4 reported moving from homosexual identification to bisexual, and 5 more to "other" (for a total of 9). Thus, a total of 33 reported what Exodus would regard as positive movement.

With 29 reporting no change (39.7% of the total), 8 reporting negative outcomes (10.9% of the total), 3 of no clear valence and 33 reporting positive outcomes (45.2% of the total), we have accounted for all 73 Time 3 cases. This profile of change summaries would be viewed positively as an outcome grid for a psychological or emotional condition that is judged difficult to treat, such as an addiction or a personality disorder. To take a seemingly less complex area, imagine conceptually that this was the outcome grid for marital counseling: an outcome from marital therapy that reported that 45% were improved, 40% were unchanged, and only 10% had gotten worse (i.e., divorced) would be viewed as an extremely compelling set of outcomes!

These outcomes are statistically significant as well. Counting the "uncertain change" cases as "no change" cases (32 no change, 8 negative change, 33 positive change), we calculated the odds ratio for positive versus negative change as 4.125, $\chi^2 = 14.05$, $p < .01$.[4] These analyses show that Exodus participants experienced statistically significant nonrandom movement between categories, with that movement obviously more toward heterosexuality than toward homosexuality.

As an outcome that is consistent with the findings that will be presented on other variables, it is notable that it would appear that almost all of the positive change occurs Time 1 to Time 2, with change from Time 2 to 3 being flat or a slight erosion. Note, for instance, that while 14 subjects had moved from homosexual to heterosexual when comparing Time 1 and 3, when comparing Time 1 to Time 2, *17 subjects* reported that same change; in other words, 3 fewer subjects must be seen as reporting the same change at Time 3 as at Time 2. This is a modest shift, though, and cannot be regarded as significant.

"Self" ratings for the Phase 1 population (all discussion in this section refers to table 7.2). For the Phase 1 subjects only, we see that under the "Total" column on the right, at Time 1, 7 participants reported themselves to be heterosexual, 9 homosexual, 8 bisexual and 14 "other." At Time 3 reported in the "Total" row at the bottom, 14 participants reported themselves to be heterosexual, 9 homosexual, 7 bisexual and 8 "other." This would appear to document a more modest trajectory of "progress" (in the terms understood by Exodus) than reported for the Whole Population, in that the homosexual group is not being depleted but some subjects are reporting movement from the bisexual and "other" categories into the heterosexual category.

Our examination of the findings within the table presents a modestly optimistic picture as well. Again presenting these findings in terms of those that report *no change, negative change, change of uncertain meaning* and *positive change*, we find:

- *No change.* In the diagonal from top left to bottom right in the table representing those individuals who at Time 1 and Time 3 reported the same categorization for themselves, we find that 5 persons said they were heterosexual at both times, 5 persons said they were homosexual at both times, 3 were bisexual at both times and 5 said they were "other" at both times, for a total of 18 of our 38 Phase 1 subjects who reported no change in self-rating.
- *Negative change.* (1) A total of 2 people at Time 1 said they were heterosexual but at Time 3 were something else (1 bisexual and 1 "other"), and (2) a total of 4 people were either bisexual (2) or "other" (2) at Time 1 but at Time 3 self-reported as homosexual, for a total of 6 Phase 1 subjects reporting negative outcomes.
- *Change of uncertain meaning.* The movement of 1 subject from bisexual at Time 1 to "other" at Time 3, and of 1 subject in the opposite direction, constitutes 2 subjects who reported change of no clear valence.
- *Positive change.* From Time 1 to 3, 1 subject reported moving to heterosexuality from homosexuality, 2 to heterosexuality from bisexuality and 6 to heterosexuality from "other" (for a total of 9). Further,

2 reported moving from homosexual identification to bisexual and 1 more to "other" (for a total of 3). Thus a total of 12 reported what Exodus would regard as positive movement.

With 18 reporting no change (47.3% of the total of 38), 6 reporting negative outcomes (15.8% of the total), 2 of no clear valence and 12 reporting positive outcomes (31.6%), we have accounted for all 38 Time 3, Phase 1 cases. These results did not attain statistical significance. This profile again would not be viewed negatively as an outcome grid for a psychological or emotional condition that is judged difficult to treat such as an addiction or a personality disorder, though the results are not as strong as for the Whole Population.

Again, it would appear among these Phase 1 subject findings that almost all of the positive change occurs Time 1 to Time 2.

"Self" ratings for the Truly Gay Population (all discussion in this section refers to table 7.3). For the Truly Gay subjects only, we see that under the "Total" column on the right, at Time 1, 4 participants reported themselves to be heterosexual, 27 homosexual, 5 bisexual and 7 "other." At Time 3 reported in the "Total" row at the bottom, 18 participants reported themselves to be heterosexual, 13 homosexual, 7 bisexual and 5 "other." This would appear to document a trajectory of "progress" (in the terms understood by Exodus) roughly comparable to that reported for the Whole Population.

Our examination of the findings within the table for our Truly Gay participants presents a *more* optimistic picture than our two prior summaries. Again presenting these findings in terms of those that report *no change*, *negative change*, *change of uncertain meaning* and *positive change*, we find:

- *No change.* In the diagonal representing those individuals who at Time 1 and Time 3 reported the same categorization for themselves (focusing only on Time 1 to Time 3 self-reports), 3 persons said they were heterosexual at both times, 9 persons said they were homosexual at both times, and 1 each was bisexual and "other" at both times, for a total of 14 of our 43 Truly Gay subjects who reported no change in self-rating.
- *Negative change.* (1) 1 person at Time 1 said he or she was heterosexual but at Time 3 was bisexual, and (2) 4 people who were bisexual

(2) or "other" (2) at Time 1 but at Time 3 were self-reporting as homosexual at Time 3, for a total of 5 Phase 1 subjects reporting negative outcomes.

- *Change of uncertain meaning.* The movement of 1 subject from bisexual at Time 1 to "other" at Time 3, and of 1 subject in the opposite direction, constitutes 2 subjects who reported change of no clear valence.
- *Positive change.* From Time 1 to 3, 11 subjects reported moving to heterosexuality from homosexuality, 1 to heterosexuality from bisexuality and 3 to heterosexuality from "other" (for a total of 15). Further, 4 reported moving from homosexual identification to bisexual, and 3 more to "other" (for a total of 7). Thus a total of 22 reported what Exodus would regard as positive movement.

With 14 reporting no change (32.6% of the total of 43), only 5 reporting negative outcomes (11.6%), 2 of no clear valence and the largest group being the 22 reporting positive outcomes (51.2%), we have accounted for all 43 Time 3 Truly Gay cases. This profile presents our most positive portrayal of change and does so among those that we would least expect to show strong evidence of change—the Truly Gay subpopulation. More than half report outcomes that must be viewed as positive, and only 5 out of 43 report negative outcomes. Again, such a pattern would be viewed extremely positively as an outcome grid for a psychological/emotional condition that is judged difficult to treat such as an addiction or a personality disorder.

These outcomes are statistically significant as well. Counting the "uncertain change" cases as "no change" cases (16 no change, 5 negative change, 22 positive change), we calculated the odds ratio for positive versus negative change as 4.400, $\chi^2 = 9.48$, $p < .01$.[5] These analyses show that the Truly Gay participants experienced statistically significant nonrandom movement between categories, with that movement obviously more toward heterosexuality than toward homosexuality.

We pause to underscore this very significant finding. Among the analyses of the two subpopulations, we obtained the strongest results indicative of change away from homosexual orientation among those who would quite reasonably be expected to show the least degree of change, our empirically derived Truly Gay subpopulation. To foreshadow the complexity of our findings, we note that this optimistic portrait of change is not repeated in our very next section on "orientation" rating, but we will then report a pattern of mostly respectable effect sizes across a range of other self-report variables.

Again as with the Phase 1 subpopulation, it would appear among these Truly Gay subject findings that almost all of the positive change occurred Time 1 to Time 2.

CATEGORICAL RATINGS FOR "SEXUAL ORIENTATION"

Overall, the categorical ratings for each subject's "sexual orientation" (apart from their "selves") present a *much* more modest portrait of positive progress in the Exodus population than do the categorical "self" ratings just discussed. Frankly, we created this different sort of self-categorization question thinking it would be more likely to reflect changes happening in this population and that the "self" question above would be more resistant to showing change. The opposite occurred.

Overall, it is clear that our instinct was correct that rating "yourself" is indeed a different question than rating "your sexual orientation" for this Exodus population, as demonstrated in the fact that at Time 1 a total of 33 rated themselves as homosexual but 51 rated their sexual orientation as homosexual. Note also that at Time 1 a total of 15 rated themselves as "other" but only 2 rated their sexual orientation as "other." The exact significance of this is difficult to tease out.

"Sexual orientation" ratings for the Whole Population (all discussion in this section refers to table 7.4). For the Whole Population on these "orientation" ratings, we see that under the "Total" column on the right at Time 1, 9 participants reported their sexual orientations to be heterosexual, 51 homosexual, 11 bisexual and 2 "other." We see much the same at Time 3 reported in the "Total" row at the bottom: 9 participants reported their sexual orientations to be heterosexual, 51 homosexual, 7 bisexual and 6 "other." This would appear to document no change whatsoever, no "progress" in the terms understood by Exodus for the Whole Population.

The analysis within the table reveals only marginal differences. Again presenting these findings in terms of those that report *no change*, *negative change*, *change of uncertain meaning* and *positive change*, we find:

- *No change.* In the diagonal from top left to bottom right representing those individuals who at Time 1 and Time 3 reported the same categorization for themselves (focusing only on Time 1 to Time 3 self-reports), 3 persons said their sexual orientations were heterosexual at both times, 39 persons reported their sexual orientations to be homosexual at both times, 4 bisexual at both times and 1 "other" at both times, for a total of 47 of 73 subjects reporting no change in their rating of their sexual orientations.
- *Negative change.* (1) 6 persons at Time 1 said their orientations were heterosexual but at Time 3 were something else (5 homosexual and 1 bisexual), and (2) 7 people who were bisexual (6) or "other" (1) at Time 1 self-reported as homosexual at Time 3, for a total of 13 of 73 subjects reporting negative outcomes.
- *Change of uncertain meaning.* The movement of 1 subject from bisexual at Time 1 to "other" at Time 3 constitutes one case reporting change of no clear valence.
- *Positive change.* From Time 1 to 3, 6 subjects reported moving to heterosexuality from homosexuality. Further, 2 reported moving from homosexual identification to bisexual, and 4 more from homosexual to "other" (for a total of 6). Thus a total of 12 reported what Exodus would regard as positive movement.

With the strong majority of subjects, 47 of 73 (64.4% of the total of 73) reporting no change, and essentially identical numbers of subjects reporting negative change (13; 17.8%) and positive change (12; 16.4%), and 1 reporting change of no clear valence, we have accounted for all 73 cases in the Whole Population. These shifts were not statistically significant. This profile presents our least positive portrayal of change.

"Sexual orientation" ratings for the Phase 1 Population (all discussion in this section refers to table 7.5). For the Phase 1 subjects only, we see a pattern similar to that for the Whole Population on these categorical ratings of sexual orientation. Under the "Total" column on the right at Time 1, 5 participants reported their sexual orientations to be heterosexual, 25 homosexual, 6 bisexual and 2 "other." We see much the same at Time 3 reported in the "Total" row at the bottom: 4 participants reported their sexual orientations to be heterosexual, 24 homosexual, 5 bisexual and 5 "other." This would appear to document little movement in the terms understood as progress by Exodus for the Phase 1 Population. Does the analysis within the table reveal anything different? Not really:

- *No change.* In the diagonal from top left to bottom right representing those individuals who at Time 1 and Time 3 reported the same categorization for themselves (focusing only on Time 1 to Time 3 self-reports), 3 persons said their sexual orientation were heterosexual at both times, 19 persons reported their sexual orientation was homosexual at both times, 4 bisexual at both times and 1 "other" at both times, for a total of 27 of 38 subjects reporting no change in their rating of their sexual orientations.
- *Negative change.* (1) 2 persons said their orientations were heterosexual at Time 1 but at Time 3 were homosexual, and (2) 3 people who were bisexual (2) or "other" (1) at Time 1 self-reported as homosexual at Time 3, for a total of 5 of 38 subjects reporting negative outcomes.
- *Change of uncertain meaning.* There were 0 subjects in this category of reporting change of no clear valence.
- *Positive change.* From Time 1 to 3, 1 subject reported moving to heterosexuality from homosexuality, 1 reported moving from homosexual identification to bisexual, and 4 more moved from homosexual to "other." Thus a total of 6 reported what Exodus would regard as positive movement.

With the strong majority of Phase 1 subjects, 27 of 38 (71.1% of the total), reporting no change, and about the same number of subjects reporting negative change (5; 13.2%) as reported positive change (6; 15.8%), we have accounted for all 38 cases in the Phase 1 population. These results did not attain statistical significance. We have no indication of significant change in this data.

"Sexual orientation" ratings for the Truly Gay population (all discussion in this section refers to table 7.6). For the Truly Gay subjects, we see the same pattern again for the orientation ratings. Under the "Total" column on the right, at Time 1, 3 participants reported their sexual orientations to be heterosexual, 36 homosexual, 2 bisexual and 2 "other." We see much the same at Time 3 reported in the "Total" row at the bottom: 5 participants reported their sexual orientations to be heterosexual, 31 homosexual, 4 bisexual and 3 "other." This would appear to document little movement in the terms understood as progress by Exodus for the Truly Gay Population. What does the analysis within the table reveal?

- *No change.* In the diagonal from top left to bottom right representing those individuals who at Time 1 and Time 3 reported the same categorization for themselves (focusing only on Time 1 to Time 3 self-reports), 1 Truly Gay person said his or her sexual orientation was heterosexual at both times, 28 persons reported their sexual orientations to be homosexual at both times, 2 bisexual at both times and 1 "other" at both times, for a total of 32 of 43 subjects reporting no change in their ratings of their sexual orientation.
- *Negative change.* (1) 2 Truly Gay persons at Time 1 said their orientations were heterosexual but at Time 3 were homosexual, and (2) 1 person who was "other" at Time 1 reported his or her orientation to be homosexual at Time 3 for a total of 3 of 43 subjects reporting negative outcomes.
- *Change of uncertain meaning.* There were 0 subjects in this category of reporting change of no clear valence.
- *Positive change.* From Time 1 to 3, 4 Truly Gay subjects reported moving to heterosexuality from homosexuality, 2 reported moving from homosexual identification to bisexual, and 2 more to "other." Thus a total of 8 reported what Exodus would regard as positive movement.

A strong majority of the Truly Gay subjects, 32 of 43 (74.4% of the total of 43), reported no change. In this category we found more subjects reporting positive change (8; 18.6%) than reported negative change (3; 7.0%). Thus we have accounted for all 43 cases in the Truly Gay subpopulation. Again, we have a mostly neutral portrayal of change, with many subjects not reporting a change in their categorical rating of their sexual orientation. More reported positive change (8) than negative (3), but this degree of change did not attain statistical significance.

These discouraging findings in the categorical ratings of sexual orientation may be interpreted in several ways, but these interpretations must be viewed as inconclusive. The interpretation most favorable to Exodus would be that the ratings of "orientation" (as opposed to "self") provided no room for the documentation of change. This is analogous to judging outcomes from depression treatment by asking subjects not to rate their depression on a sliding scale of how depressed they feel but rather to have them make a forced choice between "depressed and not depressed." Subjects might experience considerable positive change without moving out of the "depressed" self-categorization. Exodus might also argue that the stronger positive shifts in the "self" ratings were the reflection of participants shifting their self-identities in light of their sense of fundamental change occurring, even if they could not yet report their "orientation" moving from one category to another. Critics of Exodus might argue the exact opposite: That it would be the ratings of "orientation" that would provide the most sensitive measure of fundamental change, and that the "self" ratings are both more ambiguous about what is actually being measured *and* also more susceptible to shift based on ideological commitments rather than actual change in erotic attraction. Both arguments have legitimacy, but on balance we would suggest that the pattern of results presented in the balance of this chapter support the pro-Exodus interpretation by showing significant and meaningful, if not always dramatic, shifts in sexual attraction. And so we turn to our other findings.

KINSEY ONE-ITEM, TWO-ITEM AND EXPANDED RATINGS RESULTS

We present here separate tabular summaries for the Whole Population, Phase 1 Population and the Truly Gay Population. Within each of these analyses, we present the results of three comparisons of change as already discussed (see pp. 231-232):

- from our Time 1 assessment (the baseline) to Time 3 (73 subjects)
- from Time 1 to Time 2 for those cases still in the study at Time 3 (73 subjects)
- from Time 1 to Time 2 for all cases in the study at Time 2 (85 subjects).

Table 7.7. Kinsey Scores for Whole Population

	Time 1 Mean	Time 2 Mean	Time 3 Mean	Mean Diff.	N	Df	Std. Dev.	t score	2-tailed sig.	Cohen *d*
1. Kinsey 1-item Time 1 to 3	5.07		4.08	0.99	71	70	2.42	3.44	0.001	0.518
2. Kinsey 1-item Time 1 to 2 (all Time 3 cases)	5.03	4.09		0.94	70	69	2.23	3.54	0.001	0.516
3. Kinsey 1-item Time 1 to 2 (all Time 2 cases)	4.88	3.89		0.99	81	80	2.24	3.96	0.000	0.526
4. Kinsey 2-item Time 1 to 3	4.91		4.32	0.59	73	72	1.62	3.11	0.003	0.373
5. Kinsey 2-item Time 1 to 2 (all Time 3 cases)	4.91	4.37		0.54	73	72	1.45	3.19	0.002	0.342
6. Kinsey 2-item Time 1 to 2 (all Time 2 cases)	4.84	4.21		0.63	85	84	1.51	3.85	0.000	0.386
7. Kinsey Expanded Time 1 to 3	4.97		4.32	0.66	73	72	1.83	3.05	0.003	0.415
8. Kinsey Expanded Time 1 to 2 (all Time 3 cases)	4.97	4.21		0.76	73	72	1.69	3.83	0.000	0.499
9. Kinsey Expanded Time 1 to 2 (all Time 2 cases)	4.89	4.07		0.82	85	84	1.73	4.38	0.000	0.518

Legend

1. For each of the Kinsey 1-item, 2-item and Expanded scores, we present three comparisons. First, the report of Time 1 to Time 3 comparison, including only those cases presenting data for both assessments. Second, the report of Time 1 to Time 2 comparison, including only the cases also available at Time 3 (in other words, this comparison included only the same cases as in the first Time 1 to Time 3 comparison, designated "all Time 3 cases"). Third, the report of Time 1 to Time 2 comparison, including *all* of the cases that were available at Time 2 (in other words, this comparison included all of the cases available at Time 2, a larger population than those available at Time 3, designated "all Time 2 cases").

Note: In this and the analyses that follow, we number the comparisons listed in each row of the table (as in the above) to correspond with the presentation of those comparisons in the bar charts that immediately follow.

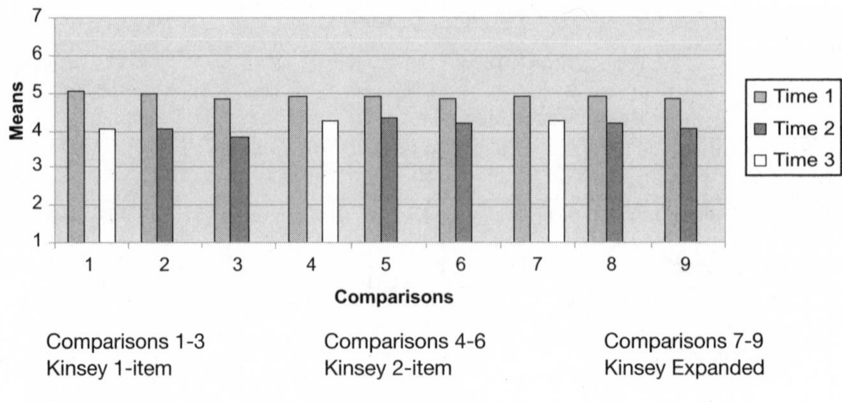

Figure 7.2. Kinsey Variables: Whole Population

Statistically significant degrees of change were obtained in all comparisons of change in the Whole Population on all three Kinsey variable types measuring sexual orientation; the two-tailed t-tests were all highly significant. It would appear that the bulk of reported change occurred from Time 1 to Time 2 rather than between Time 2 and Time 3; Time 2 to Time 3 changes were not statistically significant and are not reported here.

"Effect size," represented in the table 7.7 as "Cohen *d*," is the standardized way that behavioral scientists today compare the relative size of the effects (or changes) they observe in their studies. The effect sizes for the changes recorded in this study are moderately strong by contemporary behavioral sciences standards. Cohen defined, with considerable caution, effect sizes as "small, *d* = .2," "medium, *d* = .5," and "large, *d* = .8," cautioning that "there is a certain risk inherent in offering conventional operational definitions for those terms for use in power analysis in as diverse a field of inquiry as behavioral science."[6] A casual review of the far-right column in table 7.7 shows that the Cohen *d* effect sizes for the Kinsey one-item and expanded scores hovered around the 0.5 standard of "medium effects," and the Kinsey two-item effect sizes between small and medium. We take Cohen's caution seriously, but qualify that sense of caution by reminding the reader that we are reporting effect sizes for movement on a variable that the prevailing professional wisdom tells us *is impossible to change!* These effect sizes would be meaningful if reported as the results of any scientific study of an attempt to change any behavioral or psychological pattern, but they assume considerably more significance in light of the fact that we are reporting change on a dimension of human functioning that is supposed to be impossible to change.

The Kinsey one-item variable showed the strongest degree of change, while the Kinsey two-item and the Kinsey expanded showed less change in absolute terms. We would argue that the Kinsey one-item and Kinsey expanded variables are better indicators of the change that is really occurring in this population, because we made a mistake in the Kinsey two-item variable in our Time 2 and 3 assessments. At Times 2 and 3, we were interested in change, and so item 22, the Kinsey one-item single measure, asked about *current* sexual attraction: "22. How would you describe the gender of the persons to whom you *are* sexually attracted?" By inquiring in the present tense, "*are* sexually attracted," we were able to get a *current* measure of attraction at Time 2 or 3 against which to compare the same report at Time 1. For the two-item measure, we added a question about behavior, and here we made our mistake: when it came to asking about sexual behavior, we failed to change the tense and hence the time frame for the question. The Kinsey question about sexual behavior was "21. How would you describe the gender of the persons with whom you *have been* sexually intimate physically?" Though we did not explicitly say "in the past," by framing the question in terms of "with whom you *have been* sexually intimate physically," we encouraged respondents to include all sexual experiences in their lives, a measure completely insensitive to change. This would be parallel to asking patients being treated for depression, Have you ever been depressed? (a question that obviously would not get at change in the current experience) rather than, Are you depressed right now (after being treated)? Thus the Kinsey one-item and Kinsey expanded variables are better measures of change than the Kinsey two-item, the Kinsey one-item variable because it focuses only on current attraction, and the Kinsey expanded variable because the insensitive measure of behavior is averaged against three other measures that are sensitive to change. The Kinsey two-item variable would obviously show the least change because fully half of the averaged score is anchored to a variable that should not change at all.

Social scientists often debate the difference between statistical significance and clinical or absolute meaningfulness.[7] The two are not the same, and the distinction is perhaps best illustrated by recourse to parallel cases in pharmacological (drug) research. It is not impossible for clinically meaningful change to fail to achieve statistical significance. A drug trial, for instance, may yield distinctly positive outcomes for a subgroup within the total population studied, but because this positive outcome is averaged with the equivocal results of the total population, a statistical analysis that looks only at averaged outcomes for the whole population may miss this finding. The positive outcomes for the subgroup may only be revealed when the researchers "mine" their data in what are commonly called post-hoc analyses. Other ways in which positive outcomes may be obscured include when wide degrees of variation in outcomes render the statistical tests insensitive to the positive changes (which may occur if a drug trial produces very positive results for a subpopulation, but very negative results for other parts of the population), or when small sample sizes weaken the power of a statistical test. These are some of the ways in which our statistics may report no significant findings when in reality something real and meaningful has occurred.

The opposite result is more common in social science, however; that being when the outcomes being examined achieve statistical significance but fail to reflect clinically meaningful levels of change. All researchers understand that an increase in sample size increases the likelihood that our statistical tests will report back significant results in any comparison. Further, any measurement method that decreases the variability of our measures enhances the likelihood that significant results will be found. Thus a drug trial on thousands of patients may report that a new pain medication produced statistically significant reductions in pain over other treatments but fail to highlight that the degree of change on average was, on a 100-point rating scale, only a few points better than the effects produced by the nearest competitor. If the sample size is large enough and the degree of variance in the measure small enough, a mere 5% differential in effectiveness, a degree of change that is of little meaning from a practical perspective, may still be reported as statistically significant (and become the basis for an aggressive marketing program!). To use an illustration in the mental health realm, a new drug treatment or psychotherapy for the treatment of depression may be reported as producing statistically significant change, but may fail to move the subjects on average out of the depressed range of scores on the measure of treatment effectiveness; this would be statistically significant (they are less depressed and the difference is statistically significant) but practically or clinically of uncertain meaning.

We report here statistically significant changes, but are those changes clinically meaningful? We expect this question to be intensely debated. The best argument for clinical significance on these variables would be the following: First, if one is located at one extreme end of the Kinsey scale (7—exclusively homosexual), the most one could move would be six points (from 7 to 1) toward exclusive heterosexuality.1 For subjects on average to report about one point of change from Time 1 to Time 3 on the Kinsey one-item scale, the core measure of attraction, is to report change on average of 17% of the total possible degree of change, and this on a dimension of personal experience, sexual orientation, that is commonly regarded as impossible to change.

Second, this degree of change is reported on average even though persons who are reporting complete failure to change or even reversion to homosexual orientation (having given up on the change process and embraced homosexual orientation) are included in the calculations. In other words, subjects in the study experiencing change are being averaged with those reporting no change. This is, of course, typical.

Third, we would point to the commonsense meaning of these numerical ratings. The average Time 1 score of 5.07 on the Kinsey one-item corresponds to a rating of "largely homosexual, but more than incidental heterosexual" attraction, and the Time 3 average of 4.08 places the subjects as reporting "equal amounts of heterosexual and homosexual." Descriptively, this would appear to be, on average, a clinically meaningful shift in how these people are describing their sexual attractions.

What are the arguments that these results are not clinically meaningful?

1Kinsey created a 7-point scale of sexual orientation as discussed in chapter six, with his scale ranging from 0 (exclusively heterosexual) to 6 (exclusively homosexual). We ran into problems anchoring the scale at one end with a zero because some of our analyses treated this value as missing data rather than an actual value. Therefore, we recoded this data to range from 1 (exclusively heterosexual) to 7 (exclusively homosexual), thus keeping the same 7-point scale structure for assessing sexual orientation but shifting the point values by one.

First, any single item is open to biased reporting based on the strong moral and expectational demands that those seeking change seem to place on themselves. These ratings, in other words, may represent less a true reporting of change of the state of attraction and more the respondent's hopes for change. Second, this modest level of change is the result of over two years of effort, a modest level of change for such a long process.

We would urge the reader to withhold judgment on this issue until after reading chapter eight. We are reporting in this chapter the degree of change averaged across the entire sample. But such averages are, of course, composed of those who experienced positive change (as debated as that concept is for this topic) as well as those who experienced negative change.[8] Hence, an "average change" here is a problematic concept. In chapter eight we separate the participants into groups and discover that some experienced much more significant change (positive and negative).

Finally, it is easy in making data presentations visually to create distorted impressions of the magnitude of one's results by visually presenting data on a truncated range that does not represent the full spread of the variable measured. Figure 7.3 presents the same data we have been discussing (and presented in figure 7.2), but alters the presentation by cutting off the "empty" sections of the chart, namely the top scores (5.5 to 7) and the bottom scores (1 to 3.5). This new view presents a statistically accurate but visually (or subjectively) deceptive portrait of the magnitude of the changes we found in our data. This form of presentation increases the sense of the

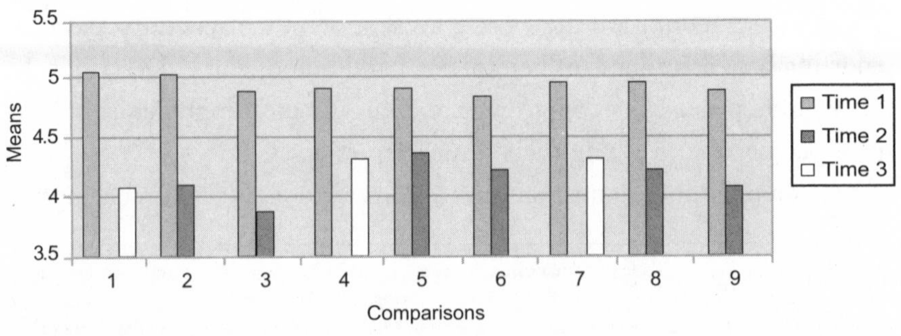

Figure 7.3. Kinsey Variables: Whole Population with "Empty" Sections Removed

magnitude or degree of change; it *looks* dramatically different when we compare figures 7.2 and 7.3.

In all of our data presentations, we have chosen to present the figures with bar charts with the y-axis showing the full range of the variable displayed in order that the absolute magnitude of the change be fairly and accurately presented.

Changes for the Phase 1 Population were more modest than for the Whole Population, and perhaps very surprisingly, than for the Truly Gay subpopulation presented later. It is common in making such comparisons to set the p-value at either 0.05 or 0.01 level. Using a 0.01 significance level, none of these comparisons achieved statistical significance, but using a 0.05 level for significance, three of the six Time 1 to Time 2 changes were significant, though none of the three Time 1 to Time 3 comparisons achieved statistical significance. In terms of Cohen effect sizes, these three statistically significant changes were in the small range of effect size.

It would appear that the Phase 1 Population experienced less change on average than the Whole Population. Two competing explanations of these findings come to mind. The first would be that change through Exodus (as discussed by Spitzer and others) is a very long-term process, and so it would make sense to see less change among the Phase 1 Population, defined as the one that had been in the actual change process for a shorter period of time (less than one year at the start of the study) than the Phase 2 Population, which had been in the actual change process for a longer period of time at the start of the study (between one and three years). For individuals who are in a long-term change process, the measurement of Time 1 to Time 3 change for Phase 1 subjects may represent too short of a process to reflect dramatic change. Alternatively, this more modest change may reflect real differences between the Phase 1 and 2 populations. Phase 2 subjects, by virtue of their longer participation in the change process, may constitute a less representative sample of those seeking change composed of those (some might say rare) individuals who gain positive gains from the Exodus process, whereas Phase 1 subjects may be a more representatively diverse population with a higher percentage of subjects unlikely to respond well to the Exodus process who have hence produced more modest results. It is worth noting, though, that when we discuss the

Table 7.8. Kinsey Scores for Phase 1 Population

	Time 1 Mean	Time 2 Mean	Time 3 Mean	Mean Diff.	N	df	Std. Dev.	t score	2-tailed sig.	Cohen *d*
1. Kinsey 1-item Time 1 to 3	4.50		4.24	0.26	38	37	2.14	0.76	0.453	
2. Kinsey 1-item Time 1 to 2 (all Time 3 cases)	4.46	4.03		0.43	37	36	1.77	1.48	0.146	
3. Kinsey 1-item Time 1 to 2 (all Time 2 cases)	4.35	3.84		0.51	43	42	1.98	1.69	0.098	
4. Kinsey 2-item Time 1 to 3	4.53		4.50	0.03	38	37	1.40	0.12	0.909	
5. Kinsey 2-item Time 1 to 2 (all Time 3 cases)	4.53	4.26		0.26	38	37	1.22	1.33	0.191	
6. Kinsey 2-item Time 1 to 2 (all Time 2 cases)	4.49	4.03		0.45	44	43	1.46	2.06	0.045	0.299
7. Kinsey Expanded Time 1 to 3	4.68		4.43	0.25	38	37	1.73	0.90	0.374	
8. Kinsey Expanded Time 1 to 2 (all Time 3 cases)	4.68	4.13		0.54	38	37	1.54	2.17	0.037	0.359
9. Kinsey Expanded Time 1 to 2 (all Time 2 cases)	4.60	3.95		0.65	44	43	1.70	2.54	0.015	0.426

Legend

1. For each of the Kinsey 1-item, 2-item and Expanded scores, we present three comparisons: First, the report of Time 1 to Time 3 comparison, including only those cases presenting data for both assessments. Second, the report of Time 1 to Time 2 comparison, including only the cases also available at Time 3 (in other words, this comparison included only the same cases as in the first Time 1 to Time 3 comparison, designated "all Time 3 cases"). Third, the report of Time 1 to Time 2 comparison, including *all* of the cases that were available at Time 2 (in other words, this comparison included all of the cases available at Time 2, a larger population than those available at Time 3, designated "all Time 2 cases").

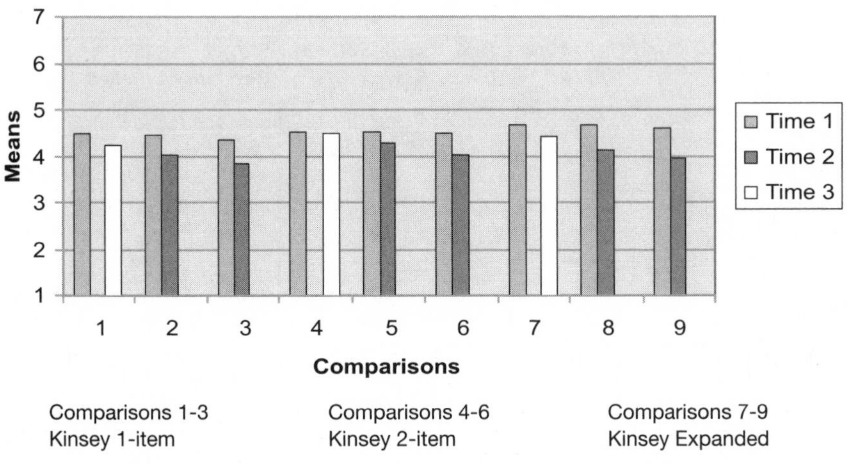

Figure 7.4. Kinsey Variables: Phase 1 Population

eleven "success cases" from the qualitative results that half of them were Phase 1 subjects, about the same ratio as that of Phase 1 subjects in the entire population.

Looking first at our Kinsey one-item Time 1 to Time 3 comparison, we note a remarkable result: The single largest average change ("mean difference" of 1.41) from any of the Kinsey one-item comparisons comes in this analysis of the population that would seem least likely to experience change at all, the subjects categorized by the rigorous standards discussed earlier as Truly Gay. These participants—who had to have self-identified as gay in the past, to have been sexually experienced predominantly with persons of their same gender, and to experience predominantly homosexual attraction—are the population that experienced the most significant change.

All of the Kinsey scale comparisons of this Truly Gay group achieved strong statistical significance. Further, it must be noted as a dramatic finding that the Cohen *d* effect sizes all surpass the 0.5 level for "medium" effect sizes and many come very close to the 0.8 level at which they would be considered "large" effects. These are, by behavioral science standards, strong findings and ones that occur in that very population where change would least be expected to occur—the Truly Gay.

Table 7.9. Kinsey Scores for Truly Gay Population

	Time 1 Mean	Time 2 Mean	Time 3 Mean	Mean Diff.	N	df	Std. Dev.	t score	2-tailed sig.	Cohen *d*
1. Kinsey 1-item Time 1 to 3	5.46		4.05	1.41	41	40	2.68	3.38	0.002	0.725
2. Kinsey 1-item Time 1 to 2 (all Time 3 cases)	5.44	4.20		1.24	41	40	2.38	3.35	0.002	0.687
3. Kinsey 1-item Time 1 to 2 (all Time 2 cases)	5.50	4.11		1.39	44	43	0.37	3.77	0.000	0.768
4. Kinsey 2-item Time 1 to 3	5.59		4.67	0.92	43	42	1.66	3.63	0.001	0.673
5. Kinsey 2-item Time 1 to 2 (all Time 3 cases)	5.59	4.85		0.74	43	42	1.56	3.14	0.003	0.571
6. Kinsey 2-item Time 1 to 2 (all Time 2 cases)	5.67	4.82		0.85	47	46	1.71	3.42	0.001	0.628
7. Kinsey Expanded Time 1 to 3	5.50		4.55	0.95	43	42	1.78	3.49	0.001	0.738
8. Kinsey Expanded Time 1 to 2 (all Time 3 cases)	5.50	4.51		0.99	43	42	1.74	3.75	0.001	0.665
9. Kinsey Expanded Time 1 to 2 (all Time 2 cases)	5.59	4.50		1.09	47	46	1.83	4.11	0.000	0.721

Legend

1. For each of the Kinsey 1-item, 2-item and Expanded scores, we present three comparisons. First, the report of Time 1 to Time 3 comparison, including only those cases presenting data for both assessments. Second, the report of Time 1 to Time 2 comparison, including only the cases also available at Time 3 (in other words, this comparison included only the same cases as in the first Time 1 to Time 3 comparison, designated "all Time 3 cases"). Third, the report of Time 1 to Time 2 comparison, including all of the cases that were available at Time 2 (in other words, this comparison included all of the cases available at Time 2, a larger population than those available at Time 3, designated "all Time 2 cases").

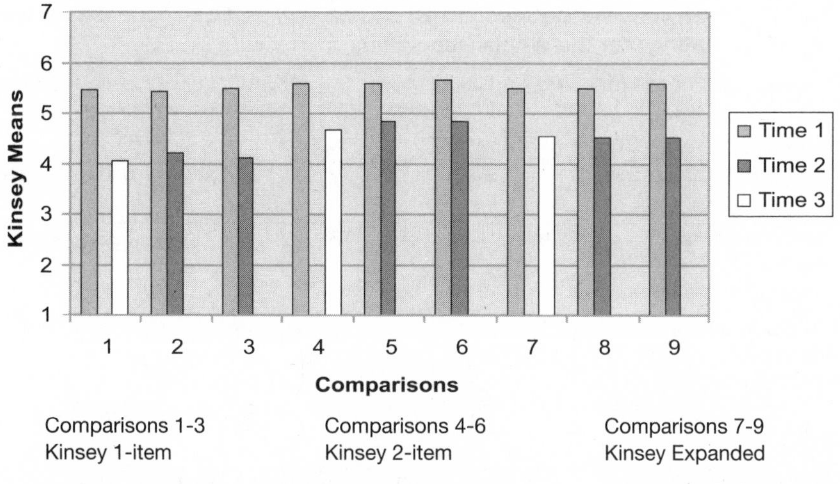

Figure 7.5. Kinsey Variables: Truly Gay Population

The Time 2 to Time 3 changes did not attain statistical significance and hence are not presented, but the trajectory of change is consistently in the direction of continuing change across the two follow-up assessments. In determining whether these statistically significant changes are clinically meaningful, all of the arguments developed earlier for the Whole Population analyses, pro and con, continue to hold. Solid arguments for the clinical meaningfulness of these changes can be made.

Summary of Kinsey findings. Statistically significant degrees of change (medium effect sizes) in the direction of movement toward heterosexuality for the Whole Population were found on the Kinsey ratings. Many of the findings for the Truly Gay subpopulation from Time 1 to Time 3 approached being large effect sizes. Less change was reported for the Phase 1 subpopulation.

Shively and DeCecco Ratings Results

The value of the Shively and DeCecco (S-D) ratings is their separation or disaggregation of changes in heterosexual and homosexual orientation ratings. Changes on the Shively and DeCecco ratings for all three of our analyses follow a stable pattern. All comparisons show statistically significant changes in the direction intended by the Exodus process (less homosexu-

Table 7.10. Shively and DeCecco (S-D) and Shively and DeCecco Expanded (S-D Exp) Ratings for the Whole Population

	Time 1 Mean	Time 2 Mean	Time 3 Mean	Mean Diff.	N	df	Std. Dev.	t score	2-tailed sig.	Cohen *d*
1. S-D Heterosex Time 1 to 3	2.45		2.79	-.34	73	72	1.35	-2.214	.030	-0.309
2. S-D Heterosex Time 1 to 2 (all Time 3 cases)	2.45	2.90		-.45	73	72	1.21	-3.226	.002	-0.420
3. S-D Heterosex Time 1 to 2 (all Time 2 cases)	2.52	2.96		-.44	85	84	1.19	-3.455	.001	-0.397
4. S-D Homosex Time 1 to 3	4.11		3.18	.93	73	72	1.39	5.679	.000	0.834
5. S-D Homosex Time 1 to 2 (all Time 3 cases)	4.11	3.12		.99	73	72	1.24	6.818	.000	0.955
6. S-D Homosex Time 1 to 2 (all Time 2 cases)	4.08	3.05		1.03	85	84	1.23	7.781	.000	0.959
7. S-D Exp Heterosex Time 1 to 3	2.48		2.84	-.36	73	72	1.15	-2.671	.009	-0.337
8. S-D Exp Heterosex Time 1 to 2 (all Time 3 cases)	2.48	2.96		-.48	73	72	1.00	-4.154	.000	-0.484
9. S-D Exp Heterosex Time 1 to 2 (all Time 2 cases)	2.57	3.04		-.47	85	84	.97	-4.417	.000	-0.447
10. S-D Exp Homosex Time 1 to 3	4.27		3.41	.86	73	72	1.17	6.288	.000	0.939
11. S-D Exp Homosex Time 1 to 2 (all Time 3 cases)	4.27	3.46		.81	73	72	1.06	6.586	.000	0.970
12. S-D Exp Homosex Time 1 to 2 (all Time 2 cases)	4.24	3.39		.85	85	84	1.02	7.598	.000	0.968

Legend

1. The Shively and DeCecco (S-D) ratings comprise two independent scores, one of heterosexuality and one of homosexuality; so also the Shively and DeCecco Expanded (S-D

Exp) ratings. For each of the S-D and S-D Exp scores, we present three comparisons: First, the report of Time 1 to Time 3 comparison, including only those cases presenting data for both assessments. Second, the report of Time 1 to Time 2 comparison, including only the cases also available at Time 3 (in other words, this comparison included only the same cases as in the first Time 1 to Time 3 comparison, designated "all Time 3 cases"). Third, the report of Time 1 to Time 2 comparison, including all of the cases that were available at Time 2 (in other words, this comparison included all of the cases available at Time 2, a larger population than those available at Time 3, designated "all Time 2 cases").

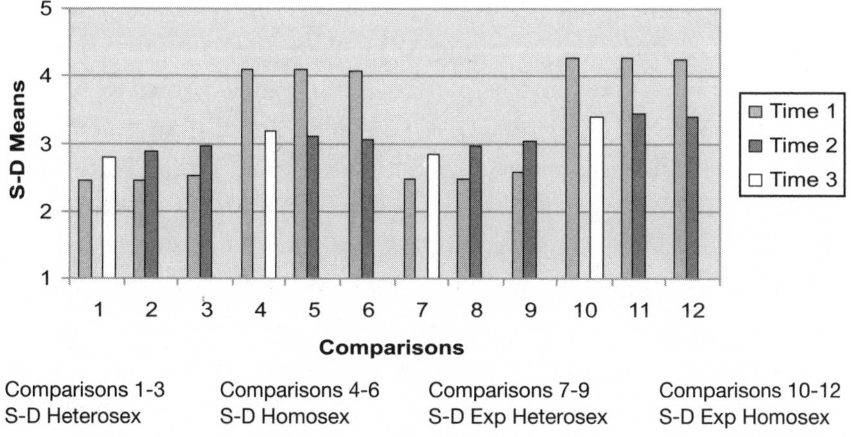

Figure 7.6. Shively and DeCecco (S-D) and Shively and DeCecco Expanded Variables: Whole Population

ality, more heterosexuality, whether from Time 1 to 3, or Time 1 to 2), and changes away from homosexual orientation are consistently, if roughly, twice the absolute magnitude of changes toward heterosexual orientation. It would appear, then, that while change away from homosexual orientation is related to change toward heterosexual orientation, the two are not identical processes.

Review of the statistical findings in table 7.10 reveal that all of the changes attained statistical significance in our 2-tailed t-tests. Further, the Cohen *d* measure of effect size indicates that changes toward being less homosexual (a decrease in reporting of homosexual orientation) were consistently in the large effect size range, while changes toward being more heterosexual (an increase in reporting of heterosexual orientation) were consistently in the medium to small effect size range. These are dramatic findings.

What of their clinical meaningfulness? To contrast the absolute magnitude of the changes reported on the Shively and DeCecco ratings (which are reported on a five-point scale) to those of the Kinsey (which are reported on a seven-point scale), note that a person reporting the absolute extreme of homosexual attraction (a rating of 5 on these scales) who experienced dramatic total change to heterosexual orientation would report moving four points (from 5 to 1) from exclusive homosexual attraction to no homosexual attraction. An average shift of one point away from homosexual attraction (approximately the average reported here) then represents a shift of about 25% of the total possible change, a shift in magnitude essentially identical to that reported on the Kinsey scales. The absolute magnitude of the changes found on these Shively and DeCecco ratings for movement away from homosexual orientation, then, almost exactly paralleled those found on the Kinsey. The average size of the movement toward heterosexual orientation, though, was about half that absolute size. In terms of statistical versus clinical significance, it appears that the same arguments made earlier for the Kinsey ratings hold for the Shively and DeCecco ratings as well.

In interpreting the Shively and DeCecco results, note that the Shively and DeCecco ratings (one for homosexual orientation, the other for heterosexual orientation) given in table 7.10 are the average of two items as discussed in chapter six. The Shively and DeCecco Expanded ratings, in contrast, are the average of four items. The "regular" Shively and DeCecco rating (in contrast to the expanded Shively and DeCecco) is the one intended by the scale authors.

One particular shift in the findings on the Shively and DeCecco ratings from the findings on the Kinsey variables merits note. Although Time 1 to Time 3 and Time 1 to Time 2 changes were all significant for the Whole Population on the Shively and DeCecco ratings, as in the Kinsey findings Time 2 to 3 changes were not significant and are not reported. But further, in the Kinsey findings we found a continuing directionality of change (what the Exodus ministries would call continuing improvement) from Time 1 through Times 2 and 3; bluntly, subjects were *better* in Exodus terms at Time 2 than Time 1, and *better* at Time 3 than Time 2. But there is no such trajectory of continuing change noted in the Shively and DeCecco ratings. Rather, there appears to be a plateauing of change if not a modest (and statistically insignificant) regression. Subjects were typically less heterosexually inclined and more homosexually inclined at Time 2 than they were at Time 3, though these differences are tiny and not of an absolute magnitude of which we can make much. In plain English the Kinsey variables reflected a continuing trajectory of "improvement" (as Exodus would view it) as you moved from Time 1 to 2 to 3, but on the Shively and DeCecco ratings, all of the change was from Time 1 to 2, with no change (or a very tiny erosion) from Time 2 to 3.

As with other findings, charitable and uncharitable interpretations of this could be made. Perhaps these findings reflect dramatic changes from Time 1 to 2 that are simply being held and consolidated through Time 3, and perhaps this is a fairly common trajectory of change. Alternatively perhaps the Time 1 to 2 changes are the result of hopeful and unrealistic self-reporting, and the Time 3 findings are beginning to reflect the erosion of confidence that change has really begun to occur.

As with the Kinsey findings, while the direction of change remained the same for the Phase 1 Population compared to the whole, the magnitude of change for the Phase 1 Population was less than that for the Whole Population. Shifts away from homosexual orientation were statistically significant for both Shively and DeCecco and Shively and DeCecco Expanded measures, but not of as large a magnitude as for the Whole Population. The shifts toward heterosexual orientation were not statistically significant for the Shively and DeCecco ratings, but two of three of the Shively and DeCecco expanded measures showed a significant shift toward heterosexual orientation, again not of as large a magnitude as for the Whole Population. Generally, shifts away from homosexual orientation were of about twice the magnitude of the shifts toward heterosexuality. Eight of the 12 comparisons in table 7.11 attained statistical significance, and the Cohen *d* measure of effect size indicates that changes toward being less homosexual were consistently in the medium effect size range while changes toward being more heterosexual were consistently in the small effect size range. These significant findings, while again not as dramatic as those for the Whole Population, are noteworthy.

Table 7.11. Shively and DeCecco (S-D) and Shively and DeCecco Expanded (S-D Exp) Ratings for the Phase 1 Population

	Time 1 Mean	Time 2 Mean	Time 3 Mean	Mean Diff.	N	df	Std. Dev.	t score	2-tailed sig.	Cohen *d*
1. S-D Heterosex Time 1 to 3	2.54		2.75	-.21	38	37	1.25	-1.038	.306	
2. S-D Heterosex Time 1 to 2 (all Time 3 cases)	2.54	2.80		-.26	38	37	.99	-1.636	.110	
3. S-D Heterosex Time 1 to 2 (all Time 2 cases)	2.63	2.85		-.22	44	43	.98	-1.530	.133	
4. S-D Homosex Time 1 to 3	3.92		3.42	.50	38	37	1.41	2.179	.036	0.427
5. S-D Homosex Time 1 to 2 (all Time 3 cases)	3.92	3.24		.68	38	37	1.09	3.881	.000	0.640
6. S-D Homosex Time 1 to 2 (all Time 2 cases)	3.90	3.20		.70	44	43	1.03	4.440	.000	0.619
7. S-D Exp Heterosex Time 1 to 3	2.57		2.78	-.21	38	37	1.01	-1.284	.207	
8. S-D Exp Heterosex Time 1 to 2 (all Time 3 cases)	2.57	2.91		-.34	38	37	.78	-2.686	.011	-0.346
9. S-D Exp Heterosex Time 1 to 2 (all Time 2 cases)	2.67	2.96		-.29	44	43	.78	-2.460	.018	-0.285
10. S-D Exp Homosex Time 1 to 3	4.11		3.64	.47	38	37	1.06	2.759	.009	0.517
11. S-D Exp Homosex Time 1 to 2 (all Time 3 cases)	4.11	3.58		.53	38	37	.87	3.758	.001	0.644
12. S-D Exp Homosex Time 1 to 2 (all Time 2 cases)	4.07	3.55		.52	44	43	.82	4.215	.000	0.603

Legend

1. The Shively and DeCecco (S-D) ratings comprise two independent scores, one of heterosexuality and one of homosexuality; so also the Shively and DeCecco Expanded (S-D

Exp) Ratings. For each of the S-D and S-D Exp scores, we present three comparisons: First, the report of Time 1 to Time 3 comparison, including only those cases presenting data for both assessments. Second, the report of Time 1 to Time 2 comparison including only the cases also available at Time 3 (in other words, this comparison included only the same cases as in the first Time 1 to Time 3 comparison, designated "all Time 3 cases"). Third, the report of Time 1 to Time 2 comparison, including *all* of the cases that were available at Time 2 (in other words, this comparison included all of the cases available at Time 2, a larger population than those available at Time 3, designated "all Time 2 cases").

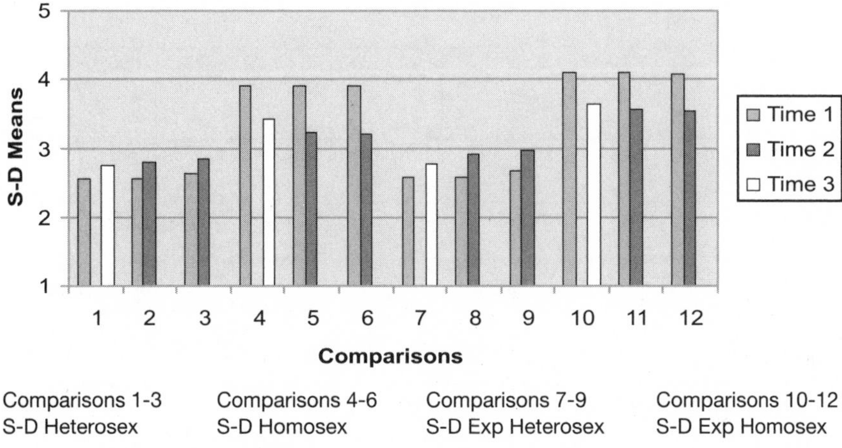

Figure 7.7. Shively and DeCecco (S-D) and Shively and DeCecco Expanded Variables: Phase 1 Population

Again, as with the Kinsey findings, the Truly Gay subpopulation showed (table 7.12) the largest gains both in shifts away from homosexual orientation and shifts toward heterosexual orientation. All comparisons were statistically significant; shifts away from homosexual orientation were of about twice the absolute magnitude as shifts toward heterosexual orientation. The Cohen *d* measure of effect size indicates that changes toward being less homosexual for this Truly Gay subpopulation were consistently in the large to very large effect size range, while changes toward being more heterosexual were consistently in the medium to medium-large effect size range. Once again, the dramatic nature of these shifts in this subpopulation that should be least expected to demonstrate such change must be noted. Very substantial movement away from homosexuality is documented here, and movement toward heterosexuality, while more modest, is nevertheless still considerable.

Table 7.12. Shively and DeCecco (S-D) and Shively and DeCecco Expanded (S-D Exp) Ratings for the Truly Gay Population

	Time 1 Mean	Time 2 Mean	Time 3 Mean	Mean Diff.	N	df	Std. Dev.	t score	2-tailed sig.	Cohen *d*
1. S-D Heterosex Time 1 to 3	2.27		2.74	-.47	43	42	1.43	-2.185	.035	-0.429
2. S-D Heterosex Time 1 to 2 (all Time 3 cases)	2.27	2.95		-.68	43	42	1.28	-3.522	.001	-0.624
3. S-D Heterosex Time 1 to 2 (all Time 2 cases)	2.19	2.89		-.70	47	46	1.22	-3.935	.000	-0.647
4. S-D Homosex Time 1 to 3	4.21		3.15	1.06	43	42	1.42	4.860	.000	1.001
5. S-D Homosex Time 1 to 2 (all Time 3 cases)	4.21	3.08		1.13	43	42	1.23	5.989	.000	1.084
6. S-D Homosex Time 1 to 2 (all Time 2 cases)	4.26	3.09		1.17	47	46	1.23	6.497	.000	1.130
7. S-D Exp Heterosex Time 1 to 3	2.28		2.78	-.50	43	42	1.21	-2.771	.008	-0.486
8. S-D Exp Heterosex Time 1 to 2 (all Time 3 cases)	2.28	2.98		-.70	43	42	1.02	-4.545	.000	-0.691
9. S-D Exp Heterosex Time 1 to 2 (all Time 2 cases)	2.23	2.94		-.71	47	46	.98	-4.984	.000	-0.706
10. S-D Exp Homosex Time 1 to 3	4.33		3.40	.93	43	42	1.21	5.037	.000	1.024
11. S-D Exp Homosex Time 1 to 2 (all Time 3 cases)	4.33	3.42		.91	43	42	1.07	5.549	.000	1.043
12. S-D Exp Homosex Time 1 to 2 (all Time 2 cases)	4.35	3.42		.93	47	46	1.05	6.049	.000	1.075

Legend

1. The Shively and DeCecco (S-D) ratings comprise two independent scores, one of heterosexuality and one of homosexuality; so also the Shively and DeCecco Expanded (S-D

Exp) ratings. For each of the S-D and S-D Exp scores, we present three comparisons: First, the report of Time 1 to Time 3 comparison, including only those cases presenting data for both assessments. Second, the report of Time 1 to Time 2 comparison, including only the cases also available at Time 3 (in other words, this comparison included only the same cases as in the first Time 1 to Time 3 comparison, designated "all Time 3 cases"). Third, the report of Time 1 to Time 2 comparison, including *all* of the cases that were available at Time 2 (in other words, this comparison included all of the cases available at Time 2, a larger population than those available at Time 3, designated "all Time 2 cases").

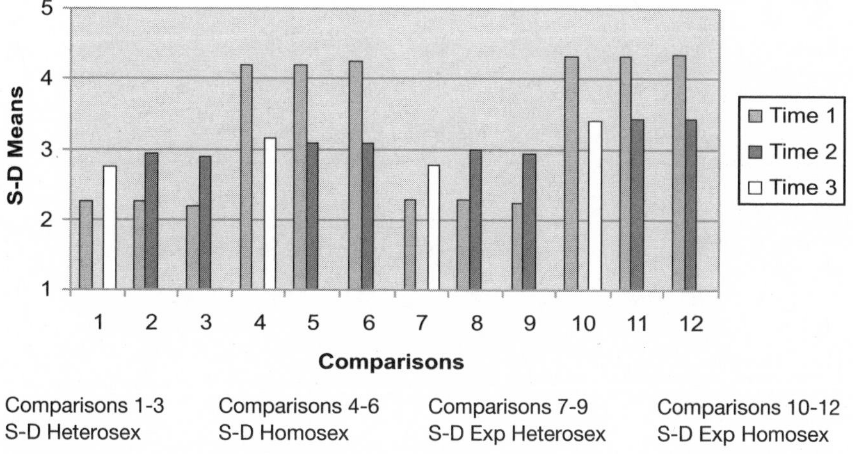

Comparisons 1-3 S-D Heterosex

Comparisons 4-6 S-D Homosex

Comparisons 7-9 S-D Exp Heterosex

Comparisons 10-12 S-D Exp Homosex

Figure 7.8. Shively and DeCecco (S-D) and Shively and DeCecco Expanded Variables: Truly Gay Population

Essentially all of the changes noted occurred from Time 1 to Time 2, with no apparent change on average from Time 2 to 3. Again, it is remarkable that the strongest findings of change on the Shively and DeCecco and Shively and DeCecco Expanded ratings would come in this Truly Gay subpopulation.

Klein Sexual Orientation Grid Ratings Results

As discussed in chapter six, we created a composite four-item Klein Sexual Orientation Grid (KSOG) score for each subject. Each Klein Grid gave us past, present and ideal scores on each of seven items (for a total of twenty-one possible scores), but our analyses showed, as expected, no significant changes at all for any of the past or ideal comparisons. We reiterate, we had

Table 7.13. Klein Sexual Orientation Grid (KSOG) (4-Item) "Present" Scores for Whole, Phase 1 and Truly Gay Populations

	Time 1 Mean	Time 2 Mean	Time 3 Mean	Mean Diff.	N	df	Std. Dev.	t score	2-tailed sig.	Cohen *d*
Whole Population										
1. KSOG 4-item Time 1 to 3	4.99		4.69	.30	73	72	.98	2.682	.009	0.256
2. KSOG 4-item Time 1 to 2 (all Time 3 cases)	4.99	4.59		.40	73	72	.73	4.604	.000	0.337
3. KSOG 4-item Time 1 to 2 (all Time 2 cases)	4.92	4.50		.42	84	83	.72	5.306	.000	0.346
Phase 1 Population										
4. KSOG 4-item Time 1 to 3	5.17		4.77	.40	38	37	1.09	2.283	.028	0.346
5. KSOG 4-item Time 1 to 2 (all Time 3 cases)	5.17	4.71		.46	38	37	.84	3.382	.002	0.415
6. KSOG 4-item Time 1 to 2 (all Time 2 cases)	5.08	4.63		.45	44	43	.80	3.722	.001	0.380
Truly Gay Population										
7. KSOG 4-item Time 1 to 3	4.95		4.71	.24	43	42	.92	1.676	.101	
8. KSOG 4-item Time 1 to 2 (all Time 3 cases)	4.95	4.58		.37	43	42	.71	3.385	.002	0.289
9. KSOG 4-item Time 1 to 2 (all Time 2 cases)	5.01	4.61		.40	47	46	.71	3.842	.000	0.321

Legend

1. For each of the Klein Sexual Orientation Grid (KSOG) scores, we present three comparisons. First, the report of Time 1 to Time 3 comparison, including only those cases presenting data for both assessments. Second, the report of Time 1 to Time 2 comparison, including only the cases also available at Time 3 (in other words, this comparison included only the same cases as in the first Time 1 to Time 3 comparison, designated "all Time 3 cases"). Third the report of Time 1 to Time 2 comparison, including all of the cases that were available at Time 2 (in other words, this comparison included all of the cases available at Time 2, a larger population than those available at Time 3, designated "all Time 2 cases").

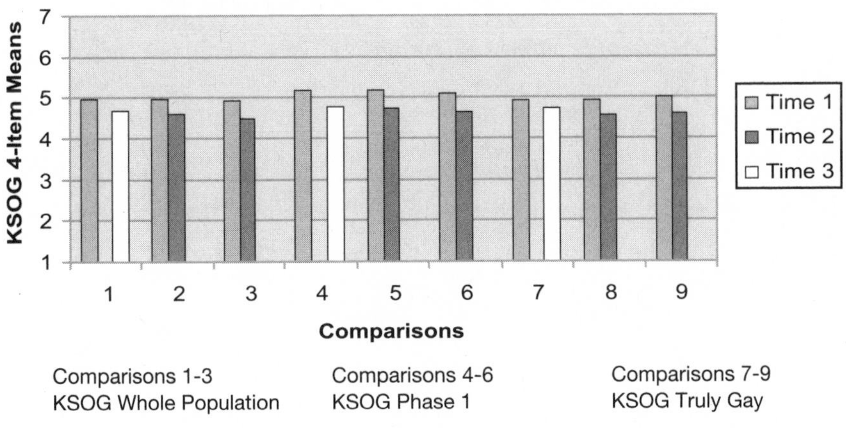

Figure 7.9. Klein Sexual Orientation Grid (KSOG) 4-Item: Whole, Phase 1 and Truly Gay Populations

no reason to believe that participant reports of their "past" ratings (which should remain stable) and of their "ideal" ratings would move, and the lack of significant changes on these confirmed our supposition. Hence, we present here only the various comparisons of the "present" scores, specifically of the four-item composite we created from the Klein's rating questions for sexual attraction, sexual fantasies, emotional preference and social preference.

Using the 0.05 level of significance, eight out of our nine KSOG comparisons (table 7.13) attained statistical significance. The Cohen *d* effect sizes for these eight significant results ranged from small to a few approaching medium effect sizes. Several contrasts to the findings reported for the Kinsey and Shively-and-DeCecco variables merit comment. First, for the first time the findings for the Truly Gay subpopulation were not the strongest of the various population findings, but rather it was in this comparison that we had one of the comparisons fail to achieve statistical significance.

More globally and significantly, however, it must be noted that the absolute magnitude of the means across time were truly modest and hard to describe as clinically meaningful. Among the eight statistically significant differences, the absolute sizes of the differences ranged from 0.30 to 0.46, this on a statistical mean of four scales scored from 1 to 7. In real terms this means that the average subject in giving four seven-point ratings each at Time 1 and Time 3 would have reported a difference of between one and two points on all four scales together to produce this outcome (e.g., ratings of 6, 6, 6, 6 at Time 1 and ratings of 5, 5, 6, 6 at Time 3 would have been an average shift that produced about a 0.50 change in the average rating). We would not be willing to argue that statistical significance here had much connection with clinical significance.

How would we explain the contrast between these changes and those reported on the Kinsey and Shively-and-DeCecco variables? One explanation might have to do with the inclusion of the "social preference" variable in our ratings. One study suggests that the Klein variables that cluster together empirically by factor analysis are behavior (which we did not use because of our sexually inexperienced participants), sexual attraction, fantasy and emotional attraction variables.[9] Our inclusion of the social preference variable may have "dampened" our findings. It is also possible that the Klein is simply less sensitive of an instrument (or the opposite may be possible—that the Kinsey and Shively-and-DeCecco measures are overly sensitive and that the Klein represents the better single measure).

YARHOUSE SEXUAL ORIENTATION THERMOMETER RESULTS

The Yarhouse Sexual Orientation Thermometer (YSOT) instrument is an unvalidated one, and so interpretation of these mixed results must be rather tentative. Generally, the changes were consistently modest on this measure. A smattering of findings achieved statistical significance at the 0.05 level (table 7.14). For those that attained significance, the Cohen *d* effect size measure depicted these shifts as small in size.

In contrast to the findings with the Shively and DeCecco ratings, the shifts toward heterosexual orientation were of about the same magnitude as the shifts away from homosexual orientation. As we have found consistently, the change that occurred was almost all from Time 1 to Time 2; Time 2 to 3 change was negligible.

Table 7.14. Yarhouse Sexual Orientation Thermometer (YSOT) Ratings for the Whole, Phase 1 and Truly Gay Populations

	Time 1 Mean	Time 2 Mean	Time 3 Mean	Mean Diff.	N	df	Std. Dev.	t score	2-tailed sig.	Cohen *d*
Whole Population										
1. YSOT Heterosex Time 1 to 3	3.95		4.52	-.57	73	72	2.29	-2.130	.037	-0.218
2. YSOT Heterosex Time 1 to 2 (all Time 3 cases)	3.95	4.38		-.43	73	72	1.61	-2.285	.025	-0.182
3. YSOT Heterosex Time 1 to 2 (all Time 2 cases)	4.16	4.58		-.42	85	84	1.65	-2.350	.021	-0.169
4. YSOT Homosex Time 1 to 3	6.25		5.78	.47	72	71	2.49	1.590	.116	
5. YSOT Homosex Time 1 to 2 (all Time 3 cases)	6.26	5.70		.56	73	72	1.86	2.553	.013	0.209
6. YSOT Homosex Time 1 to 2 (all Time 2 cases)	6.09	5.46		.63	85	84	1.92	2.986	.004	0.231
Phase 1 Population										
7. YSOT Heterosex Time 1 to 3	3.32		3.97	-.65	38	37	2.47	-1.618	.114	
8. YSOT Heterosex Time 1 to 2 (all Time 3 cases)	3.32	3.99		-.67	38	37	1.70	-2.410	.021	-0.311
9. YSOT Heterosex Time 1 to 2 (all Time 2 cases)	3.61	4.13		-.52	44	43	1.67	-2.013	.050	-0.219
10. YSOT Homosex Time 1 to 3	6.74		6.22	.52	37	36	2.89	1.100	.278	
11. YSOT Homosex Time 1 to 2 (all Time 3 cases)	6.75		5.93	.82	38	37	2.11	2.384	.022	0.320

12. YSOT Homosex Time 1 to 2 (all Time 2 cases)	6.52	5.75		.77	44	43	2.03	2.529	.015	0.292
Truly Gay Population										
13. YSOT Heterosex Time 1 to 3	3.77		4.30	-.53	43	42	2.28	-1.536	.132	
14. YSOT Heterosex Time 1 to 2 (all Time 3 cases)	3.66	4.28		-.62	47	46	1.78	-2.420	.020	-0.239
15. YSOT Heterosex Time 1 to 2 (all Time 2 cases)	3.77	4.33		-.56	43	42	1.65	-2.229	.031	-0.213
16. YSOT Homosex Time 1 to 3	6.22		5.98	.24	43	42	2.42	.652	.518	
17. YSOT Homosex Time 1 to 2 (all Time 3 cases)	6.28	5.82		.46	47	46	1.75	1.801	.078	
18. YSOT Homosex Time 1 to 2 (all Time 2 cases)	6.22	5.87		.35	43	42	1.66	1.411	.166	

Legend

1. Like the Shively and DeCecco (S-D) ratings, the YSOT scores report two independent scores, one of heterosexuality and one of homosexuality. For each, we present three comparisons: First, the report of Time 1 to Time 3 comparison, including only those cases presenting data for both assessments. Second, the report of Time 1 to Time 2 comparison, including only the cases also available at Time 3 (in other words, this comparison included only the same cases as in the first Time 1 to Time 3 comparison, designated "all Time 3 cases"). Third, the report of Time 1 to Time 2 comparison, including *all* of the cases that were available at Time 2 (in other words, this comparison included all of the cases available at Time 2, a larger population than those available at Time 3, designated "all Time 2 cases").

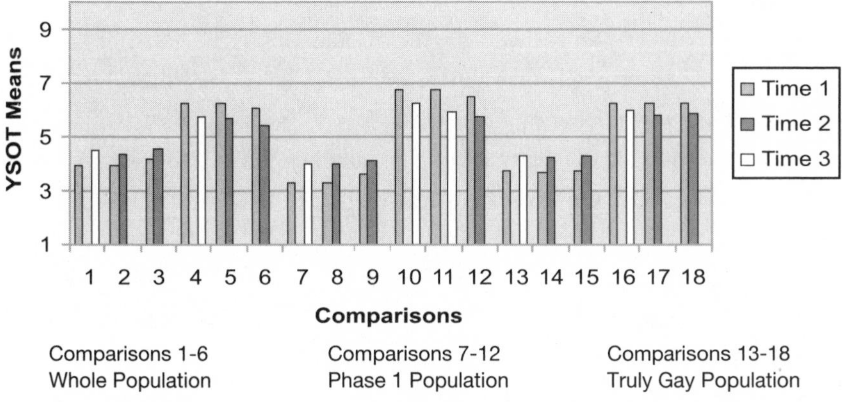

Figure 7.10. Yarhouse Sexual Orientation Thermometer (YSOT) Variables: Whole, Phase 1 and Truly Gay Populations

Conclusion and Summary

The general picture that emerges from our analyses of these data is that, on average, this population has experienced significant change away from homosexual orientation and toward heterosexual orientation. By empirically derived standards of effect size, the average movement away from homosexual orientation may be termed medium to large, and the average shift toward heterosexual orientation is small. This generalization is, of course, not true for every single test of every variable, but this is the clear trend in the data.

The most surprising single finding, and one that is replicated over several different measures, is that the population most likely on average to manifest significant change is the Truly Gay subpopulation. We constructed this subpopulation based on responses at the Time 1 assessment that indicated that the individual was above the median score for ratings of homosexual erotic attraction, for past homosexual sexual behavior and for identification as homosexual (gay or lesbian). These individuals, in other words, all reported homosexual attraction above the bisexual median of the rating scales, had been predominantly homosexually active in the past and had identified as homosexual in the past. These are rigorous classification standards. Common sense and dominant clinical professional opinion would clearly predict that these would be the research subjects least likely to report fundamental change, and yet consistently it was this group that reported the greatest degree of change.

Among the three groups we separated for analysis, the Phase 1 subpopulation (those in the change process for less than one year at the Time 1 assessment) showed the least degree of change. Even so, they reported many significant changes but not to the degree of the Truly Gay subpopulation.

The reporting and analysis of "average change" mask the results shown by particular individuals. As we will see in chapter eight, the average changes contain rather dramatic changes experienced by certain individuals.

8

Can Sexual Orientation Change?

Report of the Qualitative (and Supporting Quantitative) Analyses

THE TYPES OF ANALYSES PRESENTED IN chapter seven represent the kind of "number crunching" that is a staple of the field of psychology. But these results suffer from the kinds of limitations that are inherent in such analyses. For instance, we reported the "average" change over time on the Kinsey scores for groups as a whole (such as the average Time 1 to Time 3 change for the Whole Population on the Kinsey one-item, which averaged about one point on a seven-point scale), but such an average obscures the reality that some participants changed dramatically while others experienced negative change. The averages wash out more dramatic and positive results for certain individuals and hide negative change for others (at least in the eyes of Exodus). And some would also argue that focusing exclusively on what the numbers tell us obscures the human story of what has transpired in this population, a story less to be told in statistical averages and significance tests and more in the words that people use to tell their stories.

This chapter reports the latter type of analysis, what advocates for this type of analysis call a qualitative, as opposed to a quantitative, analysis. Such an analysis of the outcomes from the Exodus interventions gives us information different from and complementary to what a statistical analysis of single or even compound quantitative measures can provide.

We will begin by describing in straightforward terms the nature of the analysis that is presented in this chapter. Remember that we audiotaped all of the interviews (except for turning off the tape recorders when subjects were silent as they filled out the self-administered questionnaires), and then had each of these tapes transcribed. We began our qualitative analysis by reading all seventy-three (actually sixty-nine, since we had four taping malfunctions among the possible 73 Time 3 subjects) transcriptions of the Time 3 interview assessments. In this first read, we were not yet trying to categorize the reports of the participants but rather were attempting to discern if there were "natural categories" that emerged from the reports, obvious groupings of the experiences of these 73 individuals still in our study. We settled on the six categories we introduce later (see pp. 279-281).[1] Next, we returned to the transcriptions, reading them again to categorize each participant in one of the six categories. The bulk of this chapter is the report of the categorizations, and the reporting of edited transcriptions of the self-descriptions of these participants that serve to exemplify the experiences of participants in each category. Between the tabular summary of the categorizations and the sample transcripts, we present quantitative data on the subjects arrayed by the qualitative group to which we have assigned them. In other words, we separated subjects into the six qualitative categories and then went back to our data to see if the patterns of quantitative outcomes for these subjects paralleled their qualitative results. It would make no sense, for instance, to accept the reports of the "Success: Conversion" group as meaningful if, on the quantitative sexual orientation scales, these subjects reported no better results than any other group in the sample.

The validity of qualitative analysis is vigorously disputed throughout the field of psychology. For some, it gives us access to the meaningful data of human experience that responses on tests and scales cannot. For some, it simply obscures the scientifically validated outcomes in favor of unreliable anecdotal testimony. Personally, both of us lean more toward the quantitative end than the qualitative, and because of this we have insisted on reexamining our quantitative data in light of the qualitative categories as a check on the anecdotal reports and to use those reports as rigorously as possible.

What we offer here falls short of what some regard as the most rigorous way to do qualitative analysis. For example, some would urge the use of computerized content analyses of transcriptions to generate the findings without human intervention. We rejected this possibility because we did not believe such programs would give us meaningful outcomes given the structure and complexity of our data. Another approach to rigor would mandate the use of multiple highly trained raters working independently of each other, with reliability and agreement reported, in categorizing the transcriptions. The following steps might be followed for such a rigorous qualitative analysis to guarantee "objectivity" of the analysis:

- establish the final categories (we came up with six) through independent agreement of multiple raters
- train three or four independent raters for your experimental sample using test cases
- have the independent raters categorize each of your cases in your sample, noting rates of agreement
- if needed, resolve ambiguity in the categories and do the training and categorizations by independent raters again, reporting rates of agreement

We did not approach these categorizations with this level of rigor because of the types of results we see this study producing. We do not, as we articulated earlier (see pp. 121-126), know for sure that we have a representative sample for this study of the universe of people who might have a desire to change their sexual orientation from homosexuality, and we do not see that our results could meaningfully address questions such as, What percentage of people can change their sexual orientation? We do, however, see this study as meaningfully addressing the core question of whether change of sexual orientation is impossible, and of providing insight into the type of change that may be possible. For outcomes of this sort, we felt it unnecessary to strive for a higher level of rigor through such steps as already summarized.

The Six Qualitative Categories of Outcomes

We began with the creation of workable categories that would meaningfully summarize the general outcomes for these participants at the Time 3 assessment. After reading the transcriptions of the Time 3 interviews, we decided on six qualitative categories, which we defined as:

- *Success: Conversion*. The subject reports complete (or nearly complete) success or resolution of homosexual orientation issues *and* substantial conversion to heterosexual attraction. Homosexual attraction is either missing or present only incidentally and in a way that does not seem to bring about distress or undue "temptation." The person either has a successful heterosexual sex life (whether in marriage or otherwise), or reports he or she is dating and experiencing satisfactory heterosexual attraction even though not acting out sexually due to moral constraints. The subject appears to have firm confidence in the stability of change and of continuing progress. Prototype: "I'm healed; rarely experience homosexual desire to significant proportions, and enjoy a good sex life with my spouse (or am dating and am very attracted to my love interest)."

- *Success: Chastity.* The subject reports very substantial resolution of homosexual orientation issues; homosexual attraction is either missing or present only incidentally and in a way that does not seem to bring about distress or undue temptation. The person may either report some sort of asexual moderation of sexual drive of all kinds, most typically as decrease in homosexual attraction without parallel increase of heterosexual, or may report a lack of compulsion to act on (or power of) their existing homosexual drive. The subject may be uninvolved in heterosexual romantic or erotic experience altogether, or may report "thinking about" or "considering" heterosexual dating. The subject may also be actively exploring heterosexual dating but without clear and definitive experience of heterosexual desire, or may even be married with an asexual experience in the marriage (marital relationship mentioned in incidental way). He or she appears to have firm confidence in the stability of change and of continuing progress. Prototype: "I'm healed; rarely experience homosexual desire to significant proportions, and am contented to enjoy healthy male and female relationships without worrying about trying to 'become' heterosexual. God may bring about further change in the future."
- *Continuing.* The person may have experienced substantial, moderate or little diminution of homosexual attraction, but is clearly not reporting dramatic change of the type with which to be satisfied as an end product of the change process. Nevertheless, the person remains

hopeful and firmly committed to the change process, whether through Exodus, therapy, general Christian or religious resources, or even in isolation. Prototype: "It is still very much a struggle, and my sexual orientation has not changed much at all, but I am experiencing healing in many emotional ways and am confident in my path as I continue to pursue the direction I began with Exodus."

- *Nonresponse.* The subject has experienced no significant sexual orientation change. The person has *not* given up on the change process, however, but is not forcefully or confidently pursuing further change either. He or she may be confused or conflicted about which direction to turn next. The subject may have engaged in homosexual activity, but without embracing a homosexual identity. Prototype: "I have not changed my experience of sexual attraction at all. I'm discouraged and not doing much on this at present. I still want to change; maybe I just need to find a different approach. I've had a couple of homosexual affairs, but that disgusted me."
- *Failure: Confused.* The person has experienced no significant sexual orientation change and has clearly given up on the change process. However, he or she has not yet clearly reembraced gay identity and is conflicted about his or her direction. If the person reports active sexual partnerships, they are guilt-ridden and/or highly unstable and do not clearly signal a definitive embrace of homosexual identity. Prototype: "I have not changed at all and have given up on the attempt to change my orientation. I do not know what to do now, though, because I do not want to go into a gay lifestyle, but I am finding no peace and no happiness in trying to pretend I am something I am not."
- *Failure: Gay identity.* The person has clearly given up on the change process and reembraced gay identity. The person may be actively partnered, between partners, looking for a partner or even may be sexually inactive for now (this last possibility differs from the "chaste" option in that he or she has made a decision to be open to future homosexual relationships). Prototype: "Exodus was a failure; change of orientation is a myth. I gave it up, have found someone to love and am happy again."

RESULTS OF THE QUALITATIVE CATEGORIZATIONS

After establishing the six categories above, we returned again to the transcriptions, and this time assigned every case transcript to one of these six categories. Table 8.1 presents the numbers of cases in the categories to which we assigned them.

Table 8.1. Results of the Qualitative Analysis

Success: Conversion	**Success: Chastity**	**Continuing**	**Non-response**	**Failure: Confused**	**Failure: Gay Identity**
Whole Pop. 11 cases (15%) of the 73 total Time 3 cases	*Whole Pop.* 17 cases (23%) of the 73 total Time 3 cases	*Whole Pop.* 21 cases (29%) of the 73 total Time 3 cases	*Whole Pop.* 11 cases (15%) of the 73 total Time 3 cases	*Whole Pop.* 3 cases (4%) of the 73 total Time 3 cases	*Whole Pop.* 6 cases (8%) of the 73 total Time 3 cases
Phase 1 6 of 11 cases (55%) were Phase 1 subjects	*Phase 1* 7 of 17 cases (41%) were Phase 1 subjects	*Phase 1* 10 of 21 cases (48%) were Phase 1 subjects	*Phase 1* 8 of 11 cases (73%) were Phase 1 subjects	*Phase 1* 3 of 3 cases (100%) were Phase 1 subjects	*Phase 1* 3 of 6 cases (50%) were Phase 1 subjects
Truly Gay 8 of 11 cases (73%) were Truly Gay	*Truly Gay* 7 of 17 cases (41%) were Truly Gay	*Truly Gay* 12 of 21 cases (57%) were Truly Gay	*Truly Gay* 7 of 11 cases (64%) were Truly Gay	*Truly Gay* 3 of 3 cases (100%) were Truly Gay	*Truly Gay* 4 of 6 cases (67%) were Truly Gay

Note: There were four taping failures at Time 3 (two were Phase 1 and were not Truly Gay; one was a Phase 2 person who was Truly Gay, and one was Phase 2 and not Truly Gay) of the seventy-three cases total [4 of 73 Total = 5%]

In each column we present first the number and percentage of the total of cases categorized into this group out of the total of 73 (so under "Success: Conversion," we had 11 cases of the total 73 Time 3 cases that merited categorization here), followed by the number and percentage of the total that were Phase 1 subjects in this category (6 of 11 "Success: Conversion" cases [55%] were Phase 1 subjects), and finally report the number and percentage of the total in this category that were empirically assigned as Truly Gay (in this case, 8 of 11 or 73%). These findings are graphically depicted in figure 8.1.

How do these findings for outcome compare with other change efforts in the mental health field, such as marital therapy? Our two success categories (conversion and chastity; together 38%) would parallel strongly pos-

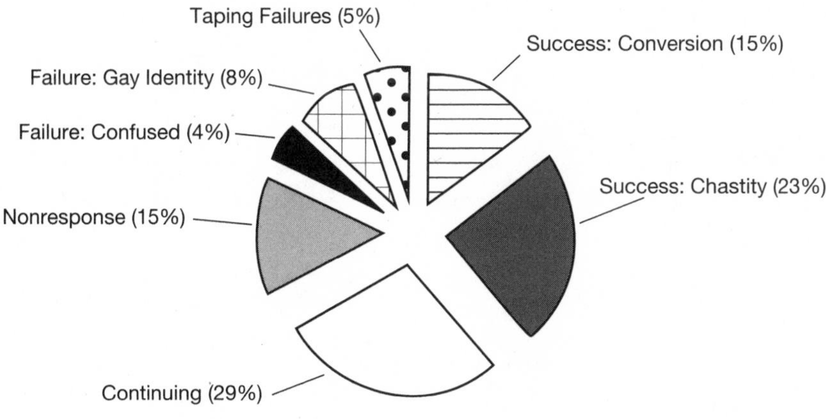

Figure 8.1. Qualitative Categorizations

itive outcomes, the continuing group (29%) would parallel an improved-but-with-room-for-continued-growth category, the nonresponders (15%) would reflect a no-change outcome, and the two failure groups (together 12%) represent negative outcomes (in the estimation of Exodus). We would contend that an outcome array like this would be regarded as highly positive and estimable in the mental health field, especially when you consider that what Exodus calls failure would not be considered failure at all by the majority of mental health professionals.

But let's not grapple with this in the abstract. It will facilitate understanding of this outcome profile to compare it concretely with another study of successful clinical intervention. Many today would construe pharmaceutical treatment of depression as a gold standard of successful intervention.[2] A very recent and rigorous published study of outcomes from such pharmaceutical treatment of depression with an enormous (2,876) sample of patients can serve as a suitable comparison for our study. The Sequenced Treatment Alternatives to Relieve Depression (STAR*D) study treated a sample of seriously depressed people in standard outpatient settings (by psychiatrists and by general practitioners) to test the effectiveness of this form of medical intervention in general clinical practice with depressed patients.[3] The researchers do not report average depression score outcomes for their subjects in a way that would be comparable to the average outcomes for our study as reported in chapter seven, but they did report two key categories of outcome: (1) "remission," which was defined as the "virtual absence of [depressive] symptoms," and (2) "response," which was defined as "a clinically meaningful reduction in symptoms."[4] The authors of the STAR*D study report that between 28% and 33% (depending on which of the two principle measures of depression reviewed) reported the remission of their depressive symptoms, with an additional 14% showing a clinical response on the more generous outcome measure, for a total of 47% of the patients showing either remission or response. This means, of course, that 53% of the subject patient population did not show a clinically meaningful response to pharmaceutical treatment, the most common method for treating depression.

The results of this ambitious and expansive study can be summarized as 33% remission or substantial success, 14% improvement and 53% non-improvement. Among our population, 38% of the subjects (15% and 23%, respectively, in the two success groups) consider themselves to have successfully changed, an additional 29% consider themselves to have experienced sufficient change such that they are continuing with the change process, and the remaining 33% report no change or return to homosexual identity. The Exodus 38% successes compare to the 33% success rate in this treatment study of depression, and the Exodus successes combined with the 29% continuing total to 67% responding, compared to the 47% responding in the STAR*D study. This would appear to provide grounds for viewing the Exodus ministry approach as representing a reasonably effective intervention into the life concerns of those presenting for change, especially when we consider that (1) sexual orientation is supposed to be immutable, while depression is one of the psychological difficulties more amenable to change, and (2) the failure outcomes in the view of Exodus are not regarded as failures at all by the secular mental health community.

A thought experiment. We have not yet spoken much about outcomes for the dropouts from our study, and fittingly so since we know little about this population. We mentioned the information we have on the dropouts in chapter five, including mentioning that we know that at least one of our dropouts was a success rather than a failure. Even so, in figure 8.2 we present a graphic representation of what our results would look like if all

29 of the subjects on which we lack qualitative information (the four taping failures and the twenty-five true dropouts) were considered to be failures of some kind. Given that this is merely a speculative exercise, we added 10 dropout subjects to the "Failure: Gay Identity" group, 10 to the "Failure: Confused" group and 9 to the "Nonresponse" group. The results then look like this:

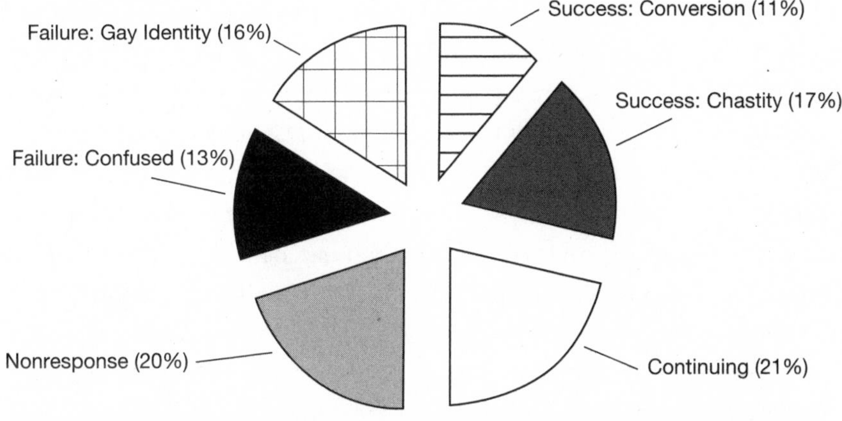

Figure 8.2. Qualitative Categorizations (with Dropouts Assumed Failures)

We would argue that even the results of figure 8.2 are fairly typical from psychotherapy outcome studies, especially those looking at populations that experience significant difficulty in changing. How would this compare to the STAR*D data mentioned earlier? In this thought experiment, our Exodus successes now drop to 28% compared to the 33% success rate in this treatment study of depression, and the Exodus successes combined with the 21% continuing total to 49% responding, compared to the 47% responding in the STAR*D study. Note that this comparison is made without considering the STAR*D dropouts as all failures, as we have for the Exodus sample dropouts.

While we are discussing dropouts and intervention failures, we want to mention one notable treatment failure. After this book manuscript was essentially complete, we received a letter from a research participant retracting his earlier reports of his status. This participant was one of the eleven "Success: Conversion" cases at Time 3, a Phase 1 participant who had been classified as Truly Gay. He reported that through the Time 3 assessments he had believed himself to be rightly reporting his successful outcomes, but that through a series of difficulties and deepening self-reflection, after the Time 3 assessment he came to realize that his homosexual orientation was in fact unchanged. He has since repudiated the Exodus movement and returned to active embrace of his gay identity.

We report briefly on this individual's testimony in the later section (see pp. 300-301) where we present representative excerpts from participant interviews. In doing so, however, we go beyond the boundaries of the data available at Time 3. Recognizing this, we have not changed this person's categorization in our data analysis because we are continuing the study and will present a follow-up analysis of the participant's continuing status at a later point. This individual is here presented as a success, but we now know that he later repudiated his prior presentation and has committed himself to the gay lifestyle. This subject is continuing in the study, and is now reporting full gay identity, and his data will be included in further reports. What we do not know, however, is the status of other subjects who may have made dramatic moves in their status in any direction—subjects may have moved from any of our categories into other categories, so this individual may be balanced by persons moving from the various failure or nonresponse categories into the success categories. This situation is not dissimilar to the movement one gets across groups in any treatment study, as when smokers who had quit return to smoking, or people experience relapses into serious emotional distress. We have faithfully represented the data from our subjects as presented in Times 1 through 3 and will continue to do so in subsequent presentations as well.

QUANTITATIVE DATA AND ANALYSIS BY QUALITATIVE CATEGORIES

Were either Phase 1 or Truly Gay subjects overrepresented or underrepresented in the six categories we have identified? For instance, it is noteworthy that all three of the "Failure: Confused" subjects were *both* Phase 1 and Truly Gay subjects. Is there a trend here? While noteworthy, the three subjects in this category are such a small sample that extreme caution must be exercised in drawing conclusions from them. A total of 57 of the original Time 1 sample of 98 subjects (58.2%) were Phase 1 subjects, and 55 of the original 98 (56.1%) were Truly Gay. At Time 3, 41 of 73 remaining subjects (56.2%; this number counts the 2 Phase 1 taping failures) were Phase 1 subjects. At Time 3, 42 (counting the 1 Truly Gay taping failure) out of 73 (57.5%) remaining subjects were Truly Gay subjects. There appears to have been no differential in sample erosion based on Phase 1 or Truly Gay status.

It would appear that there might be some slight tendency for both Phase 1 and Truly Gay subjects to be overrepresented in the three "more negative" outcome categories. Aggregating the three "more positive" change categories, we find that 47% were Phase 1 subjects (23 Phase 1 cases out of 49 total) and 55% were Truly Gay (27 Truly Gay cases out of 49 total) in these groups overall, while when we combine the three more negative outcome groups to the right in table 8.1 we find that 70% were both Phase 1 and Truly Gay cases (14 Phase 1 and 14 Truly Gay cases each out of 20 total). These were not stark differences, however, and we note that the percentages of Phase 1 and Truly Gay subjects in the most positive change category of "Success: Conversion" and in the most negative change category of "Failure: Gay Identity" were essentially equivalent.

How did the cases in each of these six categories fare on the respected measures of sexual orientation used for our quantitative analysis? Our success cases should reflect more strongly positive outcomes on our measures than the other cases, and so this quantitative examination represents an empirical test of a sort for our qualitative analyses. We summarize here that the results for the Kinsey, Shively and DeCecco, and Klein Sexual Orientation Grid measures for the cases in fact follow the approximate pattern that we would expect from the qualitative characteristics that they reported.

Success: Conversion (11 Cases)

By both statistical and absolute measures of change, these changes are remarkable (table 8.2). On the Kinsey measure, subjects reported an average Time 1 to 3 change of 3.55 points. Remember that the extreme ends of the Kinsey scale range from 7 (exclusively homosexual) to 1 (exclusively heterosexual).1 These success cases reported starting at an average Time 1

1Kinsey created a 7-point scale of sexual orientation as discussed in chapter six, with his scale ranging from 0 (exclusively heterosexual) to 6 (exclusively homosexual). We ran into problems anchoring the scale at one end with a zero because some of our analyses treated this value as missing data rather than an actual value. Therefore, we recoded this data to range from 1 (exclusively heterosexual) to 7 (exclusively homosexual), thus keeping the same 7-point scale structure for assessing sexual orientation but shifting the point values by one.

Table 8.2. Kinsey, Shively and DeCecco (S-D), and Klein Sexual Orientation Grid (KSOG) (4-Item) Scores for the Eleven "Success: Conversion" Cases from the Qualitative Analysis

Success: Conversion 11 Cases	Time 1 Mean	Time 2 Mean	Time 3 Mean	Mean Diff.	N	df	Std. Dev.	t score	2-tailed sig.
1. Kinsey 1-item Time 1 to 2	5.09	1.91		3.18	11	10	2.316	4.56	0.001
2. Kinsey 1-item Time 1 to 3	5.09		1.55	3.55	11	10	2.12	5.56	0.000
3. S-D Homosex Time 1 to 2	3.77	1.73		2.05	11	10	1.62	4.19	0.002
4. S-D Homosex Time 1 to 3	3.77		1.82	1.95	11	10	1.46	4.45	0.001
5. S-D Heterosex Time 1 to 2	2.50	4.27		-1.77	11	10	1.10	-5.33	0.000
6. S-D Heterosex Time 1 to 3	2.50		4.45	-1.95	11	10	0.72	-8.97	0.000
7. KSOG 4-item Time 1 to 2	3.61	2.93		0.68	11	10	0.77	2.95	0.015
8. KSOG 4-item Time 1 to 3	3.61		2.95	0.66	11	10	1.24	1.77	0.107

score of 5.09 on the Kinsey one-item, which corresponds to a rating of "largely homosexual, but more than incidental heterosexual" attraction score. At Time 3, they reported an average Kinsey one-item score of 1.55, the midpoint between "exclusively heterosexual" (1) and "largely heterosexual, but incidental homosexual" (2). This gives every indication of being, on average, a strong and clinically meaningful shift in how these people are describing their sexual attractions. Following the pattern of findings in the general population, the greatest portion of the change is reported to have occurred between Times 1 and 2. These findings were all highly statistically significant, but this finding should not be emphasized, because applying the t-test to a subpopulation that is preselected as success cases violates the assumptions behind the test.

The Shively and DeCecco ratings provide independent reports of the sexual attraction and emotional attraction the subject experiences to men and women *separately.* These scores range between 1 and 5 for both homosexual and heterosexual attraction. The scores reported in table 8.2, as in our earlier presentation, are averages of the person's reported sexual attraction and emotional attraction to persons of the same sex and of the other sex. As would be required for a successful conversion, these subjects reported decreased homosexual orientation and increased heterosexual attraction. On average, these subjects began at Time 1 reporting their homosexual attraction as between (3.77) "somewhat attracted homosexually" and "very attracted homosexually," and then on average *decreased* their report of homosexual attraction to between "not at all attracted homosexually" and "somewhat attracted homosexually" (at about 1.8). In complementary fashion, they reported increasing heterosexual attraction. On average, these subjects began at Time 1 reporting their heterosexual attraction as just below (2.5) "somewhat attracted heterosexually," and then on average *increased* their report of heterosexual attraction to between "somewhat attracted heterosexually" and "very attracted heterosexually" (at about 4.3, near the extreme of the scale). These findings again were all highly statistically significant, but this should not be emphasized.

The Klein Sexual Orientation Grid four-item rating was a simple numerical average of the four sexual attraction, sexual fantasies, emotional preference and social preference ratings on the Klein. Each of these Klein scores range potentially from 1 to 7, with a score of 1 indicating exclusive heterosexuality and a 7 exclusive homosexuality. On this scale, subjects reported starting out at Time 1 at just below the midpoint of 4 at 3.61 (just slightly closer to heterosexuality than homosexuality), and then moved to 2.93 or 2.95 at Time 2 and 3 respectively, a shift of less than one point on average. The findings on this scale, just as in the analysis of the more general population, present the most modest estimate of change in the population (see our earlier discussion of factors that may be involved in this outcome).

Success: Chastity (17 Cases)

The Kinsey, the Shively and DeCecco, and the Klein Sexual Orientation Grid (KSOG) (see table 8.3) present a common picture of significant movement away from homosexual orientation for this chastity group. On the Kinsey, they demonstrated significant Time 1 to Time 3 change, a

Table 8.3. Kinsey, Shively and DeCecco (S-D), and Klein Sexual Orientation Grid (KSOG) (4-Item) Scores for the Seventeen "Success: Chastity" Cases from the Qualitative Analysis

Success: Chastity 17 Cases	**Time 1 Mean**	**Time 2 Mean**	**Time 3 Mean**	**Mean Diff.**	**N**	**df**	**Std. Dev.**	**t score**	**2-tailed sig.**
1. Kinsey 1-item Time 1 to 2	4.79	3.50		1.29	14	13	1.98	2.43	0.030
2. Kinsey 1-item Time 1 to 3	5.00		3.06	1.94	16	15	1.61	4.81	0.000
3. S-D Homosex Time 1 to 2	4.06	2.62		1.44	17	16	1.22	4.86	0.000
4. S-D Homosex Time 1 to 3	4.06		2.70	1.35	17	16	0.90	6.22	0.000
5. S-D Heterosex Time 1 to 2	2.35	2.74		-0.38	17	16	1.08	-1.46	0.165
6. S-D Heterosex Time 1 to 3	2.35		2.76	-0.41	17	16	1.16	-1.46	0.163
7. KSOG 4-item Time 1 to 2	4.96	4.41		0.54	17	16	0.68	3.30	0.004
8. KSOG 4-item Time 1 to 3	4.96		4.24	0.72	17	16	0.55	5.40	0.000

move of almost two points (out of seven) away from homosexual and toward heterosexual attraction, change that is quite meaningful in absolute terms and statistically significant. Similarly, on the KSOG we see a pattern of significant Time 1 to Time 2 and Time 3 change away from homosexual and toward heterosexual. The absolute size of this change (move of about 0.50 points out of 7) is modest in contrast to the movement on the other two scales. (This is the same pattern we saw in all of our quantitative analyses.) Importantly, though, the Shively and DeCecco measure of movement toward heterosexuality does not display statistically significant movement (though the nonsignificant trend is toward heterosexuality).

The comparison between the Shively and DeCecco changes Time 1 to Time 3 for the "Success: Chastity" group of 17 cases and the 11 "Success: Conversion" cases tells the story here in a nutshell. The "conversion" group averaged about two points (on a five-point scale) of movement away from homosexual orientation and almost the same size movement toward heterosexual orientation. The "chastity" group, on the other hand, averaged slightly less than 1.5 points of movement away in the lessening of homosexual orientation but less than 0.5 points of gain toward heterosexual attraction. They experienced sizeable movement away from homosexual attraction but did not experience statistically significant growth in heterosexual attraction. This pattern of shift is exactly what we would suggest based on their self-descriptions: Comparing the conversion and chastity groups, we see that the chastity group experienced meaningful lessening of homosexual attraction (though less than that of the conversion group), but did not experience the strong movement toward heterosexual attraction of the conversion group.

Continuing (21 Cases)

The "continuing" group (those still dedicated to the change process but not yet describing themselves as having experienced meaningful change of the type they desired on entering the Exodus program) demonstrates a pattern consistent with their subjective self-description (see table 8.4). They show ambiguous change that is not, with one exception, statistically significant. The one exception is the Shively and DeCecco measure of homosexual attraction, where we find change that is strongly significant statistically (a lessening of homosexual attraction), but in absolute terms, the change of about one point on a five-point scale is modest.

Nonresponse (11 Cases)

As we would expect for this nonresponse group, none of the measures suggest significant change in any particular direction (see table 8.5). Scanning down the "mean difference" column shows absolute changes that are quite small, and none of the change measures approached anything remotely like statistical significance.

Failure: Confused (3 Cases)

Interpretation of the findings of the "Failure: Confused" group is both helped and hindered by the small size of the group (see table 8.6). Interestingly, it would appear across all three measures that the initial ratings of

Table 8.4. Kinsey, Shively and DeCecco (S-D), and Klein Sexual Orientation Grid (KSOG) (4-Item) Scores for the Twenty-One "Continuing" Cases from the Qualitative Analysis

Continuing Cases 21 Cases	Time 1 Mean	Time 2 Mean	Time 3 Mean	Mean Diff.	N	df	Std. Dev.	t score	2-tailed sig.
1. Kinsey 1-item Time 1 to 2	5.14	4.76		0.38	21	20	1.66	1.05	0.305
2. Kinsey 1-item Time 1 to 3	5.14		4.48	0.67	21	20	1.68	1.81	0.085
3. S-D Homosex Time 1 to 2	4.33	3.59		0.74	21	20	0.75	4.50	0.000
4. S-D Homosex Time 1 to 3	4.33		3.24	1.09	21	20	1.17	4.30	0.000
5. S-D Heterosex Time 1 to 2	2.33	2.88		-0.55	21	20	1.04	-2.42	0.025
6. S-D Heterosex Time 1 to 3	2.33		2.57	-0.24	21	20	1.22	-0.89	0.382
7. KSOG 4-item Time 1 to 2	5.30	4.94		0.36	21	20	0.64	2.56	0.019
8. KSOG 4-item Time 1 to 3	5.30		5.00	0.30	21	20	0.65	2.08	0.050

degree of homosexual orientation of this small group was higher than that found in any other group (including those in the next group who moved to consolidate gay identity); compare this group's Time 1 Kinsey rating of 6.33 (of a maximum of 7) to the scores averaging around or just above 5 for all of the other groups. Perhaps it is because of this high initial rating that we get no evidence of any movement whatsoever on the ratings of homosexual orientation of this group that has given up on the change process. There is no statistically significant change in any direction for this group; the statistical tests are of questionable meaningfulness with such a small sample anyway, but the lack of findings is appropriate for the ambiguous change noted.

FAILURE: GAY IDENTITY (6 CASES)

Once again, we have no statistically significant findings in the "Failure: Gay

Table 8.5. Kinsey, Shively and DeCecco (S-D), and Klein Sexual Orientation Grid (KSOG) (4-Item) Scores for the Eleven "Nonresponse" Cases from the Qualitative Analysis

Nonresponse 11 Cases	**Time 1 Mean**	**Time 2 Mean**	**Time 3 Mean**	**Mean Diff.**	**N**	**df**	**Std. Dev.**	**t score**	**2-tailed sig.**
1. Kinsey 1-item Time 1 to 2	5.18	5.00		0.18	11	10	2.09	0.29	0.779
2. Kinsey 1-item Time 1 to 3	5.20		5.70	-0.50	10	9	1.58	-1.00	0.343
3. S-D Homosex Time 1 to 2	4.05	3.45		0.59	11	10	1.02	1.91	0.084
4. S-D Homosex Time 1 to 3	4.05		3.86	0.18	11	10	0.90	0.70	0.519
5. S-D Heterosex Time 1 to 2	2.59	2.32		0.27	11	10	0.72	1.26	1.257
6. S-D Heterosex Time 1 to 3	2.59		2.36	0.23	11	10	1.03	0.73	0.729
7. KSOG 4-item Time 1 to 2	5.57	5.41		0.16	11	10	0.79	0.666	0.521
8. KSOG 4-item Time 1 to 3	5.57		5.57	0.00	11	10	0.76	0.000	1.000

Identity" group of six who have failed to change their sexual orientation and have embraced a gay identity (see table 8.7). As is fitting for a group that embraces gay identity, their Time 3 rating on the Kinsey of 6.50 (out of a possible 7.00) for homosexual identity is the highest reported average of homosexual orientation of any group at any point in time, but because of the high variability in reported scores (reflected in the high standard deviation) and the small sample size, even this change did not attain statistical significance. It is noteworthy, though, that this large move toward homosexual orientation on the Kinsey is not reflected on the other measures.

Summary of Statistical Change Findings

The bar graph in figure 8.3 provides a summary of what was found for change scores ("mean difference" in each of the preceding six tables) from Time 1 to Time 3 for each of the six outcome groups. The changes reported for each of the six groups are presented in three clusters: first for the Kinsey ratings, then for the Shively and DeCecco (S-D) Homosexual ratings, and finally for the Shively and DeCecco Heterosexual ratings. For the Kinsey a bar *above* the 0 baseline indicates a shift away from homosexuality and toward heterosexuality, while a bar *below* the 0 baseline indicates a change toward homosexuality and away from heterosexuality. For the Shively and DeCecco Homosexual ratings, a bar *above* the 0 baseline indicates a shift away from homosexuality, and a bar *below* indicates a change toward homosexuality. Finally, for the Shively and DeCecco Heterosexual ratings, a bar *below* the 0 baseline indicates a shift toward heterosexuality, and a bar *above* indicates a change away from heterosexuality. Even the most casual perusal of this table will indicate that the pattern of change is *strongly congruent* with the subjective reports of the subjects of the study. The "success" participants experienced substantial change away from

Table 8.6. Kinsey, Shively and DeCecco (S-D), and Klein Sexual Orientation Grid (KSOG) (4-Item) Scores for the Three "Failure: Confused" Cases from the Qualitative Analysis

Failure: Confused 3 Cases	Time 1 Mean	Time 2 Mean	Time 3 Mean	Mean Diff.	N	df	Std. Dev.	t score	2-tailed sig.
1. Kinsey 1-item Time 1 to 2	6.33	6.00		0.33	3	2	0.58	1.000	0.423
2. Kinsey 1-item Time 1 to 3	6.33		6.33	0.00	3	2	1.00	0.000	1.000
3. S-D Homosex Time 1 to 2	4.33	4.33		0.00	3	2	0.50	0.000	1.000
4. S-D Homosex Time 1 to 3	4.33		4.67	-0.33	3	2	1.26	-0.459	0.691
5. S-D Heterosex Time 1 to 2	2.67	1.83		0.83	3	2	0.29	5.000	0.038
6. S-D Heterosex Time 1 to 3	2.67		1.83	0.83	3	2	0.44	1.890	0.199
7. KSOG 4-item Time 1 to 2	5.58	5.17		0.42	3	2	0.14	5.000	0.038
8. KSOG 4-item Time 1 to 3	5.58		5.58	0.00	3	2	0.90	0.000	1.000

Table 8.7. Kinsey, Shively and DeCecco (S-D), and Klein Sexual Orientation Grid (KSOG) (4-Item) Scores for the Six "Failure: Gay Identity" Cases from the Qualitative Analysis

Failure: Gay Identity *6 Cases*	Time 1 Mean	Time 2 Mean	Time 3 Mean	Mean Diff.	N	df	Std. Dev.	t score	2-tailed sig.
1. Kinsey 1-item Time 1 to 2	4.50	5.00		-0.50	6	5	2.88	-0.425	0.688
2. Kinsey 1-item Time 1 to 3	4.50		6.50	-2.00	6	5	2.53	-1.936	0.111
3. S-D Homosex Time 1 to 2	4.08	4.16		-0.08	6	5	0.74	-0.277	0.793
4. S-D Homosex Time 1 to 3	4.08		4.75	-0.67	6	5	1.44	-1.136	0.307
5. S-D Heterosex Time 1 to 2	2.33	2.75		-0.42	6	5	1.50	-0.682	0.526
6. S-D Heterosex Time 1 to 3	2.33		1.75	0.58	6	5	1.59	0.896	0.411
7. KSOG 4-item Time 1 to 2	5.33	5.29		0.04	6	5	0.36	0.115	0.913
8. KSOG 4-item Time 1 to 3	5.33		6.12	-0.79	6	5	0.45	-1.763	0.138

homosexuality and toward heterosexuality, the "failure" participants experienced substantial shifts toward homosexuality and away from heterosexuality, and the "continuing" and "nonresponse" subjects in the middle experienced much less change of any kind.

Sample Narratives from Each Category

In the following we offer four examples of each category (except for the one category with three subjects), quoting from the taped transcriptions of the subjects' responses to the qualitative queries that were included in our assessments. In the following excerpts the probe questions by the interviewers are abbreviated and italicized. For example, in the Time 3 assessment, section four of the interview opened with qualitative probes of the person's sexual orientation, with the very first question asked of the subject being, "We want to begin our questions about your sexual feelings by ask-

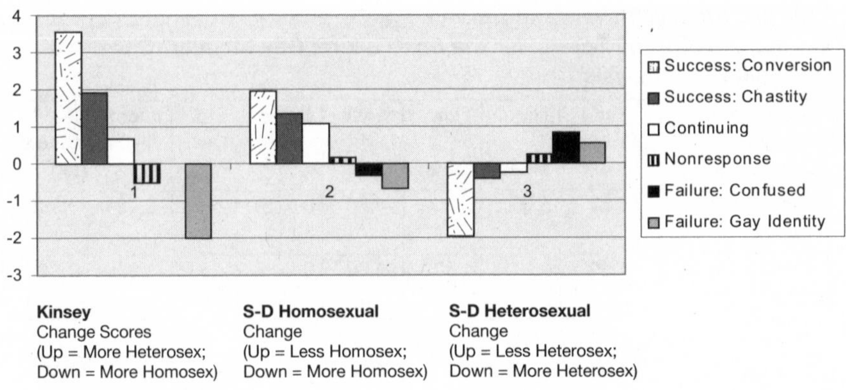

Figure 8.3. Kinsey and Shively-DeCecco Change Scores Time 1 to Time 3 for Each of the Six Outcome Groups

ing you to describe in your own words your sexual orientation as you understand it today." This probe is summarized as *What is your sexual orientation?* The exact questions as presented to the participants can be found in the "interview protocol" in the appendixes;2 a condensed version of just the qualitative questions is presented as an appendix at the end of this chapter. Very minor editing of the transcripted comments has been made to mask the identity of the subject and his or her family, and of the Exodus ministry with which he or she was affiliated, and occasionally to shorten (but not substantively alter) a long, rambling response. All of the material in the following that is not in italics is quotation from our participants.

We alert the reader to a phenomenon that we continue with in chapter nine: even among our failure cases here, we found no evidence of harm from the Exodus experience. This, of course, does not mean that such harm could not happen, but we found no evidence of such harm in these transcripts.

EXAMPLES OF "SUCCESS: CONVERSION"

Success: Conversion example 1 (male, married). *Commitment to change?* "It's stronger; the call to a life of holiness and wholeness, seeking God and knowing that [homosexuality] is not part of it. The more practical aspect

2See appendix 2 on the Internet at <www.ivpress.com>.

is seeking real happiness, which I've found in my marriage. I never found real happiness in that life." *Original major concerns?* "Sexual attraction to men and not wanting it." *How are you doing?* "Really well, light years from where I was. I'm married now, and we have a really blessed relationship in all respects. The strain and temptation of something outside of that is really gigantically diminished such that I want to be with my wife. We have a really healthy, sexual relationship. It's just a delight. I think it's unrealistic to say that I would be unresponsive to things like pornography. I mean, I just have to stay away from that like every man does. I have healthy relationships with men, my wife, other women and with God. I don't think there's an area that hasn't seen change." *Important steps in your faith journey?* "I live my faith. I am a Christian, and it's not so much a choice as a recognition of the order of life. God is God and we are his children. Life is really in this world a pursuit of knowing him. That's the main drive of my life and helping others to know him as well. It's all about God and Jesus and living life in love and obedience to him and seeing how he delights in blessing us and pouring out his abundance on our lives. It's really astonishing to pursue God as wholeheartedly as I can and to see his response. Granted, I'm still a sinner and fall short every day in any number of ways. I'm in my third year of seminary and will be an ordained priest in a few months. I'll be engaging in a life of ministry, proclaiming the freedom for which Christ set us free." *What is your sexual orientation?* "I am a heterosexual, yet I continue to suffer from some degree of sexual brokenness and unwanted sexual attraction to men."

Success: Conversion example 2 (male, married). *Is change possible?* "Absolutely." *Commitment to change?* "It's stronger. I am in full-time ministry. I see the effects of the lifestyle. I'm active in helping others out of it, that feeds my own desire to change. I am in seminary." *Original major concerns?* "I originally sought it out because I wanted to experience the joy of marriage. I just could never picture myself with a woman to be able to do that. I knew that God would not ask of me something that he wouldn't give me the strength to achieve, so I pursued the healing ministry. I wanted to be sexually attracted to women. I wanted to understand how God saw my sin and how God understood homosexuality. I wanted to experience freedom from the desires to go into the lifestyle and to live in that." *How are you* *doing?* "I think very well." *Most helpful methods?* "I was initially helped to change by a program that emphasized healing prayer and time in the Word and building nonerotic same sex friendships. From there I had minimal contact with program participants and minimal contact with the leadership, but thankfully I had been working on building my relationship with my dad. That was able to strengthen. That relationship with my dad was able to feed my sexual identity as a man. I also had the benefit of having a pretty close-knit men's prayer group that walked with me through the healing process—heterosexual guys that cared about me and loved me regardless of everything. I was also open with my fiancée about the program and why I was going through it. No, she wasn't my fiancée then. It was actually a girlfriend that I had gotten close to. She was able to give me a lot of support and at the close of the program, a few months after we finished, I proposed to her. It was really cool because she could go into our marriage knowing my biggest weakness. She has been and has given me incredible support over the last few years. She has been able to really see me heal and change. It's awesome to have her have such confidence in me and in God and in the process." *Are there particular areas where you have experienced change?* "I remember answering this question last year and saying that I wanted God to give me freedom from homoerotic dreams and freedom from the images that kept coming back into my psyche. It's been cool because that has decreased from several times a month to maybe once every three or four months. That would have been my biggest weakness, and I guess a goal for further healing is to completely eliminate the dreams altogether. Also I want to watch my eyes better." *What is your sexual orientation?* "I would define myself to be primarily heterosexual by definition of who I have sexual activity with, with latent, sporadic homosexual lust. I don't desire sexual contact as much as I did last year; I think that a vibrant sexual relationship with my wife has contributed to that." *Exodus influence?* "I think before I entered into the ministry there was a lot of anxiety, a lot of fear, a lot of guilt. I think the ministry helped me to release a lot of those things. I have always been a generally happy person, but because the healing ministry has helped me achieve an identity in heterosexual relationship with my wife, that has helped me to see the goals of becoming a father and supporting a family. Whereas marriage has its own stresses, I think that overall I'm a lot more secure. In just the heterosexual experience alone I have been freed from a lot of the lust and a lot of the guilt that comes from homoerotic behavior and masturbation and things like that that plagued me before. I probably wouldn't be married if it weren't for the healing ministry, and because of my marriage I have also been able to achieve the next level of emotional health. And the acceptance and admiration that I receive from my spouse and the support that we give to each other and the family goals that we set and attain together—all of those things are very healthy."

Success: Conversion example 3 (male, truly gay, married). *Original major concerns?* Originally just wanting freedom from homosexual addictive behavior and thought, wanting to find confidence in my own gender identity. I was pretty desperate at that point." *How are you doing?* "Very well. My life has certainly been changed." *What is your sexual orientation?* "Today, it is heterosexual." *Important steps in your faith journey?* "One would be that church is very important to me. I go on a weekly basis, twice a week actually. The reasons I go are to hear the Word of God being preached, which helps give me guidance and direction for how I try to live my life. I go to worship God through song and dance, to really experience the Lord's tangible presence, which helps me to have peace of mind and joy at church as well as on a day-to-day basis. I consider myself to be a spirit-filled believer, which some might term charismatic or Pentecostal. [We have changed denominations because] my wife and I are trying to pursue becoming licensed in that denomination."

Success: Conversion example 4 (female, truly gay, married). *Is change possible?* "Yes, I've experienced it in my own life, and I've watched others experience the same change." *Are you continuing with the process of changing orientation?* "At the present time I feel like I'm just dealing with the emotional and relational things that have come up—the emotional and relational damage I've had from those relationships. I don't have any of the same-sex attractions anymore, per se, but I have some codependent type things that I have to deal with. I'm starting to deal with pieces of sexual abuse from my past. So I'm dealing with how I got into the same-sex attractions, so in that sense I'm dealing with that. But as far as dealing with the same-sex attractions, I do not have that." *Original major concerns?* "I had attempted on my own at one point to leave the lifestyle. I went back into the lifestyle after about two years. When I felt the Lord's call on me to leave it the second time, I knew that if I was going to do it, it had to be different than the first time, and I knew that meant fellowship and support from fellow believers. At that time there was nothing in my area. I had to look outside of where I lived, and that took me to [a certain ministry]." *How are you doing?* "I believe I'm doing pretty good—I'm married. I feel like I reached the point where I was comfortable with developing relationships with males and then finding one that I felt was special enough in my life to marry. The female relationships have been a little slower in developing. In the last year that has really started to blossom. I'm really praying that the Lord would help me with that." *What is your sexual orientation?* "Heterosexual." *Most helpful methods for change?* "The Exodus group itself was the beginning of my healing. In the last year I went to a group for survivors of childhood sexual abuse and that specific group has been awesome for me. From that group and having those relationships develop for the last nine months, I've been able to go outside that group and have some confidence at forming some friendships with women. Another part would probably be my marriage, having the Exodus ministry walk beside me during that process and still walking beside me as my husband and I have some conflicts has been an awesome thing to grow in that heterosexual relationship with that support. I feel like that's a change because it's a completely different life than I've ever led before."

Success: Conversion example 5 (male, truly gay, single)—an actual failure. After completion of the Time 4 assessment (see pp. 285-286), this subject wrote a letter to retract his earlier reports of his progress; the following quotes are from this letter. He described himself as having grown up in a conservative Christian church, having come out and embraced gay identity at age sixteen to the dismay of his family and church, and reported that during his late teens, "I was a spokesperson for gay rights." In his early twenties he got involved with Exodus (and this study), and "became a spokesperson for the 'ex-gay' movement and reorientation groups such as Exodus International. In order to define my experience, I identified with different extremes of my personality at different times in my life. This is a dynamic I believe is common for men like me [gay] who do not grow up with the privilege of knowing we are acceptable to God or to our families, or even to society. We seek selfdefinition and self-acceptance through external contacts and associations." He described Exodus as instilling "an extreme value system whereby acceptance by God and subsequently by others in the group is dependent upon commitment to the process of reorientation. . . . Men are encouraged to suppress their true feelings of attraction and to 'confess' their belief in a heterosexual identity. Men who show signs of gaining ground in this pursuit are pitied, shamed or even disciplined. This extreme value system can influence how a man thinks, feels and represents himself to the outside world. . . . Personally, I do not believe that Exodus or faith-based reorientation groups are healthy or necessarily beneficial to participants."

Examples of "Success: Chastity"

Success: Chastity example 1 (female, truly gay, single). *Is change possible?* "Yes, there's been a total change in me from living in the lifestyle to no desire for that. I've also seen a number of my friends radically changed and coming out of that lifestyle and some of them even pursuing heterosexual marriage." *Is your commitment to change stronger or weaker?* "Stronger—because I found that change was possible. When I discovered that, there was more hope that I could change and really pursue everything that God has for me in the area of freedom from homosexuality and really striving after that. Now there is real hope that I don't have to live with that." *How are you doing?* "Very well. I feel like I've met or am meeting all of my goals." *What is your sexual orientation?* "Completely heterosexual with no desire to go back to the life I lived and no desire to mess around with it at all." *Where have you experienced the greatest change?* "I think the healthy same-sex relationships have really begun to establish for me what it means to be a woman. Like I said before, that was something I lacked. It's becoming a very safe thing for me to be with other women. I can look at the way they act with their families and with other women and learn from that. As far as who I am in Christ, I think the sermons in church and the prayer and Bible study have affected that greatly in a positive way." *Effect of faith on change?* "For me the most important thing in life is to pursue Christ. For me that looks very much like digging into the Word of God and just starting again to study and study and then taking what I've studied and praying through it and meditating on it and asking God to reveal what is going to affect my life today. A large part of my time is spent taking what I've learned and passing it on to the next generation. That's how important it is to me that what God has taught me and done in me is now passed on to someone else. I'm very involved in church, but to me it's all about relationship—first of all my relationship with Christ and then my relationship with my fellow church members who have really become my family. Christ has really begun to affect every aspect of life."

Success: Chastity example 2 (female, truly gay, single). *Commitment to change?* "It's stronger. God is leading me in that direction, the overall help that I've received from the ministry in the past to help me where I am now. It has been a big help, so I'm very motivated in that direction." *Original major concerns?* "Get married and just to get rid of those feelings." *How are you doing?* "The married thing is not working out too well. The goal that I had when I started is not the same goal that I have now. I used to just want God to take those feelings away, and of course I wanted to be married and 'live the normal life.' That's not my goal anymore. I don't think that was ever the goal God had for me, but it was the goal I thought he had for me. My goals now are to be more like him and to live in God's will, whatever that looks like. It does involve not being involved in homosexuality, but my goals now are to live in his holiness and to be the woman that he created from the beginning, which includes living in his will. My goal is not to be married. My goal is not to not have these feelings anymore because these are the feelings that drove me to the cross. The goal is not to get rid of the feelings, but the goal is to live in his plan for the world and for my life—as far as heterosexuality, man and woman relationships but not just that, not in the sexual realm but in the ability to relate to people in a mature way." *How helpful are methods?* "I would not consider myself 100% there, but the attractions to women definitely have reduced greatly and the attractions to men have increased proportionally. There are times when I still have those inappropriate attractions or feelings, but they continue to shift to more predominantly heterosexual. The church involvement and same-sex healthy friendships have been invaluable in the process." *What is your sexual orientation?* "Heterosexual with homosexual issues. It continues to shift to predominantly heterosexual attractions with times of homosexual attractions and a less mature way of relating to males and females."

Success: Chastity example 3 (male, single). *Is change possible?* "Yes, I think it's a matter of being committed, being serious about wanting to make a change. I think if a person is really serious about that and committed to that, then they are going to see results." *Original major concerns?* "I was just . . . had come to the end of my rope. I just thought I've got to make a change. It just seemed like something that would be worth trying. I had just come out of a five-year relationship that made me realize that this was not what I wanted anymore. It just wasn't ever going to work, and I didn't want it to work. I was supposed to be a committed Christian. I had no business being in something that was wrong from the get-go, and yet I had allowed myself to be part of it. I very much want to get married. And to get to a point where I can allow the Lord . . . I guess my thought was that the Lord was never going to honor or bless the desire of getting married if I'm living a life that's going to stop him from working in my life. I determined that if I was really serious about wanting to have a spouse, a wife, then I needed to take steps. I had to do my part for him to really hear the prayers and to honor that which I kept verbalizing that I wanted." *How are you doing?* "I am doing pretty well. I had been in singles' groups when I was younger, and I had stopped going to them for a decade. I've started going back into singles' groups at church and putting myself in a position to meet young ladies again. My goals are really the same—to continue to grow in my personal walk with the Lord but also to try to meet somebody and to spend my life in a way that is pleasing to God." *Area of desired future change?* "I would say the biggest area . . . if I were to say, 'Lord, I want you to intervene in one main area,' it would be the way I'm physically attracted to a woman. When I say that, I certainly enjoy an attractive woman, but the way that I am turned on." *What is your sexual orientation?* "I would say it is . . . This isn't a multiple choice, is it? I'm never going to say and I've never said I am a homosexual, because I don't think God made homosexuals. I would certainly say I am someone who struggles with same-sex attractions. I'm also more inclined toward heterosexual feelings than I have been for years."

Success: Chastity example 4 (male, married). *Is change possible?* "Yes, as shown by my own experience, somewhat, and the experiences of the men in the group with me and my Christian belief that we are not created that way." *Commitment to change?* "It's stronger. Being asked to be a leader helped me to make more of a commitment to the group, and being there weekly helps a great deal. Just being in the presence of other men who are trying to do the same thing I am encourages me to continue to come and continue to look at my own issues." *How are you doing?* "I'd say quite well. My goals now have changed. My main goal now is just to feel more confident around other men and also to have some deeper male friendships." *Important steps in your faith journey?* "I believe in Jesus Christ, and I believe in who he says he is in the Bible. I know that currently my relationship with him is not anywhere near what I would like it to be, but I do know and am learning about his grace and forgiveness, and he allows us to not be perfect. That has probably been the greatest thing for me in the last six months at least, just knowing that I don't have to earn his love. I don't have to do anything to receive his love. It's there. I'm in a slow process of accepting that—that I'm loved by him and I don't have to earn his love in any way and that I can't earn it." *What is your sexual orientation?* "Ninety-five percent heterosexual. Though attracted to women, occasionally I will fantasize and masturbate about being with a man. The amount of acting out has dramatically decreased. I still have those feelings sometimes, but I don't act on them nearly as often as I used to."

EXAMPLES OF "CONTINUING"

Continuing example 1 (male, married). *Is change possible?* "I would say yes, I believe that. I think that if God has given them the ability to be convicted to turn away from homosexual behavior, they can do that. I think it's definitely harder to get rid of all the feelings, but I think it's possible. I don't think it's an overnight thing." *Are you continuing with the process of changing orientation?* "Yes." *Commitment to change?* "Stronger, [due to] an increased conviction and marriage." *Original major concerns?* "Just concern for my spiritual life, conviction of the behavior being incompatible with my spiritual convictions. The goals were to become more free from the power of my desires and to become free from acting out on those desires and to find some people to talk to about this problem." *How are you doing?* "I think overall, as I look back over the grand scheme of things, I would say pretty well. I feel satisfied. I wish I could say perfect, but I'm overall satisfied—

well, I'm overall pleased. I'm not completely satisfied with where I am, but I feel like I'm improving. I think over time that things are getting better. I'm certainly in a much better place than I was prior to involvement in the Exodus group. The acting out is under control, but the desires remain and I would like for those to continue to minimize." *What is your sexual orientation?* "My sexual orientation is mostly still oriented toward males, but there is attraction to men and women. I'm definitely attracted to my wife, and we have a good sexual relationship. There is definitely still a strong desire and attraction to males." *Most helpful methods for change?* "I think they have all been very important. The support group was helpful originally, but at this point, the interactions with people who don't struggle with the same thing that I've been able to share this with have been very helpful, just close friendships. My wife has been very helpful and very useful in helping me to change." *Important steps in your faith journey?* "I believe in Jesus Christ, that he is God's Son and that he died on the cross to forgive me, to save me from my sins. That's the only way that I have any real desire or chance to be free from desires and from things that God has commanded us not to engage in. I would say in general that is my hope, and my hope is for eternal life because Christ has saved me, because I cannot save myself. Christ loves me and he is there for me. He sent his Spirit to me to convict me of my sin. I believe that God is always working in my life to change me and to make me more like Christ. When I die I will be like Christ. I'll be in heaven. I'll be liberated from all the sin and worry and pain of this existence, and this will be an existence where I will be face to face with God. I will not have to struggle with the pain of living in this world. That's my hope and my reason to exist. I have no other reason to exist other than to be in relationship with Christ and all that entails, which would be relating to his people, being in fellowship with his people, worshiping him and seeking out those who don't know them to serve them and minister to them. Through all that I have received a lot of joy. I have much contentment even being in the paths of distress and paths of pain."

Continuing example 2 (male, truly gay, married). *Is change possible?* "I believe it can be successful because God is all-powerful. I still believe that I was not born on this earth for that kind of lifestyle. It is not in the design that God has for me. It's of the evil one." *Are you continuing with the process* *of changing orientation?* "I am continuing to struggle through it, yes." *Commitment to change?* "It's weaker. Sin—not dealing with . . . sin is one thing, not obeying is another. Also unsuccessful in finding consistent accountability relationship." *Original major concerns?* "The main one was my relationship with Jesus, and the second reason was my relationship with my wife and family. God exposed my lifestyle. After that, in order to keep my marriage together and in order to be healed, I had to seek help because my life was going down the toilet. I sought to be healed and to move on in what God had for me and to be free of homosexuality." *How are you doing?* "I would say that I'm struggling, but I would say that I am making progress. At the church I now go to, the men's accountability group is slowly starting to take off. I have a ten-year-old son who I don't want to experience what I did. I want to see him know God for who God is and know how God made him and how he's supposed to be. Plus, I have a wife who is my partner." *Important steps in your faith journey?* "I feel very strong that you can't survive in this world without a relationship with Jesus Christ. I believe that he is real. I believe that even though I disobey sometimes, I believe that he is true to his Word. I believe that he is patient. On a daily basis I feel very strongly that I have to seek him or else I have trouble surviving throughout the day." *What is your sexual orientation?* "My sexual orientation right now is probably bisexual. Before I was sexually attracted mostly to men—I would say all men and not women. That is changing slowly to where I am sexually attracted to both. I'm not more sexually attracted to women than men, but the pendulum is swinging."

Continuing example 3 (female, truly gay, single). *Is change possible?* "Yes. First of all, the full understanding of what sexuality is, what's good in God's eyes and what's not good in God's eyes and that he redeems people." [Being] redeemed doesn't mean that you stay in the ways that God doesn't want you to live. It means that you are able to come out of the ways that God doesn't want you to live. The other aspect would be common sense. It's not a natural behavior. It physically doesn't fit naturally. I also can trace the origins of it in my own life, and I know that it doesn't come from genetics. I'm just encouraged by other people who have changed." *Are you continuing with the process of changing orientation?* "Yes." *Commitment to change?* "I'm trying to discern between discouragement and commitment.

I've been a bit discouraged in the last few months, but I don't think that means I'm not committed. I would say it's probably about the same." *Original major concerns?* "I would guess control of fantasy life, not fantasizing homosexually, learning how to relate to women in healthy ways. Probably also the desire for reconciliation in one specific relationship." *How are you doing?* "Slow progress, but I'd say there is progress. Actually I would say that with the first one, the fantasy thing, there's been a lot of progress in that. That's largely under control." *What is your sexual orientation?* "Leaning toward neutral. If I have any sexual inclinations, they are homosexual, but they are definitely weakening. I'm becoming more neutral—much less attraction to women, most noticed by less attraction to [women] that I meet and also less desire, less temptation toward sexual fantasy, which in my life was the big thing. I rarely got into relationships. I'm not yet attracted to men, but I'm much less attracted to women." *Most helpful methods for change?* "I think what's helping most right now is the encouragement that comes from the teaching and reminders about what's important in my relationship with God. Also encouragement from hearing testimonies of other people who are still working through things but are making progress." *Important steps in your faith journey?* "I am someone who believes that the Bible is the Word of God and that the Bible is the authoritative Word of God. I believe that Jesus who is written about in the Bible is a real person who did what it says he did. He came, he lived, he died. He rose from the dead. I believe that his death was a personal gift to me. I believe and have experienced that God is personal and powerful and can change people in terrific ways." *Influence of Exodus?* "They were very helpful, very supportive and encouraging. In terms of success I would say that they have a significant measure of success in encouraging that change can happen and that the body of Christ really does care. I can see change in my life."

Continuing example 4 (male, truly gay, single). *Is change possible?* "Yes, [because of the teaching of] Scripture." *Are you continuing with the process of changing orientation?* "Yes. I guess I still think the bottom line is that Scripture is direct in the New and Old Testament that this isn't the plan that God has in mind. Therefore, being a Christian and wanting to follow that, somehow I needed to address this issue. I think that was probably the largest factor. But I also see that there is an addictive aspect to this whole situation. There's a danger in that addiction that I wanted to recognize and address." *Commitment to change?* "I think probably at this point my number one goal is to walk in the direction that God wants me to go and see that more clearly, be more focused on that. I'm not quite as worried about the complete change in orientation as I am in doing the right thing and letting whatever else happens fall in place. [My motivation] is not incredibly strong but it's something that I'm still committed to. Maybe that's just part of the process too. It's probably been about five years that I've been involved with this whole thing. Maybe there's more of a dose of realism." *Original major concerns?* "I think initially the goal would be some kind of complete transformation and change in orientation and also to grow stronger in terms of behavior." *How are you doing?* "In terms of the first one, I haven't felt that I've really made tremendous progress. In terms of the second goal, though, I have made some progress." *What is your sexual orientation?* "I still find my attractions are for men, and it's very predominant. I understand better where it's coming from. I kind of see how a lot of different things in the past and growing up have all come together and put me in that situation, but I would still say that's largely where I'm at. I don't think there have been any significant changes in orientation. I would say it's pretty steady in terms of where I'm really at in terms of attraction. I just haven't really experienced that in the way I thought I would initially coming in to Exodus."

EXAMPLES OF "NONRESPONSE"

Nonresponse example 1 (male, truly gay, single). *Is change possible?* "Yes, I have seen people do it." *Are you continuing with the process of changing orientation?* "Yes." *Commitment to change?* "It's weaker, I think because of no contact with the ministry." *How are you doing?* "So-so." *Influence of Exodus?* "In some ways they have been successful, but a lack of a support group and the lack of contact with people with the same trouble has weakened my desire to change. I take that back—it's not my desire to change that has weakened; my desire to change is still strong, but what has weakened is my effectiveness in changing and avoiding temptation." *Important steps in your faith journey?* "I consider myself very religious. I go to church every Sunday. My church has been very supportive to my struggles. In fact they are getting ready to have a support group close to me with people from my church who may be dealing with the same issues. I am Mormon. Some members of the church have a group, which is located in Utah. That group deals with same-sex attraction as well. We are in the process of looking for someone to be trained from our church to be a group leader to support a group close to my area. I have been without a support group for about two and a half years, and it has hurt my strength and my commitment to change for lack of support, even though I have tried to do it by myself. I know and I understand that you cannot do it alone regardless of how faithful you are or how strong you think you are, your commitment to your church or your commitment to God. This is something that you need help with getting understanding, support and a commitment with a support group." *What is your sexual orientation?* "I see myself as a man who struggles with same-sex attractions. I have become active in my sexual orientation since the last interview. I have acted on my desires."

Nonresponse example 2 (male, truly gay, single). *Is change possible?* "Yes." *Are you continuing with the process of changing orientation?* "Right now I guess I'm not really working on it. I haven't given up on it, just taking a break from working on it. Yes, I am continuing it." *Commitment to change?* "It's grown weaker. Probably a lot of what I learned at [a certain ministry], my whole perspective on the issue—homosexual orientation in itself is not a sin but rather what you choose to do with it. I am really focusing on not sinning, but as far as changing the orientation, I'm a little less convinced of the necessity of that." *Original major concerns?* "My goal would have been to get rid of any sexual attraction toward men and develop sexual attraction to women." *How are you doing?* "Not especially well." *Important steps in your faith journey?* "I believe in the Bible, the Word of God, the ultimate authority. I try to live by it. I spend a good amount of time studying it and staying involved in my church. I believe it's important to be part of the body of Christ, not only to have my own relationship with God but try to be part of the body. I contribute to my church as well as to missions around the world—I give financially. I believe the Bible says to stay committed to God, and I make an effort to do that. I'm involved in Bible study and sing in the choir at church. I lead a Sunday school class. I try to look for relationships too where I can encourage people and build them up as well as finding people who can help me to grow in my relationship with

God." *What is your sexual orientation?* "I guess I feel a sexual attraction toward men, exclusively homosexual. I don't think there's been any change." *Most helpful methods for change?* "They are not very successful—a little bit of progress in some areas but overall not a lot of progress."

Nonresponse example 3 (female, truly gay, single). *Is change possible? Why?* "Yes. Psychological, physical research about behavior change, faith in God and promises God made in the Bible, examples of people who have successfully changed." *Are you continuing with the process of changing orientation?* "Yes. Because I moved, I'm not in group anymore, but I stay in touch. I have weekly contact by phone with my former small group leader." *Commitment to change?* "I moved across the country, so I guess it's weaker, but overall it's about the same." *Original major concerns?* "I had split up with my partner of ten years because we were both Christians, and we could not reconcile our faith with our lifestyle. I was overcome with grief and loss. I needed a way to express that and also to regain my footing in Christ and reset my course to follow Christ more rigidly. The most immediate goal was relief from the grief I was feeling. Second was to prevent me from getting into another relationship with a woman. Third was to really focus on becoming open to considering a romantic relationship with a man." *How are you doing?* "I'm still struggling with the grief. I have not gotten over the grief. I'm still grieving her loss. I have not gotten into another relationship with a woman. That has been very helpful. I'm more open—about 50% of the way—toward having a relationship with a man." *Influence of Exodus?* "After I finished my formal contact with [a certain ministry] and moved to the West Coast, psychotherapy has been the most important thing, second only to my ongoing contact with my small group leader and one of the members of the group. Those are the main three things that have really been helpful. I have eliminated contact with same-sex, homosexual-oriented organizations—going to bars, clubs, that kind of stuff. I have decreased the number of sexual liaisons I've had with women over the years. They are getting much rarer and very short. I am aware of potential men who could be partners. I'm aware of men I could date—where before I couldn't even tell you there was a man in the room. I'm interested in dating. I'm somewhat pursuing more relationships with men that are appropriate relationships. I would like to change my fantasy life to be more reflective of what I think is healthy sexual expression in marriage. I really need to deal with the self-esteem issue. I just don't think anybody would really want me. I am waiting for my fantasy life to change. I have not seen any significant change there. I am not comfortable with sexual contacts that are loving and supportive. They are not arousing to me. Sexual contacts that have a more dominant-submissive, sadomasochistic overlay on them are much more exciting." *What is your sexual orientation?* "Today I am mostly attracted to women. My sexual expression is very sadomasochistic in orientation. I am becoming attracted to men."

Nonresponse example 4 (male, married). *Is change possible?* "Yes, I think that I felt change going through the program I've been in the last couple of years, just learning a lot about my own background and what caused a lot of the feelings that I had. I believe that has made a difference." *Are you continuing with the process of changing orientation?* "Yes." *Commitment to change?* "Weaker, due to personal stress in my life, personal stress in my marriage, perhaps a feeling of futility in trying. I'm dealing with depression. I feel I was unable to control certain parts of my life, specifically in the area of pornography." *How are you doing?* "I don't feel I'm doing very well. I think the actions have subsided, but the feelings and temptations are still there, perhaps a little weaker, but not a lot. I think the goal for me should be to be able to handle the temptations better and to not be so overwhelmed by them." *Influence of Exodus?* "They have been helpful in helping me understand the reasons why I think and act the way I do. They have been less helpful in helping me walk it out or work it out very much because it's almost like it's a daily struggle, not a surprising one. It's more like it's a lot of textbook knowledge, but the actual living it out has been very, very difficult. They have definitely strengthened my faith. I think they focus specifically on helping people like myself realize how God loves them and that the sin in their lives is not really different than other people's sin. Society may tell them otherwise. Helping people understand that they're the same in God's sight no matter what their particular addiction may be. It is a big thing to learn. The past year, again, has been focused on realizing just how much God loves me—trying to anyway." *What is your sexual orientation?* "Heterosexual. I believe that was the way I was created and the way I was born as a heterosexual. That's how everyone is."

EXAMPLES OF "FAILURE: CONFUSED"

Failure: Confused example 1 (male, truly gay, single).3 *Is change possible?* "Yes." *Are you continuing with the process of changing orientation?* "No. It was such a long process. I think after years of struggling and trying to deal with it by change, it wasn't happening." *Influence of Exodus?* "I think that for the goals that I stated earlier of overcoming same-sex attractions, I would have to say neutral or no effect. But I think there are definite positive benefits that came out of [the Exodus program] and out of therapy and friendships and a lot of me just becoming more comfortable with who I was outside of the whole sexual realm, which had always been a problem just feeling unworthy in general. I think I've learned a lot about my self-image through [the Exodus program] and therapy and other sources. I really don't feel it had a big impact on my sexual struggle or the goal related to that. The other benefits were almost completely successful. On a scale for the other goals, I would say almost a complete success." *Important steps in your faith journey?* "I don't really think that the journey of faith has been more difficult since I tried to grapple with this issue of sexuality. I think faith is still the key to who I am and the core of who I am. I continue to attend church weekly and be active in some activities with the church. I also pray a lot, pray for strength and pray for having the revelation of Christ in my life as far as a lot of daily things go and how I interact with people and how I treat people and what my attitude is. I pray for the attitude of Christ in situations. I think it's also a different faith than I had when I was growing up, which I think a lot of times was based on a lot of fear and shame and guilt. A lot of times I feel like it's just a new day in my faith relationship." *What is your sexual orientation?* "Predominantly homosexual. I don't think there has really been any change in my sexual orientation or my attraction. I think it's been more of a change of how I'm choosing to deal with that now."

Failure: Confused example 2 (male, truly gay, single). *Is change possible?* "Not certain. Continuing." *Are you continuing with the process of changing orientation?* "No. It got too difficult, and I wanted to explore what it was like to truly love someone as I am now, to see what that was like. I couldn't do that when I was in heterosexual relationships because I was faking how

---

3Note: There are only three cases in this category, so here all three cases are presented.

I was feeling, and I was hurting myself and the girl or girls that I have dated. As a postscript, I got tired of being relationshipless." *Important steps in your faith journey?* "I would say that I have grown up in the church all of my life and through many years. I do continue to accept Christ as my Savior and seek to have him be the director of my life and have my life used as he would like it to be used. That meant for many years that I needed to subdue the feelings that I had with respect to sexual orientation, and I did that for twenty-six years. My faith has come into conflict with my attraction. I entered into Exodus to try to understand those conflicts and to overcome them through Christ's help. What I found was obviously there is no magic pill, so I stayed on that route of just beating myself up for two or three years until I got to the point where I let [it all out to] someone that I enjoy hanging out with as a friend and feel important to this person, and this has really challenged my faith a lot because this person is also a Christian. We're in the same boat together, and that made it really interesting. We cried together over our brokenness. I would say what has happened now is I'm put between another rock and a hard place. The rock is my faith and what I believe that God is calling us to, a sexual life or a celibate life. The hard place is that I care a lot about this friend of mine. I can't seem to satisfy both—wanting to be in a relationship, and a serious one, and at the same time go to church with the same person. I have friends who are common who don't understand the depth of our friendship. Right now you're catching me at a particularly bad time because I'm withdrawing a little bit from my church. It's just become very difficult because when I go I feel really bad about what I'm involved with, and yet I like the fact that I can call someone every day, and the person doesn't mind. I'm challenged between a relationship with my Savior and a relationship with someone who kind of understands where I'm coming from and gives me comfort and encourages me. I still struggle with the same issues. I'm kind of in a challenging spot right now because both seem really real. My religious life seems really real, and my friendship/relationship with this guy who is a Christian seems really real. It's very difficult to figure out what's wrong and what's right. I know it's wrong, but it's hard to figure out why I have to go back to being alone and relationshipless, a dust ball in the wind, just kind of blowing around the earth just waiting. So unfortunately my faith is taking a beating in light of my strong desire to know and be known. I hope it's not permanent." *Influence of Exodus?* "I think initially it very much strengthened my faith. It strengthened the fact that regardless of the struggle that God loves me and knows the struggle and loves me anyway and doesn't condemn. Now I would say it has a more neutral effect because I've got another influence that is coming into play. It hasn't negatively affected me. I haven't had negative repercussions from it, but it is no longer positive. It used to be positive, but now it's more neutral and it's never been negative." *What is your sexual orientation?* "I would say it would be gay or homosexual orientation. I used to think to try to make myself heterosexual, but I can't really think that to be true."

Failure: Confused example 3 (male, truly gay, married). *Are you continuing with the process of changing orientation?* "I'm not in Exodus; I don't go to any group." *Why not?* "I feel helpless and hopeless; I'm seeing no results." *How are you doing?* "Feeling empty, frustrated and hurt in relation to same-sex attractions and difficulty in my marriage. Doing badly." *Most helpful methods for change?* "Nothing has been helpful. I feel very alone. My wife is not understanding the complexity of this problem. I'm very motivated to stay with my family, but I'm not motivated anymore to be with my wife because it's not working. I don't want to lose my kids." *What is your sexual orientation?* "I am attracted to men and not really attracted to women. I am obligated to my family, which makes it very awkward and difficult because my wife is being ignored. All we do is do things for the children. We don't sleep in the same bed hardly at all. I sleep on the couch. We don't even touch each other."

EXAMPLES OF "FAILURE: GAY IDENTITY"

Failure: Gay Identity Example 1 (female, single). *Is change possible?* "No, as judged from my own personal feelings and talking to other people who have tried to go through the process." *Are you continuing with the process of changing orientation?* "No." *Important steps in your faith journey?* "I still have very much faith in God. I have found a church that's accepting of who I am and my sexuality as far as being gay or not being gay, straight or gay. My faith in God has not changed at all." *What is your sexual orientation?* "I am attracted to women and don't see that even though I made an attempt to change that it didn't change. I am accepting myself as being a lesbian and that this is my lifestyle."

Failure: Gay Identity example 2 (female, truly gay, single). *Is change possible?* "No. I would just say that it's something that I threw myself into wholeheartedly; I was honestly, fully committed to this, and I was not able to find that in my own experience at all despite giving it my complete best efforts and turning it all over to God. It didn't change." *Are you continuing with the process of changing orientation? Why not?* "No. I just came to the point where after struggling with it for a couple years and really throwing myself into the process, it didn't get better. I never felt like it went away or that it was totally changed. I felt like it was the same thing as my trying not to be a white female. It's who I am. There are some things in life that you just can't change, and trying to change them is going to be futile and result in much more pain than is necessary. I came to a place within myself and in my relationship with God where I am okay with who I am. I'm working on, instead of changing myself, working within the constructs of who I am right now to just go forward." *Important steps in your faith journey?* "I am deeply committed to the Christian faith in Christ. I would say that my spiritual life is not as active as I would like it to be. I pray frequently, read the Bible occasionally and am currently seeking out a church in my neighborhood to go to. We're in the process of visiting some in the neighborhood. So while I consider myself a deeply spiritual person and very committed to Christ, I'm not active in the Christian community right now." *What is your sexual orientation?* "I would say that I'm a lesbian. I have a partner. We've been together for over a year now, and we're in a very committed relationship." *Influence of Exodus?* "Honestly, I think that while I was in the Exodus ministry, I had much more of a problem with anxiety and depression and panic attacks than I do now several years out of it. I think I was constantly, obsessively worried that I was sinning, and he would never forgive me, and I needed to change and what I was doing was wrong. When I was in that state I was just a mess all the time. I was constantly depressed and having panic attacks almost on a daily basis because I was worried about it so much. Since I've come to the point where I've accepted who I am, that God made me this way, God allowed me to be this way, what I really need to do is just concentrate on knowing him better and living my life and being happy. All of that improved slowly. It's taken quite a lot of time, but it's gotten a whole lot better."

Failure: Gay Identity example 3 (male, truly gay, single). *Is change possible?* "Yes, I believe that God can do anything." *Are you continuing with the process of changing orientation?* "No, because it got to a degree of frustration, not being able to get past certain points, loneliness, lack of support. Probably the biggest one was the frustration level." *Important steps in your faith journey?* "What I believe at this time in my life or where I find myself at is I have finally reached a level of comfort with knowing that God loves me. I'm currently not going to a church. I'm very comfortable with my spirituality. I wouldn't consider myself religious. I still pray. I still ask God for help. I don't let the status of my sexuality rule my life. It's no longer the goal for me as I believed it was before. I feel like I missed out on a lot of other goals in my life because I tried so hard on this one. As far as spirituality is concerned, my relationship with God is probably not near as close as it was four years ago. As far as my belief of how God feels about me, it's probably twice as strong. That's really all I have to say." *Influence of Exodus?* "The ministry provided me with a lot of . . . I don't want to use the word *support* but a sense of *community.* I didn't know that there were more people like myself out there, so it gave me a sense of belonging, a sense of reality that this is a real struggle. It wasn't something that was thought up. It gave me a doorway to feel that God really did love me for who I was and not based on what level of sin I was involved in. The ministry had a big impact on my relationship with God now." *What is your sexual orientation?* "Mostly gay—my feelings are still mostly gay. I have, I believe, a healthy sexual attraction for females, which is probably something I didn't have at the beginning of my search. But my sexual orientation is still mostly gay. Shortly after our last interview I got into a relationship for about a year and a half or two years. I'm not quite sure where I was at that time as far as relationships. That just recently ended in October. That was a steady thing. I would have to say no significant changes."

Failure: Gay Identity example 4 (male, truly gay, single/partnered). *Is change possible?* "No. I've met somebody who I care about very much and they care about me. We are in a very committed and loving relationship. I have been involved in a church. I no longer feel that homosexuality is something that needs to be changed. I don't feel that it is an illness or defect." *Important* *steps in your faith journey?* "I believe in a loving God who loves all people. I don't believe that God would put his children on this earth only to have them try to change who they really are. I don't believe he would really do that, that he would create people and have them put themselves through that. I believe that Jesus died for us and that he forgives our sins and our shortcomings. Nobody is perfect; we all do wrong. I believe that there are things that are morally wrong and morally right. I don't believe in the kind of religion that judges people harshly. I feel very much in tune with my faith and with God." *What is your sexual orientation?* "Exclusively homosexual." *Influence of Exodus?* "My involvement actually, in a way, made things a little bit more difficult for me. I realized the people there were well-intentioned. I don't believe they were setting out to harm me. I believe that they believed that what they were doing was right, but I no longer believe that's true. I feel much more emotionally stable now than I did then. I was still probably going through some doubts as to who I was and what my feelings were. I feel pretty stable now."

Unsystematic Examples of Change Methods from Transcripts

What happened in these Exodus ministries that helped those subjects who report significant change to attain that change? We conclude this chapter with material which, while not systematically gathered, nevertheless may helpfully convey the qualitative sense of the impact of the Exodus change process on the participants in our study. We report first the responses of both Phase 1 (early change) and Phase 2 (longer change) to our questions about the types of methods used in their current Exodus group that helped them to change. Participant quotes are in bullets and are noted either as from males (M) or females (F), with the timing of the comment noted as either Time 1 (T1) or Time 2 (T2).

Methods Used to Promote Change

Phase 1 (early change)

1. **Group Format: Talking and Listening Openly**
    - "Being able to tell somebody no longer makes it a bondage. It's no longer a secret." (M-T1)

- "Talking, group circles—really listening to other guys and their struggle and being able to share." (M-T1)

2. Group Readings, Worship, Journaling

- "There are readings that look at some of the fundamental issues that people with this struggle in sexual addiction and sexual brokenness deal with. But Scripture as well as lay writing, and there's a small group component of hearing other people and prayer. There's a lot of emphasis on prayer and personal commitment and brokenness before the Lord, and an emphasis on grace. Also worship. Also a lot of writing and journaling and recognizing our hurt, recognizing our pain, and then an emphasis on voicing those hurts and pains to Christ and leaving them at the foot of the cross." (M-T2)
- "Reading articles and talking about the articles—articles that deal with homosexuality and male identities, with sexual addictions. With this I related to the homosexual lifestyle. Also prayer." (M-T1)

3. Individual Counseling

- "The support has definitely been there in the one-on-one counseling." (F-T1)
- "I am only in one type of therapy now and that is individual. That is a therapy-based, individual, one-on-one clinical situation working through evaluation of consistencies and inconsistencies in behavior." (F-T1)
- "The most important, I think, is very effective counseling with a Christian counselor who is experienced. Very effective teaching based on professional and exceptionally well-written texts such as *Coming Out of Homosexuality* by Bob Davies and Andy Comiskey's books *Living Waters* and *Pursuing Sexual Wholeness.*" (M-T1)

Phase 2 (longer change)

1. Group Readings and Curriculum

- "For the most part, we used an article dealing with homosexuality written by someone in the field. On occasion we used a video. Sometimes within the group, if someone had a particularly large issue that night, we might just spend the evening talking about that." (M-T1)

- "Mostly it's a course—Living Waters. I've been through it twice. It's a structured class that involved a time of worship and then there was teaching and small group time. Then there was homework, a workbook and a lot of things to read during the week." (M-T1)

2. Worship, Prayer, Scripture

- "They have so many different programs here. Praise and worship, of course, because that's always part of their programs here. . . . And of course the study of the Word and spending time in Scripture and prayer." (M-T1)
- "Teaching, prayer, honest confession and worship actually is very important." (F-T1)

3. Group Sharing and Accountability

- "Accountability within your group and your small group. Accountability with your leaders, including accountability with my pastor who is not part of this ministry." (M-T1)
- "I've also been to talk to [an Exodus ministry leader] one on one, and then there are informal drop-in groups. I did that two years ago. Informal drop-in groups—someone will talk about some aspect of homosexuality. And it's informal and people can ask questions. It's not a commitment. You come when you want to." (M-T1)

4. Didactic/Teaching Sessions

- "Half is a teaching time with a lesson about relationships or communication or faith. The other half is personal confession and transparency and asking for help and establishing accountability. Then I'm involved with a smaller men's group, which is mostly like the second part of the main meeting which is more relational and confessional." (M-T1)
- "The helpful methods that were used was . . . explaining sources, explaining why I felt the way I did. But what was really helpful was not the ministry itself. It was the statement that someone had said that

it is purely a matter of obedience to God. The Bible says that homosexuality is sin. You can be obedient or you can not be obedient. It's a matter of obedience. The ministry has given me the support I need, the weapons, the intellect to deal with it, which is important, but outside of that, I don't think recovery is possible. That's why I think that secular change ministries don't work." (M-T1)

Questions About Change

We asked several questions about change. We began with a question about how helpful their ministry has been thus far, and we followed this with questions about what areas reflect real change so far, and areas in which the person has not yet experienced real change.

How Helpful Has the Ministry Been So Far?

1. **Phase 1 (early change)**
   - "I think it has been very successful in that it has made my walk with Christ closer. It has taught me how to activate the Holy Spirit that lives within me to be able to hear that "still, small voice" of God, which is the Holy Spirit revealing and translating and showing me what God has for me. It has given me a willingness and a desire to let Christ have all my hurts and all my pains, to understand how I tick, to understand what makes me work, to understand what is wrong with me what my brokenness is, and how that can be fixed by letting Christ take those things to the cross. Well, let me put it another way, by teaching me to leave those things at the cross and let Christ have them and heal me by his shedding of blood, and the effects of those things and that brokenness within me through his resurrected power of the Holy Spirit." (F-T1)
   - "It has not been successful so far. I still have a problem with pornography, except it's not pictures, it's stories. It's part of a cycle for me when I'm really down. It's one of the things I turn to. Just like buying is, sex used to be, grass used to be, alcohol used to be—escapes. I get rid of it and stay away from it for a time, but it's a cycle. It's less likely once I'm involved again. I knew once I got in my small group, to be honest, I would have to confess it. Maybe you

want to call it pride, but I didn't want to have to confess that I'd failed to the group. So that would keep me most of the time, not always, but most of the time it would keep me away. I did miss one meeting because I was busy downloading, and then I had to go tell them the downloading was more important to me. I'm glad I didn't have to tell the whole group. I figure I would be ducking tomatoes and lemons being thrown at me." (M-T1)

2. **Phase 2 (longer change)**

  - "It's been very helpful because it's let me get my hands on materials that are helpful to read. It's opened my eyes to something like an Exodus conference and what goes on there. Again, all the additional resources that are available. It's been very helpful that way. It's successful in that it's moved me in the right direction. I still have a lot of the same problems and issues and struggles, but I'm not where I was when I came in. I think that overall the struggle is less." (M-T1)
  - "I think there has been some success. I don't have quite the same attractions for women that I had, but I still have some. I think we are getting down to some core issues now. There's been some dry times, but I think overall it's helping." (F-T2)
  - "I would say without having the opportunity to go to somewhere like [an Exodus group], I'd be struggling. I need that intermediate place between church, between the rest of the world to be able to be honest and say, 'Hey, you know, this is me, and this is where I'm at. Life's good today (or it isn't).' To be able to have somewhere to be real. Without it, I'd been still feeling a little lost or at least alone. Very helpful." (F-T2)
  - "I would say it's been very, very helpful. Very useful. They've helped me to find myself. To see where I stand. They've opened my eyes to the mood of real relationships. I've been able to bond with other guys, which I really have never been able to before. And the other guys are a lot older than me, which is kind of different. Unmet needs have been met. I've grown up. My social life has totally changed, turned around. I've become very more open with myself

with other people around. Before I was very shut off. Felt like I didn't fit in. Felt like I wasn't part of the group. I would say probably about eight or nine months before I noticed the changes." (M-T2)

- "Highly successful. I've not been involved in a homosexual relationship since then. That's very significant. I would say that my attraction to women has decreased. I'm more attracted to men. I'm not quite there yet. I have good relationships with men, which I've never done before in my life. I have friendships with men now. . . . It was very helpful to increase my relationship with God, making it closer. I feel closer to God as a result of not being in a homosexual relationship. I think that made me feel very distant from him when I was in the relationship. There was a time period during the relationship when I would go back and forth with her and when I was not with her, I certainly felt closer to God. I wanted that, and I want to keep that." (F-T2)

Areas That Reflect Real Change

We asked both Phase 1 and 2 subjects at Time 1 to describe any areas where involvement in their Exodus group has begun to produce what they feel is real change in their life (and to comment on length of time to achieve such real change).

1. Phase 1 (early change)

- "I'd say what it's doing is reminding me of God's intimate care and reminding me of his care for me—that he's gentle and he will walk with me. I guess that's basically saying it's okay to struggle. It's okay to begin walking this process of dealing with everything. It's a lot like that poem 'Footprints.'" (F-T1)
- "All of them, I guess mainly my sexual brokenness, which is my homosexuality, my lesbianism, my sexual promiscuity, because I have ran the gamut. I not only had a homosexual relationship but at the same time got involved sexually with my partner's husband, so I have ran that gamut. So that is starting to change. Masturbation, by the grace of God, has ceased as of June 6, 1998. Emotional dependency—I am becoming more dependent on God, not less depen-

dent on people. I am starting to learn what my true self is and not living out of a false self: being that alcoholic, that homosexual, that sexual promiscuous woman, that manipulative woman. Another area that has changed is finding identity in Christ and not through other people, and not idolizing other people but idolizing God and worshiping God, because emotional dependency and idolatry went hand in hand. And if anyone took an interest in me and wanted to help me in any kind of way or show me any kind of affection, especially a woman, I latched onto them and leached onto them and sucked the life out of them. And that has changed." (F-T1)

- "I haven't acted out sexually in any way since I've been going. That's been a big goal. But then it's also helped me. It's gotten under the surface, helped me see the reasons why I did the things I did. So that's been a big help too." (M-T1)

2. Phase 2 (longer change)

- "I think it took from three to six months to really start to see changes. I saw behavioral changes. I didn't struggle quite as intensely with desire or to go and act out." (M-T1)
- "I think that when I started, it was really at a time when I was still acting out pretty regularly. I think that God used it to let me know that I could struggle and still be accepted. I didn't need to be perfect to be at a given place. Worship and prayer and accountability and confession and encouragement. Changes were noticed immediately." (M-T1)
- "I'm seeing just a little bit of change now. So, it's been a little over two years. If I've seen any change, it's not very pronounced at this time." (F-T1)
- "I am no longer attracted to women in physical or sexual ways. Which if you had told me seven years ago, I would have said, 'Like, get out of my face. You are absolutely wacked.'" (F-T1)
- "The most help has been in establishing relationships, having more healthy communication with people, eliminating sexual behaviors." (M-T1)

- "I think it took from three to six months to really start to see changes. I saw behavioral changes. I didn't struggle quite as intensely with desire or to go and act out." (M-T1)

Areas in Which You Have Not Yet Begun to Experience Real Change

1. Phase 1 (early change)

- "The big one would be seeing a consistent desire to be different. There's still a part of me that says this homosexuality stuff is the cure. It's familiar. Hang on to it. I'd like for there to be more consistency, settledness and wholeheartedness toward the Lord in this area. There's not a wholeheartedness there. I'm sitting here thinking, *Is it right to expect a ministry to give you wholeheartedness toward the Lord?* I don't know if that's even an appropriate thing to expect of a ministry. I don't just expect it of them. I pray for it and know ultimately it's God that gives you the faith that you have for anything. I just ask the Lord for that with the ministry as a tool to equip." (F-T1)
- "Well just as far as the mental images and the thought life. There are still things that come up from time to time. Temptation or mental images, something that happened in the past. That still plagues me." (M-T1)
- "When I feel like I'm isolated and lonely, the urge to or the temptation to have the contact of a same-sex sexual encounter is still too much of a pull. I have, even once for about a week, have gone against my religion and everything, and failed and actually had sexual contact. I've since repented of that and realized that I've slipped and it's time to move on. Similar to any other process that people are coming out of lifestyle change." (M-T1)
- "Well, I haven't had a relationship with a woman yet. And, I'd like to someday. I haven't confronted those issues. I'm still learning about myself and that aspect of my life. Although the Lord's changing me very slowly. I'm developing friendships here in the church that are different and new, and they are with women." (M-T1)

2. Phase 2 (longer change)

- "I think still the whole idea of what is a man and how does a man relate to a woman. I have never had an attraction in a sense to women. It's a real mixed bag in that, in fact, most of the people in our group are married. That is somewhere that still seems to be far away." (M-T1)
- "I would say the biggest thing on my mind right now is self-acceptance. It's like dealing with all of this self-hate I never knew I had." (F-T1)
- "I would say [I am missing] something in the area of inner peace and confidence, kind of a natural masculinity." (F-T2)

Conclusion and Summary

This chapter brings the changes experienced by the participants in our study into considerable focus. In chapter seven we described the average quantitative outcomes reported by our participants. In this chapter we sorted participants into six outcome categories, reported their quantitative outcomes when separated into those six categories and presented sample transcripts for the types of outcomes reported.

This study has been examining the core question, Is fundamental change of homosexual orientation possible? The answer, measured over time, is yes. The American Psychological Association and others claim that change is impossible. We have produced findings here that directly challenge that claim, and have done so through following carefully over time a sample of people seeking to change their sexual orientation as professional research standards indicate.

One group in our sample, the "Success: Conversion" group, which constitutes 15% of our sample, have experienced dramatic change in lessening their homosexual orientation and strengthening their heterosexual orientation. A second group, the "Success: Chastity" group, which constitutes 23% of our sample, have experienced dramatic change in lessening their homosexual orientation and developing a sense of satisfaction in living as sexually abstinent single persons. Both groups contain a significant number of subjects who, by rigorous empirical standards, qualify as Truly Gay individuals prior to the attempted change process. A sizeable number of "Continuing" subjects have experienced some change and continue their efforts unabated.

Every psychological intervention method results in some successes and some failures; strong interventions are those that maximize successes and minimize failures in comparison to other "best practice" methods. Given that the professional wisdom is that change of sexual orientation is utterly impossible, the changes documented in this chapter are truly remarkable. Further, we believe that these results stand favorably in comparison of most well-researched psychotherapy methods for the outcomes produced.

APPENDIX: EXCERPTS OF THE QUALITATIVE PROBES FROM THE TIME 3 INTERVIEW PROTOCOL

The following are the prompts or probes that elicited the responses reported in the middle section of this chapter in the transcript summaries of the cases in the six outcome categories. Note that we jump over some questions (e.g., from 6 to 8 and 13 to 19) because we are here reporting only the qualitative probes and are omitting the quantitative questions.

Section 2, "Change Attempts," Pages 7, 9, 11, 14 of the Time 3 Interview Protocol

From page 7

1. At this point, do you believe that the attempt to change homosexual orientation or feelings can be successful? <No, Yes or Uncertain> <Follow-up> What leads you to believe this?
2. At this point, are you continuing with the process of changing your homosexual orientation or feelings? <Note: If person reports having "succeeded" and hence feels he or she is no longer in "process," ask that they answer "Yes" here.>

   ______ No <go to questions 3-4> _____ Yes <continue; questions 5-19>
3. First, let me ask an open-ended question: Why are you no longer continuing with the process of changing your homosexual orientation or feelings?

From page 9

5. With which Exodus ministry were you involved when we first interviewed you for this study?
6. Please describe the nature of your involvement with this ministry in the last six months. <If still involved, ask the following follow-up questions: 2-3 minutes.>

   What types of methods are used in your Exodus group to help you to change? (examples: group, healing prayer, mentoring, accountability)

   How are these methods helping you to change? How do these methods help you?

   Has your commitment to work with this particular ministry to seek change grown stronger, grown weaker or stayed the same? <If the respondent reports *any change (weaker or stronger)*, ask> What factors have contributed to this change in your commitment to this ministry?

From page 11

Now we return to some open-ended questions about your commitment to change.

<5 minutes maximum this page>

8. Has your commitment to the process of change, the commitment that led you to be involved with that ministry originally, grown stronger, grown weaker or stayed the same? <If the respondent reports *any change (weaker or stronger)*, ask> What factors have contributed to this change in your commitment to the process of change?
9. In your own words and as you understand it today, what is the major concern that led you to seek help from this ministry originally?
10. What goals were you attempting to achieve when you began your involvement in this ministry to address these concerns?
11. How are you doing in attaining those goals?
12. What are your goals *now* that you would like to achieve in dealing with this concern?
13. How motivated are you to continue the change process at this point in your life?

From page 14
Now we return again to some open-ended questions about your commitment to change.
<3 minutes maximum this page>

19. In your own words, could you please tell us how helpful or successful all of these methods of supporting change have been so far in helping you achieve your main goals for change as you described them earlier? <Follow-up 1> Please describe any areas where these methods of supporting change have begun to produce what you feel is real change in your life.

    < Follow-up 2> Please describe any major areas where you hoped that these methods of supporting change would help you to change, but where you feel that you have not yet begun to experience any real change in your life. In other words, tell us the areas where you are still waiting to experience change.

Section 3, "Religious Experience," Page 15 of the Time 3 Interview Protocol

Qualitative Questions
<Note: Total time 6 to 8 minutes. Goal is to get description of *current faith* and of *significant changes* in faith. If person thoroughly discusses *both* of these areas in response to the first question, then expand time frame for this one question to the full 6 to 8 minutes.>

In each interview, you have been asked about your religious or spiritual experience, and about your religious journey in life—how your beliefs and experiences had changed over the years. We want to ask some questions to help us understand your religious faith and journey since we last interviewed you. We want to begin by asking you to describe, in about 5 minutes, your current religious or spiritual life in your own words. Another way of asking this question would be to ask how, in a few brief minutes, you would describe yourself to me, someone who really does not know you, if you wanted me to understand who you are as a person of faith right now.

<Skip if covered in previous question> Could you now describe, again in about 3 or 4 minutes, any major changes in your religious experience or faith since your last interview?

As a follow-up to the previous question, how would you say the religious values of the change ministry with which you have been involved has contributed to changes in your religious experience or faith? Did they or have they contributed to strengthening your faith, to hindering it or what?

Section 4, "Sexual Orientation," Page 17 of the Time 3 Interview Protocol

<Time for this qualitative section: 5 to 7 minutes>

We want to begin our questions about your sexual feelings by asking you to describe in your own words your sexual orientation as you understand it today.

Please describe in your own words any significant changes in your sexual orientation since your last interview.

What is your understanding today of the causes of your sexual orientation?

<<Probe—Are there other factors that may have contributed to the development of your sexual orientation?>>

Section 5, "Emotional Health," Page 24 of the Time 3 Interview Protocol

Now we move to a set of questions about your "mental health." First, I would ask you to tell us, at a general level, how your mental health or emotional well-being has changed since the time of the last interview.

Has your involvement in the Exodus ministry had anything to do with any changes in your mental health or emotional well-being?

In those areas where your mental health or emotional well-being has improved or gotten better, what major factors, as you understand them, have contributed to this improvement and how?

In those areas where your mental health or emotional well-being has declined or gotten worse, what major factors, as you understand them, have contributed to this decline and how?

9

Is the Attempt to Change Harmful?

Impact on Psychological and Spiritual Functioning

"The American Psychological Association is concerned about such therapies [i.e., therapies and other interventions directed at changing sexual orientation] and their potential harm to patients."
FROM THE AMERICAN PSYCHOLOGICAL ASSOCIATION WEBSITE

"The potential risks of 'reparative therapy' are great, including depression, anxiety and self-destructive behavior."
FROM THE AMERICAN PSYCHIATRIC ASSOCIATION WEBSITE

IN CHAPTERS SEVEN AND EIGHT, WE GRAPPLED with the complex and controversial issue of change of sexual orientation, and provided strong evidence that the claim that sexual orientation change is impossible is false. Our concern in this chapter is the claim that attempts to change sexual orientation are harmful.

In discussing the rationale for this study in chapter three, we quoted from the official website of the American Psychological Association, because there we found closely linked the claimed impossibility of change and the potential harm of attempting to change. Their concern "about such therapies and their potential harm to patients" is the focal claim (or implication, really) that the attempt to change is somehow harmful. While there certainly are anecdotal suggestions that change attempts are harmful, we have found no empirically based evidence in our literature review in support of that claim (see chap. 3). But what about anecdotes of harm? We would be hypocritical to dismiss anecdotes as lacking any sort of evidentiary value; after all, it was our own attention to personal stories and anecdotes of change of orientation that sustained our interest in examining the questions of this study. We would also be inhumane to ignore the pathos of the stories of individuals who claim grave harm or even to have attempted suicide as a result of their despair over failed change attempts. We will return to a discussion of these issues at the end of the chapter because we want to engage these issues in light of the best available evidence from this current study on the factual basis for these claims. For the reader who is sure that the potential harm is grave, we request serious consideration of these findings before returning to this issue at the end.

Our scientific hypothesis for the purposes of this study was that the change attempt *would* be harmful to the individuals participating. We adopted this hypothesis because the weight of professional opinion is that the effort to change one's sexual orientation should be harmful to emotional health. The APA makes a firm prediction that *we should observe a decrement in emotional well-being as a result of involvement in the change process.* This clear prediction is one that can be falsified by clear results, which makes it an ideal scientific hypothesis.

This prediction of harm was not our personal supposition at the start of this study. In this area, we had no clear hypothesis. We expected that some would experience positive mental health outcomes as a result of their involvement in the attempt to change, that others might well experience negative psychological outcomes, especially if they experienced no change, and finally that many would likely find the experience difficult as they went through a long and challenging change effort with little societal understanding or support.

This chapter is presented in three main sections:

1. We examine the core question of harm on average across the entire sample (and our two subsamples) by examining whether those attempting to change sexual orientation report more negative psychological symptomatology, more distress, as a result of their involvement in Exodus. We used a standard and respected measure of distress, the Symptom Check List-90-Revised (the SCL-90-R),[1] to measure distress, and took as our hypothesis that scores on the SCL-90-R should show significant

movement toward worsened functioning or psychological status as a result of Exodus involvement.

2. We extended our hypothesis to spiritual functioning as well. Assuming a necessary connection between emotional and spiritual well-being and growth, and also assuming that the APA was right and change is impossible, we hypothesized that people would be negatively affected spiritually by attempting what must ultimately be utterly frustrating. Thus we hypothesized that the change attempt would produce a decrement in spiritual well-being and faith maturity as a result of involvement in the change process. For these variables, we used other standardized and respected measures—the Spiritual Well-Being Scale (SWB) and the Faith Maturity Scale (FMS).

3. We subjected our data to the hardest test we could imagine by repeating our analyses *after eliminating all subjects that have returned to acceptance of their gay identity or have otherwise stopped the attempt to change sexual orientation.* In other words, we hypothesized that harm to parts of our population might be masked by the inclusion of "more healthy" individuals who had given up on the change attempt, and so repeated our analyses including only subjects who reported a continuing commitment to the change process.

We should be clear that our second hypothesis about the change process having a negative affect on spiritual functioning (spiritual well-being and faith maturity) is *our extension* of a possible implication of the prediction of harmfulness. We draw our first hypothesis about emotional distress directly from the predictions of mental health experts; our second hypothesis is not a direct prediction from those same mental health experts but rather our exploration of a possible implication of that first hypothesis.

In all of these areas, and using the "standard to test the validity of any mental health intervention," which is that the change attempt be "followed and reported over time,"[2] *we find no evidence that the type of attempt to change sexual orientation studied here is harmful.*

Each of the following sections contains a relatively brief but "dry" review of the psychological tests used to measure psychological and spiritual well-being. These sections include discussions of how to understand the numbers we report, but reading these sections is not essential to understanding the results as we present them. The reader can skip these sections and go straight to the results if so inclined.

RESULTS FOR PSYCHOLOGICAL DISTRESS

Review of the Symptom Check List-90-Revised (SCL-90-R, or SCL). The SCL-90-R is a ninety-item self-report inventory that measures the psychological distress of the respondent.[3] It is a commercially available product widely used to monitor progress during treatment. Each item or question refers to a specific psychological symptom of distress (e.g., feeling down, not being able to sleep, mind racing or feeling anxious), with each symptom rated on a five-point scale (0-4) of degree or intensity of distress ranging from "not at all" to "extremely." The measure produces nine primary symptom dimensions and three global indexes.

The SCL-90-R is a strong measure for use in both research and clinical settings, with clear evidence of reliability and validity to support its use; indeed it appears that literally hundreds of studies have demonstrated its usefulness.[4] The results of the SCL-90-R portray the distress of the respondent on nine "primary symptom dimensions": somatization (SOM—the tendency to experience psychological symptoms as if they are physical symptoms, such as when a person experiences depression as physical fatigue); obsessive-compulsive (O-C—the tendency to engage in disruptive ritualistic thought patterns or behaviors); interpersonal sensitivity (I-S); depression (DEP); anxiety (ANX); hostility (HOS); phobic anxiety (PHOB—more extreme anxiety focused on discrete feared objects); paranoid ideation (PAR—perceptions of persecution by others); and psychoticism (PSY—the experience of more extreme forms of psychological impairment, often including hallucinations or other breaks with reality). We conducted analyses of these individual indexes, but these specific results only mirrored the results found on the global indexes we report here, and so these bulky analyses are not reported here.*

*We briefly mention a curious finding that puzzled us a bit until we figured it out. We saw across several of our analyses that our participants tended to score slightly higher on the "psychoticism" scale of the SCL than any other individual scale. This stood in considerable contrast to our subjective impressions

We focused on the SCL-90-R's three global or summary indexes of the degree of respondent distress: Global Severity Index (GSI), Positive Symptom Distress Index (PSDI) and Positive Symptom Total (PST). The SCL-90-R manual states:

> Among the three global measures, the GSI provides the most sensitive single numeric indicator of the respondent's psychological status, combining information regarding the number of symptoms and intensity of distress. The PSDI represents a pure intensity measure, in a sense "corrected" for number of symptoms; it also indicates the patient's "style" of experiencing distress. The PST reveals the number of symptoms the respondent endorsed to any degree and contributes to interpreting the global distress pattern by communicating the symptomatic breadth of the individual's psychological distress.[5]

Scores on the SCL-90-R are compared to four different norming populations. We report here comparisons against the two populations most relevant to the Exodus population: a nonpatient population and an outpatient psychiatric (or mental health) population. We ignore the other two main norming populations—psychiatric inpatients and adolescents—as they are not relevant or similar to our population.

The nonresearcher reader can think of comparisons with these two norming populations as asking different questions. Generally, any measurement assumes comparison if we are to understand its relevance. Finding out our child's temperature is 103°F is meaningful only when we know the normal temperature is 98.6°F and that it is potentially fatal for the temperature to go over 105°F. Our numbers acquire meaning when we answer the question, Compared to what? When comparing against a nonpatient population, we are asking, Is this person more distressed than the av-

---

of this population, particluarly the impressions of our clinically trained interviewers who never reported any impression of psychoticism among any of the subjects even as they observed other significant concerns (of the types reflected in the qualitative transcript excerpts in chap. 8). How then is this elevation explained? We went back and examined the specific items that comprise the psychoticcism scale and discovered (as is the case for many other well-validated psychological measures of psychoticism) that this scale is the only one that has several items related to sexual experience, specifically asking questions about sexual concerns or preoccupations., Such complaints are correlated in the general population with psychoticism, but of course people can have "sexual concerns" or "feel different sexually" without being psychotic. Thus we are confident that these minor elevations are an artifact of scale content and not truly indicative of psychoticism.

distressed than the average person on the street? When comparing against an outpatient mental health population, we are asking, How intensely is this person distressed compared to the average person currently in treatment for psychological or emotional concerns?

The SCL-90-R yields raw scores that are converted to T scores. For the reader not familiar with statistical procedures, T-score conversions are used to insure that scores on different measures can be compared easily and validly. In the case of the SCL-90-R, for instance, subjects might respond differently to eight items that sample whether the person is depressed compared to eight items that sample whether the person is psychotic. Since certain symptoms associated with depression are both more common in our experience than those of psychosis (we are more likely to feel down than to hallucinate) and because it is more socially acceptable to report symptoms of depression than of psychosis, the average person experiencing perfect emotional health might score higher on a depression scale than a psychosis scale. Further, the significance of a one- or two-point increase on that scale may differ substantially; a one-point increase in psychotic symptoms might be of grave concern, whereas a similar increase in depression symptoms might be of unclear concern.

T scores take these problems into account and provide a control for them. T scores are designed to take any measure across any range (a scale with raw scores ranging from 1 to 2 versus a scale from 1 to 1,000), with varying averages (one scale ranging from 1 to 100 might average 15 and another 85) and varying sample characteristics (one scale might tend to have people "clumping" in the low range around the average of 15 while another scale has people spread out evenly across its entire range), and *convert* the scores into a form that allows easy and valid comparisons between scales. T scores always range from 0 to 100, always have an average of 50, and the meaning of any given change in scores across scales is always comparable because the scale characteristics are reconfigured in standardized ways (e.g., 10 point changes in both depression and psychosis mean the same thing). Because the T score conversion puts scores into a normal distribution, we can interpret the T scores in terms of percentiles. Most important for our study:

- A T score of 50 means that the subject is at the average score for the norm group, with 50% of the norm group (nonpatients or mental health outpatients depending on the comparison) scoring below (with less severe emotional distress symptoms) and 50% scoring above (with more severe emotional distress symptoms).
- A T score *increase* of 10 points, from 50 to 60 points, means that the subject is one standard deviation above the average for the norm group, which means that 84% of the norm group (nonpatients or outpatients depending on the comparison) scored below (with less severe emotional distress symptoms) and 16% scored above (with more severe emotional distress symptoms).
- A T score *decrease* of 10 points, from 50 to 40 points, means that the subject is one standard deviation below the average for the norm group, which means that 16% of the norm group (nonpatients or outpatients depending on the comparison) scored below (with less severe emotional distress symptoms) and 84% scored above (with more severe emotional distress symptoms).

Our major concern in this chapter is *change* in distress, but we must also pay attention to the absolute level of distress as measured by this scale. Are the participants in the change process experiencing significant distress on an absolute basis? The publishers of the SCL-90-R state in their manual: "If the respondent has a GSI score (on Norm B, the nonpatient norm) greater than or equal to a T score of 63 . . . then the individual is considered a positive risk or a case."[6] We use this operational definition in this study.

SCL-90-R results for psychological distress. We begin with an analysis of global trends for all subjects in the study, presenting our results in two large tables, the first comparing the SCL-90-R scores of our subjects (for the Whole Population as well as for the Phase 1 and Truly Gay subpopulations) compared first against nonpatient norms (table 9.1) and then in a second table against outpatient mental health norms (table 9.2). A quick orientation for the reader to these large tables: You can scan down the table 9.1 and 9.2 columns labeled "Mean Diff." ("Mean Differences"), which is the Time 1 mean minus the Time 2 or 3 mean (depending on the comparison); in this column a positive number indicates an improvement in functioning and a negative number indicates a worsening of functioning. Generally, the changes are quite small and statistically insignificant. Statistically significant changes are noted by a number that is smaller than 0.05 in the "2-tailed significance" column; there are few of these, and *all of them show significant movement in the direction of improved mental health*. "2-tailed significance" tests are appropriate when the results could reasonably be expected to go either direction—in this case better *or* worse mental health outcomes—and so you are testing for movement in either of two directions (the "2 tails"). "1-tailed tests" are appropriate when the results could only be expected to go in one direction. The 0.05 cutoff for statistical significance is a convention in social science generally. It indicates that the statistical test calculates that the numerical difference being tested has a less than 5% likelihood of having been generated purely by chance. When the differences tested show a significance greater than 0.05, social scientists generally say that because the likelihood of the finding having been generated purely by chance is greater than 5%, it should not be seen as significant. Almost all of the changes in symptom ratings are, by this standard, not significant.

Absolute level of distress. First, we look at the absolute level of the scores reported, particularly at Time 1, to answer the question of whether our participants were already significantly distressed at the baseline or Time-1 assessment for this study. These results are best summarized in terms of three key findings.

1. The rule from the manual is that a T score of 63 on the nonpatient norms merits consideration as a "positive risk or case." On average, our subjects did not score (corporately) as a case at Times 1, 2 or 3. Their scores, mostly clustering in the upper 50s (57 to 61) range, fell short of the 63 cutoff. Since an average is composed of persons above and below the average, the fact that these averages came close to the cutoff for categorization as a case means that a fair number of our participants would have been categorized as cases.
2. A T score of 50 is average, and as previously noted, a T score of 60 means that 84% of the nonpatients norm group scored below (with less severe emotional distress symptoms) and 16% scored above (with more

Table 9.1. SCL Scores Normed on a Nonpatient Sample for Whole Population, Phase 1 Population and Truly Gay Population

	Time 1 Mean	Time 2 Mean	Time 3 Mean	Mean Diff.	N	Df	Std. Dev.	t score	2-tailed sig.
SCL Scores: Whole Population									
1. GSI Time 1 to 3	59.26[a]		58.74	0.52	73	72	13.24	0.34	0.738
2. GSI Time 1 to 2 (all Time 3 cases)	59.68	59.38		0.30	71	70	9.47	0.26	0.793
3. GSI Time 1 to 2 (all Time 2 cases)	60.35	59.53		0.82	81	80	9.18	0.80	0.427
4. PSDI Time 1 to 3	57.86		55.90	1.96	73	72	12.44	1.35	0.183
5. PSDI Time 1 to 2 (all Time 3 cases)	57.79	54.10		3.69	71	70	9.26	3.36	0.001
6. PSDI Time 1 to 2 (all Time 2 cases)	57.85	54.52		3.33	81	80	9.10	3.30	0.001
7. PST Time 1 to 3	57.48		58.21	-0.73	73	72	12.60	-0.49	0.624
8. PST Time 1 to 2 (all Time 3 cases)	57.93	59.42		-1.49	71	70	8.43	-1.49	0.140
9. PST Time 1 to 2 (all Time 2 cases)	58.59	59.37		-0.78	81	80	8.49	-0.83	0.412
SCL Scores: Phase 1 Population									
10. GSI Time 1 to 3	60.18		59.13	1.05	38	37	16.27	0.40	0.692
11. GSI Time 1 to 2 (all Time 3 cases)	61.06	58.72		2.33	36	35	11.04	1.27	0.213
12. GSI Time 1 to 2 (all Time 2 cases)	61.34	58.83		2.51	41	40	10.50	1.53	0.133

[a]There are several apparent anomalies in the data tables, but one that may appear glaring is easily explained. Some might wonder why the three means (averages) that are all reported as Time-1 means differ. For example, shouldn't there be one identical Time 1 mean on the GSI measure for the Whole Population, rather than three different means as reported: 59.26, 59.68 and 60.35? The answer is first that the means in line 3 of the table are for the 85 subjects in the study at Time 2 rather than the 73 still available at Time 3; the additional 12 subjects change the average. The mean in line 2 differs from that in line 1 because the number of subjects for which we have Time 2 data differs, as seen in the "N" (number of subjects) column which reports 73 for line 1 but 71 for line 2. This indicates that we either had invalid or missing data on the SCL at Time 2 for two subjects who were still in the study at Time 3. You will note that the slight differences run through the tables. We had 98 subjects at Time 1, 85 at Time 2 and 73 at Time 3, but did not get valid data from all subjects at each time, so these numbers represent the maximum number of data points we have at each assessment.

13. PSDI Time 1 to 3	60.08		57.11	2.97	38	37	15.86	1.16	0.255
14. PSDI Time 1 to 2 (all Time 3 cases)	60.06	53.89		6.17	36	35	10.09	3.67	0.001
15. PSDI Time 1 to 2 2 (all Time 2 cases)	59.34	53.59		5.76	41	40	9.68	3.81	0.000
16. PST Time 1 to 3	57.45		58.63	-1.18	38	37	15.16	-0.48	0.633
17. PST Time 1 to 2 (all Time 3 cases)	58.33	58.89		-0.56	36	35	10.21	-0.33	0.746
18. PST Time 1 to 2 (all Time 2 cases)	58.83	59.00		-0.17	41	40	9.82	-0.11	0.912
SCL Scores: Truly Gay Population									
19. GSI Time 1 to 3	60.65		60.23	0.42	43	42	15.82	0.17	0.863
20. GSI Time 1 to 2 (all Time 3 cases)	61.10	60.07		1.02	42	41	9.54	0.70	0.491
21. GSI Time 1 to 2 (all Time 2 cases)	61.65	60.24		1.41	46	45	9.26	1.04	0.306
22. PSDI Time 1 to 3	58.37		57.19	1.19	43	42	13.85	0.56	0.577
23. PSDI Time 1 to 2 (all Time 3 cases)	58.38	53.83		4.55	42	41	9.37	3.15	0.003
24. PSDI Time 1 to 2 (all Time 2 cases)	58.78	54.30		4.48	46	45	8.96	3.39	0.001
25. PST Time 1 to 3	58.72		59.86	-1.14	43	42	15.00	-0.50	0.621
26. PST Time 1 to 2 (all Time 3 cases)	59.17	60.19		-1.02	42	41	7.88	-0.84	0.405
27. PST Time 1 to 2 (all Time 2 cases)	59.67	60.15		-0.48	46	45	7.76	-0.42	0.678

Legend

For each of the Symptom Check List scores, we present three comparisons: First, the report of Time 1 to Time 3 comparison, including only those cases presenting data for both assessments. Second, the report of Time 1 to Time 2 comparison, including only the cases also available at Time 3 (in other words, this comparison included only the same cases as in the first Time 1 to Time 3 comparison, designated "all Time 3 cases"). Third the report of Time 1 to Time 2 comparison, including *all* of the cases that were available at Time 2 (in other words, this comparison included all of the cases available at Time 2, a larger population than those available at Time 3, designated "all Time 2 cases"). GSI refers to the most important overall score, the Global Severity Index. The other two summary scores are the PSDI, which refers to the Positive Symptom Distress Index, which measures general intensity of distress, and the PST, which refers to the Positive Symptom Total, which measures breadth of symptoms reported.

Table 9.2. SCL Scores Normed on an Outpatient Psychiatric Sample for Whole Population, Phase 1 Population and Truly Gay Population

	Time 1 Mean	Time 2 Mean	Time 3 Mean	Mean Diff.	N	Df	Std. Dev.	t score	2-tailed sig.
SCL Scores: Whole Population									
1. GSI Time 1 to 3	40.40		41.11	-0.71	73	72	13.58	-0.45	0.655
2. GSI Time 1 to 2 (all Time 3 cases)	40.69	40.04		0.65	71	70	7.16	0.76	0.448
3. GSI Time 1 to 2 (all Time 2 cases)	41.28	40.28		1.00	81	80	6.92	1.30	0.197
4. PSDI Time 1 to 3	41.67		40.68	0.99	73	72	14.21	0.59	0.555
5. PSDI Time 1 to 2 (all Time 3 cases)	41.61	37.79		3.82	71	70	8.83	3.64	0.001
6. PSDI Time 1 to 2 (all Time 2 cases)	41.74	38.33		3.41	81	80	8.90	3.44	0.001
7. PST Time 1 to 3	41.56		43.10	-1.53	73	72	13.99	-0.94	0.352
8. PST Time 1 to 2 (all Time 3 cases)	41.92	42.65		-0.73	71	70	7.88	-0.78	0.436
9. PST Time 1 to 2 (all Time 2 cases)	42.68	42.83		-0.15	81	80	7.87	-0.17	0.866
SCL Scores: Phase 1 Population									
10. GSI Time 1 to 3	41.74		42.87	-1.13	38	37	17.99	-0.39	0.700
11. GSI Time 1 to 2 (all Time 3 cases)	42.39	39.69		2.69	36	35	8.14	1.99	0.055
12. GSI Time 1 to 2 (all Time 2 cases)	42.68	39.95		2.73	41	40	7.69	2.27	0.028
13. PSDI Time 1 to 3	44.11		42.71	1.40	38	37	18.62	0.46	0.647
14. PSDI Time 1 to 2 (all Time 3 cases)	44.11	37.69		6.42	36	35	9.70	3.97	0.000
15. PSDI Time 1 to 2 (all Time 2 cases)	43.54	37.66		5.88	41	40	9.32	4.04	0.000
16. PST Time 1 to 3	42.11		44.26	-2.16	38	37	17.89	-0.74	0.462
17. PST Time 1 to 2 (all Time 3 cases)	42.83	42.22		0.61	36	35	9.39	0.39	0.698

18. PST Time 1 to 2 (all Time 2 cases)	43.54	42.63		0.90	41	40	8.95	0.65	0.522
SCL Scores: Truly Gay Population									
19. GSI Time 1 to 3	41.56		43.26	-1.70	43	42	16.99	-0.66	0.516
20. GSI Time 1 to 2 (all Time 3 cases)	41.86	40.60		1.26	42	41	7.69	1.06	0.294
21. GSI Time 1 to 2 (all Time 2 cases)	42.35	40.72		1.63	46	45	7.46	1.48	0.145
22. PSDI Time 1 to 3	42.21		42.47	-0.26	43	42	16.71	-0.10	0.920
23. PSDI Time 1 to 2 (all Time 3 cases)	42.24	37.52		4.71	42	41	9.05	3.38	0.002
24. PSDI Time 1 to 2 (all Time 2 cases)	42.70	37.93		4.76	46	45	8.69	3.72	0.001
25. PST Time 1 to 3	42.93		45.67	-2.74	43	42	17.31	-1.04	0.304
26. PST Time 1 to 2 (all Time 3 cases)	43.29	43.57		-0.29	42	41	7.70	-0.24	0.811
27. PST Time 1 to 2 (all Time 2 cases)	43.83	43.57		0.26	46	45	7.60	0.23	0.817

Legend

For each of the Symptom Check List scores, we present three comparisons: First, the report of Time 1 to Time 3 comparison, including only those cases presenting data for both assessments. Second, the report of Time 1 to Time 2 comparison, including only the cases also available at Time 3 (in other words, this comparison included only the same cases as in the first Time 1 to Time 3 comparison, designated "all Time 3 cases"). Third, the report of Time 1 to Time 2 comparison, including *all* of the cases that were available at Time 2 (in other words, this comparison included all of the cases available at Time 2, a larger population than those available at Time 3, designated "all Time 2 cases"). GSI refers to the most important overall score, the Global Severity Index. The other two summary scores are the PSDI, which refers to the Positive Symptom Distress Index, which measures general intensity of distress, and the PST, which refers to the Positive Symptom Total, which measures breadth of symptoms reported.

severe emotional distress symptoms). Thus the average scores of our population do appear elevated compared to a national norm of 50.

3. However, our participants on average were as far *below* the average for outpatient mental health norms as they were above the average for nonpatient norms. Again, as previously noted, a T score of 40 means (in mirror opposite of a score of 60) that 16% of the psychiatric outpatient norm group scored below (with less severe emotional distress symptoms) and 84% scored above (with more severe emotional distress symptoms). So it appears that our participants were on average about the same degree above (thus more distressed than) the nonpatient norm group as they were below (and thus less distressed than) the psychiatric outpatient norm group. For a specific example, the Time 1 scores for the Whole Population for the nonpatient norms ranged from a low of 57.48 to a high of 60.35 (respectively, 7.48 and 10.35 *above* the 50.00 norm for nonpatients), but also the Time 1 scores for the Whole Population for the psychiatric outpatient norms ranged from a low of 40.40 to a high of 42.68 (respectively, 9.60 and 7.32 *below* the 50.00 norm for outpatients). So, our participants appear more distressed than the nonpatient population (though not to the degree of being considered a case) but less distressed than an outpatient population.

These data overall suggest some mildly elevated psychological distress in this population, but distress that falls short of comparability to that experienced by the average outpatient mental health client. In some ways the mild levels of distress are remarkable when we consider the meager level of support these individuals feel for the difficult task they have undertaken. There is much discussion in psychological circles of the "heterosexist bias" of contemporary society,[7] but our sense from conversation with those involved in the Exodus movement is that these individuals feel remarkably beleaguered and besieged by a pervasive homosexist bias.* Certainly the majority of the "secular mental health establishment" views their project with derision. Many others manifest similar views, accepting as a given

---

*For objective evidence of this see our discussion in chap. 1 (pp. 35-37) of the progression of change in the engagement of the *Diagnostic and Statistical Manual* of the American Psychiatric Association. There we document how they have moved from homosexuality being diagnosable as a mental illness to the desire to change homosexual orientation being diagnosable as a mental illness.

that homosexual orientation cannot change and that these individuals should just accept their sexual orientation. It is not all roses on the conservative Christian side of society for these individuals either. Many of those whom secularists would expect to support the work of Exodus in fact do not; there are many conservative Christians (and nonreligious conservatives as well) who simply regard those struggling to change their homosexual orientation as depraved or degenerate persons to be dismissed or condemned rather than helped. If we think (all too simplistically) of society divided roughly between those who support full affirmation of gay lifestyle and those who repudiate it, people trying to change their sexual orientation through Exodus feel no support from the former and from very few of the latter. Thus the life situation of the typical Exodus participant is a difficult one indeed, one that might be expected (like the claims of the impact of heterosexist bias on gays and lesbians) to produce significant distress. In this context the mild average levels of distress are remarkable.

Change in distress over time. The more important issue is change, and *our analysis yields no support for the hypothesis that scores on the SCL-90-R would show significant movement toward worsened psychological functioning as a result of Exodus involvement.* Particularly on the GSI—the most important overall measure of psychological distress—we see little evidence of significant change at all in any of the three populations: the Whole Population, the Phase 1 Population or the Truly Gay Population. Scores basically stay the same. The table 9.1 and 9.2 columns labeled "Mean Diff." (mean difference) capture this. (Remember that a positive number indicates an improvement in functioning and a negative number a worsening of functioning.) Generally, the changes are quite small and statistically insignificant.

There was one area where we noted a number of statistically significant changes. For both norming groups—nonpatients and psychiatric outpatients—and for all three population groups—the Whole Population, the Phase 1 subpopulation and the Truly Gay subpopulation—the one consistently statistically significant shift was the shift in the Positive Symptom Distress Index in a direction of *less distress,* that is, clinical improvement. Remember that the PSDI is "a pure intensity measure," and so this shift means that while the number of symptoms being reported by the subjects has not changed (this is the PST), the reported intensity of the symptoms has changed for *the better* to a statistically significant degree. But we would not make much of this shift; this change, while statistically significant, is a modest one.

In summary, there is no evidence here of increased distress as "treatment outcome . . . [was] followed and reported over time."[8] Contrary to our hypothesis that "harm" would be demonstrated, we find here little evidence of harm, but instead mostly evidence of little change on average. Where we did detect evidence of statistically significant change occurring, it is toward improvement, not harm.

RESULTS FOR SPIRITUAL WELL-BEING

Review of the Spiritual Well-Being Scale. We chose to operationalize our assessment of spiritual well-being by using the Spiritual Well-Being Scale (SWBS).[9] The SWBS is a self-administered survey consisting of twenty items (ten explicitly religious and ten existential). The scale was developed for use with religious populations and is clearly worded and easy to administer, score and interpret. Subjects respond to items such as "I get strength from God" on a six-point scale from 1 (strongly agree) through 6 (strongly disagree). The SWBS was administered as one of our self-administered questionnaires, specifically as "Religious Faith Inventory 2 (SAQ 3)."

The SWBS yields three scores: a total spiritual well-being or SWB score, a subscore for religious well-being (RWB) items and a subscore for existential well-being (EWB) items. SWB scores range from 20-120, while subscales range from 10-60. The RWB subscale consists of the ten items that measure the degree to which individuals report a satisfying relationship with God (and hence are explicitly religious). The EWB subscale contains the ten items that measure a sense of identity, purpose and life satisfaction without making specific religious references. Both subscale dimensions involve transcendence of a sort. The subscales overlap (both practically and statistically).

The SWBS is probably one of the most comprehensively studied measures of religiosity.[10] The SWB score has been found to be positively correlated with measurements of purpose in life, intrinsic religious orientation, self-confidence and self-esteem. Individuals who score high on SWB tend to be less lonely and more socially skilled than those who score lower.

SWB is negatively correlated with individualism, personal freedom, loneliness and living in a large city environment. All three scores from the SWBS consistently relate to well-being, correlating positively with positive self-concept, sense of purpose in life, physical health and emotional adjustment. Consequently, SWB is negatively correlated with ill health, emotional maladjustment and lack of purpose in life.[11] These correlations are relevant to the present study.

SWBS results for spiritual well-being. As with the discussion of psychological distress and the SCL-90-R, the key to reading table 9.3 is the "Mean Diff." (mean difference) column. The mean difference is the Time 1 mean minus the Time 2 or 3 mean, so that a positive number indicates a worsening of spiritual well-being and a negative number an improvement in spiritual well-being. The statistically significant findings, though small in absolute terms, are marked by a "2-tailed significance" score of 0.050 or less.

Absolute level of spiritual well-being. Let us begin unpacking these findings by examining the absolute scores of our participants on the Spiritual Well-Being Scale. As with the SCL-90-R, we examine this in the context of how the scores of our population compare with those of other populations, the norming populations. In the *Manual for the Spiritual Well-Being Scale,* the authors of the scale summarize the norms of scale responses for different populations. A variety of Christian denominational groups, along with a norming sample of evangelical Christian college students, report higher mean scores than other reported populations. The scores of those groups ranged from just over 99 to almost 110. Unitarians reported a lower mean (82.81), adults and college students described as "ethical Christians" scored means of between 91 and 94, and a variety of mental health patient groups scored means between 77 and 87.

Our Exodus population reported SWB and EWB norms slightly below those of the Christian denominational groups and evangelical Christian college students, at approximately the same level as those described as "ethical Christians," and above the norms reported for the variety of mental health patient groups. This intermediate scoring of our population on the SWB and EWB scales is probably a reflection in part of the heterogeneous nature (religiously speaking) of our sample, with many but not all identifying as evangelical Christians. The similarity with conservative

Table 9.3. SWBS Scores for Whole Population, Phase 1 Population and Truly Gay Population

	Time 1 Mean	Time 2 Mean	Time 3 Mean	Mean Diff.	N	Df	Std. Dev.	t score	2-tailed sig.
SWBS Scores: Whole Population									
1. RWB Time 1 to 3	51.34		51.94	-0.61	73	72	5.67	-0.92	0.363
2. RWB Time 1 to 2 (all Time 3 cases)	51.09	52.22		-1.13	71	70	5.55	-1.71	0.092
3. RWB Time 1 to 2 (all Time 2 cases)	51.27	52.23		-.096	82	81	5.70	-1.53	0.131
4. EWB Time 1 to 3	44.22		45.67	-1.45	73	72	7.70	-1.61	0.111
5. EWB Time 1 to 2 (all Time 3 cases)	44.00	45.85		-1.85	71	70	5.96	-2.61	0.011
6. EWB Time 1 to 2 (all Time 2 cases)	43.80	45.54		-1.73	82	81	6.19	-2.54	0.013
7. SWB Time 1 to 3	95.17		97.28	-2.11	73	72	11.82	-1.52	0.132
8. SWB Time 1 to 2 (all Time 3 cases)	94.71	97.73		-3.02	71	70	9.67	-2.63	0.010
9. SWB Time 1 to 2 (all Time 2 cases)	94.67	97.42		-2.74	82	81	10.28	-2.42	0.018
SWBS Scores: Phase 1 Population									
10. RWB Time 1 to 3	50.66		51.95	-1.29	38	37	5.64	-1.41	0.168
11. RWB Time 1 to 2 (all Time 3 cases)	50.41	51.74		-1.33	37	36	5.54	-1.46	0.153
12. RWB Time 1 to 2 (all Time 2 cases)	50.69	51.91		-1.22	43	42	5.74	-1.40	0.170
13. EWB Time 1 to 3	42.84		46.42	-3.58	38	37	8.10	-2.72	0.010
14. EWB Time 1 to 2 (all Time 3 cases)	42.59	45.57		-2.97	37	36	6.61	-2.73	0.010
15. EWB Time 1 to 2 (all Time 2 cases)	42.79	45.19		-2.40	43	42	6.73	-2.33	0.024
16. SWB Time 1 to 3	93.08		98.07	-5.00	38	37	12.06	-2.56	0.015
17. SWB Time 1 to 2 (all Time 3 cases)	92.57	96.98		-4.41	37	36	10.77	-2.49	0.017

18. SWB Time 1 to 2 (all Time 2 cases)	93.05	96.74		-3.70	43	42	11.23	-2.16	0.037
SWBS Scores: Truly Gay Population									
19. RWB Time 1 to 3	50.77		51.31	-0.54	43	42	5.71	-0.62	0.538
20. RWB Time 1 to 2 (all Time 3 cases)	50.55	52.34		-1.79	42	41	5.85	-1.99	0.054
21. RWB Time 1 to 2 (all Time 2 cases)	50.62	52.31		-1.69	46	45	5.72	-2.00	0.052
22. EWB Time 1 to 3	43.00		44.86	-1.86	43	42	8.03	-1.52	0.136
23. EWB Time 1 to 2 (all Time 3 cases)	42.79	45.53		-2.74	42	41	6.58	-2.70	0.010
24. EWB Time 1 to 2 (all Time 2 cases)	42.57	45.26		-2.70	46	45	6.52	-2.81	0.007
25. SWB Time 1 to 3	93.36		95.82	-2.47	43	42	12.56	-1.29	0.205
26. SWB Time 1 to 2 (all Time 3 cases)	92.92	97.51		-4.59	42	41	11.08	-2.68	0.010
27. SWB Time 1 to 2 (all Time 2 cases)	92.76	97.20		-4.44	46	45	10.98	-2.74	0.009

Legend

For each of the spiritual well-being scores, we present three comparisons: First, the report of Time 1 to Time 3 comparison, including only those cases presenting data for both assessments. Second, the report of Time 1 to Time 2 comparison, including only the cases also available at Time 3 (in other words, this comparison included only the same cases as in the first Time 1 to Time 3 comparison, designated "all Time 3 cases"). Third, the report of Time 1 to Time 2 comparison, including *all* of the cases that were available at Time 2 (in other words, this comparison included all of the cases available at Time 2, a larger population than those available at Time 3, designated "all Time 2 cases"). SWB refers to the most important overall score, the Spiritual Well-Being score, which is reported last in each set. The other two scores reported are subscale scores, the RWB, which refers to the Religious Well-Being score, and the EWB, which refers to the Existential Well-Being score.

Christian groups shows up on the RWB measure, one correlated with traditional religious belief; on this subscale our population scored in the same range as the more theologically conservative and religiously active norming groups. The parallel in scoring similar to "ethical Christians" on the other two measures, EWB and the overall SWB, may in fact be apropos for some subjects in our sample, because some of our participants were involved in Exodus less out of a deeply intrinsic embrace of the conservative Christian ideologies of these ministries and more out of an ethical sense of wanting to change a sexual inclination they found morally troubling. The fact that our population reported more positive scores on all scales than the various patient samples indicates a sense of religious and spiritual strength in this population in comparison to classic patient groups.

Table 9.4. Absolute Scores on the SWBS

Population	Range of Means: RWB	Range of Means: EWB	Range of Means: SWB
Christian denominational groups	49 to 57	49 to 53	99 to 110
Evangelical Christian college students	54	51	104
Unitarians	34	49	83
Ethical Christians	43 to 47	46 to 47	94 to 97
Mental health patient groups	38 to 47	35 to 40	77 to 87
Exodus sample of this study	51 to 52	44 to 46	94 to 97

Change in spiritual well-being. Of course, the most important finding on these measures is that there is no evidence in the change scores (from Time 1 to either Time 2 or 3) that involvement in this change process causes a decline in religious or spiritual well-being. To the contrary, the reader will note from scanning down the column labeled "Mean Diff." that *every* reported mean difference is negative, indicating an improvement (however modest) in spiritual, religious and existential well-being. A number of these changes were statistically significant. Even if we take our cutoff for statistically significant change to be a more rigorous p (for probability) value of 0.01 or less (a more rigorous standard for significance of less than

1% probability that the outcome could have happened just by chance, compared to the standard 5% or 0.05), then a number of findings for existential well-being (EWB) and for the more important global measure of spiritual well-being (SWB) shifted to a statistically significant degree toward *enhanced* well-being. These shifts were, however, modest in degree and not likely to be clinically or practically meaningful.

If involvement in Exodus treatment to change sexual orientation is supposed to be detrimental to the spiritual well-being of the participants as we hypothesized as an extension of the reasoning of the American Psychological Association, we find no evidence of it in this population.

Results for Faith Maturity

Review of the Faith Maturity Scale. We wanted a measure of change in "faith maturity" for this study. The whole field of measurement of change or growth in religious faith is fraught with complexity. We are convinced that there is not one singular entity of "religion," but rather that there are different religions.[12] Hence, there will not be one generic measurement device for religion because different religious faiths construe the very meaning of growth in spirituality differently. To use an obvious example, in classic Buddhism, detachment from the concerns of the world is typically associated with maturation, and while certain varieties of Christian mysticism might parallel this pattern, most conceptions of Christian maturity foster continued passionate engagement with the concrete affairs of living.[13] Hence, we decided to use a measure of change in religious maturation that was constructed around the specific contours of Christian faith.

We used the Faith Maturity Scale[14] (FMS) in this study, embedding it as the second self-administered questionnaire, the Religious Faith Inventory 1. The scale was developed by the Search Institute of Minneapolis as part of the National Study of Protestant Congregations to assess the personal faith, denominational loyalty and determinants of a group of church attendees. Over 11,000 adults and adolescents from six Protestant denominations participated in the original research. The FMS comprises thirty-eight items that measure the degree to which one embodies the priorities, commitments and perspectives characteristic of a person with mature Christian faith. Each item is scored from 1 (never true) to 7 (always true).

The FMS was developed using a criterion-based approach by working within the Christian tradition to assemble consensus descriptions of markers of religious maturity. The authors construed faith maturity to occur along a continuum, based on the degree to which certain indicators (of faith maturity) are present. The authors attempted to balance and integrate a number of dimensions of faith, particularly balancing "vertical and horizontal" manifestations of faith, that is, transcendent (vertical or "upward") spiritual growth to greater closeness with God and the obligation as a believer to serve other human beings (the horizontal). The final product queries doctrinal beliefs, moral beliefs and a variety of life practices, from care for the poor and distressed to church service to environmental activism.

The FMS has not been widely used, but the work done in its development and validation is impressive. Reliability across the range of respondents' ages, genders, relationships to the church and denominations appears sound, and there are a number of indicators of validity.[15] Face and construct validity were addressed in the scale's construction by using a panel of experts and a criterion-based approach. FMS scores are unrelated to educational attainment or to conservative-to-liberal political orientation. There is a small but significant negative relationship between scores on the FMS and income.

The FMS authors reported that they developed a twelve-item short form as part of their validation study, finding that the twelve-item short form correlated highly with the full scale. Even though we administered the entire scale in our study, we used this short form in our data analysis. We found substantial inter-item reliability problems for a number of the items on the full FMS, but found no such problems for the twelve items used to create the short form. So we concluded that the twelve-item short form, and not the full form, demonstrated sufficient reliability to report scores from our population. Finally, we should note that FMS scores (for either the full or short forms) are reported as the average rating on each item in the scale. Since subjects respond to each item with a 1 (never true) to 7 (always true) rating, we divide the sum of their ratings by the number of items (12), so the summary scores always range between 1 and 7.

FMS results for faith maturity. Interpretation of table 9.5 parallels that of the other tables in this chapter.

Table 9.5. FMS (Short Form) Scores for Whole Population, Phase 1 Population and Truly Gay Population

	Time 1 Mean	Time 2 Mean	Time 3 Mean	Mean Diff.	N	Df	Std. Dev.	t score	2-tailed sig.
FMS Scores: Whole Population									
1. FMS Time 1 to 3	5.06		5.00	0.06	73	72	0.67	0.70	0.486
2. FMS Time 1 to 2 (all Time 3 cases)	5.06	4.99		0.07	73	72	0.52	1.16	0.249
3. FMS Time 1 to 2 (all Time 2 cases)	5.10	5.02		0.08	85	84	0.52	1.42	0.161
FMS Scores: Phase 1 Population									
4. FMS Time 1 to 3	4.97		4.95	0.02	38	37	0.76	0.20	0.841
5. FMS Time 1 to 2 (all Time 3 cases)	4.97	4.93		0.05	38	37	0.60	0.50	0.621
6. FMS Time 1 to 2 (all Time 2 cases)	5.07	5.01		0.06	44	43	0.58	0.70	0.490
FMS Scores: Truly Gay Population									
7. FMS Time 1 to 3	5.05		4.98	0.07	43	42	0.76	0.61	0.894
8. FMS Time 1 to 2 (all Time 3 cases)	5.05	5.06		-0.01	43	42	0.55	-0.07	0.945
9. FMS Time 1 to 2 (all Time 2 cases)	5.04	5.05		-0.01	47	46	0.54	-0.13	0.548

Legend

For each of the Faith Maturity Scale scores, we present three comparisons: First, the report of Time 1 to Time 3 comparison, including only those cases presenting data for both assessments. Second, the report of Time 1 to Time 2 comparison, including only the cases also available at Time 3 (in other words, this comparison included only the same cases as in the first Time 1 to Time 3 comparison, designated "all Time 3 cases"). Third, the report of Time 1 to Time 2 comparison, including *all* of the cases that were available at Time 2 (in other words, this comparison included all of the cases available at Time 2, a larger population than those available at Time 3, designated "all Time 2 cases").

Absolute level of faith maturity. We begin again with the question of what the absolute scores of our participants on the Faith Maturity Scale indicate in context of how the scores of our population compare with those of others. In the original report of the norming and validation of the FMS, the authors summarize the norms of scale responses for different populations by role in the church and by age; we reproduce their reported norms for adults in table 9.6,[16] along with that of our sample.

Table 9.6. Absolute Scores on the FMS

Population	FMS Mean
Pastors (N = 454)	5.32
Coordinators (N = 404)	4.85
Teachers (N = 3043)	4.74
Adults (N = 3582)	4.64
Ages 20-29 (N = 309)	4.46
Ages 30-39 (N = 681)	4.50
Ages 40-49 (N = 724)	4.63
Ages 50-59 (N = 660)	4.76
Exodus sample of this study	4.93 to 5.10

Our Exodus population reported FMS norms slightly below those of the pastors in the original norming study and above those of all other groups. Whether these differences in means are meaningful is unclear.

Changes in faith maturity. Again, our most important finding on this FMS measure is that there is no evidence in the change scores (from Time 1 to either Time 2 or 3) that involvement in this change process caused a decline in faith maturity as measured by the FMS. Unlike the results reported on the SWBS, we found no evidence that involvement changed faith maturity as measured by the FMS to the better. Still, we would again suggest that if involvement in Exodus treatment to change sexual orientation is supposed to be detrimental to the spiritual faith of the participants, we find no evidence of such damage or decrement in this population.

It is possible that the FMS is a measure that is highly insensitive to change, measuring a dimension of personhood that is much more like a stable, unchanging trait than a changeable state like mood. Still, one might expect that the dramatic nature of these change attempts would have a chance to alter faith maturity over the significant time frame of this study (with up to four years or more elapsing between Times 1 and 3), but we see no such change here.

A Stronger Test: Focusing Only on Those Subjects Continuing with the Change Process

For all of the above analyses, we conducted analyses on our entire sample, which included people continuing with the Exodus change process, those continuing the change process but without involvement in Exodus, participants who were demoralized and unsure of what they were doing in this area, and those who had rejected the idea of change and had embraced their gay identity. We realized after producing the previously discussed analyses of the entire population that the stronger test of our hypothesis would come from an analysis exclusively focused on those continuing with the change process and excluding all others. The hypothesis generated from the American Psychological Association was that involvement in such a change process would be harmful, so the strongest test of the hypothesis would focus only on those subjects still involved in the project of change.

We chose as our inclusion-exclusion criterion to create for this group a single yes-no question in the Time 3 interview protocol. Section two, question two of the Time 3 interview asked: At this point, are you continuing with the process of changing your homosexual orientation or feelings? Of the 73 subjects at Time 3, 59 answered yes; they were continuing with the change process. *The significance of this response rate by itself is remarkable.* On average, subjects at Time 3 were three to four years into the change process, a process that should, according to contemporary thinking, be utterly fruitless and damaging. Nevertheless, 59 of 73, or 81%, were still committed to the change attempt. Even if we go back to the original sample size of 98 and estimate that 75% of the 25 dropouts from the study have discontinued the attempt, we are then presented with the estimate that 65% of the original sample were still committed to the change attempt.[17] This is a remarkable continuation rate for those engaged in a process that is so frequently called impossible.

Our focus here is change in the various measures of well-being. We took as our hypothesis from the mental health establishment that scores on the SCL-90-R, the SWBS and the FMS should all show significant movement toward *worsened functioning* as a result of Exodus involvement. We repeated the previously discussed analyses, but this time with a unique subpopulation, namely those who reported that they were indeed continuing with the change process. Now looking only at those actually continuing the change process, what did we find?

Tables 9.7, 9.8 and 9.9 present Time 1 to Time 3 change data only (since the inclusion variable was a response to a Time 3 question). We present in separate tables the findings for the Whole Population (table 9.7), Phase 1 Population (table 9.8) and Truly Gay Population (table 9.9). The data for the SCL-90-R, the SWBS and the FMS are all presented together in each table for each distinct population.

Earlier, we discussed the significance of the absolute scores for each of these three major scales; we will not reexamine these issues because the earlier discussion of the absolute scores applies equally to these reports.

Our hypothesis was that involvement in this change process for sexual orientation would be harmful, with the strongest test of the hypothesis coming from an examination only of those subjects still involved in change. From this data set, however, *we find no evidence of movement in a harmful direction as a result of Exodus involvement.* Contrary to the clear predictions of the American Psychological Association regarding psychological distress and contrary to our extension from that prediction to a prediction of negative spiritual outcomes, scores on all of these measures show little indication of change over time. This is particularly striking for the SCL-90-R and SWBS scores, as these indexes are designed to be sensitive to change.

Distress and Dropouts

Is it possible that the change process caused certain members of our research population such significant distress that they dropped out of the study, thus removing from our study evidence of the harmfulness of the change process? This is indeed possible. We present here the data most relevant to that question, looking only at psychological distress as measured by the SCL-90-R. Remember that our sample started out as 98 individuals at Time 1, dropped to 85 at Time 2 (a loss of 13, who we here call Time 2 dropouts), and then to 73 at Time 3 (a loss of 12, who we here call Time

Table 9.7. Symptom Check List-90-Revised (SCL-90-R, or SCL), Spiritual Well-Being Scale (SWBS) and Faith Maturity Scale (FMS) Time 1 to Time 3 Results for Only Those Subjects Continuing in the Exodus Change Process: Whole Population

	Time 1 Mean	Time 3 Mean	Mean Diff.	N	Df	Std. Dev.	t score	2-tailed sig.
SCL Scores Time 1 to 3: Nonpatient Norms for Continuing Population								
1. GSI Time 1 to 3	57.76	57.80	-0.03	59	58	13.32	-0.02	0.984
2. PSDI Time 1 to 3	56.76	55.10	1.66	59	58	13.05	0.98	0.332
3. PST Time 1 to 3	56.22	57.47	-1.25	59	58	12.78	-0.75	0.454
SCL Scores Time 1 to 3: Outpatient Norms for Continuing Population								
4. GSI Time 1 to 3	39.24	40.54	-1.31	59	58	14.20	-0.71	0.483
5. PSDI Time 1 to 3	40.61	40.17	0.44	59	58	15.10	0.22	0.826
6. PST Time 1 to 3	40.32	42.54	-2.22	59	58	14.44	-1.18	0.242
SWBS Scores Time 1 to 3: Continuing Population								
7. RWB Time 1 to 3	51.88	52.90	-1.02	59	58	5.22	-1.50	0.140
8. EWB Time 1 to 3	45.00	45.80	-0.80	59	58	6.80	-0.90	0.372
9. SWB Time 1 to 3	96.50	98.31	-1.81	59	58	10.38	-1.34	0.186
FMS Scores Time 1 to 3: Continuing Population								
10. FMS Time 1 to 3	5.09	5.10	-0.01	59	58	0.64	-0.08	0.936

Legend

For the SCL-90-R scores, GSI refers to the most important overall score, the Global Severity Index, PSDI refers to the Positive Symptom Distress Index and PST refers to the Positive Symptom Total. For the Spiritual Well-Being Scale, SWB refers to the most important overall score, the Spiritual Well-Being score, which is reported last in each set; the other two scores reported are subscale scores, the RWB, which refers to the Religious Well-Being score, and the EWB, which refers to the Existential Well-Being score. FMS refers to the average score on the Faith Maturity Scale (12-item short form).

Table 9.8. Symptom Check List-90-Revised (SCL-90-R, or SCL), Spiritual Well-Being Scale (SWBS) and Faith Maturity Scale (FMS) Time 1 to Time 3 Results for Only Those Subjects Continuing in the Exodus Change Process: Phase 1 Population

	Time 1 Mean	Time 3 Mean	Mean Diff.	N	Df	Std. Dev.	t score	2-tailed sig.
SCL Scores Time 1 to 3: Nonpatient Norms for Continuing Population								
1. GSI Time 1 to 3	58.62	58.62	0.00	29	28	17.47	0.00	1.000
2. PSDI Time 1 to 3	59.03	56.69	2.35	29	28	17.28	0.73	0.471
3. PST Time 1 to 3	56.14	58.48	-2.35	29	28	16.37	-0.77	0.447
SCL Scores Time 1 to 3: Outpatient Norms for Continuing Population								
4. GSI Time 1 to 3	40.90	43.38	-2.48	29	28	19.75	-0.68	0.504
5. PSDI Time 1 to 3	43.17	42.90	0.28	29	28	20.48	0.07	0.943
6. PST Time 1 to 3	41.14	44.93	-3.79	29	28	19.63	-1.04	0.307
SWBS Scores Time 1 to 3: Continuing Population								
7. RWB Time 1 to 3	50.83	52.75	-1.92	29	28	5.94	-1.74	0.093
8. EWB Time 1 to 3	43.17	45.59	-2.41	29	28	7.38	-1.76	0.089
9. SWB Time 1 to 3	93.58	97.95	-4.67	29	28	11.75	-2.00	0.055
FMS Scores Time 1 to 3: Continuing Population								
10. FMS Time 1 to 3	4.93	4.94	-0.01	29	28	0.78	-0.08	0.941

Legend

For the SCL-90-R scores, GSI refers to the most important overall score, the Global Severity Index, PSDI refers to the Positive Symptom Distress Index and PST refers to the Positive Symptom Total. For the Spiritual Well-Being Scale, SWB refers to the most important overall score, the Spiritual Well-Being score, which is reported last in each set; the other two scores reported are subscale scores, the RWB, which refers to the Religious Well-Being score, and the EWB which refers to the Existential Well-Being score. FMS refers to the average score on the Faith Maturity Scale (12-item short-form).

Table 9.9. Symptom Check List-90-Revised (SCL-90-R, or SCL), Spiritual Well-Being Scale (SWBS) and Faith Maturity Scale (FMS) Time 1 to Time 3 Results for Only Those Subjects Continuing in the Exodus Change Process: Truly Gay Population

	Time 1 Mean	Time 3 Mean	Mean Diff.	N	Df	Std. Dev.	t score	2-tailed sig.
SCL Scores Time 1 to 3: Nonpatient Norms for Continuing Population								
1. GSI Time 1 to 3	58.74	59.38	-0.65	34	33	16.17	-0.23	0.817
2. PSDI Time 1 to 3	57.32	57.18	0.15	34	33	14.55	0.06	0.953
3. PST Time 1 to 3	56.97	59.03	-2.06	34	33	14.61	-0.77	0.447
SCL Scores Time 1 to 3: Outpatient Norms for Continuing Population								
4. GSI Time 1 to 3	40.00	43.03	-3.03	34	33	18.09	-0.98	0.336
5. PSDI Time 1 to 3	41.12	42.88	-1.77	34	33	17.82	-0.58	0.568
6. PST Time 1 to 3	41.21	45.15	-3.94	34	33	18.21	-1.26	0.216
SWBS Scores Time 1 to 3: Continuing Population								
7. RWB Time 1 to 3	52.15	53.13	-0.98	34	33	4.80	-1.19	0.244
8. EWB Time 1 to 3	44.53	45.97	-1.44	34	33	6.95	-1.21	0.235
9. SWB Time 1 to 3	96.27	98.71	-2.44	34	33	10.33	-1.38	0.178
FMS Scores Time 1 to 3: Continuing Population								
10. FMS Time 1 to 3	5.14	5.14	-0.00	34	33	0.71	-0.04	0.968

Legend

For the SCL-90-R scores, GSI refers to the most important overall score, the Global Severity Index, PSDI refers to the Positive Symptom Distress Index and PST refers to the Positive Symptom Total. For the Spiritual Well-Being Scale, SWB refers to the most important overall score, the Spiritual Well-Being score, which is reported last in each set; the other two scores reported are subscale scores, the RWB, which refers to the Religious Well-Being score, and the EWB, which refers to the Existential Well-Being score. FMS refers to the average score on the Faith Maturity Scale (12-item short form).

3 dropouts). Table 9.10 looks at the SCL-90-R scores for the 13 Time-2 dropouts at Time 1, and the 12 Time-3 dropouts at Time 2, in each case this being the last set of data we have on those subjects.

Table 9.10. SCL-90-R Scores for Dropouts at Time 2 and Time 3

	GSI	PSDI	PST	N
1. Time 1 SCL-90-R for Time 2 Dropouts: Nonpatient Norms	67.23 (10.43)	63.00 (9.50)	64.23 (9.27)	13
2. Time 1 SCL-90-R for Time 2 Dropouts: Outpatient Norms	48.23 (12.69)	48.38 (12.38)	49.00 (12.64)	13
3. Time 2 SCL-90-R for Time 3 Dropouts: Nonpatient Norms	62.58 (15.57)	57.83 (12.23)	61.17 (14.73)	12
4. Time 2 SCL-90-R for Time 3 Dropouts: Outpatient Norms	43.58 (12.01)	42.58 (12.38)	46.17 (14.19)	12

Earlier we reported that the Exodus participants scored about as far below the psychiatric outpatient norms for psychological distress as they scored above the nonpatient norms (see p. 342). That pattern shifts a bit in these data. That characterization still appears to hold for the Time 3 dropouts (the last two rows of table 9.10), but the Time 2 dropouts scored a few points higher on average at Time 1 than those who stayed in the study on nonpatient norms, actually scoring at around the 63 standard set by the scale authors for being judged a "clinical case." Further, in comparison to the psychiatric outpatient norms, the Time 1 dropouts scored close to the norm for this sample. This would appear to indicate that the Time 1 dropouts were considerably distressed. Unfortunately, because they dropped out, we have no further information about their status.

It is easy to imagine starkly different interpretations of this finding, modest as it is. Those opposed to attempts to change sexual orientation might well argue that this is the evidence of harm that they anticipated; it would appear that the change process produced significant distress and was fruitless for these individuals. On the other hand, proponents of change could argue that (1) because we have no further information on these individuals, we have no basis on which to conclude that they were unsuccessful in the change process, but more important that (2) these findings should be interpreted as indicating that the long and difficult change process, one that according to its proponents involves confrontation with very difficult emotional realities, requires a certain "psychological hardiness" or resilience, and that individuals without sufficient external supports or internal strength (or motivation) would be the ones to become distressed and drop out (i.e., the distress preexisted and was the cause of dropout, rather than treatment per se causing distress).

We conclude that we have insufficient empirical evidence to decide between such interpretations based on this data alone, but the broader pattern of data reported in this chapter *does not* appear to support the hypothesis that it is the change process, in and of itself, that produces clinical distress and psychological harm.

Anecdotes of Harm, Risk and Expanded Informed Consent

We found no empirical evidence in this study to support the claim that the attempt to change sexual orientation is harmful. To return to the topic we introduced in chapter three and again at the start of this chapter, what then are we to make of the widely reported anecdotes of the harm caused by such attempts to change? To make this very concrete, here are two such anecdotes, presented by an individual who attests to Christian faith, who is an outspoken critic of change attempts and who himself claims to have attempted and failed at such a change:

> Mark B. was a young man who accepted his sexual orientation "until he became a Christian" and was told on the basis of these texts [i.e., the biblical texts that condemn homosexual conduct as discussed in chapter two] that he couldn't both be a Christian and a gay man. Mark committed suicide and wrote this suicide note to God: "I just don't know how else to fix this." Mary Lou Wallner, one of our most faithful Soulforce volunteers, was led by these texts to condemn her lesbian daughter, Anna, who hanged herself. Mary Lou now says, "If I can just steer one person away from the pain and anguish I've been living, then maybe Anna's death will have meaning."[18]

Again, we would be hypocritical to claim, contend or argue that anecdotes per se have no evidentiary value; after all, it was our own attention to personal stories and anecdotes of change that led us to pursue the questions of this study. We would also be inhumane to ignore the obvious tragedy of such stories. But should such anecdotes foreclose the option of the individual choosing to attempt orientation change?

What are the issues embedded in thinking through these issues? First, anecdotes have traditionally been understood as having little evidentiary value in comparison to systematically gathered empirical evidence. For instance, innumerable ineffective treatments for serious concerns and diseases have been promulgated on the basis of anecdotes of miracle cures, from snake oil to faith healing to ineffective natural remedies. Such anecdotes of cure may themselves be fraudulent or inaccurate. They may also be genuine—miracle (and near-miracle) cures do happen—but may be either (1) *unrepresentative* (the person may really have been cured by the snake oil for some idiosyncratic reason, but that remedy may have absolutely no benefit on average to the general public) or (2) *spurious* (the person may have been healed from their disease due to factors that had nothing to do with the consumption of snake oil but rather with some other medicine or substance they ingested or supernatural intervention).

Anecdotes of harm must be treated similarly. Anecdotes of miraculous cure and of ineffectiveness or harm exist for just about every intervention around. Anecdotes simply cannot provide us with a *representative* picture of the effectiveness and consequences of an intervention, and thus anecdotes must be viewed in the context of the findings of systematic research.[19] Further, in the specific context of the issue of harm to homosexually orientated individuals attempting change, we must ask the difficult question of whether a true case of a person committing suicide (or experiencing any other type of harm) after unsuccessfully attempting change is actually attributable to the change attempt. After all, people who commit suicide may make attributions for their own behavior that are not completely accurate. Suicidally depressed individuals may not be reliable interpreters of their own behavior, as some have experienced when counseling parents devastated by the suicide death of a teenage child who leaves a note blaming the parents for his or her actions. Many mental health professionals have had to grapple with the aftermath of a patient committing suicide and leaving some indication that the professional failed him or her in providing effective treatment, when the professional may in fact have provided competent care, but care which can never attain perfect success. All of this leaves us saying that anecdotes cannot be ignored, but also that they cannot be privileged above systematic research.

Second, such anecdotes of harm from the attempt to change must be counterbalanced against counteranecdotes, specifically the type that circulate in ministry circles of individuals who experience despair in the gay community because they do not know that the possibility of an alternative to the gay lifestyle exists. The reality is that members of the gay community experience elevated risk for suicide and for many other types of psychological distress compared to the general population. Susan Cochran, a distinguished psychologist and epidemiologist who is also a lesbian, recently published an analysis of the impact on mental health of status as gay, lesbian or bisexual. Her conclusion on occurrence of psychological distress is that, in all of the studies she had reviewed, "researchers found some evidence for elevated risk when lesbian, gay, and bisexual individuals are compared with heterosexual respondents."[20] The variables on which risk was elevated included addictions, anxiety, depression and suicidality.

What are we to make of this empirically elevated risk?* Cochran argued that the most likely cause of this elevated risk is the stress of living in a rejecting, heterosexist culture.† This is a plausible hypothesis, but it is also a hypothesis for which conclusive proof is yet forthcoming and for which the best support is merely indirect. Proponents of Exodus approaches to understanding of the homosexual condition would claim that elevated distress may be intrinsic to the homosexual condition because that is not how God intended persons to live, and many of those who give personal testimony in support of Exodus report living in various forms of despair themselves in the gay community before finding freedom through Exodus. Are anecdotes of harm the only anecdotes deserving to be heard? We cannot give ear only to one type of anecdote.

Third, treatment decisions must be made according to a thoughtful and informed benefit-risk analysis. As we all have come to know thanks to "side effects disclaimers" for prescription medications, all treatments and interventions have potential risks. The question cannot be simply, Are there any risks? but rather, How do I weigh the potential gains from this

---

*Note that such elevated risk does nothing to establish that all gay or lesbian persons are at such risk.

†And we note that our book is likely to be taken as a contribution to the cultivation of such a hateful culture even though we do not intend it to be so and support civil tolerance of different moral choices in a pluralistic and democratic culture.

intervention against its potential risks? Such assessments are made yet more complicated when the human subjectivity of the values assigned to the various benefits and risks are factored in. For a pharmaceutical intervention, the risk of a 0.05% probability of death must be weighed against the degree of personal distress caused by, for example, a chronic pain condition; this is no easy choice. In the specific case we are examining, the outcome of "accepting your sexual orientation" will be weighed very differently by the person who believes such an orientation to be a human condition that is morally indistinguishable from heterosexual orientation *versus* the person who believes sincerely that homosexual conduct is immoral or unnatural (or that a "normal" or "traditional" family is the only acceptable option for finding fulfillment). Anecdotes alert us to risks in making such difficult benefit-risk analyses, but only systematic research can actually provide a strong evidence base for such decisions.

As we briefly consider ethical and professional practice issues in light of therapies and paraprofessional ministries that address sexual orientation concerns, we note that side effects are a concern in any intervention program and may or may not become an ethical concern depending on how severe or enduring those side effects are and whether they are the experience of the vast majority of participants.[21] In a discussion of how consequences of treatment play a role in informed consent, Thomas Grisso and Paul Appelbaum discuss *high benefit/low risk* treatment, *low benefit/high risk* treatment, and *low to moderate benefit/low to moderate risk* treatment.[22] We found no empirical evidence in this study that would place Exodus ministry approaches in a *high-* or even *moderate-risk* treatment approach, and we found evidence of *moderate benefit* in a range of areas that matter to ministry participants.

This study offers the first systematically gathered information available on a sample (though a sample that is not conclusively representative) of those attempting to change their sexual orientation. We note again that our study is not of psychotherapy or reparative therapy but of a diverse group of methods used by a number of different Exodus ministries, but also note that the mental health professional organizations have cast broadly their denunciations of reparative therapy to include religious interventions like those studied here. In this study we have found on average no evidence that involvement in this change process produces harm.

Conclusion

The findings presented in this chapter represent significant evidence supporting the rejection of our hypothesis that the change process causes harm. "The American Psychological Association is concerned about such therapies [i.e., therapies and other interventions directed at changing sexual orientation] and their potential harm to patients."[23] This study finds no evidence to support these concerns; specifically, we find no meaningful evidence that the attempt to change sexual orientation through the Exodus ministries causes harm.

10

Conclusion

> COOPER: Alan Chambers is the president of Exodus International, an organization that claims to turn gay people straight, and Mark Shields is with the Human Rights Campaign, a gay advocacy group. Gentlemen, I appreciate you being on the program. . . .
>
> Mark, you know people who have been through this kind of therapy. Some call it reparative therapy. In your experience, does it work?
>
> SHIELDS: Again, absolutely not. Every bit of evidence we've seen is that it does not work. And at the Human Rights Campaign, we believe the only choice there is about being gay is, you know, whether or not you choose to be open and honest about it, if that's how you were born.
>
> I think that people have the choice that they can try and hide that or try and deny that piece of themselves, but ultimately, that's not healthy for them or for their loved ones.
>
> COOPER: But Mark, if someone is not happy being gay, as Alan clearly wasn't as a child, what's wrong with him trying to change?
>
> SHIELDS: You know, again, the mental health professionals tell us that, in trying to change or fix something that's not broken, you can actually cause a great deal of harm to yourself and ultimately to those that are around you.
>
> "Anderson Cooper 360 Degrees," CNN, February 6, 2007

IN CONDUCTING THIS STUDY WE FOUND empirical evidence that change of homosexual orientation may be possible through involvement in Exodus ministries, either (1) in the form of an embrace of chastity with a reduction in prominence of homosexual desire, or (2) in the form of a diminishing of homosexual attraction and an increase in heterosexual attraction with resulting satisfactory heterosexual adjustment. These latter individuals regard themselves as having changed their sexual orientation; the former regard themselves as having reestablished their sexual identities to be defined in some way other than by their homosexual attractions.

Further, we found little evidence of harm incurred as a result of the involvement of the participants in the Exodus change process. These findings would appear to contradict the commonly expressed view of the mental health establishment that change of sexual orientation is impossible and that the attempt to change is highly likely to produce harm for those who make such an attempt.

In concluding this report, we want to briefly review our study, summarize the core of our findings, be clear about what we are claiming and anticipate criticisms of the study.

What Questions Were We Trying to Answer in This Study?

We were attempting to answer two questions: Is change of sexual orientation (specifically homosexual orientation) possible? Is the attempt to change sexual orientation harmful? These questions were framed in the context of strong declarations by aspects of the mental health community that change of sexual orientation is impossible, and that the attempt to change is harmful. The means we examined for seeking sexual orientation change was not professional psychotherapy per se but rather a set of religious ministries that use a combination of spiritual and psychological methods.

In fact, these strong declarations by the mental health community allowed us to frame our hypotheses in terms of the strong absolutes urged by our field: we hypothesized, first, that change of sexual orientation is impossible, and, second, that the attempt to change is harmful. The logic of scientific inquiry then drives us, based on our results, to reject both hypotheses and to conclude that change of sexual orientation is *not* impossible, and that the attempt to change sexual orientation is *not* harmful.

What Is Unique About This Study?

As we argued in chapter four, this is the first prospective and longitudinal study (reporting on multiple assessments at Times 1, 2 and 3) of a respectably large and arguably representative sample of those seeking to undergo change in sexual orientation via religiously mediated means. Further, this study utilized a compound array of respected, established and well-validated self-report measures of sexual orientation, psychological distress, and other variables to measure the outcomes of interest.

We proposed six key criteria for empirical respectability for a study of this kind:

- prospective—that is, beginning assessment with individuals that are starting the change process and watching the results unfold, in contrast to methods that ask participants to reflect on change experiences that happened in their pasts
- longitudinal—that is, follow participants over time with multiple assessments rather than simply sampling their status at one static moment in time
- representative sample of the population
- use the best contemporary self-report measures of sexual orientation and of psychological distress, and use multiple measures
- large subject population
- sample subjects in different Exodus groups

We argued in chapter four that we succeeded strongly in the prospective and longitudinal nature of the study. Few studies in the literature have been prospective and longitudinal. In this alone, this study stands out. We succeeded in using the best contemporary measures of sexual orientation and psychological distress, and in sampling different Exodus groups. We are confident that ours is the most representative sample of a wide array of individuals seeking help through Exodus that has ever been compiled, but we cannot be sure that our sample is completely representative. As we emphasized, no one really knows what a representative sample of homosexual individuals would really look like. Finally, while our study is one of the larger studies in this area and must be taken seriously on this account, the sample is not as large as we had hoped.

As discussed in chapter four, there are two points on which we expect to draw particular criticism and where this study falls short of the empirical ideal. We did not use a true experimental design, and we did not use psychophysiological measures to assess sexual arousal and orientation. We argued previously that implementation of a true experimental design, with random assignment of blind subjects to experimental treatment conditions, including placebo controls, would have been patently impossible to implement given the unique nature of Exodus ministries, the long time frame for change and the unique characteristics of the participant population. We also argued that the use of psychophysiological measures to assess sexual arousal and orientation was pragmatically impossible given the dispersed nature of our sample and the limitations of our funding, morally unacceptable to the bulk of our research participants, and not justified given the current state of understanding of the reliability and validity of the method itself. While we might admit that in an ideal world with unlimited funding and no reality constraints conducting a true experiment and including psychophysiological measures to assess sexual arousal might strengthen our conclusions to some degree, we believe that the methods we chose in this study were necessary and more than adequate to the questions we were pursuing.

What Did We Find?

We found sufficient evidence to conclude that change of sexual orientation is *not* impossible, and that the attempt to change sexual orientation is *not* harmful on average. Here we quickly summarize our key findings.

Quantitative analysis of sexual orientation outcomes. In chapter seven we presented our quantitative analyses of changes in sexual orientation, just as one would the results of psychotherapy or drug trials, by looking at average changes over time on the various outcome measures. The general picture that emerged from these analyses was that, on average, this population had experienced significant movement away from homosexual orientation and toward heterosexual orientation. Many of these average changes achieved the standards of statistical significance adopted by our field.

But were these shifts meaningful? The best answer comes from looking at empirically derived standards of effect size. By the standards used to judge whether psychotherapy and drug interventions are meaningful, the answer would appear to be yes, these changes were meaningful. The effect sizes of the average movement away from homosexual orientation may be termed medium to large, and the average shift toward heterosexual orientation small.

Our most surprising single finding was that the subpopulation from this study that was most likely on average to manifest significant change was the Truly Gay subpopulation. We constructed this subpopulation based on responses at the Time 1 assessment that indicated that the individual was above the median score for ratings of homosexual erotic attraction, for past homosexual sexual behavior and for identification as homosexual (gay or lesbian). These individuals, in other words, all reported homosexual attraction above the bisexual median of the rating scales, had been predominantly homosexually active in the past and had identified as homosexual in the past.

Common sense and dominant clinical professional opinion would clearly predict that these would be the research subjects *least* likely to report fundamental change, and yet consistently, it was this group that reported the greatest degree of change. For instance, we might note the argument of Robert Epstein that some people do change, but that the ones who can and do are probably lower in genetic determination of sexual orientation, are probably less truly gay.[1] While this is a credible hypothesis, our evidence does not support this conclusion; our Truly Gay subpopulation had as strong or stronger change outcomes as the population as a whole. Unless the degree of genetic determination of homosexual orientation has no bearing on degree of immersion in homosexual identity and lifestyle, our data are incompatible with Epstein's hypothesis.

Phase 1 subjects were somewhat less likely to experience success than other subjects. Phase 1 subjects were those that were one year or less into the change process at the time of our first, baseline assessment; Phase 2 subjects were those that had already been in the change process for between one and three years. There are a number of possible ways to interpret this finding. One, the one that would seem the most credible to us, would be that individuals who are experiencing more difficulty in the initial stages of the change process would be more likely to drop out, so that any sampling from those who have endured into the second and third years of pursuing change would mean that you are including disproportionately in your sample individuals who are more likely to report success from their efforts to change.

Qualitative analysis of sexual orientation outcomes. In chapter eight we presented our qualitative analyses and some post hoc (after the fact) quantitative analyses of our findings. Participants were categorized on the basis of their self-reports in interviews in one of six categories; we report the percentages in each category in parentheses:

- "Success: Conversion" (15%): The subject reports considerable resolution of homosexual orientation issues and substantial conversion to heterosexual attraction.
- "Success: Chastity" (23%): The subject reports homosexual attraction is either missing or present only incidentally and in a way that does not seem to bring about distress.
- "Continuing" (29%): The person may have experienced diminution of homosexual attraction, but is not satisfied and remains committed to the change process.
- "Nonresponse" (15%): The person has experienced no significant sexual orientation change. The subject has *not* given up on the change process, but may be confused or conflicted about which direction to turn next.
- "Failure: Confused" (4%): The person has experienced no significant sexual orientation change and has given up on the change process but without yet embracing gay identity.
- "Failure: Gay Identity" (8%): The person has clearly given up on the change process and embraced gay identity.

We explored how such a pattern of results compares to outcomes in other change efforts in the mental health field, arguing that our two success categories (conversion and chastity; together 38%) would parallel strongly positive outcomes, the continuing group (29%) would parallel an improved-but-with-room-for-continued-growth category, the nonresponders (15%) would reflect a no change outcome, and the two failure groups (together 12%) represent negative outcomes (in the estimation of Exodus). We argued further that an outcome array similar to this would be regarded as respectable in the mental health field. Interventions such as psychotherapy or drug treatments always have successes, improvers, nonresponders and some negative outcomes. It is particularly notable that

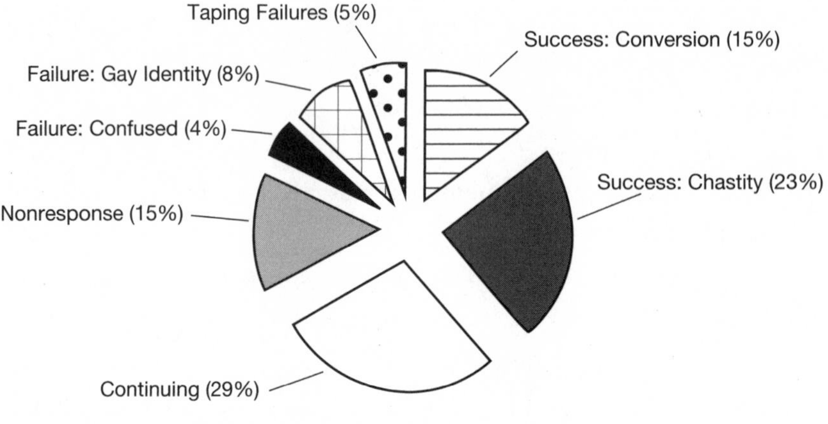

Figure 10.1. Qualitative Categorizations

what Exodus calls failure would not be considered failure at all by the majority of mental health professionals, in that an embrace of same-sex erotic orientation would be seen as the most positive outcome by most psychologists today.

We explored further the meaning of our findings by examining the quantitative outcomes for our subjects when divided into these general outcome groups. In other words, instead of looking at global outcomes of the entire population averaged together, which can mask remarkable outcomes, we returned to our quantitative outcome measures by outcome group and presented a summary of these findings in figure 10.2. These outcomes are exactly as would be predicted if our qualitative categorization were valid.

Outcomes for harm. In chapter nine we examined evidence for the Exodus process causing harm to these participants. Our analysis yielded no support for the hypothesis that our participant's scores on the SCL-90-R, our respected measure of psychological distress, would show significant movement toward worsened psychological functioning as a result of Exodus involvement. Generally, the changes noted were small and statistically insignificant, with one exception: For all three population groups—the Whole Population, the Phase 1 subpopulation, and the Truly Gay subpop-

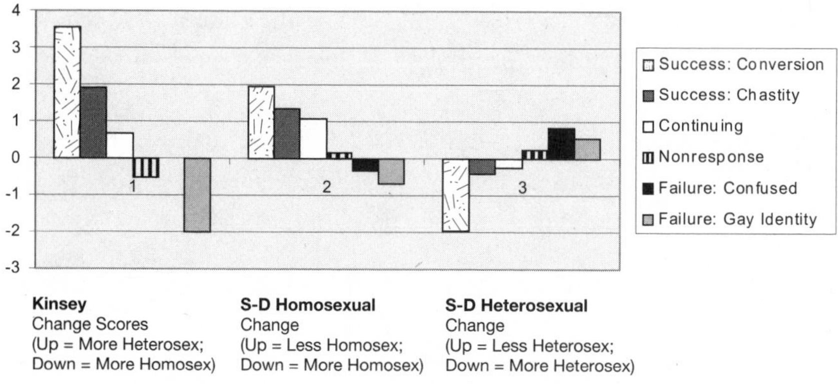

Figure 10.2. Kinsey and Shively-DeCecco Change Scores Time 1 to Time 3 for Each of the Six Outcome Groups

ulation—the one consistently statistically significant shift was the shift in the Positive Symptom Distress Index in a direction of *less distress*. In other words, as a result of Exodus involvement, participants reported that their intensity of distress symptoms changed for *the better* to a statistically significant degree (though this shift was modest in absolute terms).

So, contrary to our hypothesis that harm would be demonstrated, we found little evidence of harm. Where we did detect evidence of statistically significant change occurring, it was toward a diminishing or lessening of psychological symptoms and distress (i.e., improvement), and not toward greater harm.

We then examined a more rigorous hypothesis. Recognizing that some might suppose that the good mental health of those who had embraced their gay identities might be masking (by averaging out) the decaying mental health of those seeking change, we analyzed our data gain including only those subjects who reported at Time 3 continuing down the path of seeking sexual orientation change. Surely, we reasoned, if the attempt at the change process was going to be harmful, it would be harmful to those continuing to pursue change over a period of years.

Contrary to these expectations, we found no evidence of movement toward increased distress or other evidence of harm as a result of Exodus involvement. Contrary to the clear predictions of the American Psychological Association regarding psychological distress, scores showed little indication of change over time.

Also in chapter nine we examined results for spiritual well-being and faith maturity. We found no evidence that involvement with the Exodus change process produced negative outcomes in these areas.

WHAT DID WE *NOT* FIND?

In addition to clarifying what we did find, it is equally important to clarify what we did not find. Given the controversial and volatile nature of discourse about this highly controversial topic, it is likely that commentators of all sorts will draw varying conclusions about this work, and so we want to give our best logical take on what we believe would be improper or illicit conclusions to draw from this study.

First, we found that some respondents experienced significant, meaningful change of sexual orientation in this sample, but we did not find that everyone (or anyone) can change. The fact that some human beings can break the four-minute mile barrier establishes that running a four-minute mile is not impossible, but that same fact does not establish that anyone (every human being) can break the four-minute mile barrier. So also our findings firmly refute any notion that change of sexual orientation is impossible. Saying that change is not impossible in general is not the same thing as saying that everyone can change, that anyone can change or that change is necessarily possible for any given individual.

Second, while we found that a part of our research population experienced success to the degree that it might be called (as we have here) "conversion," we have insufficient evidence to conclude that these changes are categorical, resulting in uncomplicated, dichotomous and unequivocal reversal of sexual orientation from utterly homosexual to utterly heterosexual. Most of the individuals who reported that they were heterosexual at Time 3 did not report themselves to be without experience of homosexual arousal, and they did not report heterosexual orientation to be unequivocal and uncomplicated. Sexual orientation for the individuals in this study (and indeed for most of us) may be considerably more complicated than commonly conceived, involving a complex interplay of what we are instinctively attracted to, what we can be attracted to with proper attention and focus, what we choose to be attracted to based on how we structure our interpersonal environments, our emotional attachments, our broader psychological functioning, (of course) our religious and moral beliefs and values, and many more factors. We believe the individuals who presented themselves as heterosexual success stories at Time 3 are heterosexual in some meaningful but complicated sense of the term.

Some would immediately challenge us that any change short of complete conversion to uncomplicated (and caricaturish) heterosexuality with total eradication of homosexual attraction means that claims of successful change are a sham. By this standard, any admission that these participants experience any homosexual arousal means that claims of success are an illusion. Are people who still have any level of homosexual attraction still gay?

As we discussed in chapter six and elsewhere, we reject the stance that any reoccurrence of homosexual attraction signifies that the person has "not really changed." This is simply too stringent a stance to pass the test of generalization to other conditions. We would not say that couples who have experienced positive gains from relational therapy but still have distressing conflict have not changed for the better, that a person who still experiences craving for an addictive substance has not defeated the addiction, or that the person who still struggles with occasional milder dysphoria has not overcome major depression. On the other hand, the general concern here is not without merit as an argument. Take what might be regarded as the paradigm case: the phenomenon of the "ex-ex-gay," who (1) experiences clear homosexual orientation ("gay"), (2) attempts change and claims healing/change ("ex-gay"), and (3) then later reverts back to an embrace of homosexual identity and lifestyle ("ex-ex-gay"), while reporting that his or her earlier reports of change were coerced, insincere responses to a heterosexist climate that were made despite stable, enduring, unaltered homosexual attraction. It must be acknowledged that this person never shifted from being homosexually orientated. This, however, begs the question, in that the fact that such a person experienced inadequate change on which to reestablish a new ground of sexual identity cannot establish that others were not able to make that shift in a way that is satisfying and meaningful.

Third, these findings do not refute the anecdotal reports of specific individuals that they could not change. But then neither do the anecdotal reports of persons who could not change refute the reality that some of the individuals in this study did experience quite significant change.

Fourth, the change results documented in this study are the results of a set of diverse, religiously based intervention programs, and hence these findings do not speak directly to the issue of the effectiveness of professionally based psychotherapy interventions, what are commonly called reparative or conversion therapies. Psychotherapy delivered by a mental health professional was a part of the total "package" experienced by some individuals in this study, but we are unable to tease out the impact of such therapy from the more general context of change. Though this study does nothing direct to establish evidence for the effectiveness of professional reparative or conversion therapies, however, to the degree that the contemporary mental health field regards such conversion therapies as discredited[2] on the presumptive basis that it is impossible to change sexual orientation, these results may and perhaps should open the door for a reconsideration of the possible efficacy of such therapies. In other words, as we argued in chapter three, professional conversion therapies are being regarded as discredited not because a positive evidential base exists proving that such therapies are unsuccessful, but rather in spite of a considerable (though imperfect) research base suggesting that such treatments produce positive outcomes some of the time with some individuals. At least in part, the credibility of this argument is grounded in a general acceptance of the claim that sexual orientation is immutable. The present results suggesting that some change is possible undermine this core assertion, which may contribute to a reexamination of whether professional conversion therapies ever succeed.

Fifth, the fact that we documented positive outcomes from religiously mediated interventions does not constitute evidence of divine intervention in the lives of these individuals. Participants in Exodus rely on God's help in the change process, call out for that help, and often attribute significant change to divine intervention or blessing. But do these results then stand as "proof" of God's intervention in these lives? As scientists, we have to say that we can draw no such conclusion from this study. It is logically possible that we captured a snapshot of God's divine power on display in the lives of some of these individuals, but other explanations are possible as well. It is possible that the religious dimension in the Exodus program merely energizes and directs higher levels of participant motivation and drive for change according to completely naturalistic laws of human behavior. Further, nothing in the pattern of evidence uniquely and exclusively points to divine agency. The change processes behind the successful outcomes in this study may be natural or supernatural.

Sixth, we cannot validate that the significant changes experienced by the Exodus successes in this study are permanent or utterly pervasive. We discussed in chapter eight the case of the individual who has returned to full gay identity after being classified as a success at Time 3. The same fate could await other (or even all) of our other successful cases. But alternatively, it is logically possible that the opposite could happen—that individuals classified at Time 3 as failures could yet become Exodus successes. It must be remembered that all reports of outcomes in behavior change intervention studies are provisional, at this time. Persons cured of addictions relapse; individuals who alter their behavior lapse back into old patterns. That an individual is free of a type of distress at one assessment does not guarantee that the change will endure.

Seventh, we cannot shed light on the provocative and important question of which methods employed by these Exodus groups were the effective element producing change. We did not produce clear evidence regarding which methods are successful and which are not. First, we did not have a large enough subject sample to allow us to untangle the effects produced by different aspects of the packages of interventions that different participants experienced in different groups. Second, we did not implement a methodology for our study that would allow us to "dismantle" the complex packages used in these ministries to test specific elements alone or in combination. Such dismantling studies require carefully controlled packages of interventions, and we here studied the results of whatever participants experienced in their ministries (and beyond).

Eighth, we did not find evidence to conclude which subject variables predict success or failure, and so we cannot say that those with certain characteristic are more (or less) likely to change. Here we simply lacked a sufficiently large sample to allow us to conduct such analyses with confidence. Even so, it was with considerable surprise that we uncovered the results showing that changes in the Truly Gay subsample were as great as or greater than that of the sample as a whole; this was contrary to what we had supposed.

Ninth, despite our finding that on average participants experienced no harm from the attempt to change, we cannot conclude that specific individuals are not harmed by an attempt to change. It is important to remember here that life is dangerous and filled with potential harm. When pharmaceutical companies test drugs or other medical interventions, they do not actually seek to prove that the interventions are utterly benign, but rather that the incidence of potential harm is not larger than chance or placebo. At this writing, the Food and Drug Administration of the U.S. federal government has just lifted the longstanding ban on silicone breast implants. Dramatic anecdotal reports had circulated for years of significant harm to individuals who had received such implants, but research has apparently now established that these negative outcomes are not occurring in the implant population beyond the base probabilities of such events. Similarly, our findings from this first-ever study to examine reports of psychological distress prospectively and longitudinally have produced no evidence of harm on average to this population.

Specific individuals may claim to have experienced harm from the attempt to change, and those claims may be legitimate. Genuine and tragic harm may indeed result from intervention methods that are inept, harsh, punitive or otherwise ill-conceived. Additionally, specific individuals may be psychologically fragile in such ways that well-meaning interventions that would not cause harm to most other persons may be traumatic to those persons. It is also necessary to say that claims of harm may be ideologically based and exaggerated for the sake of foreclosing the option of the attempt to change.

What Are the Implications of This Study?

Obviously, the limitations of this study combined with the provocative nature of its findings suggest the value of further study of this complicated issue. The complications of conducting such research are immense, however, and we do not need to reiterate those complications here. So our first implication of this study is the call for further research.

Second, and at much greater length, we want to argue that these results suggest the importance of respecting the autonomy and right of self-determination of individuals who, because of their personal values, religious or not, desire to seek change of their sexual orientation as well as of those who desire to affirm and consolidate their sexual orientation. A general principle of respect for client/patient autonomy and self-determination is a common feature of the ethics codes of all of the major mental health professional organizations. The American Psychological Association's Code of Ethical Principles of Psychologists, for example, includes recognition of the value of self-determination among its *General Principles:* "Psychologists respect the dignity and worth of all people, and the rights of individuals to privacy, confidentiality, and self-determination."[3]

Douglas Haldeman is one who has explicitly applied this principle of autonomy and self-determination to the issue of attempted change of sexual orientation for religious clients:

> Some believe that it is easier to find a new religious affiliation than to change or repress one's sexual orientation; thus, they will attempt overtly or subtly to guide the client in this direction. This may be an inappropriate choice for the individual as well as a disruptive element in the therapeutic environment. Similarly, some religious counselors may be at risk for ignoring the client's realities because of a scripturally induced rigidity about the way in which people should live their lives. . . . Psychology's responsibility is not to contravene its own database or its own policies by supporting treatments founded in the conception of lesbian, gay, and bisexual people as mentally ill or incapable of fulfilling, productive lives. Nor, however, should psychology deny individuals the right to therapeutic support in making the accommodations necessary to living lives that are consonant with their personal values.[4]

Though there are aspects of Haldeman's argument with which we disagree, he seems to be voicing a stance of respect for client autonomy, respect for the role of religious and moral belief as a core value in the lives of many, and (perhaps) respect for the right of professionals to explore disparate methods as long as professional care is taken to guard clients from harm. We affirm this stance.

But many actively resist including conversion therapy or ministry approaches such as Exodus in a discussion of possible options for clients who are distressed about their sexual orientation. The American Psychiatric Association, for instance, claims to support client autonomy, but in its denunciation of reparative therapy, states:

> Many patients who have undergone "reparative therapy" relate that they were inaccurately told that homosexuals are lonely, unhappy individuals who never achieve acceptance or satisfaction. The possibility that the person might achieve happiness and satisfying interpersonal relationships as a gay man or lesbian is not presented, nor are alternative approaches to dealing with the effects of societal stigmatization discussed.[5]

The oddity of this statement is first its seemingly omniscient declaration that many clients of reparative therapy are never presented or told certain things, but more important that it fails to advocate that (1) clients/patients be told, in the interest of full disclosure, that there is evidence that homosexual individuals continue to manifest heightened risk of various forms of psychological distress in all studies of these populations, and (2) clients/patients be told, in the interest of full disclosure, about the evidence that exists (reviewed in chapter three, to which this study adds considerably) that change of sexual orientation may be possible for some.

Even more forcefully, Gonsiorek argues:

> When clients request that psychologists perform activities of uncertain or questionable appropriateness, then the requirements for careful discussion and judgment become more complex. Client choice properly functions as an aspect of informed consent and not as a substitute for ethical decision making and practice standards. . . . A client's request for conversion therapy is a questionable request. It is questionable in terms of ethics, efficacy, and possible harm among other concerns. It is nonsense to assert that in requests for conversion therapy, respect for diversity requires that psychologists abdicate these complex duties and considerations. I also believe it is dangerous for the client, the psychologist, and the profession. . . . At their core, conversion therapies seek to legitimize the use of psychological techniques and behavioral science to enforce compliance with religious orthodoxy. The dilemma resists solution because it cannot be solved. Either psychology is co-opted into abdicating its ethical principles, professional practice standards, and

> scientific base, or it soundly rejects the enforcement of religious orthodoxy as a legitimate goal of psychological practice. . . . The American Psychological Association has developed a tradition of operating with a "big tent" philosophy, welcoming into its fold all psychologists For the most part, this philosophy has served the association well. . . . I suggest, however, that there are natural limits to this philosophy and that conversion therapies are an example.[6]

Gonsiorek clearly calls for the complete foreclosure of the option for clients of attempting sexual orientation change. We, on the other hand, based on the best scientific evidence including the present study, want to keep options open for individuals experiencing significant conflict between their erotic attractions and their personal values.

We are not alone in this stand. Robert Perloff, a past president of the American Psychological Association and Distinguished Service Professor Emeritus of Business Administration and Psychology at the Graduate School of Business at the University of Pittsburgh, recently championed the right of client self-determination in a paper titled "Free to Choose," where he argued:

> I am here as the champion of one's right to choose. . . . It is my fervent belief that freedom of choice should govern one's sexual orientation. . . . If homosexuals choose to transform their sexuality into heterosexuality, that resolve and decision is theirs and theirs alone, and should not be tampered with by any special interest group—including the gay community.[7]

Perloff, who is also a Fellow of Division 44: Society for the Study of Gay and Lesbian Concerns of the American Psychological Association, stands against those voices who would seek to silence patients who express an interest in reorientation therapy.

> The individual has the right to choose whether he or she wishes to become straight. It is his or her choice, not that of an ideologically driven interest group. . . . To discourage a psychotherapist from undertaking a client wishing to convert, for reasons I will explain, [is] anti-research, anti-scholarship, and antithetical toward the quest for truth. . . . To deny a client the opportunity to engage in a psychotherapeutic experience is potentially harmful to the client, who may well have emotional problems and mental health roadblocks independent of that client's sexual orientation.[8]

Perloff concluded that "the research on sexual conversion is . . . a work in progress, an open question." This study adds substantial evidence that change of orientation is indeed possible for some persons, and that the risks of harm have been exaggerated.

Beyond this conceptual appeal, what would this mean in practice? Mental health professionals are to be informed by the best science available, and we have to return to science as the common language shared by stakeholders who come from a range of ideological viewpoints in these discussions. Scientific findings will inform our ethical reasoning and professional conduct, particularly findings about the possibility of change and the risks of harm inherent in the attempt to change. The findings from this study certainly support keeping a range of ministry and professional options open to clients who experience same-sex attraction and who may benefit from hearing about a number of intervention modalities. We would do well to put as much information in the hands of the consumer as possible so that they are able to make informed decisions and wise choices among treatment options.

To that end, we would argue for "expanded" informed consent, as previously discussed by Yarhouse.[9] Medical ethics has long moved away from *simple* or *implied* consent ("Doctor knows best") to *informed* consent.[10] That is, when individuals seek help for a range of clinical concerns, they should be given information that is deemed by the average person to be sufficient for making an informed decision about a course of treatment. According to Thomas Grisso and Paul Appelbaum,[11] the client's right to choose treatments that may or may not work has a long history in medicine. Further, there is a recognized tension in ethics between promoting well-being and respecting autonomy. Clients may elect to choose that which puts them at risk for distress. What has arisen from this ethic is a desire to maximize what clients need to know in order to give informed consent. As was mentioned above, this typically means that they should receive information that the average client would deem relevant to their treatment decision, sufficient to empower a voluntary choice by a person competent to make such a choice.

In light of the controversies and confusion surrounding reorientation therapy and religion-based ministries, we favor offering clients a more in-depth discussion (hence, "expanded" or "advanced" informed consent) of the array of issues involved in such a choice. This could start with discussion of the major theories as to the causes of same-sex attraction and homosexual orientation as well as a discussion of why these experiences are distressing to this particular client/patient. We also urge offering a discussion of the possible professional therapies that are available (including gay-affirming integrative treatment, sexual identity management approaches,[12] behavior management approaches that focus on celibacy, and reorientation or reparative therapies), as well as of religion-based ministry options and the potential benefits and drawbacks of these approaches. This must also include discussion of the range of percentages of positive outcomes from attempted change of sexual orientation (discussed in chapter three), that there are inadequate grounds in the empirical research to give a solid estimate of the probabilities of successful change because the existing research (including this study) has been conducted with samples of insufficient size and uncertain representativeness to ground firm probabilistic statements, and that there is considerable debate about the nature and meaning of that change.

The potential for harm from the attempt to change should also be discussed (including the evidence from this new study), but this discussion should also be broadened to a include discussion of potential benefits of the change attempt as well. In addition to the potential benefits, risks and costs of the interventions they are considering, clients should also be told of the potential benefits, risks and costs of *not* attempting the intervention; in the case of homosexuality, for example, we do not know what the potential risks would be for conservative religious clients of limiting treatment options to only those therapy approaches that aim to integrate experiences of same-sex attractions into a gay identity. Clients should be informed that there is well-established research associating homosexual orientation with elevated risk of psychological distress, and that there are competing interpretations of these elevations. They should be told that the present study, the best to date, found no evidence of significant harm on average to its participants. They should further be told that there are anecdotes of serious harm (including suicide) associated with the change attempt, but also that there are anecdotes of significant gain from successful change.

Unfortunately, most psychologists seem underinformed about the possibility of change of sexual orientation, and also seem prejudicially inclined to believe that the attempt to change has a high probability of being harmful (and that there are no significant risks attached to not attempting to change).[13] Clients should be given a fair and broad representation of the types of information that support an array of views, and empowered to make their own choices. Anything short of this risks repathologizing clients who experience same-sex attraction and request change by viewing them as incapable of making choices among treatment options.

Respect for the autonomy and self-determination of clients, regard for diversity of viewpoints in a pluralistic culture, and the existing body of scientific research (including, now, the present investigation) all favor the viability of religion-based change ministries. To the extent that negative professional attitudes toward the various reorientation therapies are grounded in the raw assertion that orientation change is impossible, this study serves to undermine that pessimism. This is not meant to diminish the experiences of those in the gay community who see such programs as highly political or even personally offensive, but is a call for fairness, professionalism and ethical practice on behalf of a diverse and pluralistic culture, as well as a similarly diverse client population.

WHAT ARGUMENTS WILL BE USED TO DISMISS THIS STUDY?

We expect the most frequent and perhaps potent negative response to this study to be raw cynicism and incredulity. Such responses are becoming increasingly common. A recent "research study" (an opinion poll, really) linked conversion therapy for sexual orientation with "angel therapy," "orgone therapy," pyramids, crystals, alien abduction, past and future lives therapies, and rebirthing therapies. All were declared "discredited" approaches based on this poll.[14] This seems to represent a rhetorical strategy of shaming and ridicule rather than serious discourse; it seems tendentious for conversion therapy for sexual orientation, with its long and significant history in many facets of the mental health community, to be linked and associated with various bizarre and aberrant forms of change methods. This may represent the kind of response our results are destined to generate. It is common today to believe that sexual orientation change is impossible, and for many this belief may be impervious to refutation by the presentation of either anecdotes of change or by the kinds of empirical evidence offered here. There is perhaps no effective response to such cynicism.

We expect, second, to be attacked and dismissed as biased researchers, with descriptors such as homophobic, heterosexist, fundamentalist, fanatic, extremist and so forth applied liberally to us. We would respond that there are few neutral researchers on such controversial issues. Note, for example, that many of the contributors to the September 2004 theme issue of the journal *The Counseling Psychologist* on the relationship between religion and homosexual behavior were themselves gay, lesbian or bisexual, and none of the contributors were to our knowledge traditionalist Christians. This issue of *The Counseling Psychologist* was built around the lead article by Lee Beckstead and Susan Morrow, and Beckstead has been public that as background to his study of the phenomenon of conversion therapy in the religiously conservative Latter-day Saints (Mormon) church world, he has struggled with the personal conflict of his Mormon upbringing and his same-sex attractions, a struggle resulting in his departure from the Mormon Church and full embrace of gay identity.[15] We are grateful to have someone like Beckstead contributing to discourse on this issue, but it does point out that "neutrality" is not required for admission to the discussion. If LGBT authors and scholars are not neutral but nevertheless contribute freely to the professional discussion and research in this area, should not the same courtesy be extended to traditionalist Christian researchers or others of varying perspectives? Are only those who advocate for gay-affirming approaches to this topic to be allowed to speak and contribute to this topic?

Third, we expect the limitations of the current study to be expounded as grounds for dismissing the findings. Critics will claim that our study sample was large but not large enough, was a quasi-experimental rather than experimental design, sampled a wide range of subjects but did not prove that the sample was representative, used many measures of sexual orientation but not the right ones, misused or misapplied some of the measures used,[16] failed to use psychophysiological measures of sexual arousal patterns, and on and on. Again, we explained our decision-making on each of these specific points in chapter six and stand by the decisions made to conduct the most methodologically sophisticated study of sexual orientation change to date.

In the 1970s, Michael Mahoney, a well-respected psychologist regarded as a rising star in the field of cognitive psychotherapy, conducted an unauthorized experiment that nearly resulted in his expulsion from the American Psychological Association.[17] As the editor of a scientific journal, he sent out for review facsimile manuscripts that he constructed so that the putative results reported in the manuscripts either conformed to or clashed with the preestablished professional opinions of the scientists selected as manuscript reviewers. In other words, all reviewers received manuscripts that were identical in terms of introduction, methods sections and references cited, but some versions reported results that were congruent with the theoretical viewpoints and expectations of the reviewers, while other versions reported results that were *incongruent* with the theoretical viewpoints and expectations of the reviewers. The methodologies used in the facsimile studies, it must be emphasized, were the same. Mahoney documented that reviewers critiquing manuscripts that reported results that conformed with their expectations had many fewer complaints about the methodologies of the manuscript they received and were much more likely to regard the manuscript as meriting publication. In contrast, reviewers critiquing manuscripts that reported results that clashed with their expectations had many criticisms about the methodologies of the manuscript they received and tended to recommend against publication. In other words, reviewers tended to go easy on the manuscript reporting results in accord with their expectations, and tended to "rip apart" the manuscript that reported results that clashed with their expectations. Mahoney reported that the net result was that even though the reviewers were critiquing manuscripts reporting identical methodologies, the reviewers gave harsher recommendations against publication when the manuscripts they reviewed clashed with their expectations.

No one is immune to such tendencies. We have tried to critique evenhandedly the research in all areas, noting in chapter three, for instance, the many limitations of the research on change of sexual orientation, and in chapter six the limitations of the existing methods for conceptualizing and measuring sexual orientation. This study is not above criticism methodologically, and we have tried to be the first to articulate what we regard as fair criticisms of our study. But we do expect this study to be greeted with various claims that because the study was not rigorous enough on issue X, its findings should be dismissed. We must resist such responses. There are no formulaic rules for judging how far a study must deviate from perfection before its results no longer deserve consideration. Our study is short of perfect; so also is all scientific inquiry, particularly psychological inquiry, and particularly inquiry into such a controversial subject. This is an imperfect but strong study, which in many respects is the most rigorous ever conducted, and its results should be taken seriously.

Fourth, we expect our results to be dismissed on the basis of bias in the self-report of the individuals studied. Our research participants, it will be argued, cannot be trusted to report their experience rightly and truthfully. They will be maligned as parroting the claims of a repressive religious system and a heterosexist society. We would respond first that we have attempted to urge, over and over, the value of honest report of their experience. One of the virtues of long-term follow-up as conducted in this longitudinal study is that we can expect that, if false presentation is present, that individuals will become more likely over time to report their true status, and we are committed to reporting those results honestly.

It is also critical to note that almost the entire fabric of human research is built on the reliability and validity of self-report. We ingest new headache medications because we trust the self-report of subjects in clinical trials that their headaches are lessened by a new medication; we rely on new medicines or psychotherapies for depression because we trust the report of individuals that they are less depressed. This area is arguably different in some important respects, particularly in that homosexual lifestyle is the subject of vigorous moral, religious and political debate today, and reporting that you are less headachy or depressed is surely less subject to intense pressure and scrutiny than those others reports. Even so, we have no indication that any of the participants in our study are political pawns or parrots, but rather that they are struggling, honest human beings grappling with personal situations and experiences of immense complexity, and that they have told us the truth about their personal experiences.

To this criticism we would note finally that it was in recognition of this potential criticism that we did not rely on simple, dichotomous reports of whether the participants are "straight or gay," but rather inquired about the specifics of their experiences of sexual attraction, fantasy, infatuation and so forth. We found our participants to be transparent in reporting their experience when asked in detail, for instance, about the frequency and intensity of sexual attraction to persons of the same and opposite sex.

Fifth, it is not impossible that individuals will emerge after the publication of this study who claim to have been in the study and to have been falsely represented, pressured to present themselves as if they were completely healed and so forth. We may even have individuals come forward saying they were subjects in the study and dropped out because the research was biased or making other accusations. We have already addressed this issue of the problematic status of anecdotal reports in chapters two and three. The recent ruling by U.S. Food and Drug Administration on silicone breast implants stands as a compelling example of the risks of grounding judgments in anecdotes. The original rulings that led to the removal of silicone breast implants were based on the tragic anecdotes of immune system disruption that some individuals (and their lawyers) claimed to be the result of such implants, and only years of research established that there was insufficient evidence that the implants were causally related to the negative health sequelae of the patients/plaintiffs in these cases. Only by examining normative results over multiple subjects can the true connections between interventions and outcomes be charted. This is why we took strides to encourage ongoing participation in the study, so that the results could be reported in the context of the overall study itself, which in the end is much more valuable and credible in terms of empirical findings than are anecdotal reports as such.

Sixth, we will be criticized for inflating the success statistics of this study by combining two types of success cases: chastity and conversion. Chastity in the minds of many is not success. We have already discussed this matter at length from a Christian theological and moral perspective in chapter two. Our situation here is not unlike that in marital and couple therapy, where one has to judge whether an outcome of an amicable divorce is a treatment success or failure. It of course depends on what one believes about divorce and the premium one places on successful preservation of a marital relationship. In chapter two we argued that most traditionalist Christians do not regard miraculous and unequivocal conversion to heterosexuality as a moral necessity for living a righteous life, but rather that release from undue preoccupation with and involvement in same-sex relationships and a positive embrace of chastity (sexual purity) *is* a moral necessity for the righteous life approved by God. Recall that this group reported average decreases in same-sex attraction that were moderate to large in terms of effect sizes. So the picture is not of individuals begrudgingly refraining from sexual behavior; rather, they are not experiencing attraction to the same sex to the same degree they had been previously, and this is making chastity presumably more attainable and less demanding in terms of emotional or psychological demands placed on them.

CONCLUSION

In the end we believe we have provided evidence that change of homosexual orientation may be possible through involvement in Exodus ministries. The change may take the form of a reduction in homosexual attraction and behavioral chastity; it may also take the form of a reduction in homosexual attraction and an increase in heterosexual attraction with what might be described as satisfactory heterosexual adjustment. Those who report chastity regard themselves as having reestablished their sexual identities to be defined in some way other than by their homosexual attractions. Those who report a heterosexual adjustment regard themselves as having changed their sexual orientation.

We also found little evidence that involvement in the Exodus change process was harmful to participants in this study. Taken together, these findings would appear to contradict the commonly expressed view of the mental health establishment that change of sexual orientation is impossible and that the attempt to change is highly likely to produce harm for those who make such an attempt.

Notes

Chapter 1: The Controversy

[1]American Psychological Association, "Answers to Your Questions About Sexual Orientation and Homosexuality." Retrieved April 4, 2005, from www.apa.org/pubinfo/answers.html.

[2]Karl, Popper (1958). *The logic of scientific discovery.* London: Routledge & Kegan Paul.

[3]For example, Hooker, E. (1963). *The adjustment of the male overt homosexual, in the problem of homosexuality in modern society,* rev. ed. H. M. Ruitenbeek. New York: E. P. Dutton; Kinsey, A. C., Pomeroy, W. B., & Martin, C. E. (1948). *Sexual behavior in the human male.* Philadelphia: W. B. Saunders; Kinsey, A. C., Pomeroy, W. B., Martin, C. E. & Gebhard, P. H. (1953). *Sexual behavior in the human female.* Philadelphia: Saunders; Bell, A. P., & Weinberg, M. S. (1978). *Homosexualities: A study of diversity among men and women.* Bloomington: Indiana University Press; Bailey, J. M. & Pillard, R. C. (1991). A genetic study of male sexual orientation. *Archives of General Psychiatry, 48,* 1089-1096.

[4]Jones, Stanton L. (1994). "A constructive relationship for religion with the science and profession of psychology: Perhaps the boldest model yet," *American Psychologist, 49*(3), 184-199.

[5]Adapted from Jones (1994), and Jones, Stanton L., & Hostler, H. R. (2005). The role of sexuality in personhood: An integrative exploration. In W. R. Miller & H. D. Delaney (Eds.). *Human nature, motivation, and change: Judeo-Christian perspectives on psychology* (pp. 115-132). Washington, DC: American Psychological Association.

[6]Brooke, John H. (1991). *Science and religion: Some historical perspectives.* Cambridge: Cambridge University Press; Lindberg, David C. (1992). *The Beginnings of western science: The European scientific tradition in philosophical, religious, and institutional context, 600 B.C. to A.D. 1450.* Chicago: University of Chicago Press; Lindberg, David C., & Numbers, R. L. (Eds.). (1986). *God and nature: Historical essays on the encounter between Christianity and science.* Berkeley: University of California Press.

[7]Aguinis, H., & Aguinis, M. (1995). Integrating psychological science and religion. *American Psychologist, 50*(7), 541-542; Cox, B. L. (1995). Belief vs. faith. *American Psychologist, 50*(7), 541; Ward, L. C. (1995). "Religion and science *are* mutually exclusive." *American Psychologist, 50*(7), 542-543.

[8]Jones (1994), p. 2000.

[9]Sampson, E. E. (2000). Reinterpreting individualism and collectivism: Their religious roots and monologic versus dialogic person-other relationship, *American Psychologist, 55*(12), 1425.

[10]Sampson (2000), p. 1426.

[11]Redding, R. E. (2001). Sociopolitical diversity in psychology: The case for pluralism. *American Psychologist, 56*(3), 205-215.

[12]Redding (2001), p. 206.

[13]Midgley, M. (1992). *Science as salvation: A modern myth and its meaning.* London: Routledge, p. 13.

[14]O'Donohue, W. (1989). The (even) bolder model: The clinical psychologist as metaphysician-scientist-practitioner. *American Psychologist, 44,* 1460-1468.

[15]Meehl, Paul E. (1993). Philosophy of science: Help or hindrance? *Psychological Reports, 72,* 710.

[16]McClay, W. M. (1997). Filling the hollow core: Religious faith and the postmodern university. In G. Wolfe (Ed.). *The new religious humanists: A reader.* New York: Free Press, p. 235.

[17]Several post hoc examples are explored in Jones and Hostler, (2005).

[18]Jones (1994).

[19]London, Perry. (1986). *The modes and morals of psychotherapy* (2nd ed.). Washington, DC: Hemisphere.

[20]Jones (1994), p. 194.

[21]Jones (1994), p. 194.

[22]Jones (1994), p. 195.

[23]We review this evidence in Jones, S. L., & Yarhouse, M. A. (2000). *Homosexuality: The use of scientific research in the church's moral debate.* Downers Grove, Ill.: InterVarsity Press. We update this review in Jones, S. L., & Kwee A. W. (2005). Scientific research, homosexuality, and the church's moral debate: An update. *Journal of Psychology and Christianity, 24*(4), 304-316.

[24]We review this in evidence in Jones & Yarhouse (2000), and Jones & Kwee (2005), and would contrast our review to the distressingly flawed review by Hyde, Janet S. (2005). "The genetics of sexual orientation" (pp. 9-20). In Hyde, Janet S. (Ed.). *The biological substrates of human sexuality.* Washington, DC: American Psychological Association.

[25]Demir, E., & Dickson, B. J. (2005). *Fruitless* splicing specifies male courtship behavior in *Drosophilia. Cell, 121*, 785-794.

[26]Roselli, C. E., Larkin, K., Schrunk, J. M., & Stormshak, F. (2004). Sexual partner preference, hypothalamic morphology and aromatase in rams. *Physiology & Behavior, 83*, 233-245.

[27]Byne, W., Tobet, S., Mattiace, L. A., Lasco, M. S., Kemether, E., Edgar, M. A., Morgello, S., Buschbaum, M. S., & Jones, L. B. (2001). The interstitial nuclei of the human anterior hypothalamus: An investigation of variation with sex, sexual orientation, and HIV status. *Hormones and Behavior, 40*, 86-92.

[28]Bearman, P. S., & Bruckner, H. (2002). Opposite-sex twins and adolescent same-sex attraction. *American Journal of Sociology, 107*(5), 1179-1205.

[29]This section is adapted from Yarhouse, M. A. (2004). Reorientation or identity synthesis? Metaphysical reflections on the current ethical debate. *Christian Bioethics, 10*(4), 239-257.

[30]Stein, E. (1999). *The mismeasure of desire: The science, theory and ethics of sexual orientation.* New York: Oxford University Press. Quote p. 97.

[31]Stein (1999), p. 97.

[32]Laumann, E. O., Gagnon, J. H., Michael, R. T., & Michaels S. (1994), *The social organization of sexuality.* Chicago: University of Chicago Press.

[33]Sullivan, A. (1995). *Virtually normal: An argument about homosexuality.* New York: Random House, pp. 188-189.

[34]Troiden, R. R. (1989). The formation of homosexual identities. *Journal of Homosexuality, 17*, 1-2, 43-73.

[35]Laumann et al. (1994). *The social organization of sexuality.*

[36]Shively, M. G., & DeCecco, J. P. (1977). Components of sexual identity. *Journal of Homosexuality, 2*, 41-48.

[37]Althof, Stanley E. (2000). Erectile dysfunction: Psychotherapy with men and couples. In S. R. Leiblum & R. C. Rosen (Eds.). *Principles and practices of sex therapy* (3rd ed.) (pp. 242-275). New York: Guilford.

[38]Schaeffer, K. W., Hyde, R. A., Kroencke, T., McCormick, B., & Nottebaum, L. (2000). Religiously-motivated sexual orientation change. *Journal of Psychology and Christianity, 19*(1) 61-70; Schaeffer, K. W., Nottebaum, L., Smith, P., Dech, K., & Krawczyk, J. (1999). Religiously-motivated sexual orientation change: A follow-up study. *Journal of Psychology and Theology, 27*, 329-337; Shidlo, A., & Schroeder, M. (1999, August). Changing sexual orientation: Empirical findings on conversion therapies. Paper presented at the meeting of the American Psychological Association, Boston, Mass.; and Spitzer, R. L. (2001, May). Two hundred subjects who claim to have changed their sexual orientation

from homosexual to heterosexual. In Bialer, P. A. (Chair), *Clinical issues and ethical concerns regarding attempts to change sexual orientation: An update*. Paper presented at the annual meeting of the American Psychiatric Association, New Orleans, LA, May 9, 2001.

[39]Laumann et al. (1994). *The social organization of sexuality,* chap. 8.

[40]Greenberg, David F. (1980), *The construction of homosexuality.* Chicago: University of Chicago Press, pp. 455-481.

[41]Herdt, Gregory. (1996). "Developmental discontinuities and sexual orientation across cultures." In D. P. McWhirter, S. A. Sanders & J. M. Reinisch (Eds.). *Homosexuality/heterosexuality: Concepts of sexual orientation.* New York: Oxford University Press, pp. 208-236.

[42]For example, see Cass, V. C. (1979). "Homosexual identity formation: A theoretical model." *Journal of Homosexuality, 4*(2), 219-235.

[43]Yarhouse, M. A., & Tan, E. S. N. (2004). *Sexual identity synthesis: Attributions, meaning-making, and the search for congruence.* Lanham, MD: University Press of America. See also Yarhouse, M. A., Tan, E. S. N., & Pawlowski, L. M. (2005). Sexual identity development and synthesis among LGB-identified and LGB-dis-identified persons. *Journal of Psychology and Theology, 33*(1), 3-16; Yarhouse, M. A., Pawlowski, L. M., & Tan, E. S. N. (2003). Intact marriages in which one partner disidentifies with experiences of same-sex attraction. *American Journal of Family Therapy, 31,* 375-394; Yarhouse, M. A., & Seymore, R. L. (2006). Intact marriages in which one partner dis-identifies with experiences of same-sex attraction: A follow-up study. *American Journal of Family Therapy, 34,* 1-11.

[44]McDonald, G. J. (1982). Individual differences in the coming out process for gay men: Implications for theoretical models. *Journal of Homosexuality, 8*(1), 47-60.

[45]Sophie, J. (1986). A crucial examination of stage theories of lesbian identity development. *Journal of Homosexuality, 12*(2), 39-51.

[46]American Psychiatric Association. (1952). *Diagnostic and statistical manual of mental disorders.* Washington, DC: American Psychiatric Association. The citations for subsequent editions are the same except for edition number and dates as follows: 2nd ed. *(DSM-II),* 1968; 3rd ed. *(DSM-III),* 1980; 3rd ed. rev. *(DSM-III-R),* 1987; 4th ed. *(DSM-IV),* 1994; 4th ed. text rev. *(DSM-IV-TR),* 2000.

[47]*DSM-II,* p. 44

[48]*DSM-III,* p. 281

[49]*DSM-IV-TR,* p. xxxi

[50]*DSM-IV-TR,* p. 582

[51]Jones (1994), p. 189.

[52]Abel, G., Barlow, D., & Blanchard, E. (1977). Gender identity change in a transsexual: An exorcism. *Archives of Sexual Behavior, 6*(5), 394.

[53]Abel et al. (1977), p. 394.

[54]Pattison, E., & Pattison, M. (1980). "Ex-gays": Religiously mediated change in homosexuals. *American Journal of Psychiatry, 137,* 1553-1562.

[55]Spitzer, R. L. (2003). Can some gay men and lesbians change their sexual orientation? 200 participants reporting a change from homosexual to heterosexual orientation. *Archives of Sexual Behavior, 32*(5), 403-417.

[56]American Psychological Association, "Answers to Your Questions About Sexual Orientation and Homosexuality." From <www.apa.org/pubinfo/answers.html>. Retrieved August 8, 2005.

[57]Post (1993). Psychiatry and ethics: The problematics of respect for religious meanings. *Culture, Medicine and Psychiatry, 17*(3), 363-383. Quote p. 364.

[58]Post (1993), p. 364.

[59]Gallup Foundation. (1996). *Religion in America: Gallup Report No. 236.* Princeton, NJ: Author. Quote p. 37.

[60]Gallup Foundation (1996), p. 20.
[61]Post (1993), p. 370.

Chapter 2: Understanding the Population

[1]Gallup, G. (2001). *The Gallup poll: Public opinion 2001.* Wilmington, DE: Scholarly Resources, Inc.

[2]E.g., Kristof, Nicholas. (2003, March 4). God, Satan and the media. *The New York Times*, A25.

[3]Jones, S. L. (1994). A constructive relationship for religion with the science and profession of psychology: Perhaps the boldest model yet. *American Psychologist, 49*(3), 184-199; Shafranske, E. (Ed.), (1996). *Religion and the clinical practice of psychology.* Washington, DC: American Psychological Association; Preussler, D., Butman, R., & Jones, S. L. (1998). Diversity matters: Religion and the practice of clinical psychology, (pp. 233-253). In C. Belar (Ed.), *Sociocultural and individual differences* (*Comprehensive clinical psychology* vol. 10). A. Bellack & M. Hersen (Eds.). New York: Elsevier Science.

[4]Adapted from Jones, S. L., and Hostler, H. R. (2005). The role of sexuality in personhood: An integrative exploration. In W. R. Miller & H. D. Delaney (Eds.). *Human nature, motivation, and change: Judeo-Christian perspectives on psychology* (pp. 115-132). Washington, DC: American Psychological Association.

[5]For a reasonably balanced presentation of the array of views that call themselves Christian, from ultra-conservative to liberal, see Holben, L. R. (1999). *What Christians think about homosexuality: Six representative viewpoints.* North Richland Hills, TX: BIBAL Press.

[6]Letham, Robert. (2004). *The Holy Trinity.* Phillipsburg, NJ: Presbyterian & Reformed.

[7]Bynum, C. W. (1995). *The resurrection of the body in western Christianity, 200-1336.* New York: Columbia University Press.

[8]Greeley, Andrew. (1991). *Faithful attraction: Discovering intimacy, love and fidelity in American marriage.* New York: Tor Books. *Faithful Attraction* reports the results from two major studies of marriage sponsored by the magazine *Psychology Today* and executed by the Gallup organization, along with findings from numerous other resources, including the results of the annual General Social Survey, which is conducted by the National Opinion Research Center.

[9]Some portions of this section are adapted from chap. 5 and other chapters of Jones, S. L., & Jones, Brenna. (1993). *How and when to tell your kids about sex: A life-long approach to shaping your child's sexual character.* Colorado Springs, CO: NavPress..

[10]This iconic function of sexuality could be argued to be somewhat similar to the symbolizing function of sexuality in Vajrayana Buddhism as discussed in Jones, S. L., & Hostler, H. R. (2005). The role of sexuality in personhood: An integrative exploration. In W. R. Miller & H. D. Delaney (Eds.). *Human nature, motivation, and change: Judeo-Christian perspectives on psychology* (pp. 115-32). Washington, DC: American Psychological Association.

[11]The lack of civil punishment for the male sexual partners of the unmarried woman (who was presumed to be a virgin, Deuteronomy 22:22-21) appears to be an artifact (1) of a social context in which independent dating (with its opportunities for sexual experimentation) did not exist and which prized virginity and the married estate, and hence which actually offered little opportunity for premarital sex to occur; and (2) of a system of jurisprudence which placed great emphasis upon the testimony of at least two witnesses (Deuteronomy 17:6; 19:15) in cases which could result in the death penalty (as a constraint on spurious executions); in "crimes of passion" there are typically no other witnesses except the paramours, and the testimony of the woman would by itself be insufficient by this testimonial standard to result in the death penalty for the male participant.

[12]See Gagnon, Robert A. J. (2001). *The Bible and homosexual practice.* Nashville: Abingdon, for a comprehensive treatment of the biblical texts from a conservative Christian perspective.

[13]Gagnon (2001).

[14]Judges 19:22-30 contains a parallel story to the Sodom narrative.

[15]Gagnon (2001).

[16]Packer, J. I. (2003, January). "Why I walked: Sometimes loving a denomination requires you to fight." *Christianity Today,* pp 46-50

[17]Pannenberg, Wolfhart. (1996, November 11). Homosexual experience. *Christianity Today,* p. 36.

[18]MacNutt, Francis. (2001). *Homosexuality: Can it be healed?* Jacksonville, Fla.: Christian Healing Ministries, p. 57.

[19]MacNutt (2001).

[20]Adams, Jay E. (1973). *The Christian counselor's manual.* Grand Rapids: Baker.

[21]Payne, Leanne. (1996). *The broken image: Restoring personal wholeness through healing prayer.* Grand Rapids: Baker, p. 59.

[22]Bergner, Mario. (1995). *Setting love in order.* Grand Rapids: Baker.

[23]See NARTH's website at http://narth.com/index.html.

[24]This section is adapted from Yarhouse, Mark A., Burkett, Lori A., and Kreeft, Elizabeth M. (2002). Paraprofessional Christian ministries for same-sex attraction and behavior. *Journal of Psychology and Theology, 30*(3), 209-227.

[25]Blair, R. (1982, April). Ex-gay. A paper presented at the annual meeting of the Christian Association for Psychological Studies, Atlanta, GA.

[26]The fourteen steps of HA are (1) We admitted we were *powerless* over our homosexuality and that our emotional lives were unmanageable. (2) We came to believe the love of God, *who forgave us and accepted us* in spite of all that we are and have done. (3) We learned to see purpose in our suffering, that our failed lives were under God's control, who is able to bring good out of trouble. (4) We came to believe that God had *already broken the power of homosexuality* and that He could therefore restore our true personhood. (5) We came to perceive that we had accepted *a lie* about ourselves, an illusion that had trapped us in a false identity. (6) We learned to claim our true identity that, as humankind, *we are part of God's heterosexual creation* and that God calls us to *rediscover that identity in Him through Jesus Christ,* as our faith perceives Him. (7) We resolved to entrust our lives to our loving God and *to live by faith,* praising Him for our new unseen identity, confident that it would become visible to us in God's good time. (8) As forgiven people free from condemnation, we made a *searching and fearless moral inventory of ourselves,* determined to root out fear, hidden hostility and contempt for the world. (9) We admitted to God, to ourselves, and to another human being, *the exact nature of our wrongs* and humbly asked God to remove our defects of character. (10) We willingly *made direct amends* wherever wise and possible to all people we had harmed. (11) We determined *to live no longer in fear of the world,* believing that God's victorious control turns all that is against us into our favor, bringing advantage out of sorrow and order from disaster. (12) We determined *to mature in our relationships with men and women,* learning the meaning of a partnership of equals, seeking neither dominance over people nor servile dependency on them. (13) We sought, through confident praying and the wisdom of Scripture, for *an ongoing growth in our relationship with God* and a humble acceptance of his guidance for our lives. (14) Having made a spiritual awakening, we tried to *carry this message* to people in homosexuality with a love that demands nothing and to practice these steps in all our lives' activities, as far as lies within us (www.ha-fs.org/The_Program/p2010_articleid/26).

[27]Homosexuals Anonymous, "Statement on Philosophy," http://www.ha-fs.org/Home/p2010_articleid/5. Retrieved March 23, 2007.

[28]See the Courage website at http://www.couragerc.org. Retrieved March 22, 2007.

[29]"Welcome to the Courage Community," Courage. Retrieved March 23, 2007, from http://www.couragerc.org/index.htm.

[30]"Article Six: The Sixth Commandment," Christus Rex et Redemptor Mundi. Retrieved February 23, 2007, from www.christusrex.org/www1/CDHN/sixth.html
[31]"The Five Goals," Courage. Retrieved February 26, 2007, from http://couragerc.net/TheFiveGoals.html.
[32]Harvey, J. (1987). *Homosexuality: New directions for pastoral care*. San Francisco: Ignatius, pp. 156-158.
[33]Harvey (1987), p. 158.
[34]"Policy Statements: Statement on Homosexuality," Exodus International. Retrieved March 23, 2007, from http://exodus.to/content/view/34/118/.
[35]"Who We Are," Exodus International. Retrieved December 23, 2005, from www.exodus.to/about_exodus.shtml.
[36]"Is Homosexuality Genetic?" Exodus International. Retrieved March 23, 2007, from http://exodus.to/content/view/41/87/.
[37]"Basic Beliefs," Keys Ministries. Retrieved December 2005 from www.keysministry.com/#beliefs.
[38]"Doctrinal Statement," First Stone Ministries. Retrieved February 26, 2007, from www.firststone.org/index.php?option=com_content&task=view&id=198&Itemid=70.
[39]"Our Programs," Love in Action. Retrieved February 26, 2007, from www.loveinaction.org/default.aspx?pid=84.
[40]"What Is Living Waters?" Desert Streams Ministries. Retrieved March 23, 2007, from http://desertstream.org/programslivingwaters1.htm.
[41]"Who We Are: Our Ministry," Mastering Life Ministries. Retrieved February 26, 2007, from http://masteringlife.gospelcom.net/index.php.
[42]"Essays: Definition of Healing," Eagles' Wings. Retrieved February 26, 2007, from www.ewm.org/archives/000013.html.
[43]Homepage, First Stone Ministries. Retrieved December 2005 from www.firststone.org.
[44]"Welcome to Living Hope Ministries!" Living Hope Ministries. Retrieved March 23, 2007, from http://www.livehope.org/modules.php?op=modload&name=FAQ&file=index&my-faq=yes&id_cat=4&categories=Living+Hope+Ministries&parent_id=0.
[45]"The Truth about Ex-Gay Ministries," OutFront. Retrieved December 23, 2005, from www.outfront.org/library/exgay.html.

Chapter 3: Rationale for the Study

[1]American Psychological Association, "Answers to Your Questions About Sexual Orientation and Homosexuality," APA Online. Retrieved August 8, 2005, from www.apa.org/pubinfo/answers.html. Emphasis added.
[2]"Position Statement on Psychiatric Treatment and Sexual Orientation," American Psychiatric Association. Retrieved December 12, 2005, from www.psych.org/archives/news_room/press_releases/rep_therapy.cfm. Interestingly, the full sentence is "There is an APA 1997 Fact Sheet on Homosexual and Bisexual Issues which states that 'there is no published scientific evidence supporting the efficacy of "reparative therapy" as a treatment to change one's sexual orientation.' " This is a curiously noncommittal statement; rather than saying as a scientific organization "There is no evidence," the Psychiatric Board says, "There is a Fact Sheet that says there is no evidence." We would agree: "There is a Fact Sheet that says there is no evidence," but the deeper question is whether the statement that "there is no evidence" is true. As we will explore in this chapter, it is obviously a false statement; the published scientific research may be contested in various ways, but it exists and all points to the possibility of change.
[3]See, for example, Jones, S. L., & Yarhouse, M. A. (2000). *Homosexuality: The use of scientific research in the Church's moral debate*. Downers Grove, IL: InterVarsity Press. Earlier, we wrote Jones, S. L., &

Workman, D. (1989). Homosexuality: The behavioral sciences and the church. *Journal of Psychology and Theology, 17*(4), 213-225; and Jones, S. L. (1989, August 18). Homosexuality according to science. *Christianity Today, 33*(11), 26-29.

[4]Throckmorton, W. (2002). Initial empirical and clinical findings concerning the change process for ex-gays. *Professional Psychology: Research and Practice, 33*(3), 242-248; Yarhouse, M. A. (1998). Group therapies for homosexuals seeking change. *Journal of Psychology and Theology, 26*(3), 247-259. See also our review in Jones & Yarhouse (2000).

[5]This table is reproduced from Jones, S. L., & Yarhouse, M. A. (2000). *Homosexuality: The use of scientific research in the church's moral debate.* Downers Grove, Ill.: InterVarsity Press, p. 123. References for the studies cited are Bieber, I., Dain, H. J., Dince, P. R., Drellich, M. G., Grand, H. G., Gundlach, R. H., Kremer, M., W, Rifkin, A. H., Wilbur, C. B., & Bieber, T. B. (1962). *Homosexuality: A psychoanalytic study.* New York: Basic Books; Cantom-Dutari, A. (1974). Combined intervention for controlling unwanted homosexual behavior. *Archives of Sexual Behavior, 3,* 367-325; Freeman, W., and Meyer, R. G. (1975). A behavioral alteration of sexual preferences in the human male. *Behavior Therapy, 6,* 206-212; Hadfield, J. A. (1958, June 7). The cure of homosexuality. *British Medical Journal,* 1323-1326; Hatterer, L. (1970). *Changing heterosexuality in the male: Treatment for men troubled by homosexuality.* New York: McGraw-Hill; Kaye, H. E., Berl, S., Clare, J., Eleston, M. R., Gershwin, B. S., Gershwin, P., Kogan, L. S., Torda, C., & Wilbur, C. B. (1967). Homosexuality in women. *Archives of General Psychiatry, 17,* 626-634; McConaghy, N. (1970). Subjective and penile plethysmograph responses to aversion therapy for homosexuality: A follow-up study. *British Journal of Psychiatry, 117,* 555-560; MacIntosh, H. (1994). Attitudes and experiences of psychoanalysts. *Journal of the American Psychoanalytic Association, 42*(4), 1183-1207; MacCulloch, M. J., & Feldman, M. P. (1967). Aversion therapy in management of 43 homosexuals. *British Medical Journal, 2,* 594-597; Masters, W. H., & Johnson, V. E. (1979). *Homosexuality in perspective.* Boston: Little, Brown; Mayerson, P., & Lief, Harold I. (1965). Psychotherapy of homosexuals: A follow-up study of nineteen cases (pp. 302-344). In Judd Marmor (Ed.). *Sexual inversion: The multiple roots of homosexuality.* New York: Basic Books; Schwartz, M. F., & Masters, W. H. (1984). The Masters and Johnson treatment program for dissatisfied homosexual men. *American Journal of Psychiatry, 141,* 173-181; Socarides, C. W. (1978). *Homosexuality.* New York: Jason Aronson; van den Aardweg, G. (1985). *On the origins and treatment of homosexuality.* Westport, CT: Praeger.

[6]This table is reproduced from *Journal of Psychology and Theology 26*, no. 3 (1998) and was previously reproduced as table 5.2, p. 131, in Jones and Yarhouse (2000). References for the studies cited are: Eliasberg, W. C. (1954). Group treatments of homosexuals on probation. *Group Psychotherapy, 7,* 218-226; Hadden, S. B. (1958). Treatment of homosexuality in individual and group psychotherapy. *American Journal of Psychiatry, 114,* 810-815; Hadden, S. B. (1966). Treatment of male homosexuals in groups. *International Journal of Group Psychotherapy, 16,* 13-22; Singer, M., & Fischer, R. (1967). Group psychotherapy of male homosexuals by a male and female co-therapy team. *International Journal of Group Psychotherapy, 17,* 44-52; Litman, R. E. (1961). Psychotherapy of a homosexual man in a heterosexual group. *International Journal of Group Psychotherapy, 11,* 440-448; Truax, R. A., Moeller, W. S., & Tourney, G. (1970). The medical approach to male homosexuality. *Journal of the Iowa Medical Society, 60,* 397-403; Truax, R. A., & Tourney, G. (1971). Male homosexuals in group psychotherapy. *Diseases of the Nervous System, 32,* 707-711; Birk, L. (1974). Group psychotherapy for men who are homosexual. *Journal of Sex and Marital Therapy, 1,* 29-52.; Beukenkamp, C. (1960). Phantom patricide. *Archives of General Psychiatry, 3,* 282-288; Mintz, Elizabeth E. (1966). Overt male homosexuals in combined group and individual treatment. *Journal of Consulting Psychology, 30,* 193-198; Johnsgard, K. W., & Schumacher, R. M. (1970). The experience of intimacy in group psychotherapy with male homosexuals. *Psychotherapy: Theory, Research, and Practice, 7,* 173-176; Stone,

W. N., Schengber, J., & Seifried, F. S. (1966). The treatment of a homosexual woman in a mixed group. *International Journal of Group Psychotherapy, 16,* 425-432; Pittman, F. S., & DeYoung, C. D. (1971). The treatment of homosexuals in heterogeneous groups. *International Journal of Group Psychotherapy, 21,* 62-73; Munzer, J. (1965). Treatment of the homosexual in group psychotherapy. *Topical Problems of Psychotherapy, 5,* 164-169; Finney, J. C. (1960). Homosexuality treated by combined therapy. *Journal of the Society of Therapists, 6,* 27-34; Covi, L. (1972). A group psychotherapy approach to the treatment of neurotic symptoms in male and female patients of homosexual preference. *Psychotherapy and Psychosomatics, 20,* 176-180.

[7]MacIntosh, H. (1994). Attitudes and experiences of psychoanalysts. *Journal of the American Psychoanalytic Association, 42*(4), 1183-1207.

[8]MacIntosh (1994), p. 1189. According to MacIntosh, post-hoc analyses suggest that the change rate for male homosexuals is not significantly different (two-tail *t*-test, p = .45) from the 27% change rate reported by Irving Bieber and his colleagues over thirty-five years ago in *Homosexuality: A Psychoanalytic Study* (New York: Basic Books, 1962).

[9]MacIntosh (1994), p. 1188, table 2.

[10]MacIntosh, H. (1997). Factors associated with outcome of psychoanalysis of homosexual patients. *British Journal of Psychotherapy, 13,* 358-368.

[11]MacIntosh (1997), p. 365.

[12]Goetze, R. M. (1997). *Homosexuality and the possibility of change: A review of 17 published studies.* Toronto, Canada: New Direction for Life.

[13]NARTH can be contacted at www.narth.org or via Dr. Joseph Nicolosi at 818-789-4440.

[14]Nicolosi, J., Byrd, A. D., & Potts, R. W. (2000). Retrospective self-report of change in homosexual orientation: A consumer survey of conversion therapy clients. *Psychological Reports, 86,* 1071-1088.

[15]Nicolosi et al. (2000), p. 1079, table 1.

[16]Shidlo, A., & Schroeder, M. (2002). Changing sexual orientation: A consumers' report. *Professional Psychology: Research and Practice, 33*(3), 249-259.

[17]Shidlo & Schroeder (2002), p. 252.

[18]Yarhouse, M. A., Burkett, L., & Kreeft, E. (1999, April). Competing models for shepherding homosexual persons. A paper presented at the Christian Association for Psychological Studies National Conference, Colorado Springs, CO.

[19]Pattison, E., & Pattison, M. (1980). "Ex-gays": Religiously mediated change in homosexuals. *American Journal of Psychiatry, 137,* 1553-1562.

[20]Douglas Haldeman, in his bitingly dismissive review of this study, states, "The Pattisons do not explain their sampling criteria, nor do they explain why 19 of their 30 subjects refused follow-up interviews." On the one hand, Haldeman does have a valid point; it is curious that nineteen refused interviews, and equally curious that the Pattisons give us no indication of why. On the other hand, Haldeman is incorrect in stating that sampling criteria were not explained; the criteria were simple—select individuals who had changed orientation. It is possible that the nineteen nonparticipants refused because they had not really changed and were threatened by the prospect of close scrutiny. An alternative hypothesis would be that they did not desire to relive a painful past with a stranger. (Haldeman, D. C. [1994]. The practice and ethics of sexual orientation conversion therapy. *Journal of Consulting and Clinical Psychology, 62,* 224.)

[21]Pattison & Pattison (1980), p. 1554.

[22]Schaeffer, K. W., Hyde, R. A., Kroencke, T., McCormick, B., & Nottebaum, L. (2000). Religiously-motivated sexual orientation change. *Journal of Psychology and Christianity, 19*(1), 61-70.

[23]Schaeffer et al. (2000), p. 68.

[24]Schaeffer, K. W., Nottebaum, L., Smith, P., Dech, K., & Krawczyk, J. (1999). Religiously-motivated

sexual orientation change: A follow-up study. *Journal of Psychology and Theology, 27*(4), 329-337.

[25]Althof, S. E. (2000). Erectile dysfunction: Psychotherapy with men and couples. In S. R. Leiblum and R. C. Rosen (Eds.). *Principles and practices of sex therapy* (pp. 242-275). (3rd ed.). New York: Guilford.

[26]This study was first presented and came to the wide attention of the public as Spitzer, R. L. (2001, May). Two hundred persons who claimed to have changed their sexual orientation. In P. A. Bialer. *Clinical issues and ethical concerns regarding attempts to change sexual orientation: An update*. A paper presented at the annual meeting of the American Psychiatric Association, New Orleans, Louisiana. The study was later published as Spitzer, R. L. (2003). Can some gay men and lesbians change their sexual orientation? Two hundred participants reporting a change from homosexual to heterosexual orientation. *Archives of Sexual Behavior, 32*(5), 403-417.

[27]Spitzer (2003), p. 415.

[28]Hooker, E. (1963). The adjustment of the male overt homosexual. In H. M. Ruitenbeek (Ed.). *The problem of homosexuality in modern society.* New York: E. P. Dutton. We discuss this case extensively in Jones & Yarhouse (2000).

[29]*Archives of sexual behavior, 32*(5), 419-468.

[30]Klein, D. F. (2003). Initiating treatment evaluations. *Archives of Sexual Behavior, 32*(5), 443. (Peer commentaries on Spitzer)

[31]Wainberg, M. L., Bux, D., Carballo-Dieguez, A., Dowsett, G. W., Dugan, T., Forstein, M., Goodkin, K., Hunter, J., Irwin, T., Mattos, P., McKinnon, K., O'Leary, A., Parsons, J., & Stein, E. (2003). Science and the Nuremberg Code: A question of ethics and harm. *Archives of Sexual Behavior, 32*(5), 419-468. (Peer commentaries on Spitzer)

[32]Haldeman, D. C. (1994). The practice and ethics of sexual orientation conversion therapy. *Journal of Consulting and Clinical Psychology, 62,* 221-227.

[33]Haldeman (1994), p. 223.

[34]Bieschke, K. J., McClanahan, M., Tozer, E., Grzegorek, J. L., & Park, J. (1999). Programmatic research on the treatment of lesbian, gay, and bisexual clients: The past, the present, and the course for the future. In R. M. Perez, K. A. DeBord & K. J. Biesche (Eds.). *Handbook of counseling and psychotherapy with lesbian, gay, and bisexual clients* (pp. 309-335). Washington, DC: American Psychological Association. Quote p. 313.

[35]Zuriff, G. E. (1997, April). Psychology's sexual dis-orientation. *The World & I*, 299-311.

[36]American Psychological Association, "Answers to Your Questions About Sexual Orientation and Homosexuality." Retrieved August 5, 2003, from www.apa.org/pubinfo/answers.html.

[37]Green, R. (1988). The immutability of (homo)sexual orientation: Behavioral science implications for a constitutional (legal) analysis. *The Journal of Psychiatry and Law, 16*(4), 537-575.

[38]Burr, C. (1993, March). Homosexuality and biology. *The Atlantic Monthly,* pp. 47-65.

[39]Myers, D. G. "Sexual Orientation." Retrieved August 5, 2003, from www.davidmyers.org/sexorient/textbksumm7e.html. Myers also states, "the feelings [of homosexual orientation] typically persist, as do those of heterosexual people—who are similarly incapable of becoming homosexual (Haldeman, 1994, 2002). Most of today's psychologists therefore view sexual orientation as neither willfully chosen nor willfully changed. . . . [T]he way one is endures" and "sexual orientation is biologically influenced [and hence] an enduring identity, not a choice."

[40]Green (1988). See also Green, R. (1987). *The "sissy boy" syndrome and the development of homosexuality.* New Haven, CT: Yale University Press; LeVay, S. (1991). A difference in the hypothalamic structure between heterosexual and homosexual men. *Science 253,* 1034-1037.

[41]See Jones & Yarhouse (2000); and Jones, S. L., & Kwee, A. W. (2005). Scientific research, homosexuality, and the church's moral debate: An update. *Journal of Psychology and Christianity, 24*(4), 304-316.

[42]Byne's studies are reviewed in Jones & Kwee (2005). Scientific research, homosexuality, and the church's moral debate: An update. *Journal of Psychology and Christianity, 24*(4), 304-316. The full citations for Byne's work are Byne, W., Lasco, M. S., Kemether, E., Shinwari, A., Jones, L. B., & Tobet, S. (2000). The interstitial nuclei of the human anterior hypothalamus: Assessment for variation in volume and neuronal size, density and number. *Brain Research, 856*, 254-258; and Byne, W., Tobet, S., Mattiace, L. A., Lasco, M. S., Kemether, E., Edgar, M. A., Morgello, S., Buschbaum, M. S., & Jones, L. B. (2001). The interstitial nuclei of the human anterior hypothalamus: An investigation of variation with sex, sexual orientation, and HIV status. *Hormones and Behavior, 40*, 86-92.

[43]In the words of Byne et al. (2001), these "sex related [brain] differences may also emerge later in development as the neurons that survive become part of functional circuits" (p. 91). Specifically, the brain differences could be attributed to "a reduction in neuropil within the INAH3 [the specific hypothalamic area studied] in the homosexual group" as a result of "postnatal experience."

[44]Tozer, E., & McClanahan, M. (1999). Treating the purple menace: Ethical considerations of conversion therapy and affirmative alternatives. *Counseling Psychologist, 27*, 738-739.

[45]Nichols, M. (2000). Therapy with sexual minorities. In S. R. Leiblum & R. C. Rosen (Eds.). *Principles and practice of sex therapy* (pp. 335-367) (3rd ed.). New York: Guilford, p. 352.

[46]Nichols (2000), p. 353.

[47]Nichols (2000), p. 353.

[48]Nichols (2000), p. 357.

[49]"Appropriate Therapeutic Responses to Sexual Orientation," APAOnline. Retrieved August 8, 2005, from www.apa.org/pi/lgbc/policy/appropriate.html. The official citation for the print version of this resolution is DeLeon, P. H. (1998). Proceedings of the American Psychological Association, Incorporated, for the legislative year 1997: Minutes of the annual meeting of the council of representatives, August 14 and 17, Chicago, Illinois; and June, August and December 1997 meetings of the board of directors. *American Psychologist, 53*, 882-939.

[50]APA actually omits the Davison reference, which should have been Davison, G. (1991). Constructionism and morality in therapy for homosexuality. In J. Gonsiorek & J. Weinrich (Eds.). *Homosexuality: Research implications for pubic policy* (pp. 137-148). Thousand Oaks, CA: Sage Publications. The other two references are: Haldeman, D. C. (1994). The practice and ethics of sexual orientation conversion therapy. *Journal of Consulting and Clinical Psychology, 62*, 221-227. Letters to the editor. (1997, January 23), *Wall Street Journal*, p. A17.

[51]"Answers to Your Questions About Sexual Orientation and Homosexuality," APAOnline. Retrieved August 8, 2005, from www.apa.org/pubinfo/answers.html.

[52]Yarhouse, M. A. (Chair). (2000, August). Gays, ex-gays, ex-ex-gays: Examining key religious, ethical, and diversity issues. A symposium conducted at the meeting of the American Psychological Association, Washington, DC. A similar symposium was organized the following year and held at the American Psychiatric Association: Bialer, P. A. (Chair). (2001, May 9). Clinical issues and ethical concerns regarding attempts to change sexual orientation: An update. A symposium conducted at the annual meeting of the American Psychiatric Association, New Orleans, LA.

[53]Haldeman, D. C. (2000, August). Gay rights, client rights: The implications for sexual orientation conversion therapy. In M. A. Yarhouse (Chair). Gays, ex-gays, ex-ex-gays: Examining key religious, ethical, and diversity issues. A symposium conducted at the annual meeting of the American Psychological Association, Washington, DC.

Chapter 4: Methodology for This Study

[1]See Kendall, P. C., Holmbeck, G., & Verduin, T. (2004). Methodology, design, and evaluation in psychotherapy research. In M. J. Lambert (Ed.). *Bergin and Garfield's handbook of psychotherapy and*

behavior change (5th ed., pp. 16-43). New York: John Wiley.

[2]Spitzer, Robert L. (2003). Can some gay men and lesbians change their sexual orientation? 200 participants reporting a change from homosexual to heterosexual orientation. *Archives of Sexual Behavior, 32*(5), 403-417.

[3]See Kendall, Holmbeck & Verduin (2004), p. 20.

[4]Alford, G. S., Wedding, D., & Jones, S. L. (1983). Faking "turn-ons" and "turn-offs": The effects of competitory covert imagery on penile tumescence response to diverse extrinsic sexual stimulus materials. *Behavioral Modification, 7*(1), 113.

[5]Alford, Wedding & Jones (1983), p. 113.

[6]Alford, Wedding & Jones (1983), p. 123.

[7]Laws, D. R., & Holmen, M. L. (1978). Sexual response faking by pedophiles. *Criminal Justice and Behavior, 5*, 343-356.

[8]Plaud, J. J., & Martini, J. R. (1999). The respondent conditioning of male sexual arousal. *Behavior Modification, 23*(2), 254-268.

[9]Kaine, A., Crim, M., & Mersereau, G. (1988). Faking sexual preference. *Canadian Journal of Psychiatry, 33*, 384.

[10]Wilson, R. J. (1998). Psychophysiological signs of faking in the phallometric test. *Sexual Abuse: A Journal of Research and Treatment, 10*(2), 113-126.

[11]McAnulty, R. D., & Adams, H. E. (1991). Voluntary control of penile tumescence: Effects of an incentive and a signal detection task. *The Journal of Sex Research, 28*(4), 557-577.

[12]Delizonna, L. L., Wincze, J. P., Litz, B. T., Brown, T. A., & Barlow, D. H. (2001). A comparison of subjective and physiological measure of mechanically produced and erotically produced erections (Or, is an erection an erection?). *Journal of Sex and Marital Therapy, 27*, 21-31.

[13]Koukounas, E., & Over, R. (2001). Habituation of male sexual arousal: Effects of attentional focus. *Biological Psychology, 58*, 49-64.

[14]Laumann, E. O., Gagnon, J. H., Michael, R. T., & Michaels, S. (1994). *The social organization of sexuality.* Chicago: University of Chicago Press, p. 37.

[15]Hooker, E. (1963). The adjustment of the male overt homosexual. In H. M. Ruitenbeek (Ed.). *The problem of homosexuality in modern society.* New York: E. P. Dutton, p. 142.

[16]We discuss this more thoroughly in Jones, S. L., & Yarhouse, M. A. (2000). *Homosexuality: The use of scientific research in the church's moral debate.* Downers Grove, IL: InterVarsity Press, pp. 70-80. See also Jones, S. L., & Kwee, A. W. (2005). Scientific research, homosexuality, and the church's moral debate: An update. *Journal of Psychology and Christianity, 24*(4), 304-316.

[17]Bailey, J. M., & Pillard, R. C. (1991). A genetic study of male sexual orientation. *Archives of General Psychiatry, 48*, 1081-1096; and Bailey, J. M., Pillard, R. C., Neale, M. C., & Agyei, Y. (1993). Heritable factors influence sexual orientation in women. *Archives of General Psychiatry, 50*, 217-223.

[18]Janet Hyde makes all of the most common mistakes in her flawed review; Hyde, J. S. (2005). The genetics of sexual orientation. In J. S. Hyde (Ed.). *The biological substrates of human sexuality* (pp. 9-20). Washington, DC: American Psychological Association.

[19]Bailey & Pillard (1991), p. 1092.

[20]First discussed in Jones, S. L., & Yarhouse, M. A. (1997). Science and the ecclesiastical homosexuality debates. *Christian Scholar's Review, 26*(4), 446-477; and then in more detail in chap. 3 of Jones & Yarhouse (2000).

[21]Bailey, J. M., Dunne, M. P., & Martin, N. G. (2000). Genetic and environmental influences on sexual orientation and its correlates in an Australian twin sample. *Journal of Personality and Social Psychology, 78*(3), 524-536.

[22]Bailey, Dunne & Martin (2000), p. 534.

[23]Bailey, Dunne & Martin, (2000), p. 534.

[24]Bearman, P. S., & Brückner, H. (2002). Opposite-sex twins and adolescent same-sex attraction. *American Journal of Sociology, 107*(5), 1179-1205.

[25]Hooker (1963), p. 142.

[26]See chap. 5, particularly pp. 148-151, of Jones & Yarhouse (2000) .

[27]"The arrangements vary: Professors serve as consultants, are paid by companies to perform clinical trials on potential drugs, or are given stock in the companies. A professor also might have a financial stake in a patent on a product being marketed by the company." Mangan, K. S. (1999, June 4). Medical professors see threat in corporate influence on research. *Chronicle of Higher Education,* p. A15.

[28]Academic Senate, University of California. APM-010, proposed revision of the academic freedom statement. Retrieved August 5, 2003, from <www.universityofcalifornia.edu/senate/assembly/jul2003/jul2003ii.pdf>. Quotations from footnote 1 of the revision.

[29]Laumann et al. (1994).

[30]The results of the CHSLS were later published as Laumann, E. O., Elingson, S., Mahay, J., Paik, A., & Youm, Y. (Eds.). (2004). *The sexual organization of the city.* Chicago: University of Chicago Press.

[31]For example, Bell, A., & Weinberg, M. (1978). *Homosexualities.* New York: Simon & Schuster; Bell, A., Weinberg, M., & Hammersmith, S. (1981). *Sexual preference: Its development in men and women.* Bloomington: Indiana University Press; Harry, J. (1982). *Gay children grown up: Gender culture and gender deviance.* New York: Praeger; Green, R. (1987). *The "sissy boy" syndrome and the development of homosexuality.* New Haven, CT: Yale University Press; and McWhirter, D., & Mattison, A. (1984). *The male couple.* Englewood Cliffs, NJ: Prentice-Hall.

[32]Discussed in Laumann et al. (1994), pp. 58-60; see their SAQs on pp. 670ff. Note also the following conclusion: "for controversial topics, such as opinions about abortion or marijuana [which pale before personal conversion from homosexuality!], participants gave more socially-desirable responses in face-to-face interviews, moderate amounts in telephone interviews, and the least amount in questionnaires," in Hill, C. E., & Lambert, M. J. (2004). Methodological issues in studying psychotherapy processes and outcomes. In M. J. Lambert (Ed.). *Bergin and Garfield's handbook of psychotherapy and behavior change* (5th ed., pp. 84-135). New York: John Wiley, p. 102.

[33]Parker, G., Tupling, H., & Brown, L. B. (1979). A parental bonding instrument. *British Journal of Medical Psychology, 52,* 1-10; discussed subsequently in Fischer, J., & Corcoran, K. (Eds.). (1994). *Measures for clinical practice: A sourcebook* (2nd ed.). New York: Free Press.

[34]Laumann et al. (1994), p. 67.

[35]Laumann et al. (1994), pp. 67-68.

[36]For the Code of Ethics and Practice for Research Associates form see appendix 1 at <www.ivpress.com>.

[37]For the Description of Research Methods see appendix 2 at <www.ivpress.com>.

[38]For the Voluntary Consent and Agreement for Project Exodus Research Participation form, see appendix 3 at <www.ivpress.com>.

[39]For the follow-up contact information see appendix 4 at <www.ivpress.com>.

[40]Regarding the receipt for payment see appendix 5 at <www.ivpress.com>.

[41]For the Limits of Confidentiality form see appendix 3 at <www.ivpress.com>.

[42]American Psychological Association (2005). Answers to your questions about sexual orientation and homosexuality. From <www.apa.org/pubinfo/answers.html>. Retrieved August 8, 2005.

Chapter 5: Our Sample

[1]Kendall, P. C., Holmbeck, G., & Verduin, T. (2004). Methodology, design, and evaluation in psy-

chotherapy research. In M. J. Lambert (Ed.). *Bergin and Garfield's handbook of psychotherapy and behavior change* (5th ed., pp. 16-43) New York: John Wiley, p. 28.

[2]Brückner, H., & Bearman, P. (2005). After the promise: The STD consequences of adolescent virginity pledges. *Journal of Adolescent Health, 36,* 272.

[3]Laumann, E. O., Gagnon, J. H., Michael, R. T., & Michaels, S. (1994). *The social organization of sexuality.* Chicago: University of Chicago Press, p. 578, table B.2.C.

[4]Laumann et al. (1994), p. 578, table B.2.D.

[5]Laumann et al. (1994), p. 580, table B.2.G.

[6]Laumann et al. (1994).

[7]Laumann, E. O., Ellingson, S., Mahay, J., Paik, A., & Youm, Y. (2004). *The sexual organization of the city.* Chicago: University of Chicago Press. Laumann, in a personal communication with Stanton Jones, July 1999, suggested that we follow more closely his newer methodology than what he reported in the NHSLS study, as he and his colleagues had worked out several issues in how to phrase questions in their improved methodology. His research team kindly sent us a copy of the survey they were currently using in 1999.

[8]Bell, Alan P., & Weinberg, Martin S. (1978). *Homosexualities: A study of diversity among men and women.* New York: Simon & Schuster, p. 207.

[9]Laumann et al. (1994), p. 180, table 5.1D.

[10]Laumann et al. (1994), p. 315, table 8.4.

[11]Laumann et al. (1994), pp. 340-341.

[12]Laumann et al. (1994), pp. 340-341.

[13]Laumann et al. (1994), p. 343, table 9.14.

[14]Laumann et al. (1994), pp. 340-341.

[15]Laumann et al. (1994), pp. 340-341.

[16]Laumann et al. (1994), p. 336, table 9.7.

[17]Laumann et al. (1994), p. 338, fig. 9.3.

[18]Laumann et al. (1994), p. 332, table 9.5.

[19]Laumann et al. (1994), p. 331, table 9.4.

[20]Laumann et al. (1994), p. 332, table 9.5.

Chapter 6: Understanding and Measuring Change of Sexual Orientation

[1]Haldeman, D. C. (1994). The practice and ethics of sexual orientation conversion therapy. *Journal of Consulting and Clinical Psychology, 62,* 221-227.

[2]Chung, Y. Barry, and Katayama, Motoni. (1996). Assessment of sexual orientation in lesbian/gay/bisexual studies. *Journal of Homosexuality, 30*(4), 49-62.

[3]Sell, R. L. (1997). Defining and measuring sexual orientation: A review. *Archives of Sexual Behavior, 26,* 643-658.

[4]Kinsey, A. C., Pomeroy, W. B., Martin, C. E., & Gebhard, P. H. (1953). *Sexual behavior in the human female.* Philadelphia: W. B. Saunders, quoted in Sell (1997), p. 651.

[5]Greenberg, D. (1988). *The construction of homosexuality.* Chicago: University of Chicago Press; Smith, M. (1996). Ancient bisexuality and the interpretation of Romans 1:26-27. *Journal of the American Academy of Religion, 64,* 223-256; Gagnon, R. A. J. (2001). *The Bible and homosexual practice.* Nashville: Abingdon.

[6]In this section we draw most directly on Sell (1997).

[7]Karl Maria Benkert, cited in Sell (1997), p. 646.

[8]Kinsey, A. C., Pomeroy, W. B., & Martin, C. E. (1948). *Sexual behavior in the human male.* Philadelphia: W. B. Saunders; Kinsey et al. (1953).

[9]Laumann, E. O., Gagnon, J. H., Michael, R. T., & Michaels, S. (1994). *The social organization of sexuality.* Chicago: University of Chicago Press; Jones, S. L., & Yarhouse, M. A. (2000). *Homosexuality: The use of scientific research in the church's moral debate.* Downers Grove, IL: InterVarsity Press. Kinsey did not attempt to obtain a representative sample; rather, he oversampled Protestants, college-educated persons and those who were incarcerated (some of whom were sex offenders).

[10]Sandfort, T. G. M., Theo, G. M., de Graaf, R., Bijl, R. V., & Schnabel, P. (2001). Same-sex sexual behavior and psychiatric disorders: Findings from the Netherlands mental health survey and incidence study (NEMESIS). *Archives of General Psychiatry, 58*(1), 85-91. Specifically, they said, "Respondents were asked verbally whether that had sexual contact in the preceding year and the gender of their partner(s). If the respondent had had sex with someone of the same gender (exclusively or not), he or she was categorized as homosexual. Other sexually active people were categorized as heterosexual" (p. 86). It is worth noting that this method of categorizing resolves all of the ambiguity of sexual orientation by making same-gender sex the absolute determinant of homosexual identity, thus categorizing all bisexual people as homosexual. The reverse would never occur—where all persons who engage in heterosexual sex would be thereby categorized as heterosexual.

[11]E.g., Bem, S. L. (1981). *Bem sex-role inventory: Professional manual.* Palo Alto, CA: Consulting Psychologists Press; Bem, S. (1985). Androgyny and gender schema theory: A conceptual and empirical integration. In T. B. Sonderegger (Ed.). *Nebraska symposium on motivation 1984: Psychology and gender* (pp. 179-226). Lincoln: University of Nebraska Press.

[12]Shively, M. G., and DeCecco, J. P. (1977). Components of sexual identity. *Journal of Homosexuality, 3,* 41-48.

[13]Sell (1997); see p. 647 on desire versus behavior, and p. 648 on the variety of terms for "attraction."

[14]Klein, F., Sepekoff, B., & Wolf, T. J. (1985). Sexual orientation: A multi-variable dynamic process. *Journal of Homosexuality, 11,* 35-49.

[15]Laumann et al. (1994), p. 285.

[16]Greenberg (1988).

[17]Herdt, G. (1981). *Guardians of the flutes.* New York: McGraw-Hill.

[18]Gangestad, S. W., Bailey, J. M., & Martin, N. G. (2000). Taxometric analyses of sexual orientation and gender identity. *Journal of Personality and Social Psychology, 78,* 1109.

[19]Haslam, N. (1997). Evidence that male homosexuality is a matter of degree. *Journal of Personality and Social Psychology, 73,* 862.

[20]Gangestad, Bailey & Martin (2000).

[21]Cochran, S. D. (2001). Emerging issues in research on lesbians' and gay men's mental health: Does sexual orientation really matter? *American Psychologist, 11,* 931-941. Quote p. 932, fn 1.

[22]Bailey, J. M., Dune, M. P., & Martin, N. G. (2000). Genetic and environmental influences on sexual orientation and its correlates in an Australian twin sample. *Journal of Personality and Social Psychology, 78*(3), 524, 525, 526.

[23]This and following quotes are from Sell (1997), pp. 655-656.

[24]Hamer, D. H., Hu, S., Magnuson, V. L., Hu, N., & Pattatucci, A. M. L. (1993). A linkage between DNA markers on the X chromosome and male sexual orientation. *Science, 261,* 320-326. Hu, S., Pattatucci, A. M. L., Patterson, C., Li, L., Fulker, D. W., Cherny, S. S., Kruglyak, L., & Hamer, D. H. (1995). Linkage between sexual orientation and chromosome Xq28 in males but not in females. *Nature Genetics, 11,* 248-256. It is worth parenthetical note that for the last decade these findings have been criticized for failing replication by other laboratories outside of Hamer's own laboratory. Only recently has another genetic scan study emerged from Hamer's lab: Mustanski, B. S., DuPree, M. G., Nievergelt, C. M., Bocklandt, S., Schork, N. J., & Hamer, D. H. (2005). A genomewide scan of male sexual orientation. *Human Genetics, 116,* 272-278. Unnoticed among the ill-founded publicity

accorded this study was the finding that these researchers had definitively refuted Hamer's earlier findings. See Jones, S. L., & Kwee, A. W. (2005). Scientific research, homosexuality, and the church's moral debate: An update. *Journal of Psychology and Christianity, 24*(4).

[25]Sell (1997), p. 656.

[26]Sell (1997), p. 656.

[27]Shively & DeCecco (1977), pp. 41-48.

[28]See Bem (1981).

[29]Sell (1997), p. 656.

[30]Sell, R. L. (1996). The Sell assessment of sexual orientation: Background and scoring. *Journal of Gay, Lesbian and Bisexual Identity, 1,* 295-309.

[31]Sell (1996); see scoring instructions on p. 305, and the cited scoring table on p. 307, fig. 3.

[32]If this description of the method confuses the reader, we invite you to consult Sell's original description of his method; our simplification is the result of hours of poring over a very confusing method.

[33]Klein, F. (1978). *The bisexual option: A concept of one hundred percent intimacy.* New York: Arbor House.

[34]Klein, F. (1980). Are you sure you're heterosexual? Or homosexual? Or even bisexual? *Forum,* 41-45.

[35]Klein, F., Sepekoff, B., & Wolf, T. J. (1985). Sexual orientation: A multi-variable dynamic process. *Journal of Homosexuality, 11*(1-2), 35-49. Klein continued to advocate for the KSOG in other publications, but did not really add new empirical evidence in support of its utility; e.g., see Klein, F. (1990). The need to view sexual orientation as a multivariable dynamic process: A theoretical perspective. In D. P. McWhirter, S. A. Sanders, & J. M. Reinisch. (Eds.). *Homosexuality/heterosexuality: Concepts of sexual orientation* (pp. 277-282). Oxford: Oxford University Press.

[36]Wayson, P. (1983). A study of personality variables in males as they relate to differences in sexual orientation. Doctoral dissertation. (As reported by Klein, Sepekoff & Wolf [1985]).

[37]Sell (1997), pp. 643-658.

[38]Weinrich, J. D., Snyder, P. J., Pillard, R. C., Grant, I., Jacobson, D. L., Robinson, S. R., & McCutchan, J. A. (1993). A factor analysis of the Klein Sexual Orientation Grid in two disparate samples. *Archives of Sexual Behavior, 22,* 157-168.

[39]Weinrich, J. D., & Klein, F. (2002). Bi-gay, bi-straight, and bi-bi: Three bisexual subgroups identified using cluster analysis of the Klein Sexual Orientation Grid. *Journal of Bisexuality, 2*(4), 109-139.

[40]Sell (1997), p. 656.

[41]Klein, Sepekoff & Wolf (1985), pp. 40-41.

Chapter 7: Can Sexual Orientation Change? *Report of the Quantitative Analysis*

[1]Bailey, J. M., & Pillard, R. C. (1991). A genetic study of male sexual orientation. *Archives of General Psychiatry, 48,* 1081-1096. Bailey, J. M., Pillard, R. C., Neale, M. C., & Agyei, Y. (1993). Heritable factors influence sexual orientation in women. *Archives of General Psychiatry, 50,* 217-223.

[2]Kendler, K. S., Thornton, L. M., Gilman, S. E., & Kessler, R. C. (2000). Sexual orientation in a U.S. national sample of twin and nontwin sibling pairs. *American Journal of Psychiatry, 157*(11), 1843-1846.

[3]Spitzer, R. L. (2003). Can some gay men and lesbians change their sexual orientation? 200 participants reporting a change from homosexual to heterosexual orientation. *Archives of Sexual Behavior, 32*(5), 403-417.

[4]McNemar's test, calculated as $[(P\text{-}N)-1]^2$ / (P-N), where P = positive changes and N= negative changes; Schlesselman, J. (1982). *Case-control studies.* New York: Oxford University Press.

[5]Schlesselman (1982).

[6]Cohen, J. (1988). *Statistical power analysis for the behavioral sciences* (2nd ed.). Hillsdale, N.J.: Erl-

baum, p. 25. There is some debate about the use of effect-size calculations with repeated tests of the same population, and the consensus regarding such tests is that when you have such repeated tests (repeated measures or correlated designs) you should use the original standard deviations of each sample separately to compute the effect size. We have not reported these separate standard deviations in table 7.7 but rather the composite standard deviation generated by the t-test.

[7]This issue is discussed frequently throughout the authoritative Lambert, M. J. (Ed.). (2004). *Bergin and Garfield's handbook of psychotherapy and behavior change* (5th ed.). New York: John Wiley. In this section we discuss "clinical meaningfulness" not in the technical statistical sense of "clinical significance" as developed by Neil Jacobson and Paula Truax. To determine "clinical significance" by the Jacobson-Truax criteria, you need to know the test-retest reliabilities for each scale and the 90% or 95% confidence intervals for change, and secondly you need to know the statistical mid-point between populations (in this case heterosexuals and homosexuals) on the scales. With this information you can classify each subject as to whether their score changed to a reliable degree yielding clinically significant improvement, deterioration or no change. This essential psychometric information is not available for the scales used in this study.

[8]See Lambert, M. J., & Ogles, B. M. (2004). *The efficacy and effectiveness of psychotherapy* (pp. 139-193). In M. J. Lambert (Ed.). *Bergin and Garfield's handbook of psychotherapy and behavior change* (5th ed.). New York: John Wiley, p. 157.

[9]Weinrich, J. D., & Klein, F. (2002). Bi-gay, bi-straight, and bi-bi: Three bisexual subgroups identified using cluster analysis of the Klein Sexual Orientation Grid. *Journal of Bisexuality, 2*(4), 109-139.

Chapter 8: Can Sexual Orientation Change? *Report of the Qualitative (and Supporting Quantitative) Analyses*

[1]Obviously, we can make no claim that the six categories that "emerged" were dictated only by a tabula-rasa reading of the transcripts and that our preconceptions had no impact on these categorizations. We would state clearly, as discussed in chap. 2 and elsewhere, that we were open to and indeed (to some degree) expected to see two different types of success from the involvement of these participants in the Exodus process—movement toward heterosexual orientation and chastity/celibacy. Our theological convictions led us to construe this as a possibility. It was not predetermined, though, that the "data" would fall out in this form, and so we tried to bracket our expectations and let the data speak for itself. We would contest that the supporting empirical analyses of the results from these groups support the veracity of our categorizations.

[2]Obviously, comparison of homosexual orientation to a psychological and psychiatric disorder like depression will be offensive to some. We do not intend by this comparison to argue for a return to the pathologizing of homosexuality. We cannot put the size and nature of our results for a psychosocial intervention in reasonable context, however, without suitable comparisons, and this one seems apt.

[3]Trivedi, M. H., Rush, A. J., Wisniewski, S. R., et al. (2006). Evaluation of outcomes with citalopram for depression using measures-based care in STAR*D: Implications for clinical practice. *American Journal of Psychiatry, 163*(1), 28-40. The parallels to our testing Exodus intervention in their "natural settings" for ministry rather than constructing some sort of artificial experimental context are worth noting.

[4]Trivedi et al. (2006), p. 28.

Chapter 9: Is the Attempt to Change Harmful? *Impact on Psychological and Spiritual Functioning*

[1]Derogatis, Leonard R. (1994). *SCL-90-R: Administration, scoring and procedures manual.* Minneapolis: National Computer Systems. Note: Since 1994, NCS has been acquired by Pearson Assess-

ments, and the SCL-90-R and related support materials are available through Pearson Assessments at <www.pearsonassessments.com/tests/scl90r.htm>. Retrieved August 2005.

[2]American Psychological Association, "Answers to Your Questions About Sexual Orientation and Homosexuality," APA Online. Retrieved August 8, 2005, from <www.apa.org/pubinfo/answers .html>.

[3]Derogatis (1994).

[4]This evidence is surveyed in the manual of the instrument and will not be summarized here. See ibid.

[5]Ibid., p. 57.

[6]Ibid., p. 58.

[7]For example, see Cochran, S. D. (2001). Emerging issues in research on lesbians' and gay men's mental health: Does sexual orientation really matter? *American Psychologist, 11*, 931-941.

[8]American Psychological Association, "Answers to Your Questions About Sexual Orientation and Homosexuality," APA Online. Retrieved August 8, 2005, from <www.apa.org/pubinfo/answers .html>.

[9]Paloutzian, R. F., & Ellison, C. W. (1991). *Manual for the Spiritual Well-Being Scale*. Nyack, NY: Life Advance; Paloutzian, R. F., & Ellison, C. W. (1982). Loneliness, spiritual well-being and quality of life. In L. A. Peplau & D. Perlman. (Eds.). *Loneliness: A sourcebook of current theory, research, and therapy* (pp. 224-237). New York: Wiley Interscience; Bufford, R. K., Paloutzian, R. F., & Ellison, C. W. (1991). Norms for the Spiritual Well-Being Scale. *Journal of Psychology and Theology, 19*(1), 56-70; Ellison, C. W., & Smith, J. (1991). Toward an integrative measure of health and well-being. *Journal of Psychology and Theology, 19*(1), 35-48. This discussion of the Spiritual Well-Being Scale and of the Faith Maturity Scale to follow are based on the descriptions developed by H. R. Hostler in an unpublished Wheaton College dissertation titled "Exploring religious experience: Spiritual development during attempted sexual orientation change," June 2004.

[10]Ellison & Smith (1991) report that test-retest reliability coefficients were .93 for SWB, .96 for RWB, .86 for EWB over a one-week period. Internal consistency alpha coefficients ranged from .89-.94 for SWB, .82-.94 for RWB and .78-.86 for EWB across seven studies with over nine hundred participants. These coefficients suggest that the SWBS and subscales have high reliability and internal consistency. Further research by the scale's authors confirms a two-factor structure. The SWBS is not without its limitations, which include social desirability and measurement sensitivity, some statistical problems with distribution of scores, and varying reports on the underlying factor structure; see Bufford, Paloutzian & Ellison (1991), as well as Ledbetter, M. F., Smith, L. A., Vosler-Hunter, W. L., & Fischer, J. D. (1991). An evaluation of the research and clinical usefulness of the Spiritual Well-Being Scale. *Journal of Psychology and Theology, 19*(1), 49-55; and Ramanaiah, N. V., Rielage, J. K., & Sharpe, J. P. (2001). Spiritual well-being and personality, *Psychological Reports, 89*, 659-662.

[11]Paloutzian & Ellison (1982), n. 15.

[12]Jones, S. L. (2000). Religion and psychology: Theories and methods. In A. Kazdin. (Ed.). *Encyclopedia of psychology* (Vol. 7, pp. 38-42). Washington, DC: American Psychological Association; and New York: Oxford University Press.

[13]Jones, S. L., & Hostler, H. (2005). The role of sexuality in personhood: An integrative exploration. In W. R. Miller & H. D. Delaney. (Eds.). *Human nature, motivation, and change: Judeo-Christian perspectives on psychology* (pp. 115-132). Washington, DC: American Psychological Association.

[14]Benson, P. L., Donahue, M. J., & Erickson, J. A. (1993). The Faith Maturity Scale: Conceptualization, measurement, and empirical validation. In M. L. Lynn & D. O. Moberg. (Eds.). *Research in the social scientific study of religion* (Vol. 5, pp. 1-26). Greenwich: JAI Press.

[15]Ibid. See also Sanders, J. L. (1998). Religious ego identity and its relationship to faith maturity. *Journal of Psychology, 132*(6), 653-658.

[16]Benson, Donahue, & Erickson (1993); means on the FMS are reported in table 6 (p. 14) and table 9 (p. 18).

[17]98-73 = 25 dropouts. If 75% of the dropouts are those who have discontinued the change attempt (leaving room for others who were successful but were weary of being studied, the one deceased participant, and those who were continuing the change process but had simply become lost to follow-up contact), that would mean that an additional 18 (75% of 25) had stopped the change attempt, leaving the percentage continuing as 59 divided by 91 (73 + 18 = 91), and 59/91 = 65%.

[18]Mel White, *What the Bible says—and doesn't say—about homosexuality.* Lynchburg, VA: Soulforce, p. 7, available at <www.soulforce.org/main/whatthebiblesays.shtml>.

[19]This matter has been discussed recently in a most provocative way in Wright, R. H., & Cummings, N. A. (Eds.). (2005). *Destructive trends in mental health: The well-intentioned path to harm.* New York: Routledge. The authors in this volume conclude that psychology (and the mental health field in general) have been undiscerning in allowing ideology rather than careful research to guide clinical practice. "Reparative therapy" for change of sexual orientation is one of their main topics in this volume.

[20]Cochran, S. D. (2001). Emerging issues in research on lesbians' and gay men's mental health: Does sexual orientation really matter? *American Psychologist, 11,* 934.

[21]Yarhouse, M. A., & Throckmorton, W. (2002). Ethical issues in attempts to ban reorientation therapies. *Psychotherapy, 39*(1), 66-75.

[22]Grisso, T., & Appelbaum, P. S. (1998). *Assessing competence to consent to treatment.* New York: Oxford.

[23]American Psychological Association, "Answers to Your Questions About Sexual Orientation and Homosexuality," APA Online. Retrieved August 8, 2005, from <www.apa.org/pubinfo/answers .html>. Emphasis added.

Chapter 10: Conclusion

[1]Epstein, R. (2006, February-March). Do gays have a choice? *Scientific American Mind,* 51-57.

[2]Norcross, J. C., Koocher, G. P., & Garofalo, A. (2006). Discredited psychological treatments and tests: A delphi poll. *Professional Psychology: Research and Practice, 37*(5), 515-522.

[3]The American Psychological Association's Code of Ethics is available to all at http://www.apa.org/ethics/code2002.html retrieved December 2005. Quote from General Principle E.

[4]Haldeman, D. C. (2004). When sexual and religious orientation collide: Considerations in working with conflicted same-sex attracted male clients. *The Counseling Psychologist, 32,* 691-715. Quote p. 713.

[5]http://www.psych.org/archives/news_room/press_releases/rep_therapy.cfm retrieved 12/28/05

[6]Gonsiorek, J. C. (2004). Reflections from the conversion therapy battlefield. *The Counseling Psychologist, 32,* 750-759. Quote pp. 755-756

[7]From http://narth.com/docs/perloff.html; accessed June, 2005

[8]Ibid.

[9]Yarhouse, M. A. (1998). When clients seek treatment for same-sex attraction: Ethical issues in the "right to choose" debate. *Psychotherapy, 35*(2), 234-259.

[10]Grisso, T., & Appelbaum, P. S. (1998). *Assessing competence to consent to treatment.* New York: Oxford University Press. According to the authors, the historical shift from simple or implied consent to informed consent occurred as "the courts focused on clients' right to make autonomous decisions, suggesting the importance of being able to select desired options, as well as to reject disfavored ones" (p. 6).

[11]Grisso & Appelbaum (1998), *Assessing competence.*

[12]Sexual identity therapy is a promising sexual identity management approach that reaffirms client autonomy and self-determination in the process of seeking personal congruence, so that individuals are

supported in living (through their behavior and identity) in ways that are consistent with their beliefs and values. See Throckmorton, W., & Yarhouse, M. (2006). Sexual identity therapy: Practice guidelines for managing sexual identity conflicts. White paper distributed through the Center for Vision and Values, Grove City College, Grove City, PA. The paper is available at http://www.sexualidentity.blogspot.com/.

[13]Kilgore, H., Sideman, L., Amin, K., & Bohanske, B. (2005). Psychologists' attitudes and therapeutic approaches toward gay, lesbian, and bisexual issues continue to improve: An update. *Psychotherapy, 42*(3), 395-400. There is evidence, however, that when presented with relevant clinical vignettes generalists are more likely than specialists in gay, lesbian and bisexual concerns to support as ethical client-directed therapy goals to change same-sex behavior or orientation. See Liszcz, A. M., & Yarhouse, M. A. (2005). Same-sex attraction: A survey regarding client-directed treatment goals. *Psychotherapy, 42*(1), 111-115.

[14]Norcross, Koocher & Garofalo (2006).

[15]Beckstead, who grew up as a member of The Church of Jesus Christ of Latter-day Saints, said much of his youth was spent torn between his religious upbringing and his sexual feelings. "My Mormon background was my Mormon foreground. My entire life was spent asking, 'Am I gay or am I Mormon? Am I good or am I evil?' " Beckstead said. That moral debate, Beckstead said, led to his eventual departure from the church and allowed him to come to terms with other parts of his identity. "Who I am sexually was wrapped up in my religion. I had to disassociate from the church and the things they're trying to do against me and my partner,' he said." Benson, A. (2004, April 20). Panel breaks the silence about LGBT issues. *The Daily Utah Chronicle.* Retrieved February 5, 2007, from http://media.www.dailyutahchronicle.com/media/storage/paper244/news/2004/04/20/News/Panel.Breaks.The.Silence.About.Lgbt.Issues-665697.shtml?sourcedomain=www.dailyutahchronicle.com&MIIHost=media.collegepublisher.com.

[16]Such as using a summary score for the Klein Sexual Orientation Grid when Klein urged researchers not to use such a summary score, as we discussed in chap. 6.

[17]As recounted in Mahoney, M. (1976). *Scientist as subject.* Cambridge, MA: Ballinger, pp. 93ff.

Name Index

Subject Index